A Worker Justice Reader

Essential Writings on Religion and Labor

Interfaith Worker Justice

Edited by Joy Heine, Director
Religious Perspectives on Work Project, Interfaith Worker Justice

Cynthia Brooke
Director of Communications, Interfaith Worker Justice

ORBIS BOOKS
Maryknoll, New York 10545

Founded in 1970, Orbis Books endeavors to publish works that enlighten the mind, nourish the spirit, and challenge the conscience. The publishing arm of the Maryknoll Fathers and Brothers, Orbis seeks to explore the global dimensions of the Christian faith and mission, to invite dialogue with diverse cultures and religious traditions, and to serve the cause of reconciliation and peace. The books published reflect the views of their authors and do not represent the official position of the Maryknoll Society. To learn more about Maryknoll and Orbis Books, please visit our website at www.maryknollsociety.org.

Library of Congress Cataloging-in-Publication Data

A worker justice reader : essential writings on religion and labor / provided by Interfaith Worker Justice ; compiled by Joy Heine, project director.
    p. cm.
 Includes bibliographical references.
 ISBN 978-1-57075-875-1 (pbk.)
 1. Work – Religious aspects. 2. Labor – Religious aspects. 3. Labor movement – Religious aspects. I. Heine, Joy. II. Interfaith Worker Justice (Organization)

 BL65.W67W69 2010
 201'.73 – dc22

                    2009037732

This worker justice reader is dedicated to workers. It is a compilation of some of the best writings on work, labor, and economics, incorporating religious perspectives. The authors of these works are the people who have stood in solidarity with workers, have put workers struggles into words or have reflected theologically on work. It is a work in progress.

Contents

Preface

Why aren't we learning about worker justice in our seminaries? This was the first question asked at the end of Interfaith Worker Justice's initial Seminary Summer program, a summer internship in which seminary and rabbinical students work with labor unions to help workers improve wages, benefits and working conditions.

Since 2000, Interfaith Worker Justice (IWJ) has been engaging young leaders in seminaries, rabbinical schools, undergraduate schools and Muslim training programs through its summer internship programs, school year internships, campus groups, and Seminarians for Worker Justice groups. In addition, IWJ has helped convene faculty concerned about worker justice to discuss ways to prepare students to connect their faith with economic justice struggles facing the nation. A combination of faculty initiatives and student encouragement has produced many new courses and classes on worker justice. A sampling of course outlines can be found at www.iwj.org.

But more courses need to be developed and taught if we are to adequately prepare religious leadership to support workers, employers and congregations in being effective witnesses in the world. The *Worker Justice Reader* has been compiled to assist faculty in teaching courses on worker justice. Our experience in working with students over the years suggests that those being prepared for nonprofit and religious leadership know little about the economy, labor unions and the struggles of workers in low-wage jobs. They may know a little bit more about faith-body teachings on worker justice, theological perspectives on work or prophetic leadership, but additional background is useful.

Consequently, this text has been compiled with the average student in mind. We have included a variety of articles on an array of worker justice related topics. The *Reader* can be used as the core text for a full course on worker justice or sections can be assigned for a class or two.

Although there are hundreds of articles that could have been included, we have had to make choices about which articles would be most helpful in providing a broad overview. Nonetheless, you may come across articles that you think are particularly useful for students or better than the ones included. If so, please tell us.

Ten years ago there were only two or three courses on worker justice taught in religious training schools. Today there are several dozen. Let's hope for several hundred in the coming years.

May the *Reader* be of service in equipping religious and nonprofit leaders.

Kim Bobo
Executive Director
Interfaith Worker Justice

1 Crisis for U.S. Workers

Introduction

U.S. workers are facing a crisis. Despite working longer hours and being increasingly productive, wages and benefits for many workers are decreasing. Workers in low-paying jobs cannot earn enough to feed their families, often have no health insurance or paid vacations or sick leave and usually have no retirement savings.

This section begins with the excellent overview of the crisis found in the executive summary of the book *The State of Working America 2006/2007*. This yearly report published by the Economic Policy Institute analyzes how workers are faring in the U.S.

The rest of the articles address why U.S. workers are in crisis. One key cause for the decline in wages and benefits is the decline in the numbers and power of unions. In order to understand the importance of unions, read the introductory "Why Unions Matter," developed by Interfaith Worker Justice.

In order to understand why unions have declined over the past few decades, we highly recommend "Taking It to the Next Level," Chapter Five of Andy Stern's 2006 book *A Country That Works: Getting America Back on Track*. (Alas, IWJ was not able to receive permission to reprint this chapter, so please seek this out in your local bookstore.) Stern is the President of the Service Employees International Union (SEIU), the fastest-

growing union in the U.S. Stern led the development of the Change to Win coalition. Although many union leaders disagree with his decision to break away from the AFL-CIO, his analysis of many problems in the labor movement and the inadequacies of existing labor laws are shared by many labor leaders.

Globalization is clearly one major cause of the decline of wages and benefits in the U.S. In "Globalization and Its Impact on Labor," Dr. Pamela Brubaker, a professor of religion at California Lutheran University, examines globalization's meaning and how it is impacting workers. Dr. Brubaker crafted this piece for the reader based on material from her book *Globalization at What Price? Economic Change and Daily Life*.

Globalization has not only reduced wages for workers in the U.S. by exporting jobs and forcing U.S. workers to compete with workers earning pennies, but has restructured work in other countries, driving many workers to seek work in foreign lands. "U.S. Demand for Immigrant Labor and Its Impact," written by Ana Bedard, a doctoral student at Loyola University in Chicago, focuses on the need for immigrants in the U.S. She spent more than fifteen years organizing around fair housing for immigrants and people with little income. This is a summary of her thesis, rewritten specifically for this *Reader*.

The State of Working America: Executive Summary

Economic Policy Institute (2006)

Introduction: Life and times in the new economy

Starting in 1995, a new and important change occurred in the U.S. economy: productivity – the output of goods and services per hour worked – began to grow more quickly. After growing 1.4 percent per year since the mid-1970s, productivity growth accelerated to 2.5 percent a year from 1995 to 2000, and then jumped to 3.1 percent a year from 2000 to 2005. The post-1995 shift in productivity growth, partly attributed to the diffusion and more efficient use of information technology, has sometimes been labeled the "new economy." Because productivity growth provides the basis for rising living standards for everyone, its acceleration is an unequivocally positive development for the economy.

Yet, despite this unequivocally beneficial development, many Americans report dissatisfaction with where the economy seems to be headed, and many worry about their own and their children's well-being. These concerns have led some policy makers and economists to ask: why aren't people happier about the economy? The question seems reasonable to those who follow the top-line numbers of the economy, such as the growth of the total economy (e.g., gross domestic product), the stock market, or corporate profits. The question is easily answered, however, for those who follow and report on the data that fill the chapters in this book.

Our findings show that while faster productivity growth creates the potential for widely shared prosperity, if that potential is to be realized, a number of other factors have to be in place. Those factors include labor market institutions (such as strong collective bargaining), an appropriate minimum wage, and, importantly, a truly tight labor market, all of which are necessary to ensure that the benefits of growth reach everyone, not just those at the top of the wealth scale.

When these institutions are weakened or absent, growth is likely to bypass the majority of working families. The chapters that follow elaborate this story in greater detail by examining trends in incomes, mobility, wages, jobs, wealth, and poverty, and by placing recent developments in their historical, regional, and international context.

Family income: "New economy" drives a wedge between productivity and living standards

A family's income is, of course, one of the most important determinants of their economic well-being. Most working families depend on their income to meet their immediate consumption needs (like food and gas), to finance longer-term investments in goods and services (like housing and education), and to build their savings.

Many families face two separate but related challenges regarding the growth of their real incomes: (1) post-2000 wage stagnation, especially among middle- and lower-income families, and (2) the gap between income and productivity growth. Despite the fact that the most recent economic expansion began in late 2001, the real income of the median family fell each year through 2004, the most recent available data. Between 2000 and 2004, real median family income fell by 3 percent, or about $1,600 in 2004 dollars.

The post-2000 income trends stand in stark contrast to the extent and pattern of family income growth in the latter 1990s. Then, during a period of uniquely tight job markets, full employment conditions compelled employers to more broadly share the benefits of accelerated productivity growth. Between 1995 and 2000, output per hour grew 2.5 percent per year, while real median family income grew 2.2 percent annually. Importantly, the income growth of less-advantaged groups proved to benefit the most from the availability of more and better jobs fostered by the tight labor market. Real median income was up 2.9 percent per year for African Americans, 4.6 percent for Hispanic families, 2.3 percent for young families (family head: 25-34 years old), and 3.1 percent for single-mother families.

The post-2000 reversal of these favorable trends was a function of diminished employment opportunities, not just during the recession, as we would expect, but over the protracted jobless recovery that followed. This decline in median income during the initial years of expansions appears to be more the norm than the exception in recent recoveries. Over both the 1980s and 1990s recovery, it took seven years for median family income to regain its peak, far longer than in earlier cycles.

In fact, when it comes to income growth over the past generation, the extent of a family's prosperity is largely the result of their placement in the income scale, with the richest families experiencing the fastest income growth. Between 1979 and 2000, for example, the real income of households in the lowest fifth grew 6.1 percent; the middle fifth was up 12.3 percent; the top fifth grew 69.6 percent; and the average income of those in the top 1 percent grew by 183.7 percent.

Higher inequality shows up whether we look at consumption or income. Although inequality is not driven by tax changes, lowering the tax burden on the wealthy has demonstrably exacerbated the problem.

Greater inequality has also been generated by an expansion of capital income and an increased concentration of capital income among the very highest income families. Whereas the top 1 percent received 37.8 percent of all capital income in 1979, their share rose to 49.1 percent by 2000 and rose further to 57.5 percent in 2003 (most recent data). This shift toward greater concentration of capital income reflects an increase in the share of income flowing to corporate profits and that profit rates in 2005 are the highest in 36 years (excepting 1997). If the pre-tax return to capital (i.e., profit rate) in 2005 had remained at its 1979 level, then hourly compensation would have been 5 percent higher in the corporate sector, equivalent to an annual transfer of $235 billion dollars from labor to capital (measured for 2005).

One way that middle-income families have kept their incomes rising over the past few decades has been for women in general and wives in particular to enter the paid labor market. Among married-couple families with children, for example, middle-income wives added over 500 hours of work to total family work hours between 1979 and 2000. While this has been a positive force for women's economic independence, it has also put a strain on the need to balance work and family.

Income-class mobility: How much is there?

Another important dimension of income and living standards involves income-class mobility. How much progress do families typically make in terms of income growth over their lifetimes? To what extent are children's economic fates determined by the income position of their parents? And is there more or less such mobility in the United States versus other advanced economies?

In fact, we find significant income correlations between parents and their children, implying that income-class mobility is at least partially restricted by a parent's position in the income scale. For example, one recent study finds the correlation between parents and children to be 0.6. One way to view the significance of this finding is to note that it implies that it would take a poor family of four with two children approximately nine to 10 generations – over 200 years – to achieve the income of the typical middle-income four-person family. Were that correlation only half that size – meaning income differences were half as persistent across generations – it would take four to five generations for the poor family to catch up.

In a similar vein, we find that sons of low-earning fathers have slightly less than a 60 percent chance of reaching above the 20th percentile by adulthood, about a 20 percent chance of surpassing the median, and a very slight chance – 4.5 percent – of ending up above the 80th percentile.

In other words, the extent of income mobility across generations plays a significant role in the living standards of American families. It is, for example, a key determinant of how many generations a family will be stuck at the low end of the income scale, or snugly ensconced at the high end.

Our folklore often emphasizes the rags-to-riches, Horatio-Alger-like stories that suggest that anyone with the gumption and smarts to prevail can lift themselves up by their bootstraps and transverse the income scale in a single generation. The reality in the United States, however, shows much less mobility than such stories suggest. Surprisingly, international comparisons reveal less mobility in America than other countries with comparably advanced economies. For example, one study reveals the intergenerational income correlations in Finland, Sweden, and Germany to be 0.22, 0.28, and 0.34, respectively, compared to the U.S. correlation of 0.43. Note that these are countries that U.S. economists often criticize for their extensive social protections – each one has universal health coverage, for example – yet their citizens experience greater mobility than do our own.

Another important dimension of the mobility story is the question of how it has evolved over time. One reason this is so important relates back to our findings regarding income inequality. The growth of inequality between two time periods, say between the late 1970s and today, is of less concern if mobility is up, thus offsetting the greater distances between income classes.

The evidence reveals, however, that mobility is either flat or diminished over the very period when inequality has been on the rise. For example, one study shows that the intergenerational correlation between fathers' and sons' income has grown from 0.32 to 0.58 (higher correlations imply less mobility). Another study shows that the share of families remaining in the top fifth of the income scale for 10 years went from 49.1 percent in the 1970s to 53.1 percent in the 1990s.

What explains the lack of mobility here in the United States? Certainly unequal education opportunities and historical discrimination play a role. As such, opportunities for advancement are limited for those with fewer economic resources. For example, we show that children from wealthy families have much greater access to top-tier universities than kids from low-income families, even once innate skills are taken into account. We also find wealth concentration to be correlated across generations, and this creates another impediment to the upward mobility of the economy's "have-nots." For instance, about two-thirds of children whose parents were in the lowest fifth of the wealth scale ended up in the bottom 40 percent as adults.

Wages: Growth stalls while productivity and compensation diverge

The major development in the labor market in recent years has been the stunning disconnect between the rapid productivity growth and pay growth, especially given the rapidity of productivity's growth and the how stunted pay growth has been in the past several years.

Also of great concern is the tremendous widening of the wage gap between those at the top of the wage scale, particularly corporate chief executive officers, and other wage earners. The importance of these two developments cannot be overstated because wages and salaries make up about three-fourths of total family income, and as such, are the primary driving force behind income growth and income inequality. Over the 1995-2005 period, productivity grew a remarkable 33.4 percent, and over half of that growth has occurred since 2001. This pace of productivity growth far exceeded that of the earlier period from 1973 to 1995. However, despite enormous growth in productivity, wages for the typical worker and for those with either a high school diploma or a college degree were about the same in 2005 as in 2001.

By comparison, pay did rise in the earlier period from 1996 to 2001, fueled by the higher productivity and

the progressive drop in unemployment to 4.0 percent by 2000. Moreover, the wage momentum carried forward through 2001 and into 2002, despite rising unemployment. The wage momentum from the late 1990s is important to understand when looking at trends over the 2000-05 period – all of the wage growth from the 2000-05 period occurred within the first two years. The poor job creation during the early 2000s recession and its lackluster recovery eventually knocked wage growth down so that prices rose at least as fast. This was the case even in 2005, when the unemployment rate fell to 5.1 percent.

In short, historically high productivity growth and historically low unemployment have benefited compensation and wages very little. While productivity grew 33.4 percent between 1995 and 2005, benefits (health and pension) grew less than half that much and wages for typical workers grew one-third as much as productivity. After 2001, there has been basically no wage improvement for typical workers regardless of significant gains in productivity.

Digging a little deeper into these trends, we find that women are much more likely to earn low wages than men. In 2005, 29.4 percent of women earned poverty-level wages or less, significantly more than the share of men (19.9 percent). Women are also much less likely to earn very high wages. In 2005 only 10.1 percent of women, but 17.6 percent of men, earned at least three times the poverty-level wage. The proportion of minority workers earning low wages is substantial – 33.3 percent of black workers and 39.3 percent of Hispanic workers in 2005. Minority women are even more likely to be low earners – 37.1 percent of black women and 45.7 percent of Hispanic women in 2005.

The trend in the share of workers earning poverty-level wages corresponds to the patterns previously described: momentum in reducing poverty-level work began in the late 1990s, continued until 2002, then dissipated. So, although the share of workers earning poverty-level wages actually fell from 25.1 percent to 24.5 percent in the 2000-05 period, this progress came in the first two years of that period and then partially reversed. Among blacks the increase in low-wage work after 2002 was large enough to reverse the progress from 2000 to 2002.

A historical look at wage inequality shows that it has worsened considerably over the past three decades. The deterioration in real wages from 1979 to 1995 was both broad and uneven. Wages were stagnant or fell for the bottom 60 percent of wage earners over the

1979-95 period and grew modestly for higher-wage workers – over 16 years the growth was just 5.0 percent at the 80th percentile and 10.9 percent to 13.9 percent at the 90th and 95th percentiles, respectively.

More recently, the importance of the late 1990s full-employment labor markets that provided across the board wage increases contrast with the most recent 2000-05 period. Starting in the early 1990s low-wage workers experienced either wage growth more than or comparable to that of middle-wage workers, so that the expanding wage gap between the middle and bottom lessened and then stabilized. Tight labor markets along with increases in the minimum wage in the early and late 1990s, combined with the drop in unemployment in the late 1990s, can explain this trend.

There are three key elements of wage inequality. One is the gap at the "bottom," meaning the difference between median-wage and low-wage workers. Another measure of wage inequality takes into account the "top half" gap, that is, between high-wage (90th or 95th percentile wage earners) and middle-wage earners. The third element is the gap at the very top, i.e., the growth of wages for those in the upper 1 percent, including chief executive officers (CEOs). These three elements have had differing historical trajectories. The gap at the bottom grew in the 1980s but has been stable or declining ever since, whereas the "top half" wage gap has persistently grown since the late 1970s. The very highest earners have done considerably better than other workers for at least 30 years, but they have done extraordinarily well over the last 10 years.

Explaining these shifts in wage inequality requires attention to several factors that affect low-, middle-, and high-wage workers differently. The experience of the late 1990s is a reminder of the great extent to which a low unemployment rate benefits workers, especially low-wage earners. Correspondingly, the high levels of unemployment in the early and mid-1980s and again in recent years have disempowered wage earners and provided the context in which other forces – specifically, a weakening of labor market institutions and an increase in globalization – could drive up wage inequality. Significant shifts in the labor market, such as the severe drop in the real value of the minimum wage and de-unionization, can explain one-third of the growth in wage inequality. Similarly, the increasing globalization of the economy – immigration, trade, and capital mobility – and the employment shift toward lower-

paying service industries (such as retail trade) and away from manufacturing can explain, in combination, another third of the total growth in wage inequality. Macroeconomic factors also played an important role: high unemployment in the early 1980s greatly increased wage inequality, the low unemployment of the late 1990s reduced it, and high unemployment in recent years has renewed it.

The shape of wage inequality shifted in the late 1980s as the gap at the bottom – i.e., the 50/10 gap between middle-wage workers at the 50th percentile and low-wage workers at the 10th – began to shrink. However, over the last few years, this progress against wage inequality at the bottom has been halted among men and wage inequality at the bottom among women has resumed its growth. This reversal is partially the effect of the jobless recovery and the still-remaining shortage of jobs and partially a result of the continued drop in the real value of the minimum wage. The greatest increase in wage inequality at the bottom occurred among women and corresponded to the fall in the minimum wage's value over the 1980s, the high unemployment of the early 1980s, and the expansion of low-wage retail jobs. The positive trend in this wage gap over the 1990s owes much to increases in the minimum wage, low unemployment, and the slight, relative contraction in low-paying retail jobs in the late 1990s. The wage gap at the top half – the 90/50 gap between high- and middle-wage earners – continued its steady growth in the 1990s and early 2000s but at a slightly slower pace than in the 1980s. The continuing influence of globalization, de-unionization, and the shift to lower-paying service industries ("industry shifts") can explain the continued growth of wage inequality at the top.

The erosion of the extent and quality of employer-provided benefits, most notably pensions and health insurance, is an important aspect of the deterioration in job quality for many workers. Employer-provided health care coverage eroded from 1979 until 1993-94, when it stabilized, and then began falling again after 2000 through 2004 (the latest data). In fact, coverage dropped from 69.0 percent in 1979 to 55.9 percent in 2004, with a 2.9 percentage-point fall just since 2000. Employees have absorbed half the rise in costs for employer-provided health premiums (not counting any of the higher deductibles or co-pays paid by employees) since 1992, even though their share of costs in that year was just 14 percent. Employer-provided pension coverage tended to rise in the 1990s but receded by 2.8 percentage points from 2000 to 2004 to 45.5 percent,

5.1 percentage points below the level in 1979. Pension plan quality also receded, as the share of workers in defined-benefit plans fell from 39 percent in 1980 to just 19 percent in 2003. Correspondingly, the share of workers with a defined-contribution plan (and no other plan) rose from 8 percent to 31 percent.

Young workers' prospects are another good barometer of the strength of the labor market. Wages actually fell for all entry-level workers since 2000, whether high school or college educated, male or female. This contrasts to the extremely strong wage growth for each of these groups from 1995 to 2000, when wages rose roughly 10 percent for entry-level high school men and women, 20.9 percent for entry-level college men, and 11.7 percent for college women.

Unionized workers earn higher wages than comparable non-union workers and also are 18.3 percent more likely to have health insurance, 22.5 percent more likely to have pension coverage, and 3.2 percent more likely to have paid leave. The erosion of unionization (from 43.1 percent of blue-collar men in 1978 to just 19.2 percent in 2005) can account for 65 percent of the 11.1 percentage-point growth of the blue-collar/white-collar wage gap among men over the 1978-2005 period.

The real value of the minimum wage has been steadily falling in real terms, thereby causing the earnings of low-wage workers to seriously fall behind those of other workers and contributing to the rise in wage inequality. Those affected by the lower minimum wage make important contributions to their family's economic well-being. For instance, minimum wage earners contribute 58 percent of their family's weekly earnings; in 43 percent of the affected families the minimum wage earner generated all of the family's earnings. Moreover, there are 7.3 million children living in the families that would benefit from a modest minimum wage increase. While minorities are disproportionately represented among minimum wage workers, 60 percent are white. These workers also tend to be women (59 percent of the total) and concentrated in the retail and hospitality industries (46 percent of all minimum wage earners are employed in those industries, compared to just 21 percent of all workers).

Conversely, the 1980s, 1990s, and 2000s have been prosperous times for top U.S. executives, especially relative to other wage earners. Over the 1992-2005 period the median CEO saw pay rise by 186.2 percent, while the median worker saw wages rise by just 7.2 percent. In 1965, U.S. CEOs in major companies earned 24 times more than an average worker; this ratio grew to 300 at the end of the recovery in 2000. The fall in the stock market reduced CEO stock-related pay (e.g., options), but by 2005 CEO pay had recovered to the point where it was 262 times that of the average worker. The lion's share of the gains for the top 1 percent in the pay scale accrued to the upper 10 percent of that elite group (i.e., those in the 99.9th percentile). Of the 3.6 percentage-point gain in the share of all earnings that the top 1 percent experienced between 1989 and 2000, 3.2 of them accrued to very upper tier.

The jobs of the future will require greater education credentials, but not to any great extent. In 2004, the occupational composition of jobs required that 27.7 percent of the workforce have a college degree or more. This share will rise by just one percentage point, to 28.7 percent, by 2014, according to BLS projections.

Jobs: Diminished expectations

Strong job creation that fully utilizes the available workers and skills in our workforce is a critical component to a strong, lasting, and equitable recovery. A robust job market is what is needed to ensure that the proceeds of economic growth are broadly shared. By that measure, the current recovery has fallen short. As is well known, this recovery, which began in late 2001, was a "jobless recovery" well into 2003. That is, real gross domestic product was expanding, but we were losing jobs on net for a year and a half into the expansion (net jobs refer to the number of jobs created minus the number of jobs lost).

Historically, it took just less than two years – 21 months – to regain the prior employment peak; in this current cycle, it took almost four years (46 months). Since then, we have consistently added jobs on net, but at a slower rate than in past recoveries. As of this writing the current cycle is five years old and employment is up 1.9 percent since the last cyclical peak. Comparatively, employment growth for the five-year period of the 1990s cycle was 7.1 percent and the historical average for cycles of this length was 10 percent.

This record of historically weak job creation is costly for the economy and for workers. Lackluster job creation is partially responsible for the ongoing disjuncture between overall economic growth and the wages and incomes of working families, as shown in earlier chapters. The resulting lower rates of employment and lack of wage pressures translate into lost output and forgone increases in living standards.

Depressed employment rates are usually a sign of weak labor demand. Since the 2001 peak, employment rates are down 1.4 percentage points for men and 1.3 percentage points for women. However, there have been debates as to whether employment rate declines have been a cyclical response to weak demand or if they represented a structural change. Since young college graduates are a group with high attachment to the job market, they make a good test case for whether the low employment rates are related to weak demand as opposed to a voluntary decline in employment (i.e., cyclical vs. structural).

The employment rate of young college graduates fell 3.5 percentage points from 2001 to mid-2003 – in step with the recession and jobless recovery. In 2003, when employment started to pick up, this rate also increased significantly. Young college graduates (ages 25 to 35) who had at least a bachelor's degree, and in some cases, an advanced degree, would have been highly motivated to secure employment. Now that employment rates are rebounding, it seems the cyclical responses may have dominated structural ones.

The unemployment rate is, in a historical sense, relatively low – 4.8 percent as of this writing. Unemployment rates that prevailed during the expansion of the late 1990s into 2000 – when the annual unemployment rate was 4.0 percent – were considerably lower. For most of the current recovery, the relatively low unemployment rates have not been particularly good indicators of the actual slack that existed throughout the labor market, particularly in the first several years.

Persistent long-term unemployment has been another problem over this cycle. Shares of those unemployed 27 weeks or longer, as a share of total unemployment, were unusually high, especially given the relatively low unemployment rates that prevailed throughout the 2001 recession and recovery. As of this writing, the unemployment rate varied over the past year between 4.6 and 5.0 percent, and the average share of long-term unemployment was 18.4 percent. By comparison, the historical share of long-termers associated with this range of unemployment was just 10.8 percent.

It is still the case that those with less education disproportionately bear the brunt of economic downturns, but it is also the case that higher levels of education no longer provide the same protection against cyclical forces as in prior downturns. This was evident with depressed employment rates of young college graduates, and it is also evident in long-term unemployment woes associated with this latest cycle.

The share of educated long-termers increased 2.8 percentage points from 2000 to 2005, while the share decreased by 5.4 percentage points for those with less than a high school diploma.

Job growth has been too tepid to boost living standards for most workers – even as the economy expanded and labor productivity posted some impressive gains over this recovery. Hopefully the economy is poised to generate robust job creation and tight labor markets akin to those in the late 1990s, finally transforming output growth and strong worker productivity into broadly shared prosperity.

Other trends of note regarding jobs:

- Two industrial sectors have been especially hard hit: manufacturing employment, which is off 16 percent, and the information sector, which includes telecommunications, is down 17 percent from peak employment levels of 2001.

- Blue-collar workers made up 43.3 percent of long-term unemployment shares in 1989; in 2005 the share was 33.1 percent. Corresponding white-collar shares went from 31.0 percent to 38.9 percent.

- "Perma-temping," that is, the percent of temporary agency workers who have been on the same work assignment for a year or more, increased from 24.4 percent in 1995 to 33.7 percent in 2005.

- Employment rates for men and women at least 55 years old have trended upward since the early 1990s, and the trend even continued over the 2001 recession – the only age cohort to do so.

Wealth: Unrelenting disparities

Wealth and its accumulation are very important to a family's financial stability. Wealth, for example, enables a family to invest in a home, education, and retirement. In the short term, wealth reserves can help a family through difficult times, such as job loss. Wealth accumulation and debt often go hand-in-hand – for example, wealth as well as debt can be generated by home ownership. The ability of families to accumulate wealth and manage their debts is critical. This chapter dissects the two components that make up wealth or net worth – assets and liabilities.

Wealth is unequally distributed, more so than wages or incomes. Moreover, wealth has become more concentrated at the top of the distribution over time. In 2004, those in the top 1 percent of the wealth scale held over one-third of all wealth. The top fifth controlled 84.7 percent of all wealth in the United States, while the bottom 80 percent could claim only 15.3 percent of the country's total wealth in 2004. Over the 1962-2004 period, the wealth share held by the bottom 80 percent shrank by 3.8 percentage points, and that 3.8 percent share of wealth shifted to the top 5 percent of households. Over time wealth inequality has increased – as measured by the ratio of the wealthiest 1 percent to median wealth. In the early 1960s, the wealthiest Americans held 125 times that of the median wealth holder; in 2004 the wealthiest held 190 times more. As the wealthiest continue to thrive, many households are left behind with little or nothing in the way of assets and often have significant debt. Approximately one in six households had zero or negative net wealth.

Second, the notion that a vast majority of American households are greatly invested in the stock market is erroneous. Less than half of all households hold stock in any form, including mutual funds and 401(k)–style pension plans. From 2001 to 2004, the share of households holding stock declined – for the first time since 1989 – from 51.9 percent to 48.6 percent. Moreover, of those households that held stock, just 34.9 percent had stock holdings of $5,000 or more.

Furthermore, the ownership of stocks was particularly unequal. In 2004, the top 1 percent of stockowners held 36.9 percent of all stocks, by value, while the bottom 80 percent of stockholders owned less than 10 percent. Additionally, stocks are a bigger part of the asset portfolio for wealthier households. For those in the top 1 percent of the wealth distribution, stock assets made up over 21 percent of their total assets, while stocks consisted of just 4.8 percent of all assets for households in the middle fifth of the wealth distribution. While stock performance is very important, on a daily basis it does not significantly affect average households.

Another key observation is that household debt has consistently trended upward, and it was over 130 percent of disposable personal income in 2005. As expected, debt-service burdens continued to plague lower-income families disproportionately and they increased from 2001 to 2004. By 2004, a middle-income family spent about a fifth of their income to service their debt. Approximately one in four low-income households had debt-service obligations that exceeded 40 percent of their income, as did 13.7 percent of middle-income households.

The opportunity to start anew through fair and reasonable bankruptcy laws is crucial for those who are faced with insurmountable debt. Personal bankruptcy filings soared at the end of 2005 just before new, stricter laws went into effect. For the year, nine out of every 1,000 adults declared personal bankruptcy. Only time will tell how the new laws will affect the number of bankruptcy filings, and ultimately how families will cope with large debt burdens often caused by the loss of employment, unmanageable medical bills, or divorce.

That wealth differs considerably by race is another primary observation of this analysis. Median wealth of white households is 10 times that of black households. Home ownership rates also vary considerably by race. Less than half of black and Hispanic households own their homes, when 72.7 percent of white households do. While approximately one-in-six households had zero or negative net wealth, broken down by race the numbers diverge considerably – 13.0 percent of white households compared to 29.4 percent of black households have zero or negative net wealth.

Other key findings from this chapter include:

- Wealth inequality is greater than income inequality: The top 1 percent, next 9 percent, and bottom 90 percent shares of income were 16.9 percent, 25.6 percent, and 57.5 percent, respectively in 2004. Shares of wealth were 34.3 percent, 36.9 percent, and 28.7 percent, respectively.

- Average wealth held by the top 1 percent was close to $15 million, while it was $81,000 for households in the middle-fifth of the wealth distribution.

- Approximately 30 percent of households have a net worth of less than $10,000.

- About half of those in the bottom quarter of the income distribution own their homes, while 88.9 percent in the top quarter of the income distribution own homes.

Poverty: Rising over the recovery as the job market stalls

We next move to the other end of the wealth spectrum and examine the problem of poverty in America.

One of the most important challenges in discussing poverty in America is definitional. What, precisely, characterizes poverty in the U.S. economy? The government has an official definition, but it is widely considered to be an outdated benchmark (the 2005 threshold for a family of four was $19,961). The official thresholds have fallen well behind income growth among middle and higher income families, creating a situation wherein the poor are by definition more economically isolated. For example, the poverty line for a family of four was 48 percent of median family income in 1960; now it is 29 percent.

That said, trends in poverty are still revealing of changes in the living standards of our most economically vulnerable families. After falling steeply throughout the latter 1990s, poverty rates increased not only in the recessionary year of 2001, but in each year through 2005 (most recent data available), from 11.3 percent in 2000 to 12.6 percent in 2005, when 37 million persons, including 13 million children, were in poverty. This is the first time that poverty rose through each of the first three years of a recovery, another indicator of the narrow distribution of growth over this recovery. If we use a threshold of "twice poverty" (i.e., double the poverty line), then the increase over the 2000-05 period went from 29.3 percent to 31.0 percent (about 91 million persons were below "twice poverty" in 2004).

Given their lower incomes, poverty rates for minorities are consistently higher than those of whites. The rate for African Americans, for example, was at least three times that of whites through 1989. However, poverty among blacks and Hispanics was much more responsive than for whites to the faster and more broadly distributed income growth during the 1990s, and by 2000 the poverty rate for blacks was the lowest on record, though even then more than a fifth of blacks were poor (22.5 percent).

Tight job markets played a critically important role in poverty reduction in the latter 1990s, as overall poverty fell by 2.5 percentage points, with much larger declines for minorities: 6.8 points for blacks and 8.8 points for Hispanics. Yet, even under the best macroeconomic conditions, many poor families will need extra help to escape poverty. In the latter 1990s, for example, the push of welfare reform and the pull of strong labor demand drew many single mothers into the job market. And for many of these women, full employment conditions helped generate significant wage gains in percentage terms. But even hourly wage gains of about a third, from around $6 to around $8 dollars an hour, do not provide enough income for these families to meet their basic consumption needs. Fortunately, significant work supports – public benefits tied to work – were added or expanded over the 1990s. In the early 1990s, the highest benefit level under the Earned Income Tax Credit for a family with at least two children rose from about $1,700 to about $4,000 in 1995 dollars. The minimum wage was also

increased, and more resources were devoted to health and child care subsidies.

The last point is an important one in thinking about the steps policy makers need to take to diminish poverty amid the plenty in the U.S. economy. With both the economy and social policy pushing hard in the same direction, poverty was significantly reduced in the 1990s. The 2000s, by contrast, reveal a different picture. The policy levers from the earlier period were largely still in place, but the absence of full employment meant that a critical piece of the puzzle was missing, and poverty rose over these years.

Regional analysis: Shared experiences, crucial differences

National trends in wages, incomes, poverty, and employment, as well as other economic indicators discussed throughout this book often vary greatly by region and by state. This chapter examines the economy through a regional lens. A regional focus is important because regional data more accurately represent economic circumstances faced by workers in a particular area. While not explicitly discussed in this chapter, state specific analyses and data can be found at www.earncentral.org/swx.htm.

The four census regions are used throughout this chapter: Northeast, Midwest, South, and West. While the division into these regions for economic purposes is not perfect (dividing such intertwined states as Pennsylvania and Maryland or New Mexico and Texas), the differences between them are notable and thus provide some useful insights regarding regional variation.

This chapter begins by contrasting the early 1990s recession with the 2001 downturn. A regional perspective clearly shows that the early 1990s labor market slump disproportionately affected two areas of the country: the Northeast region and the state of California. The 2001 downturn was more geographically pervasive as there were just a few states that did not experience employment losses over the 2000 to 2003 period.

Job losses in the Northeast and California in the 1990s recession contributed to unemployment rates that rose earlier and faster in those areas compared to the rest of the country. Reflecting widespread job losses over the 2000-03 period, regional increases in unemployment were also prevalent during that time. However, the rates increased the fastest for the Midwest and California and rates increased the most for the Midwest for the latter recession.

Over the current cycle, the growth in long-term unemployment rates by region were very similar at the onset of the recession – 2001 to 2002. However, further into the cycle, different regional patterns emerged as long-term unemployment worsened much more in the Midwest relative to the other regions.

This result clearly relates to the regional impact of manufacturing job loss. One of the key factors in the recent recession and jobless recovery was the continued loss of employment in the manufacturing sector – especially for areas that have a heavy reliance on this sector. However, of the 35 states that had fewer jobs in 2003 than in 2000, 20 experienced job growth outside of manufacturing. For example, while Arkansas lost 14.2 percent of manufacturing jobs, all other industries grew by 2.1 percent.

Job loss and increases in unemployment resulted in wage stagnation. In the West North Central division (Midwestern states west of the Mississippi), for example, low wage growth slowed from 3.1 percent annually from 1995 to 2000 to less than 1 percent annually from 2000 to 2003. There were some states, primarily in the Northeast, where wage growth was faster in the 2000 to 2003 period than between 1995 and 2000, but the overall picture was one of wage stagnation.

The federal minimum wage – fixed at $5.15 – has not been raised since 1997. Tired of waiting for a federal hike, advocates at the state level have taken up the fight to increase state minimum wages. The number of states with minimum wages higher than the federal level has quadrupled, from five in 1997 to 21 in 2004, and as of this writing over a quarter of the workforce resides in states with minimum wages above the federal level. More campaigns are on the near horizon.

International comparisons: How does the United States stack up?

The more market-driven U.S. economic model is often deemed superior to European economic models. The evidence of U.S. supremacy is often made by the singular assertion that the United States is the richest country in the world. While it is true that, in per capita terms, the United States is quite wealthy, a comparative analysis as to how the U.S. economy stacks up to other advanced economies must take into consideration a broader set of criteria.

International comparisons are made between 20 countries all belonging to the Organisation for Economic Co-operation and Development (OECD). Comparing the U.S. economy to similar economies facing the same global conditions with respect to trade, investment, technology, and the environment provides an independent yardstick for gauging economic outcomes derived from different economic models. It is important to note that what is commonly referred to as the "European model" is actually many different economic models. Not only is each country unique, but unique occurrences – like the integration of East Germany – need to be taken into account. Many of the countries evaluated here are less market driven and more "interventionist" than the U.S. economic system, and much insight can be drawn from a general comparative analysis.

A main determinant of an economy's standard of living is its productivity, which can be relatively measured by the amount of gross domestic product (GDP) per hour worked. In terms of GDP per hour worked, in 2004 several European countries caught up to or surpassed U.S. levels of productivity. For example, looking at productivity relative to the United States (U.S.=100), five countries are above or equal to U.S. levels – Norway (125), Belgium (113), France (107), Ireland (104), and the Netherlands (100).

The growth rate of productivity is also important, and the United States is currently enjoying an extremely productive economy. In the current cycle (2000-05), U.S. productivity grew at 2.5 percent, and the United Kingdom came in second at 2.0 percent. However, as this book's discussion of family income and wages shows, the workforce responsible for this high level of productivity has not been able to enjoy the fruits of their very productive labor. Simply put, earnings have been stagnant for the majority of workers throughout this cycle.

The United States is one of the richest countries in the world. Per capita income in the U.S. was $39,728, but, perhaps surprisingly, that posting was second to Norway's $41,804. Many other economies have very respectable – all above $30,000 – per capita incomes, including Ireland, Switzerland, Austria, Canada, Australia, Denmark, Sweden, Netherlands, Finland, Belgium, and the United Kingdom. Many Europeans and Canadians view their social protections as factors that raise their living standards and as such are unmeasured and not captured in income measures. A main reason why per capita incomes in Europe are generally below U.S. levels is because Europeans, relative to those in the U.S., seem to value leisure over the consumption of more goods.

While the United States is one of the wealthiest countries, it also has the highest degree of inequality of the OECD countries analyzed. The gap between richest and poorest is largest in the United States – whether measured in terms of Gini coefficients or the ratio of high earners (90th percentile) to low earners (10th percentile), the United States' inequality stands out. Low-income earners in the United States not only earn relatively lower incomes than their OECD counterparts, but they also are worse off because of limited social policy and safety nets. Access to health care is a good example.

The United States spends more on health care (whether measured as a percentage of gross domestic product or per capita spending) than any of these other countries. The United States spent 15.0 percent of its GDP on health care in 2003 – 30 percent more than the next highest spender (Switzerland at 11.6 percent). Ireland (7.4 percent), Austria (7.5 percent), and Finland (7.5 percent) spent the lowest percentages of GDP on health care. Even with such high spending, 46 million people in the United States do not have health insurance, and access to health care is much more limited than in the countries of its economic peers. In Canada, Japan, and Europe there is essentially universal health care coverage.

Perhaps surprisingly, the income advantages and high health spending in the United States do not produce better outcomes relative to other developed countries regarding life expectancy, infant mortality, and poverty. The United States has the lowest life expectancy, the highest infant mortality rates, and the highest overall and child poverty rates of all the countries studied. The relatively poor performance of the United States in these categories is symptomatic of the high degree of economic inequality and unequal access to health care in the United States.

Other important insights to come out of this chapter:

- The U.S. unemployment rate in 2004 was above 10 and below nine of the 20 countries examined in this analysis.

- A breakdown in per capita income shows that, while U.S. productivity is an important determinant of relatively higher U.S. incomes, even more significant is that Americans simply work more annual hours.

- European vacation time is mandated, usually four to five weeks worth, while there is no mandated vacation time in the United States.

- U.S. labor costs are not necessarily more prohibitive, as relative U.S. manufacturing labor costs are below that of seven European countries.

Conclusion

America's working families continue to work hard to make ends meet, improve their living standards, and create better opportunities for their children. New economy or old, this remains the case today much as it was a century ago.

Yet there are clearly aspects of today's economy that make it historically unique. Some of these tilt against the bargaining power of American workers: increased global trade, less union membership, and more low-skilled and high-skilled immigration. There are fewer favorable social norms that guide employer behavior or support policies that provide adequate safety nets, pensions, and health care arrangements.

Other new forces in play have the potential to lift the living standards of working families in ways hardly seen in this country for 30 years. Most important of these is a new, stronger productivity growth regime and a brief encounter with full employment in the latter 1990s that showed that, once workers' bargaining power gets a boost, the benefits of this regime shift in productivity growth can be broadly shared.

In other words, the biggest challenge in what many have called the new economy is not growth per se, but rather how growth is distributed. Of course, economists and policy makers will be concerned with whether the economy is growing as fast and efficiently as it can, and they might turn to greater investments in public and private capital stock, more research and development, monetary policy that stresses full employment, and the educational upgrading of the workforce.

Yet, if the findings in the hundreds of tables and figures that follow can be reduced to one observation, it would be that, when it comes to an economy that is working for working families, growth in and of itself is a necessary but not a sufficient condition. The growth has to reach the people: the bakers need to benefit from bread they create each day of their working lives.

The benchmarks by which we judge the economy must reflect these distributional concerns, and we must construct policies and institutions to address them. If we do not – if our enhanced productive capacity continues to benefit mostly the wealthiest Americans – we risk sacrificing bedrock principles that have historically defined the American economic experience.

WHY
UNIONS
MATTER

Interfaith Worker Justice (2007)

Many people of faith and good will want to support workers in their efforts to improve wages, benefits and working conditions, but they don't understand why workers want to be represented by unions. Young people especially may not even understand what a union is and why many workers are interested in forming unions.

All workers should have the right to form a union without fear and harassment. Interfaith Worker Justice believes that in general unions are good for society. This does not mean that every union is perfect or that every workplace needs a union. But for those concerned about justice for workers, it is important to understand why many workers want to join unions, the union benefit for workers, the role of unions in society and the difficulties workers face in forming unions. It is also important to build relationships with labor unions in order to jointly push for shared values of justice and dignity for workers, and to uphold the rights of workers who choose to form unions.

Why Workers Join or Organize Unions

Workers want a voice in decisions

All workers want to be involved in decisions that affect their lives, and yet many find themselves and their suggestions routinely ignored or rejected. Many feel that they are denied the right to talk and think when they enter the workplace. Management, who controls their basic livelihood, discourages workers' participation in the company decision-making process. This is especially frustrating to workers regarding issues such as the scheduling of hours, workloads and ways to make the work more effective.

Workers want a safe working environment

Unions create safer working environments in two ways. They help to improve the conditions in which employees work, which reduces injuries; secondly, they encourage workers to report and seek care for the injuries that they suffer on the job. Unions help to correct the company's priorities so that the worker's welfare and safety on the job are seen as integral to the company rather than a liability to profits.

Because there are so many dangerous jobs, workers form unions to protect themselves. Farm workers form unions to reduce their exposure to pesticides, and to get drinking water and access to bathrooms in the field. Nursing home workers form unions to combat back injuries, frequently caused by chronic understaffing in nursing homes. Poultry workers form unions to address the repetitive motion injuries that plague the industry.

When accidents do happen, workers need to be able to report the injuries to the company so they can receive treatment or Workers Compensation. Unions give workers the voice they need to report their injuries because union contracts help to ensure that a worker can't be fired or denied compensation for a workplace injury. This is especially important at dangerous jobs, where occasional accidents are inevitable. An injured worker seems more like an obstacle than a human being to an employer that is more concerned with the bottom line than with worker welfare. Companies have a business incentive to find ways to sever ties with injured workers rather than provide care and compensation so that an employee can go back to work. Unions help to counteract this business pitfall by strengthening workers' voices and creating clear regulations that the employer must follow when confronted with injured employees.

Workers want living wages

Although wages are frequently not one of the first reasons cited by workers for forming a union, adequate pay is a reflection of the value a company places on its workforce. Workers need good wages to meet their families' needs and live with dignity. All workers should be able to feed, clothe and house their families on their wages. And yet, too many are forced to turn to soup kitchens and shelters for emergency help. Families should also have adequate income to provide for their children's education as well as their own retirement years. Union wages improve and strengthen working families' communities.

Workers want comprehensive benefits

Unless (or until) the United States provides comprehensive health care to all residents, workers must turn to the places of employment to provide health insurance. Unfortunately, nearly 53 million people are without health insurance as of 2009. Most of these uninsured are workers in low-wage jobs and their family members. Over half of all nursing-home workers are without health insurance because it is either not offered by their employer or the co-payments are too high. Unions place a high priority on securing health insurance coverage for workers.

Workers want and deserve other benefits such as paid vacation, paid holidays and secure pensions. These are benefits for which unions advocate. Although there are nonunionized workplaces that offer good benefits in industries that require limited amounts of training, a union is often the difference between having and not having benefits.

Workers want job security

As companies outsource, downsize and shift from permanent to contingent employees, workers have grown concerned about their job security. People want assurance that companies won't outsource their job to some cheaper group, another state or even another country. Unions can't guarantee job security, but contracts negotiated by unions attempt to create some level of security in every contract they negotiate.

Workers who are not in unions or employed by the government are working "at will" – in other words, at the will of the employer. An employer can legally fire anyone for any reason so long as the reason isn't in direct violation of a federal law regarding discrimination. Because an employer can fire someone for virtually any reason, such as having a "bad attitude" or negligible tardiness, employees who work "at will" have very little job security.

Workers want fairness in the workplace

Workers want to know what the rules are, what the consequences are for breaking those rules and what the appeal (grievance) process is for alleged rule violations. Some personnel policies clearly outline them. Most don't. Too often workers follow the policies while the employers do not.

Without a personnel policy that acts as a binding contract, or a union contract that makes the rules and procedures clear, workers feel vulnerable to the whims of supervisors. Promotions, raises, penalties and dismissals often feel random and unfair.

> " We had no consistent personnel policies. People were fired and there were no grievance procedures. New people were hired and given more vacation days than others. Everything was based on who the supervisors liked.

What is the union "benefit"?

Unionized workers have a voice in the workplace

By helping secure a contract that outlines rules, procedures and a structure for addressing workers' concerns, unions provide a counterbalancing power to management in the workplace. Workers can't always secure everything they want, but they are assured a more structured means for addressing problems.

Unionized workers earn more money and better benefits

According to the Bureau of Labor Statistics, in 2008 the union pay advantage was 22 percent higher for all workers, and it is even larger for people of color and women.

Unionized workers are more likely to have health insurance

Union members are also more likely to have health plans that include dental, prescriptions and eyeglass coverage. In 2006, 80 percent of union workers in the private sector had employer provided medical care benefits, compared with the 49 percent of nonunion workers. Many unions are fighting to preserve or establish affordable co-payments for health insurance. Unionized workers are more likely to have short-term disability benefits, as well.

Unionized workers are more likely to have retirement benefits

In 2008, most union members, 77 percent, have defined-benefit coverage plans, compared with only 20 percent of non-union workers.

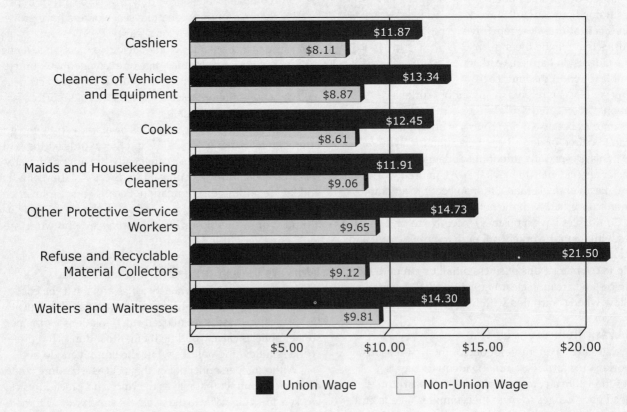

Union Representation Means Better Pay

Average Hourly Earnings by Occupations, 2006

Occupation	Union Wage	Non-Union Wage
Cashiers	$11.87	$8.11
Cleaners of Vehicles and Equipment	$13.34	$8.87
Cooks	$12.45	$8.61
Maids and Housekeeping Cleaners	$11.91	$9.06
Other Protective Service Workers	$14.73	$9.65
Refuse and Recyclable Material Collectors	$21.50	$9.12
Waiters and Waitresses	$14.30	$9.81

■ Union Wage   □ Non-Union Wage

Source: Barry T. Hirsch and David A. MacPherson, *Union Membership and Earnings Data Book*, BNA, 2007. Prepared by the AFL-CIO.

Smithfield Foods Workers Struggle 15 Years for Union Representation

Smithfield Foods is the largest hog killing and processing plant in the world, and in 1994, workers at their North Carolina Tar Heel plant attempted to organize for better wages and more safety in the workplace. After 15 years, workers finally approved a contract with the United Food and Commercial Workers (UFCW) in July 2009. Smithfield launched such a dishonest and brutal anti-union campaign that courts ruled to throw out the results of two elections in 1994 and 1997. Smithfield employed tactics like spying on workers' union activities, confiscating union materials, threatening to fire workers who voted for the union, threatening to freeze wages and to shut down the plant. One employee was beaten by Smithfield police on the day of the 1997 election – tactics which invalidated the union elections. Workers were too intimidated by Smithfield Foods to vote honestly. After a court ruling restricted the communication that Smithfield and the UFCW had with the workers, a fair election was finally won for the workers at the Tar Heel Plant.

When Workers Want to Form a Union

Workers talk with one another

Workers don't usually know that they want a union. They just know they are unhappy about working conditions. Frequently, workers seek to change conditions by talking with supervisors, participating in organized input groups or filing formal complaints. Most workers who organize turn to unions only after they've tried other means for gaining a legitimate voice in the workplace.

Contact is made with a union

The person who makes the initial contact with a union varies. Sometimes a worker knows a friend who knows someone in a union. Other times, workers contact the local labor council to find out which union should be contacted. In other settings, union organizers are out, talking with workers in particular industries and come across workers who want to organize a union.

An organizing committee is built

Because most workers don't know what unions are or do, unions build an organizing committee to help educate them. If there is not enough interest in even forming an organizing committee, it is probably not a place where workers will vote for a union.

Cards are signed

In the U.S., the way workers indicate to companies that they would like to be represented by a union is by signing "an authorization card." This card authorizes the union to operate on the workers' behalf.

In most Canadian labor jurisdictions, if a majority of the workers in a company sign authorization cards, the company is required by law to negotiate a contract with that union.

In the United States, a company may recognize the cards as indicating the will of the workers and negotiate with the union, which can be done as a community-group supervised election. Or the company may choose to have a government-supervised election. The former is referred to as "majority sign up." The latter is referred to as "an NLRB election." NLRB stands for National Labor Relations Board, the government agency that oversees union elections. At least 30 percent of the workers must sign cards before the NLRB will schedule an election.

An election is held

If the employer insists on an NLRB election, there may well be delays before the workers actually get to vote. Many employers challenge who is eligible to vote, claiming that certain workers shouldn't be included in the "bargaining unit." Only after all the challenges are resolved can the workers actually vote. If more than 50 percent of the workers vote to be represented by the union, the company is legally obligated to negotiate "in good faith" with the union.

Once a Union Is Formed

Negotiating a contract

Once the company recognizes the union (via majority sign up) or the workers win an NLRB election, the company and union must negotiate a contract which spells out terms of employment for those workers eligible for the contract. Often the workers elect their bargaining committee. Usually, the union bargaining team is composed of leaders from the organizing committee and union representatives familiar with contracts and bargaining.

Negotiating a contract is referred to as collective bargaining. When relations between unions and management are decent, contracts can usually be agreed to in a relatively short period of time – a few days, a few weeks, or at most a few months. Negotiations that drag on longer than a few months usually do so because a company does not want a contract. Unfortunately, even after workers vote in favor of forming a union, 52 percent of their workplaces remain without a contract a year later and 37 percent still lack a contract two years later.

Enforcing the contract

A union contract sets forth the terms of employment and a grievance mechanism for dealing with disagreements. A shop steward is the person who assists workers in filing grievances and using the grievance process. The union has a legal obligation to assist workers in the process. A shop steward is usually a worker who has special training in understanding the contract.

Renewing the contract

Because contracts are for specific periods of time, such as one year or three years, the contract will "come up for renewal." For most union-management relations, this is a fairly straightforward process. In other situations, it can become contentious.

What role do unions play in U.S. society?

Advocating for Public Policy

Many union members have bumper stickers that say, "UNIONS – The Folks that Brought You the Weekend" Well, it's true. Many of the public policies we take for granted, such as prohibitions on child labor, the eight-hour workday, social security, pension protections and the minimum wage were fought for and won by the labor movement and its allies in the religious community.

As important as religious involvement is in public policy advocacy for workers, progress can be achieved more effectively in partnership with a strong labor movement. Workers, especially workers in low-wage jobs, need a strong public policy voice that can counteract the powerful, well-financed business interests that too often dominate public policy.

Currently, unions are advocating increases in the minimum wage, health coverage for uninsured Americans, protections for social security, labor law reform, stronger enforcement of the Occupational Safety and Health Act and expanded protections for immigrant workers.

Raising the Wage Floor for All Workers

Union members gain higher wages through collective bargaining, a process that creates a wage floor that benefits all workers, especially workers in low-wage jobs. Frequently even nonunion employers raise wages to retain good workers and to dissuade the rank and file – non-management employees – from organizing.

Between the mid-'40s and the early-'70s, when labor unions were at their strongest, real wages rose consistently. At the beginning of the 21st century, however, unions represent only 12 percent of the workforce. Their decline is clearly a contributing cause to the overall decline of wages and benefits of all workers.

During the debates about bailing out the struggling American automobile industry, a plan for providing $14 billion in emergency loans to the carmakers was scuttled after opponents in the U.S. Senate insisted that unionized autoworkers must agree to massive pay and benefit cuts. In the heated rhetoric of the day, the fault for the meltdown of our economy was falsely attributed to "overpaid" unionized workers. But in the real world, the divide between the rich and the rest of us has become a gaping canyon, with income inequality higher than it has been than at any point since the 1920s.

The economic program we need must create living-wage jobs that allow workers to support themselves and their families in dignity, not in poverty. Unions are not the problem, and they must be part of the solution. Workers create wealth, and must be allowed a fair share of what they create.

Challenging Gross Disparity of Wages

The ratio of Chief Executive Officer (CEO) pay to worker pay in the U.S. is the most disproportionate of any industrialized nation in the world. CEO pay in the U.S. was 344 times the average worker's wages in 2008. By comparison, CEO pay in other industrialized countries is only 10 to 25 times that of the rank and file.

The salaries of CEOs in the U.S. are excessive because of a culture of greed and the decline of unions. Union bargaining not only raises the wage floor for average workers; it limits the excess of management's salaries by decreasing the amount of money that may be used for such. Thus, unions are one means by which to attain more equitable and just salaries.

Difficulties Faced by Workers Who Choose to Form Unions

Unfortunately, U.S. workers face a very hostile climate for organizing unions. Workers who choose to organize for a collective voice on the job are often viewed as disloyal troublemakers. This is true even in some religious institutions that claim to protect workers' rights to organize.

According to a 2009 study by Kate Bronfenbrenner, 53 percent of all working Americans would vote to join a union if they had the opportunity to do so without risking their jobs. However, workers are afraid. The weak laws alone are bad enough for those who choose to organize but a sophisticated, multi-million-dollar industry has developed to consult and advise employers on how to oppose unions. More than 80 percent of companies faced with union organizing efforts hire help to wage anti-union campaigns. No other industrialized nation has such a vibrant union-busting industry or weaker labor protections.

Ex-union buster, Martin Jay Levitt outlines the kind of unsavory tactics used against workers who want to unionize.

> Union busting is a field populated by bullies and built on deceit. A campaign against a union is an assault on individuals and a war on truth. As such, it is a war without honor. The only way to bust a union is to lie, distort, manipulate, threaten, and always, always attack. The law does not hamper the process. Rather it serves to suggest maneuvers and define strategies. Each "union prevention" campaign, as the wars are called, turns on a combined strategy of disinformation and personal assaults. (from prologue of Confessions of a Union Buster, 1993)

U.S. Labor law is dominated by the National Labor Relations Act (NLRA) and the Taft-Hartley amendments. The original National Labor Relations Act was passed in 1935 to improve workers' living standards by increasing the power of unions. Over the course of the next 65 years, the intent of the law has been changed via amendments to the Act and various judicial and administrative decisions that weaken the power of unions. The Taft-Hartley amendments to the NLRA, passed in 1947, strengthened managers' abilities to oppose unions. The amendments permitted the employers to campaign against union representation as long as there was "no threat of reprisal or force or promise of benefit."

What happens to workers who attempt to organize?

- Ninety-one percent of employers require employees to attend a one on one meeting with their supervisors where they are told why unions are bad and why they should vote against a union.
- Fifty-one percent of employers illegally coerce union opposition through bribes and favors.
- Thirty percent of employers illegally fire pro-union employees.
- Forty-nine percent of employers threaten to eliminate all workers' jobs if they join together in a union.

Most of this anti-union activity occurs after the workers have signed cards indicating they want to be represented by a union, and before the official NLRB-supervised election. If the point of an election is to determine what workers really want, then it would seem that both sides – union and management – should be able to present their cases fairly. But given the laws, the anti-union campaigns, and the control that employers have over workers' lives, the cases are not presented evenly. In effect, the time between signing cards and holding an election appears to be a time to scare workers into voting against unions.

Anti-union activities have become so

prevalent that an initiative was introduced in early 2006 by the 110th Congress to further employees' freedom to choose and pursue union representation. The Employee Free Choice Act, as the initiative is known, calls for stronger penalties for violations of the election process that occur between union card signing and the NLRB-supervised election, mediation and arbitration for stalled contract negotiations and union formation through majority sign-up.

Whether there is an NLRB-supervised election, card-check recognition or a community-sponsored election, the principles of fairness and respect for one another must be maintained by all parties, employees and employers alike.

After an election or card-check recognition, it is important for the union and management to negotiate a contract, a set of rules and expectations regarding wages, working conditions and other basic issues that sets terms on which both sides can agree. The contract is where employers, and employees, differing perspectives get resolved.

According to the law, all parties must bargain "in good faith." Although it is difficult to prove that someone isn't bargaining in good faith, experience has shown that if everyone really wants to negotiate a contract, it can be done in a relatively short period of time. When negotiations drag out for long periods of time, it usually means that there are irresolvable differences of opinion or that management does not want a contract. Because one key goal of unions is to negotiate contracts, it is seldom unions that create long delays. It is possible that a union would not agree to a particular contract proposal.

If a union and management cannot come to some agreement over a contract, union members can vote to go on strike. In a strike, workers withhold their labor for a certain period of time in order to put pressure on the company to negotiate a contract. During a strike, workers lose their wages and are ineli-

gible for public benefits such as unemployment insurance or food stamps (unless they were previously eligible). Although much publicized, strikes actually occur in only a small percentage of contract negotiations. In fact, most workers will strike only as a last resort because of the burden it places on themselves and their families.

Under the law, there are two different kinds of strikes. One is an unfair labor practice strike, and the other is an economic strike. For example, if a company fired three union supporters for their union activities, the union members could vote to go out on strike. This would be an unfair labor practice strike. If a company proposed reducing workers' pay by $1 per hour, the workers might vote to go on strike and it would be an economic strike.

Even though workers have the "right to strike," if they go out on an economic strike, under the terms of current U.S. labor law they can be permanently replaced. This right to strike, but right to lose your job, is one of the oddities of U.S. labor law. No other industrialized nation allows companies to permanently replace striking workers.

Though it is technically legal in the U.S., permanent replacement of striking workers is not ethical. Most religious bodies in the U.S. have publicly condemned the practice of permanently replacing striking workers because it upsets the balance of power between employees and employers.

Equally despicable is the practice of locking out workers before a contract can be settled. In a few situations, when workers attempt to negotiate a contract, management decides that things aren't going well and it simply locks the doors and refuses to let the workers in. Replacement workers are then hired to take the place of the locked-out workers. This practice, called a "lockout," has received little public attention, but is thoroughly outside the ethical principles outlined by the various faith traditions.

What about....

What about union corruption?

Unions, like religious bodies, are made up of human beings with all their flaws and frailties. There is some corruption in unions, as there is some within religious bodies. And, wherever corruption or greed is uncovered, it must be cleaned up. For that purpose, most unions have rigorous procedures to combat corruption. When a local union is found to be corrupt, the national leadership will take over control of the local until it can be cleaned up and an election of new leaders held. As wrong as union corruption is, it is unfortunate that it receives so much front page media attention in comparison to the important justice work done by unions to raise wages, benefits and working conditions for workers in low wage jobs.

What about union violence?

When workers are locked out, their jobs moved overseas or their economic livelihood threatened, it is understood that some people might respond with anger. But violence is something all national labor leaders abhor. Across the country, union members practice and preach nonviolence. And while there may always be some workers who act out their anger, this is not the modus operandi of unions.

When union-busting consultants want to denigrate unions they describe them as violent and show photos of violence on a picket line. Violence is wrong, whether it is workers on a picket line, security guards harassing picketers or companies causing economic violence against workers.

What about racism and sexism?

Racism and sexism are sins shared by unions and the religious community. The leaderships of the AFL-CIO and Change to Win hold as a key goal ensuring full participation for all in work, in society and in unions. Although much still needs to be done, the AFL-CIO has made significant progress in making its leadership more closely reflect its membership. Part of this may be due to a change the AFL-CIO made to its constitution meant to significantly develop the race and gender diversity of its leadership. Upon its establishment in 2005, Change to Win instituted three positions on its leadership council specifically meant to further race and gender diversity on the council.

Are unions really needed?

Maybe not, if the world were perfect and all employers were fair and honest. But even if employers were perfect, workers might still want to organize. Human beings have the God-given right to participate in decisions that affect their lives. Workers care deeply about their jobs and want a voice in workplace decisions.

We live in an economic society devoted more to the bottom-line than to people. Most corporate decisions that hurt workers are not driven by malice, but rather a desire to increase profits or compete in a very competitive global market. In this changing economy, individual workers need an organized voice to challenge the priorities of companies.

In our society, unions are the primary vehicles for worker representation. Over the years, unions have proved themselves as advocates for justice in society. Many workers view unions as advocates for justice now, and for the future. As unions stand for justice in the workplace and the society at large, the religious community should stand with them.

Interfaith Worker Justice
1020 W. Bryn Mawr, 4th Fl.
Chicago, IL 60660-4627
Phone: (773) 728-8400
Fax: (773) 728-8409
www.iwj.org

Globalization and Its Impact on Labor

Pamela K. Brubaker (2007)

The term *globalization* was first used in the late 1960s or early '70s to refer to "rapidly expanding political and economic interdependence," particularly between Western states. In their introduction to the globalization debate, David Held and Anthony McGrew define globalization as "the expanding scale, growing magnitude, speeding up and deepening impact of interregional flows and patterns of social interaction." They point out that the process of globalization is "deeply divisive" and "vigorously contested" because a significant portion of the world's population is largely excluded from its benefits.[1]

Our lives and communities are being changed by the impact of globalization. Ulrich Beck points out that *"we have been living for a long time in a world society*, in the sense that the notion of closed spaces has become illusory." For instance, there is the "ongoing revolution of information and communications technology," something most of us understand from the impact of computers and the Internet on our lives. We also have some awareness of the expansion and greater density of international trade when we notice where products we purchase are made. Beck calls this "globality." He distinguishes this from *globalism*, which is "the ideology of rule by the world market, or the ideology of neoliberalism."[2]

The central value of neoliberalism is competition, which is best expressed through the "free market." The ideas and policies in the "standard neo-liberal toolkit" have to do with the market, the state, corporations, unions and citizens. The market is to make major social and political decisions. The state should voluntarily reduce its role in the economy. Corporations are to have complete freedom. Unions are to be restrained and citizens given much less rather than more social protection. Susan George states that one of the greatest achievements of neoliberalism's proponents is that "they have made neoliberalism seem as if it were the natural and normal condition of humankind."[3] Margaret Thatcher had been influenced by neoliberalism, and when she became prime minister of Great Britain in 1979, she instituted a neo-liberal program that she called TINA – There Is No Alternative. Ronald Reagan, elected to the U.S. presidency a year later, began the neoliberal transformation of the U.S. economy.

Processes of Globalization

The Field Guide to the Global Economy offers a straightforward definition of economic globalization as "the flows of goods and services, capital and people across national borders."[4] Factors contributing "to the emergence of a single global market for capital, goods, and services" are a decrease in the cost of transportation and communication, as well as reduction of import tariffs, quotas and foreign exchange controls.[5] Thomas Friedman contends that globalization is "largely a technology-driven phenomenon," with the development of communication, transportation and computer technology inevitably and naturally leading to globalization.[6] But Peter Marcuse cautions that developments in technology and developments in the concentration of power, "often lumped together under the rubric of globalization," are distinct. Furthermore, he asserts that "the link between advances in technology and the concentration of economic power is not an inevitable one."[7] Rather, it is changes in the rules that enable this concentration.

The nature of present-day globalization is capitalist. What is particularly distinctive about capitalism is its focus on profit seeking, the accumulation of capital and the private ownership of the means of production. The term "capital" was not in use before the 1600s. It refers to that factor of production – "tools, equipment, factories, raw materials, goods in process, means of transporting goods and money" – that is used for production for profit. A share of profit is then devoted to the production of other goods and the process is repeated over and over, resulting in the accumulation of more and more capital.[8]

Global Economic Institutions. The post-World War II push to globalize the world's economies was led by three institutions, created at the 1944 United Nations Monetary and Financial Conference in Bretton Woods, New Hampshire: the World Bank, the International Monetary Fund (IMF) and the General Agreements on Tariffs and Trade (GATT). Henry Morgenthau, U.S. Secretary of the Treasury and president of the conference, said that its purpose was "the creation of a dynamic world economy in which the peoples of every nation will be able to realize their potentialities in peace and enjoy increasingly the fruits of material progress on an earth infinitely blessed with natural resources."[9]

An International Trade Organization had been proposed at the Bretton Woods meeting. However, its creation was blocked by the U.S. Congress, which thought it would harm U.S. interests. (It was seen as too friendly to labor and "third world" countries.) The General Agreement on Tariffs and Trade (GATT) was organized in its place. GATT was a framework for ongoing negotiations on reduction in tariffs to expand trade. During the 50 years between 1947 and 1997, tariffs dropped from almost 40 percent to around 4 percent, which greatly stimulated the process of globalization.[10]

After successive rounds of GATT, the World Trade Organization (WTO) was established in 1995 as the institution responsible for setting and enforcing the rules of trade. Its jurisdiction expanded from tariff reduction to "nontariff barriers" to trade, such as health, environmental and other public-interest regulations, and laws that give an advantage to local firms over foreign ones. Other new areas are Trade-Related Investment Measures (TRIMs), the elimination of barriers to the system of internal cross-border trade of product components among TNCs, and Trade-Related Intellectual Property Rights (TRIPs), which set enforceable global rules on patents, copyrights and trademarks (like pharmaceuticals). Particularly troubling is the WTO's unprecedented dispute resolution system. Unlike GATT, WTO rulings are automatically binding and do not require unanimous consent to be adopted. All dispute panel meetings are closed, and their activities and documents confidential. If a law is found to violate WTO agreements, countries either have to change it or face trade sanctions. This process offers no protection of due process, nor is citizen participation permitted.[11]

Expanding trade. Some data will sketch the changes in scope and intensity of present-day globalization. In the one-hundred-year period from 1870 to 1973, the percentage of world output of goods and services that were exports grew from 5 percent of the total to 12 percent. Then in just two decades – from 1973 to 2002 – it nearly doubled, now accounting for 24 percent of total production. (As we examine the types of goods and services that are traded, readers might want to think about their own purchasing patterns.) Of the goods traded across borders, the largest segment is made up of cars, trucks and car parts (8.4 percent), petroleum products (8.3 percent), textiles, footwear and clothing (6.2 percent); these three segments alone account for close to one-fourth of the total. Services that are traded include tourism and travel, banking

and insurance, education and training, communications and information services, advertising, entertainment, and legal services. The export of services from the U.S. rose from 17 percent of U.S. exports in 1980 to 30 percent in 2002; only 21 percent of the world's exports are services.[12]

Transnational corporations. Economist Peter Dicken asserts that up until about three decades ago, international economic integration was "shallow," exhibited mainly in "arm's length trade in goods and services between independent firms and through international movements of portfolio capital." In contrast, economic integration is now "deep," "organized primarily by transnational corporations" and extending to "the level of production of goods and services." Transnational corporations (TNCs) are key actors in the present form of globalization, enough so that some call this form corporate globalization. Dicken offers a useful definition of a TNC as "a firm which has the power to coordinate and control operations in more than one country, even if it does not own them." He refers to this process of coordination and control as "a spider's web of collaborative relationships," or "production chains." These are either producer or buyer driven. "Producer-driven chains" are characterized by strong control of the process from the TNC's administrative headquarters. Examples include the automotive and computer industry. In "buyer-driven chains," retailers, brand-named merchandisers, or trading companies play the crucial role in setting up decentralized production networks in a many different exporting countries. Examples include the apparel and shoe industry.[13]

According to the United Nations, the number of TNCs has grown from around 7,000 in 1970 to some 64,000 in 2003, a nine-fold increase in a little more than three decades. In addition to 870,000 affiliates, TNCs operate through hundreds of thousands of links, which include subcontracts, licensing agreements and strategic alliances between parent companies and other entities. Nike would be a prime example of this approach.[14] Van Drimmelen points out, "In 1970 a typical large US company earned 10-20 percent of its income from abroad; now many earn at least half their profits outside the US."[15]

Two-thirds of the world trade in goods and services is accounted for by TNCs. As much as one-third of this trade consists of transactions taking place within an individual TNC. In other words, parts are sent to another country for assembly (which counts as an export for the sending country, an import for the receiving one), and then the assembled part is returned for sale (counting as an import for the country which originally sent out the parts). Van Drimmelen notes that there is colossal secrecy about the way in which these "internal transfer prices are established and used," because this is an excellent way to minimize taxation. "Even governments often regard such matters as internal to the TNC." It is estimated that all this TNC activity – two-thirds of world trade – accounts for just 5 percent of the world's employment. However, TNCs control about one-third of the world's productive assets (capital). They generate about half of the greenhouse gas emissions, which contribute to global warming. Mining and commercial logging by some TNCs play a part in deforestation.[16]

Just 200 of these 60,000 or so TNCs dominate global economic activity. Between 1983 and 2002, the growth in world gross domestic product was 179.5 percent; the sales of top 200 TNCs grew 215 percent, while their assets grew 655.9 percent. Their combined sales counted for 28 percent of world GDP, but their employees made up less than 1 percent of the world's labor force. Of the top 100 economies in the world, only 48 are countries; 52 are corporations.[17] This raises the concern that the concentration of economic power threatens the sovereignty of nation-states.

Free Trade Zones. The creation of exporting processing zones (EPZs) in "developing" countries enabled TNCs to outsource much of their production. This complements a shift to export-oriented agriculture. People pushed off the land by this change become the labor force for the EPZs. At the end of the 20th century, there were over 100 export processing zones in 51 countries, which produce manufactured goods for export. These zones are set-aside areas within a country, with relaxed environmental and labor regulations and reduced taxes and tariffs. "The preferred labor force in these zones is female, very young and with little or no previous work experience." Most of these women are migrants from rural areas of the country, which are called "supporting agricultural regions." ("The single most important effect of foreign investment in export production is the uprooting of people from traditional modes of existence. … transforming people into migrant workers and, potentially, into emigrants." About 3 percent of the global population – 175 million people – are migrants.) Countries establish these zones to improve their international economic position and to get hard currency for debt servicing. Although these zones were supposedly dedicated to free trade, states would give subsidies to the industries

in these zones and "ensure labor tranquility through repressive tactics."[18]

In some cases, these export processing zones were the forerunners to development of free trade areas. This meant that the zones were no longer limited to certain areas of the country. Instead, the entire country became a free trade zone. Mexico under NAFTA is an example.

Mark Weisbrot charges that NAFTA made "it easier and more profitable for U.S. corporations to relocate to Mexico," which "increases their bargaining power against workers who try to organize unions. A study commissioned by the labor secretariat of NAFTA found that the agreement did in fact have that effect." (Mexican workers lost out too; for every four farm jobs lost, only one job was added in the export processing zones.)[19]

Weisbrot rightly claims that these cases support the charge that globalization is "a means of moving economic decision-making away from elected bodies such as congresses and parliaments, and placing more authority in the hands of unelected, unaccountable institutions such as the IMF, NAFTA or the transnational corporations themselves." Corporate campaign contributions are used to gain votes for free trade agreements opposed by constituents. A report from Public Citizen documents a total of $2.8 million given to a handful of members of the House of Representatives, whose votes led to the surprise passage of the Central American Free Trade Agreement (CAFTA) in July 2005.[20] This undermines the institutions that have alleviated the worst excesses and irrationalities of the market: the social safety net, environmental legislation, and various forms of financial regulation.

Impacts of Globalization

China and India are seen as globalization's big winners, particularly by advocates like Tom Friedman. He tells the story of globalization in a way that focuses on the winners and encourages others to follow in their path. Others tell the story in a way that focuses on those who lose out and offer policies for a fairer globalization or alternatives like localization.

Both China and India have experienced dramatic economic growth, accompanied by reduction in extreme poverty. China's growth has been more than 10 percent a year for several years. India has grown 8 percent for the past three years; its large technology companies 30-40 percent. China increased its exports from $14 billion in 1980 to $365 billion in 2002, more than a third of which goes to the U.S. However, neither India nor China followed the trade and investment liberalization policies of the Washington consensus. However, there are "losers" in India and China, too. Neither has significantly decreased child mortality, a key indicator of human development.[21] China continues to experience protests, which sometimes turn violent, over loss of farmland to industrial and commercial development. Wages are low and working conditions poor in its special processing zone where many of its exports are produced.

Income and job loss. People in other countries, the U.S. as well as many "developing" countries, have suffered job losses to China and India. India, for instance, is the main "developing-country destination" for U.S. service-sector outsourcing. "Global economic growth is increasingly failing to translate into new and better jobs that lead to a reduction in poverty," according to a December 2005 report by the International Labor Organization (ILO).[22]

A 2004 report from Oxfam International studied conditions in twelve countries – Bangladesh, Chile, China, Colombia, Honduras, Kenya, Morocco, Sri Lanka, South Africa, Thailand, Great Britain and the United States – for a report on women workers in global supply chains. They found that millions of women who work at the start of the supply chain – picking fruit, sewing garments – which source supermarkets and clothing stores, fuel growth in national exports but "are systematically being denied their fair share of the benefits brought by globalization." Oxfam holds "big brand companies and retailers" responsible for driving down employment conditions and charges them to "radically alter the way they work with producers and in negotiating deliveries and prices." During the past twenty years, "corporate rights are becoming ever stronger, while poor people's rights and protections at work are being weakened, and women are paying the social costs." States need to better enforce labor laws and guarantee workers' rights.[23]

Real wages in the United States rose only 7 percent on average between 1990 and 2003. During that same period, corporate profits increased 103 percent and CEO pay 274 percent. In 1982 the gap between average CEO pay and worker pay was just 42-to-1; by 2005 it was over 262-to-1. Average wages for workers with no education beyond high school are far lower today (adjusted for inflation) than they were in the 1970s. Many economists assign as much as 25 percent

of the increase in U.S. wage disparity to globalization, due to import competition from low-wage countries or employers exploiting a larger pool of low-wage labor in the U.S. The U.S. trade imbalance is a good indication of import competition. Between 1980 and 2005, the annual trade deficit in goods grew from $25 billion (less than 1 percent of GDP) to $717 billion (6 percent of GDP). U. S. manufacturing employment dropped from 18.7 million to 14.5 million during this same period. It is true that some manufacturing jobs are lost because of automation. However, the Economic Policy Institute found that between 1998 and 2003 (a period of dramatic job loss), 59 percent of the drop was due to the trade imbalance, or about 1.8 million jobs. Only about one-fourth of the laid-off manufacturing workers find new jobs that pay as well or better than their old jobs, according to the Department of Labor. Stiglitz points out that during this same period, "median household income – the income of the family at the center, the true middle middle-class family – fell by some $1,500, adjusting for inflation, or around 3 percent."[24]

Families living on edge. The Project on Global Working Families recently published the results of a decade of research in *Forgotten Families*. They found that "Around the world, families are increasingly living on the edge." It has become increasing difficult or impossible for employed adults "to care for themselves and their families' health and well-being," because of their working conditions. The movement of jobs from country to country "has spurred a downward spiral in working conditions." This puts parents in a position where they are forced "to make untenable choices between caring for their children adequately and earning the income they need for their families to survive and have a chance at thriving." Research found that "these experiences are devastatingly common" worldwide.[25]

Conclusion

As long as capital and transnational corporations are free to roam the globe for cheap labor and lax labor and environmental laws, we are caught up in a "race to the bottom." The rules of the game must change. I want to propose that we envision a global society in which there is "sufficient, sustainable livelihood for all." This criterion from the Evangelical Lutheran Church in America's "Social Statement on Economic Life" is a useful alternative to the rapacious logic of economic globalization.[26]

Senator Byron Dorgan (D-ND) introduced Senate

Bill 3485, "The Decent Working Conditions and Fair Competition Act," to address this race to the bottom. (The House version, introduced by Representative Sherrod Brown (D-OH), is House Bill 5635.) If passed, it will prohibit the import, export or sale of "sweatshop goods" in the U.S. This bill would, for the first time, hold corporations legally accountable to respect the labor laws of the countries where their goods are manufactured. The bill, as written, includes fines of up to $10,000 for each violation, and allows competitors and investors the right to sue for damages against corporations for violating the law. It also includes provisions for sweat-free procurement standards as conditions for all federal government purchases. A March 2006 Harris poll showed that three-quarters of Americans support protection of worker rights.[27] Worker rights in the U.S. need protection, too. For instance, the right to unionize is increasingly threatened by decisions of the National Labor Relations Board. Without protection of worker rights, there will be no "sufficient, sustainable livelihood for all."

End Notes

1. This article is adapted from my book *Globalization at What Price?: Economic Change and Daily Life* (Pilgrim Press, 2001). David Held and Anthony McGrew, eds., *The Global Transformations Reader: An Introduction to the Globalization Debate* (Polity Press, 2000), 1, 3-4.

2. Ulrich Beck, "What Is Globalization?" in Held and McGrew, eds., *The Global Transformations Reader*, 100-102.

3. Susan George, "A Short History of Neo-Liberalism, Conference on Economic Sovereignty in a Globalizing World," March 24-26, 1999, available at www.globalexchange.org/campaigns/econ101/neoliberalism.htm.

4. Sarah Anderson and John Cavanagh with Thea Lee and the Institute for Policy Studies, *Field Guide to the Global Economy*, revised and updated (The New Press, 2005), 5.

5. Rob van Drimmelen, *Faith in a Global Economy: A Primer for Christians* (World Council of Churches, 1998), 7.

6. Thomas L. Friedman, *The Lexus and the Olive Tree: Understanding Globalization* (Farrar, Straus and Giroux, 1999), 357.

7. Peter Marcuse, "The Language of Globalization," *Monthly Review* 52, no. 3 (July-August, 2000).

8. E.K. Hunt and Howard J. Sherman, *Economics: An Introduction to Traditional and Radical Views*, Fourth Edition (Harper and Row, 1981), 21; Robert Heilbroner, *The Nature and Logic of Capitalism*. (W.W. Norton, 1985).

9. Morgenthau cited in David Korten, "Sustainability and the Global Economy," in Howard Coward and Daniel Maguire, eds., *Visions of a New Earth: Religious Perspectives on Population, Consumption, and Ecology* (State University of New York Press, 2000), 29.

10. Van Drimmelen, *Faith in a Global Economy,* 39.

11. Lori Wallach and Michelle Sforza, *Whose Trade Organization?: Corporate Globalization and the Erosion of Democracy* (Public Citizen, 1999), 115-18. Van Drimmelen, *Faith in a Global Economy,* 53.

12. Anderson and Cavanagh, *Field Guide*, 12-13, 19.

13. Peter Dicken, "A New Geo-economy," in Held and McGrew, eds., *The Global Transformations Reader*, 252-55.

14. Anderson and Cavanagh, *Field Guide*, 68.

15. Van Drimmelen, *Faith in a Global Economy*, 22-23.

16. Ibid., 38, 41-43.

17. Anderson and Cavanagh, *Field Guide*, 68, 69.

18. Altha Cravey, *Women and Work in Mexico's Maquiladoras* (Rowman and Littlefield, 1998), 6.

19. Mark Weisbrot, *Globalization: A Primer* (Center for Economic and Policy Research, 1999), online at www.cepr.net/content/view/338; Marla Dickerson, "Placing Blame for Mexico's Ills," *Los Angeles Times*, July 1, 2006. Also, over 25 percent of these jobs left for lower-wage countries between 2000-2004. Robert Scott and David Ratner, "NAFTA's Cautionary Tale," Economic Policy Institute, Issue Brief #214, 2005, online at www.epi.org/content.cfm/ib214.

20. Weisbrot, *Globalization*; Global Trade Watch, "Dangerous CAFTA Liaisons: Members of Congress Providing Decisive Votes on Trade Deal Receive Jump in Corporate Campaign Cash" (Public Citizen, 2006), online at www.citizen.org/documents/CAFTA_Liaisons_Report.pdf.

21. UNDP, *Human Development Report 2005: International Cooperation at a Crossroads* (United Nations, 2005), 4.

22. Anderson and Cavanagh, *Field Guide*, 34; ILO Press Room, "Globalization failing to create new, quality jobs or reduce poverty," December 9, 2005.

23. Kate Raworth, *Trading Away Our Rights: Women working in global supply chains*, Oxfam International, 2004, 4.

24. Anderson and Cavanagh, *Field Guide*, 42-44, 56; "Documenting the Evidence of the Failed NAFTA-WTO 'Trade' Model," Global Trade Watch, October 2006; Joseph Stiglitz, *Making Globalization Work* (W.W. Norton, 2006), 45.

25. Dr. Jody Heymann, *Forgotten Families: Ending the Global Crisis Confronting Children and Working Families in the Global Economy* (Oxford University Press, 2006), 189-90.

26. The ELCA Social Statement "Sufficient, Sustainable Livelihood for All" is available online at www.elca.org.

27. The Harris poll is available at the website of the National Labor Committee, www.nlc.net. The status of the bill, "The Decent Working Conditions and Fair Competition Act," can be tracked at www.thomas.gov.

U.S. Demand for Immigrant Labor and Its Impact

Ana Bedard (2007)

Introduction

One in seven U.S. workers is foreign-born. Out of the 21 million total, seven million are undocumented and 1.5 million are legal temporary workers. Congress wrangled over immigration reform in 2006, igniting national debate on undocumented immigration, and although President Bush signed a bill authorizing construction of 700 miles of fence along the 2,100 mile U.S.-Mexico border, the debate over undocumented immigration continues. The debate is multifaceted and includes cultural, economic and moral issues. This article seeks to shed light on the economic aspect of the debate, focusing on the U.S. demand for immigrant labor and its impact on the U.S. economy.

Two words of caution before proceeding: First, although impact on U.S. citizens is an important piece of an overall moral evaluation of the situation, it is only one part. Conclusions about what should be done should not be based solely on this discussion. A proper moral evaluation must take into account other factors such as immigrants' well-being and the United States' moral responsibility for its international policies and actions. Second, to discuss the impact of immigrant labor does not imply that immigrants alone are responsible for the impact. There are structural causes for immigration as well as individual decisions, and furthermore some of those structural causes are rooted in the U.S. economy. The U.S. shares responsibility for the situation.

In this article, I examine the demand for and impact of immigrant labor in the U.S. economy. I am particularly interested in the impact of immigrant labor on the U.S. workforce. Many contend that immigrant workers take jobs from Americans and depress wages. Is this true? Or is immigrant labor good for U.S. labor markets and the economy over all? I do not focus on consumer prices, because cheaper prices come with a steep cost, low wages, and I do not have space to treat that subject adequately.

To summarize my findings briefly, the literature indicates that there is a demand for immigrant labor embedded in the U.S. economy. It also indicates that the impact of immigrant labor on the U.S. economy has a positive aspect: immigrant workers infuse needed labor in a country in which the native workforce growth is slowing and in sectors of the economy in which decreasing numbers of native workers are willing to work. However, there is a cost to U.S. workers who compete most directly with the great number of unskilled, uneducated immigrant workers. According to some research, this cost is minimal: workers without high school degrees have experienced wage losses of only 1-3 percent. However, other research has estimated a 9 percent loss of earnings for high school dropouts.

The Secure Fence Act passed in 2006 seeks to limit immigration flows. It is debatable to what extent limiting immigration flows would actually protect wages and working conditions of low-skilled workers. And it will certainly hurt the U.S. economy overall. The scholarly evidence suggests that the U.S. as a whole would benefit from continued infusion of immigrant labor into the work force. It also suggests that the wages and working conditions of the poorest workers must be attended to. An immigration policy which takes both of these into account should seek to improve the working conditions of poor workers in the U.S. overall, rather than pitting them against each other. Given the coincidence of labor interests of all poor workers, if both native and immigrant workers practice solidarity, they may be able to build coalitions that create new U.S. labor policies that benefit all low-wage workers.

Industrialized Nations' Demand for Immigrant Labor

There are numerous reasons for a person's decision to migrate. They include an economic "push," or difficult economic conditions in the sending country. They include an economic "pull" from the receiving country, or a demand for immigrant labor. Migration is also fostered by globalization, due to social, cultural and economic ties between countries and to social dislocations caused by the transition from traditional to global economic structures. In addition, migration is fostered by social capital, or the social ties that assist migrants to establish themselves in their new country. Massey, Durand and Malone outline the major lines of migration theory in *Beyond Smoke and Mirrors*, indicating that the many theories are not so much contradictory as complementary.[1] Each theory explicates a facet of a person's decision to migrate. For the purposes of the question at hand, I focus here on the economic pull.

Theorists under the broad category of "world-systems theory" specify that international migration is promoted by structural factors in the globalized economy. Among the factors is the polarization of economies in highly industrialized nations, which results in the proliferation of unskilled, low-paid work. According to Saskia Sassen, economic polarization is due in part to the flight of manufacturing and the downgrading of the manufacturing jobs that stayed behind. It is also due to growth in the highly-skilled service sector, which creates an accompanying low-skill service sector both directly in the form of low-skill jobs in high-end companies and firms, and indirectly through an increased demand on the part of the highly-paid workers for unskilled services such as dog-walking, cleaning, yard-work, and coffee shop workers.[2]

Labor market segmentation theory complements world-systems theory. Although the market segmentation model was in its beginning stages considered "anathema to neoclassical economists,"[3] William Dickens and Kevin Lang note that it has subsequently received significant attention from the mainstream,[4] and that the dual labor market model is a "useful simplification" whose application provides a "surprisingly accurate description of the empirical [wage] distribution."[5] According to the labor segmentation model, the economies of highly developed nations can be broadly divided into two sectors: a capital-intensive "primary" labor market with highly-paid, highly-skilled, permanent positions and a labor-intensive "secondary" labor market with low-wage, unstable, temporary, unskilled or semi-skilled positions which lack upward mobility.

Michael Piore explains that employers turn to migrants to fill positions in the expanded secondary market, because that expansion has coincided with a contraction in the number of native workers willing to work in the secondary sector.[6] This contraction is due to the demographic and cultural changes which shrink the traditional pools of entry-level workers – women, teenagers and rural dwellers. One factor causing fewer women to accept low-level positions is the entry of women into the workplace: many women now pursue careers rather than temporary jobs which supplement a husband's income. One factor influencing the decline in teenage workers is increasing educational requirements; another is a decline in birth rates. Finally, rural dwellers are no longer available in the same numbers in highly developed countries because of previous urbanization.

U.S. Demand for Immigrant Labor

How does this play out in the United States? In order to answer, I would like to first offer a general overview of the immigrant workforce in the United States. In 2004 the U.S. admitted 450,000 immigrants as legal permanent residents (most of whom entered the workforce) and another 174,000 as temporary workers.[7] That same year 562,000 undocumented immigrants entered the country; they now represent one-third of all immigrants residing in the U.S.[8] Over 21 million workers are foreign-born, representing 14.5 percent of the labor force. One-third of all foreign-

1. Douglas S. Massey, Jorge Durand and Nolan Malone, *Beyond Smoke and Mirrors: Mexican Immigration in an Era of Economic Integration* (Russell Sage Foundation, 2002).

2. Saskia Sassen, "The New Labor Demand in Global Cities," in Michael Peter Smith, ed., *Cities in Transformation: Class, Capital, and the State* (Sage, 1984), 139-171.

3. Aristide R. Zolberg, "Review of *Birds of Passage*," *International Migration Review* 15, no. 1/2 (Spring – Summer 1981), 404.

4. William Dickens and Kevin Lang, "The Reemergence of Segmented Labor Market Theory," *American Economic Review* 78, no. 2 (May 1988), 129.

5. Ibid., 133.

6. Michael Piore is an often cited proponent of labor market segmentation and one of its first theorists. See Michael Piore, *Birds of Passage: Migrant Labor and Industrial Societies* (Cambridge University Press, 1979).

7. Jeffery S. Passel and Robert Suro, *Rise, Peak and Decline: Trends in U.S. Immigration 1992 – 2004* (Pew Hispanic Center, 2005), 29. According to U.S. immigration policy, the U.S. has a global limit of 290,000 immigration visas per year, with a cap of 20,000 immigrants per country yearly. In actuality, however, the U.S. provides many more immigration visas, since various classes of immigrants (most notably family members) are exempt from the numerical limitations. Roger Daniels, *Guarding the Golden Door* (Hill and Wang, 2004), 134-136.

8. First statistic in Jeffery S. Passel, Robert Suro, *Rise, Peak and Decline*, 29. Second statistic in Jeffery S. Passel, *The Size and Characteristics of the Unauthorized Migrant Population in the U.S.: Estimates Based on the March 2005 Current Population Survey* (Pew Hispanic Center, March 7, 2006), 4.

born workers are undocumented (7.2 million).[9] Even though many immigrants are highly educated, immigrants as a whole are less educated than native-born workers: nearly half of all workers over age 24 without high school diplomas are immigrants. Most of the uneducated immigrants are from Mexico and Central America.[10]

Immigrants are disproportionately represented in low-wage industries in the U.S. Even though immigrants as a whole comprise 14 percent of all U.S. workers, they comprise 20 percent of low-wage workers.[11] Undocumented immigrants, who are 5 percent of the workforce, are concentrated in low-wage professions. They comprise 24 percent of farm laborers, 17 percent of building cleaners and maintenance workers, 14 percent of construction workers, and 12 percent of food preparation workers.[12] Workers from Mexico and Central America, who make up 78 percent of the undocumented population, are concentrated in eight low-skilled sectors of the economy, comprising about half of the workers in the following industries: construction, restaurants, landscaping, agriculture, food manufacturing, services to buildings and dwellings, textile, apparel and leather manufacturing and private households.[13] Native and other foreign-born workers, in contrast, comprise only 15 percent of the workers in those occupations.

Immigrant workers earn less than native workers. Overall, foreign-born workers earn 10 percent less than their native counterparts, adjusted for educational attainment and experience. Workers from Mexico and Central America earned 27 percent less than their counterparts, adjusted for educational attainment and

experience.[14] However, these statistics do not necessarily indicate that immigrant workers are dragging wages down for other low-wage workers. Numerous studies, discussed below, have been performed regarding the impact of immigrant workers on native wages. They have not been unified in their conclusions. However, there is consensus in the literature that immigrant labor is important for the health of the U.S. economy overall.

Immigrants and Economic Growth

The concentration of immigrants in low-wage work confirms that the U.S. has a demand for low-wage workers which is filled by immigrants, as suggested by world-systems and labor segmentation theories. A study by the Immigration Law Center confirms that immigrants supplement a dwindling native workforce. It shows that without recently arrived immigrant laborers, thirteen occupational categories where immigrants are concentrated would have experienced a collective shortfall of over 500,000 workers and eleven job categories would have experienced a seven percent contraction in the labor force during the 1990s, even if all unemployed natives with recent experience in those categories had been re-employed.[15]

A November 2005 study by the Congressional Budget Office (CBO) indicates that the rate in U.S. labor force growth is decreasing because of demographic and cultural changes. It projects a significant slowdown in the growth in the U.S. labor force in the next decade due largely to the retirement of the baby-boom generation. It attributes it additionally to a decline in the rate at which women are entering the workforce and to a historical decline in labor force participation of men.[16] The CBO concludes:

"The baby-boom generation's exit from the labor

9. The first statistic is from 2004, found in United States Congressional Budget Office, *The Role of Immigrants in the U.S. Labor Market* (Washington, D.C.: November, 2005), 1. The second is from 2005 and is found in Passel, *The Size and Characteristics of the Unauthorized Migrant Population in the U.S.*, 13.

10. Congressional Budget Office, *The Role of Immigrants in the U.S. Labor Market*, 1.

11. Randy Capps, Michael Fix, Jeffery S. Passel, Jason Ost, and Dan Perez-Lopez, *A Profile of the Low-Wage Immigrant Workforce* (Urban Institute, 2003).

12. Passel, *Size and Characteristics*, 11.

13. Country of origin statistic from Passel, *Size and Characteristics*, 5. Information on labor sectors from Congressional Budget Office, *The Role of Immigrants in the U.S. Labor Market*, 14. Sectors listed in descending order of Mexican/Central American worker concentration.

14. Congressional Budget Office, *The Role of Immigrants in the U.S. Labor Market*, 17.

15. Rob Paral, *Essential Workers: Immigrants Are a Needed Supplement to the Native-Born Labor Force* (American Immigration Law Foundation 2005), downloaded from www.ailf.org/ipc/essentialworkersprint.asp on December 4, 2006.

16. The labor force growth rate in the next ten years is projected to be only half of what it was from 1950 to 2004. Congressional Budget Office, *The Role of Immigrants in the U.S. Labor Market*, 25. There is debate about the decline of male participation, but there is a fair amount of research focusing on the decreasing male retirement age, attributed in part to improved pensions and disability insurance.

force could well foreshadow a major shift in the role of foreign-born workers in the labor force. Unless native fertility rates increase, it is likely that most of the growth in the U.S. labor force will come from immigration by the middle of the century." [17]

The deceleration in the labor growth rate is problematic for the U.S. economy for several reasons. It is problematic because a smaller labor force means lower productivity, or a slowing economy. And a slowing economy is problematic because it is harder to run. When economic growth shrinks, the economy's "economic speed limit," or "the pace at which the economy can grow without fueling inflation" – shrinks. [18] Furthermore, according to the *Economist*, "Any fall in America's economic speed limit will have serious consequences. Financial markets could be rattled as investors lower their expectations for future profit growth. American assets may look less attractive to foreigners. And economic policy will become decidedly more complicated." [19] In addition, a slowing economy spells shrinking revenue for the federal government. This has implications for all sorts of social programs, but a shrinking Social Security pool tops the list of worries. A smaller pool of workers means that fewer people are shouldering the responsibility for a growing pool of retirees, as the Baby Boom generation starts retiring.

Immigrants help to maintain a vibrant United States economy through filling necessary positions that would otherwise go unfilled by Americans, and they do so through growing the economy. The economy grows through the influx of workers, because, "In economic terms, a larger labor force increases the productivity of the existing capital stock and induces new investment in response to higher returns." [20] In other words, labor attracts capital.

Economist Giovanni Peri concludes that overall, the presence of immigrant labor increases U.S. workers' incomes by 1.1 percent. [21] On the whole, immigrant

labor is beneficial to the U.S. economy. Immigrant workers cause a rise in wages overall. Immigrant workers fill job vacancies in the low-wage economic sector. In addition, they create new jobs and grow the economy through creating additional consumer demand and attracting more capital. A growing economy is more manageable than a shrinking one, and a growing economy averts a shrinking federal budget and an accompanying need to cut federal spending levels for social programs.

Impact on Low-Wage Workers

On the negative side, however, there is indication that an influx of immigrant labor has a negative impact on those workers who compete most directly with them, namely low-wage, low-skilled workers. The extent of this impact is still being debated. [22] Economist David Card is a leading proponent of the position that immigrant labor has a minimal negative impact on native workers. In 1990 he studied the impact of the Mariel boatlift on Miami's economy. [23] The Mariel boatlift refugees increased the number of workers in Miami by 7 percent in short period. [24] Card chose to study Miami because it was controlled for economic demand: workers immigrated there for reasons exogenous to the demands of the local economy; they moved there because it was the closest city to Cuba. Comparing the Miami economy before and after Mariel to the economies of other U.S. cities in the same time periods, Card reached the surprising conclusion that the influx of workers had virtually no impact on either wages or unemployment among low-skilled native workers. [25]

Other economists disagree with Card. George Borjas argued that Card's methodology (mirrored subsequently by others) was inadequate, because it did not take into account native flight from cities with

17. Ibid.

18. *Economist*, "A Falling Speed Limit," December 28, 2006, 17.

19. Ibid.

20. Giovanni Peri, "Migrants, Skills and Wages: Measuring the Economic Gains from Immigration," *Immigration Policy in Focus* 5, no. 3 (American Immigration Law Foundation, March 2006), 2, downloaded from www.ailf.org/ipc/infocus/2006_skillswages.shtml on December 15, 2006.

21. Ibid., 6.

22. Roger Lowenstein has done an incisive journalistic study of the academic debate which has influenced my analysis here. Roger Lowenstein, "The Immigration Equation," *New York Times Magazine*, July 9, 2006.

23. David Card, "The Impact of the Mariel Boatlift on the Miami Economy," *Industrial and Labor Relations Review* 4, no. 2 (January 1990): 245–257.

24. Due to the demographics of the Mariel population, the population of unskilled workers increased by much more. The average education level was 11.3 years of schooling, a half a year lower than that of blacks in Miami at the time. Ibid., 247–248.

25. Ibid.

significant immigrant arrivals.[26] Native workers leave or decline to move to immigrant-rich cities, seeking economic opportunities elsewhere. The economic impact of immigrant influxes is thus diffused nationally, and so it must be studied nationally. In addition, immigrants must be compared to natives with similar amounts of experience rather than solely similar educational levels, as Card had done. Borjas contends that immigrant workers compete directly with native workers. Borjas' calculations show that a 10 percent influx in immigrant workers results in a 3-4 percent reduction in average weekly earnings for low-wage native workers, with a 9 percent reduction in earnings among high school dropouts over 20 years.

The Congressional Budget Office notes the limitations of Borjas' approach, naming principally that it "overstates the long-run impact of immigration on native workers' earnings" because it fails to take into account that immigrant workers' presence stimulates a further demand for workers.[27] Giovanni Peri has developed an analysis that uses Borjas' nationwide approach while taking this factor into account. He also takes into account the differences in occupational distribution of workers within the same educational groups and the impact of immigrant labor on wages overall. Peri's contention is that immigrant workers are not interchangeable with native workers. Rather, they fill specific segments within work sectors, taking positions within those sectors that are not being taken by native workers. They act as a complementary labor force, not a competitive one. According to Peri's calculations, U.S. incomes increased by a net of 1.1 percent, and incomes of native workers without high school diplomas decreased by only 1.2 percent decrease in the 1990s.[28]

In a 2001 analysis, Card finds another weakness in Borjas' analysis. By his calculations, there is no relationship between immigration and intercity mobility rates of native workers.[29] An influx of unskilled immigrants does not lead to native flight; it leads rather to an increase in the population of unskilled workers. And yet, new immigrants are not simply replacing native workers: according to Card's study, immigrant inflows led to a mere half percentage point increase in unemployment rates in the 1980s. In addition, Card calculates that the negative impact of the immigrant influx was minimal: a 1-3 percent loss in wages.[30]

Conclusion: Immigrant Labor and Justice for the Working Poor

Even given the limitations of Borjas' approach, his research cannot be discounted. Economists continue to debate and research the impact of immigrant labor on the native population. One body of research, represented by Borjas, suggests that immigrants compete directly with U.S. workers and that limiting immigration would significantly improve wages of low-skilled workers. Another, represented by Card and Peri, suggests that immigrants complement the U.S. labor force, and that to limit the influx of immigrants would not have a significant impact. Given that all agree that there is at least a minimal negative impact on low-skilled workers and in the absence of a consensus to the contrary, it is wise to take concerns about wage depreciation seriously.

There is reason to be concerned about even a slight negative impact on U.S. workers: those affected are those who can least afford any decrease in wages. The average hourly wage rate in the U.S. as adjusted for inflation has barely changed since 1979: it is about $7.50 an hour.[31] A full-time worker at $7.50 an hour will earn $15,000 a year – which is $3,000 less than the poverty threshold for a family of four. The condition of low-wage workers in the United States must be improved, whether through immigration reform or other measures.

The literature does not indicate, however, that immigration reform is the best way to do so. It indicates that overall, immigration at current levels is beneficial to the U.S. economy (even though much of it is not legally recognized). Nonetheless, in order to ensure that the whole is not benefited at the expense of the most vulnerable, a liberal immigration policy must be accompanied by labor policies that improve the wages and working conditions of all low-skilled workers in the United States.

---

26. George Borjas, *Heaven's Door* (Princeton University Press, 1999).

27. Although they do not name Borjas by name, they are addressing his methodology. Congressional Budget Office, *The Role of Immigrants in the U.S. Economy*, 24.

28. Giovanni Peri, 6.

29. David Card, "Immigrant Inflows, Native Outflows, and the Local Market Impacts of Higher Immigration," *Journal of Labor Economics* 19, no. 1 (January 2001): 22–64.

30. Ibid., 58.

31. Congressional Budget Office, *Changes in Low-Wage Labor Markets between 1979 and 2005* (Washington, D.C.: December 2006), 19.

Pastor and Marcelli, recognizing that African-Americans are a significant number of the low-wage workers, argue for partnership between immigrants and African-Americans. They suggest that the two groups can together create the political will to create economic policies that benefit the working poor. However, in order to do so, they must have an ethic of solidarity. In their words,

> *"It is rational for African-Americans to be less restrictionist toward immigration than a simple competitive labor-market perspective might suggest, especially because such a restrictionist position would weaken coalitional possibilities on other is-sues and/or may fan prejudicial attitudes that will diminish political and policy gains later. … It may be useful to move away from debates around immigration (e.g. enforcement) policy per se and focus instead on immigrant (e.g. integration) policy that can lift up all communities."* [32]

Solidarity is not an easy prescription for either group, and indeed the solidarity must go both ways. However, as suggested by Pastor and Marcelli, poor immigrants and poor Americans have common interests and could be potentially powerful allies in fighting for economic justice for all.

---

32. Manuel Pastor, Jr. and Enrico Marcelli, "Somewhere Over the Rainbow? African Americans, Unauthorized Mexican Immigration, and Coalition Building," *The Review of Black Political Economy* 31, no. 1 (Summer – Fall 2003): 127.

2 Religion-Labor History

Introduction

This section outlines the history of religion and labor, highlights a few specific events in this history, explains the labor laws enacted over the past 200 years and shares a few examples of the history of religion and labor from two people actively involved in this movement.

The first piece was developed by Regina Botterill, former Assistant Director of IWJ, to highlight important events in the relationship between religion and labor history.

The next piece, "Negro Labor and the Church," comes from the 1929 book *Labor Speaks for Itself on Religion: A Symposium of Labor Leaders Throughout the World*. The author of the piece is A. Philip Randolph, an African American and the first president of the Brotherhood of Sleeping Car Porters Union. His piece specifically speaks to labor's perspective on the religious community's involvement with workers.

"Religion and Labor: Then and Now" is taken from the book *Organized Labor and the Church: Reflections of a "Labor Priest"* by Monsignor George G. Higgins (with William Bole). Higgins was a champion of workers' rights and a leading figure for Catholics on

social justice issues in Washington, D.C., and was one of the founding board members of IWJ. He dedicated his life in service to the cause of workers organizing to improve their working conditions.

Father Edward Boyle presented his chapter, "At Work in the Vineyard: The Jesuit Labor Apostolate," as a conference talk. Father Boyle chairs the last existing Labor Guild in the Archdiocese of Boston. He is also President of the Massachusetts Interfaith Committee on Worker Justice.

"No Shvitz: Your One-Stop Guide to Fighting Sweatshops" was developed by the Progressive Jewish Alliance, a non-profit organization in Los Angeles. This powerful group of Jewish leaders dedicated to justice develops resources and provides opportunities for the Jewish community to engage in social justice issues.

"Charles Stelzle and the Workingmen's Department," by Richard Poethig, was originally written for the journal of the Presbyterian Church (U.S.A.), *Church & Society* – for a special issue devoted to the theme of "The Church and the Working Poor" (January/February 2003). This article highlights the life of one of the key religious advocates of workers' rights.

Historic Highlights of the Religion-Labor Movement

Interfaith Worker Justice (1999)

The Anti-Slavery Movement

The first link between religion and labor in America started in the antebellum south and could fill volumes of books, chronicling how belief and faith in God compelled Africans to refuse their station in life as slaves.

With pride, hope, and dreams of a better life, courageous Africans and white abolitionists fought against the longest abuse of human labor ever witnessed in America and in the modern world, because they were determined that it was their God-given right to be free and to be treated as human beings.

The most well-known opposition of the peculiar institution included Harriet "Moses" Tubman, the most famous conductor of the Underground Railroad. Churches, both Black and White throughout the south and north were common "stations" for the Underground Railroad, where runaways would hide in the church during the day and travel at night.

Some used their pens to declare their convictions that the institution of slavery was not in accordance with God's commandments, including Rev. Samuel E. Cornish and John Russworm, who published the first black newspaper, Freedom's Journal, while Frederick Douglass and David Walker and many others published works that advocated freedom.

Those with a vested interest in slavery recognized the intricate role that religion played in the anti-slavery movement. Governor John Floyd of Virginia blamed insubordination and insurrection among Africans due to Northern travelers and "black preachers" creating uprisings by teaching that "God is no respecter of persons" and that "the black man was as good as the white," in his message to the Virginia legislature on December 6, 1831. Virginia and the Carolinas' night patrols were on the prowl to interrupt services at "church meetings" held in obscure places on the plantations, to prevent any plots for escape or rebellion.

There are many examples throughout the annals of history of the ties between religion and labor including the Methodist General Conference declaration in 1784 that slavery was "contrary to the golden laws of God." This declaration, though suspended a year later, is credited with having sparked some slave owners to free their slaves as a declaration of religious conviction. There were the Emancipating Baptists who were opposed to slavery, as well as the early formed African churches like the African Methodist Episcopal Church, that gave stinging rebukes of slavery.

The Pullman Strike of 1894

The strike of workers at the Pullman Palace Car Company in Pullman, Illinois – home of the passenger car – is one of the more famous events in labor history. The company and town were founded and owned by entrepreneur George M. Pullman, who created the community for his employees, then just outside Chicago. During the Depression of 1893, the company fired a large number of workers and reduced wages without reducing the amount of rent payments.

Workers of the American Railway Union called a strike because even after business picked up again and some of the laid-off workers were rehired, nothing was done to raise wages or reduce rent payments. With government injunctions and federal troops, Pullman and the association of railway managers crushed the strike which ended in violence. The company refused to rehire workers, blacklisting many and having hundreds arrested on federal and local charges.

Though no one from the religious community publicly supported the workers, Rev. William Carwardine, the minister of First Methodist Episcopal Church in Pullman wrote a complete account of the strike so that people outside of Pullman could learn the stories not being told by the newspapers.

Rev. Carwardine was active with the Pullman Relief Committee which gathered food, clothing and money for strikers, and became director of the Homeseekers' Association, an organization that found jobs and homes for workers who had been blacklisted. Less than two decades later, religious organizations began to take an even more active public position to help workers.

Labor Temple

In 1910 Minister Charles Stelzle of The Presbyterian Church established the Labor Temple in New York in response to industry workers' needs. Stelzle had extensive experience working with organized labor.

Throughout its history, Labor Temple viewed supporting efforts to secure dignity and justice in the workplace an essential part of Christian teaching. The Temple was often used as a base for strike activity. An employment bureau was set up, and Presbyterian businessmen around the city notified Labor Temple when they had news of job openings.

Seminary students from Union Theological Seminary also came to Labor Temple to provide part-time assistance, and received practical training in return. Next came ecumenical organizations who stood for worker justice.

The Brotherhood of Sleeping Car Porters

The ties between the civil rights movement and labor can be linked directly to the efforts of the great labor and civil rights leader A. Philip Randolph (1889-1979). Randolph was greatly influenced by his father, Rev. James Randolph and his denomination, the African Methodist Episcopal (A.M.E.), recognized as a center of black radical politics since the 18th century.

Heavily influenced by his father's religious convictions, Randolph was able to become a serious labor and civil rights leader. Randolph earned respect from both labor and congregations with the establishment of The Brotherhood of Sleeping Car Porters and his victory over the notorious Pullman Palace Car Company that had already defeated the American Railway Union during the Pullman Strike of 1894.

After federal control of the railroads ended in 1920, Pullman created a company union to stifle outside organization efforts. In 1925, Randolph officially launched The Brotherhood with the large labor population of Black men who landed jobs as porters. For the thousands of Blacks migrating north, this was considered a very prestigious occupation.

Pullman struck back with a spy system, threats and firings, but The Brotherhood continued to struggle for 12 years. The Brotherhood's courageous battles won the admiration of many labor and liberal leaders, including the American Federation of Labor (AFL), when prior to that half the affiliates of the AFL barred blacks from membership.

Though initially timid, the churches and the "Negro" press eventually joined the NAACP and local members of the National Urban League in supporting the Brotherhood.

The Brotherhood won its first major contract with the Pullman Company in 1937. The following year, Randolph removed his union from the AFL in protest against its failure to fight discrimination in its ranks and took the brotherhood into the newly formed Congress of Industrial Organizations (CIO).

When the AFL and CIO merged in 1955, Randolph was made a vice president and member of the executive council of the combined organization. Randolph and others formed the Negro American Labor Council in 1960 to fight discrimination within the AFL-CIO.

Religion and Labor Council of America

The National Religion and Labor Foundation, later known as the Religion and Labor Council of America, was founded in 1932. It was established in an attempt to apply religious social teachings to economic and industrial life by supporting labor in the United States. Members were of different faiths and various labor unions.

The Foundation had three main activities. Production of a monthly newsletter that provided membership with news of the foundation's work and of relevant developments in both the religion and labor worlds. Second, was the organization of various community-centered Religion and Labor "Fellowships" where members could meet and discuss issues of concern about labor. Lastly, educational work in seminaries and schools of religion was also an important focus for the Foundation. Annually, the foundation sponsored Inter-Seminary Conferences at both the AFL and CIO national conventions.

The foundation encouraged the labor movement to keep its focus on justice and the general welfare. The newsletter covered the Montgomery bus boycott, and other activities of Rev. Dr. Martin Luther King Jr. and A. Philip Randolph, and on the need for the labor and civil rights movements to be mutually supportive.

The Catholic Worker Movement

The Catholic Worker movement began in the 1930's with the creation of the Catholic Worker newspaper. Dorothy Day and Peter Maurin, started the paper to advocate for social change and raise Catholic consciousness of the religious ideals that provided the foundation for that change.

The Catholic Worker Movement viewed unions as a legitimate and helpful way to ensure justice for workers. Many Catholic Workers joined strikers on picket lines, organized consumer boycotts, served as third party mediators between workers and management, and helped unions organize many kinds of workers.

The Catholic Worker's biggest involvement with labor came during the 1936-1937 New York Maritime strike. During the strike, Catholic Workers set up a special Catholic Worker headquarters on the docks where they provided strikers with food and shelter.

Former Catholic Workers, Fathers Carl Hensler, Charles Owen Rice, and Jerome Drolet made great contributions to CIO organizing, especially among Catholics in Pittsburgh and New Orleans. John Cort, a one-time Catholic Worker, founded the Association of Catholic Trade Unionists (ACTU), an organization of Catholic workers that was actively supportive of the trade union movement. The Catholic journal, Christian Front, later known as Christian Social Action, was also founded by former Catholic Workers who were supportive of the labor movement. Catholic Worker houses in Baton Rouge, Houston, and elsewhere continue to be actively involved in building ties with labor.

The Farm Worker Movement

Religious involvement with the farm workers began in the 1920's with day care centers for young children of laborers on the East coast sponsored by the Council of Women for Home Missions. Direct service programs were expanded in 1926 when the newly created National Migrant Ministry, a ministry related to the National Council of Churches, began providing health, vocational training and religious services at labor camps.

By 1939, migrant ministry programs had been established in 15 states. By the 1950's, the California Migrant Ministry was experimenting with ministry in areas on the outskirts of established towns where farm laborers had settled, called "rural fringe" areas, to promote justice and self-determination among farm workers through the cooperative efforts of a team made up of a pastor and a community organizer.

The California Migrant Ministry was strengthened by the training they received from Fred Ross and Cesar Chavez (1927-1993), who were both trained by Saul Alinsky of the Industrial Areas Foundation. The rela-

tionships that grew between the California Migrant Ministry staff, Fred Ross and Cesar Chavez paved the way for CMM's involvement with labor when Chavez formed the National Farm Workers Association and asked for religious support during its first strike against grape growers in 1965.

The religious presence on the picket lines (including 1965 and 1973) let growers and others in power know that community people were concerned and were watching the actions of both the farm workers and the growers and helped to prevent workers and others from resorting to violence.

In an attempt to spread the news of the plight of farm workers, religious leaders joined Cesar Chavez and farm workers in a march from union headquarters in Delano, California, to the state capital in Sacramento during Lent of 1966. Influenced by the religious tradition of pilgrimages, Chavez envisioned a march that would also help solidify support for farm workers. Thousands of marchers, among them clergy and people who identified with the march's religious symbolism, joined the 67 original marchers along the way. Ten thousand people converged on Sacramento on Easter Day 1966.

Religious support for farm workers also came in the form of denominational and faith body resolutions, which paved the way for more recent involvement, including the boycott of Campbell's Soup products to help pressure Campbell's to negotiate a contract with the Farm Labor Organizing Committee, a farm workers' union representing workers in the Midwest and North Carolina. The reorganized National Migrant Ministry, now called the National Farm Worker Ministry, continues to encourage the religious community's involvement with farmworker issues and the farmworker unions.

Martin Luther King Jr. & the Sanitation Workers' Strike

The sanitation workers' strike in 1968 galvanized the labor and religious movements. Rev. Dr. Martin Luther King was killed while supporting 1,300 striking garbage workers in Memphis, Tennessee.

In late 1967, the nearly all African-American Memphis' sanitation workers established a local chapter of the American Federation of State, County, and Municipal Employees to improve wages and working conditions, but the city refused to recognize them. The workers decided to strike on Feb. 12, 1968. Religious and community leaders asked for and received support from Dr. King. "We are tired of working our hands off and laboring every day and not even making a wage adequate with the daily basic necessities of life," said Dr. King to 17,000 people at Mason Temple, March 18, 1968. Dr. King called for a huge downtown march and boycott.

"The question is not what will happen to me if I stop and help these men," said Dr. King at a march on April 3. "The question is, if I do not stop to help the sanitation workers, what will happen to them? That's the question." The next day, Dr. King was assassinated on his hotel balcony. Four days later, his wife, Coretta Scott King led 19,000 people in a silent memorial march through Memphis. Eight days later, the city recognized the union and signed a contract to improve their wages and benefits.

Jewish Labor Committee

The Jewish Labor Committee was founded in 1934 by leaders of the International Ladies' Garment Workers' Union, the Amalgamated Clothing Workers of America, the Workmen's Circle, the Jewish Daily Forward Association, and other kindred groups to challenge the rise of Nazism in Europe.

In the 1950's, the Committee's focus changed to fight prejudice and discrimination among American workers. The Committee established 25 local committees to combat intolerance around the United States and Canada. These committees worked closely with local labor and other community groups to develop multi-ethnic and inter-religious solidarity among workers and within the larger community. Since that time, the Committee has evolved into a permanently established community relations and worker advocacy organization.

Jewish religious and cultural traditions demand an attitude of fairness toward workers and an active commitment to social justice. This imperative has led many to take an active role in programs and policies that lead to a more just and equitable society, such as the struggle to organize or to secure adequate wages and working conditions. American Jews and the American labor movement have been close allies for many years, with a shared commitment to pursuing a just, fair and stable community and society.

Catholic Labor Schools

The Catholic Labor Schools were a means by which Catholic labor union members, their families and fellow workers could learn about the special care and concern the teachings espoused for workers in its social encyclicals, *Rerum Novarum* and *Quadregesimo Anno*.

The Labor School movement was encouraged by the Social Action Department of the National Catholic Welfare Conference, now the United States Catholic Conference, as a way to train union rank and file leaders in the social teachings of the Church and provide practical skills for building and maintaining effective unions. Courses were added which were of special appeal to union leaders, who also became students. The Labor Schools provided support, training and resources for priests through the innovative programs.

Labor Schools were organized by local parish priests, the Association of Catholic Trade Unionists, dioceses and Catholic colleges. It is estimated that more than 150 labor schools were established from 1936 through 1956. The Labor Schools gave labor union members and leaders the spiritual and moral base for their work in the unions. There is one remaining Catholic labor school: the Labor Guild of Boston.

The March on Washington

Despite A. Philip Randolph's earlier success, there continued to be troubles for blacks in organized labor. Randolph's fights inside the AFL-CIO began in the late 1950s, during a time of harsh economic recession that was disproportionately affecting blacks. Martin Luther King Jr. was becoming more prominent and the Montgomery bus boycott was heating up in Alabama.

This led to Randolph becoming a director of the March on Washington for Jobs and Freedom, which brought more than 250,000 people to the capital on Aug. 28, 1963, to demonstrate support for civil-rights policies for African Americans. Randolph's ties to organized labor provided a crucial link to the march. Although AFL-CIO president George Meany refused to endorse the march, trade unions provided key organizational and financial support.

After the march, Randolph, Martin Luther King Jr. and other leaders met with President Kennedy and within a year, the Civil Rights Act of 1964 was signed. Over the next decade, Randolph became entrenched as the elder statesman of the civil rights movement.

Negro Labor and The Church

A. Philip Randolph (1929)

The only representative of the Negro race to contribute to this volume was born in 1889 in Crescent City, Florida. In a very literal sense he was a product of the church, for his father was a minister. He early evidenced a passionate desire to learn and finally won admission to the College of the City of New York. He had to earn his way and the only position available was that of elevator operator. Together with Chandler Owen he organized the First Union of Elevator Operators and Starters in New York. By hard outside work he succeeded in completing his college course. He early joined the Socialist Party and became an effective writer of pamphlets such as "Terms of Peace and the Dark Races," "The Truth about Lynching." He has taught at the Rand School of Social Science and lectured widely in forums. He is editor of The Messenger, a Negro periodical of distinction. His greatest achievement, however, has been as general secretary of the Brotherhood of Sleeping Car Porters. To him more than any other is due the foundation and success of this union which is doing so much to maintain and improve the position of the porters of America.

The African Negro Church, like most primitive tribal forms of religious worship, was built around taboos, totems and fetishes. The slave trade tore asunder the socio-religious-political institutional arrangements and transplanted, with the African slave, in the Western world, all of the religious mechanisms the African possessed in his native land.

The early slave religious worship in the Americas, a distinctly New-world environment, was a virtual replica of the African tribal forms. But, naturally, this outward manifestation of religious similarity could not persist. The dominant religion of the New World, Christianity, decreed the doom of African animism.

In the Americas, religious worship in the alleged civilized form, among the slaves, began in the established white churches. This was the mandate of the slave owners, so as to prevent and render unnecessary clandestine religious gatherings of the slaves, that might have, incidentally, served as convenient occasions for fermenting insurrections against the whites, and plots for escape in the Underground Railroad.

Doubtless, the slave owners' fear of rebellion among the slaves rested on sound grounds; for there had already been 25 recorded slave insurrections in the Colonies before the Revolution. The slave regime had been deeply stirred and shaken into a hectic feverish fear of slave uprisings, led by General Gabriel, in 1800; Denmark Vesey, in 1822; and Nat Turner, in 1831. As a precaution against recurrent slave revolts, rigorous and oppressive laws were enacted against the assemblies of slaves, following these efforts of black bondmen to secure their freedom.

Although the entrance of a Negro into a wealthy and beautiful temple of religion of white Americans today may severely test and strain their profession of belief in the Christ's ethic, because of the tribal Nordic outcry of superiority against all Alpines, Mediterraneans, Mongoloids and Negroids, the African slave enjoyed the blessings of the Christian doctrine, beside their white masters, in order that they (the slaves) might not engage in mischievous and sinister conspiracy against the holy order of Southern slavery. Thus, the black and white Churches were practically one under the slave power.

The formal Negro Church was born as a protest against discrimination in the white church, as was the case with the African Methodist Episcopal Church; or it had been set up by white missionaries, or it was the result of too large a congregation in the white church, which divided invariably into black and white groups or into separate religious bodies by, for and of Negroes.

The foregoing brief historical account of the Negro Church shows that its background is both proletarian and revolutionary. In the North, it was composed of Negroes escaped from slavery through the Underground Railroad, Negroes who bought their freedom, and Negroes who had been freed by the passage of laws for the abolition of slavery in the Northern Colonies. The Black Church was led by former slave preachers, such as Lott Carey, who organized the African Missionary Society, and Richard Allen, who founded the African Methodist Episcopal Church as a protest against persecution by the whites in their churches. The Negro Church in the North prayed and struggled and fought for freedom of the slaves in the South.

It may not be amiss to observe here, also, that before the Civil War, there were probably not a half dozen Negro churches, if any, in the South. They were banned on the grounds of being places of gatherings of slaves which constituted a menace, unless supervised by whites, to the safety and security of slavery.

The early Negro Church then championed the cause of freedom for the black bondmen. During the Reconstruction period, Negro churches served as centers of agitation for the validation and enforcement of civil and political rights of the freed men, and black religious leaders rang the changes for the political and civil liberty of the black proletariat who constituted practically 99 percent of the Negro population.

But with the coming of freedom, the Negro lost the security of his maintenance in terms of food, clothing and shelter, which was assured under the slave regime. He must now find employment in which to make wages, with which to purchase food, clothing and shelter, upon which his life depended. His first thought, then, was the getting of a job. The economic reward of the job was a secondary consideration. Next to the question of getting a job, was the matter of preparation for the new demands which were manifesting themselves as a result of the march of the industrialization of the South. That the Negro might not be the flotsam and jetsam of a new industrial era which was rapidly assuming ascendancy in America, as a result of the American industrial revolution, Booker T. Washington, great American educator, conceived the Tuskegee Idea, and sought, with the aid of white philanthropists, to create black artisans, to take their places in the building of industrial America. His was the vision of a prophet. He wrought more nobly and wisely than he knew. But under the stress of the industrial and commercial profit system, which was more and more functioning through gigantic trusts and mergers as a result of the increasing concentration of productive capital into fewer and fewer hands, the Negro, like the white worker, began to realize that in order to sell his labor at a favorable wage level, besides industrial training, he needed economic power, which came only from organization.

Thus, the Negro worker, as a result of economic necessity, began thinking in terms of collective bargaining. During the Reconstruction period, Negro workers had organized a National Negro Labor Union, which unfortunately fell under the leadership of Negroes whose political philosophy took precedence over the economic, and resulted in sacrificing the economic movement to political expediency. Negro workers had also entered the Knights of Labor, and began joining international unions of the American Federation of Labor, as soon as that body was formed.

While the Negro Church comprehended the struggle of the black workers for jobs and the industrial educational preparation for jobs, it did not readily grasp the nature, scope and meaning of the Negro workers' economic efforts to raise their wages, shorten hours of work, and improve working conditions. Only the job-getting and the industrial training efforts met with no resolute resistance, for white Northern philanthropists had shown themselves greatly favorable to Negro industrial education. Probably one cogent reason for the Negro preachers' indifference and opposition to the organization of Negro workers for economic advantage, in many cases, was that the powerful white capitalists who had sometimes appeared as friendly philanthropists, themselves opposed black wage earners organizing as they opposed the organizing of white wage earners. Moreover, organized labor had become anathema in the eyes of the Negro generally, because of the feeling that Negro workers were discriminated against by white labor unions, both with respect to securing jobs under the control of unions and union cards in order to get union jobs. This feeling among Negroes was not without foundation, for there are several international unions that still prevent Negro workers from joining them. It is well to note in this connection, however, that the American Federation of Labor, as a National Body, in convention after convention, has gone on record as opposed to all forms of discrimination among workers because of color, race, creed or nationality. But, of course, international unions are autonomous and usually determine their own constitutional policies, which may or may not be favorable to the inclusion of certain race groups in their bodies. This short-sighted policy of some international trade unions will be corrected by the organization of Negro workers, despite discrimination; and the forces of industrial necessity and education will develop in the white workers a recognition of the fact that their interests are common with the black workers and that the salvation of the workers of both races are bound irretrievably together.

The attitude of the Negro Church toward labor may be best viewed concretely in relation to the movement to organize the Pullman porters. Fundamentally, one cannot accurately aver that the Negro Church is either for or against organized labor. Although it is fair to add that it is rare to find a Negro preacher who is committed to the philosophy of labor unionism. Of course, white preachers are not numerous either who can be counted upon to champion the cause of the trade union, although many may express general sympathy with the principle of collective bargaining, which they regard as having sufficient latitude to include company unions, variously known as employee representation plans, works councils, shop committees, industrial democracy parliaments, and congresses. Upon discussing a company union, in contrast to a trade union, with the average preacher, white or colored, one readily discovers, among the large majority, a very definite misunderstanding of the difference between these two economic structures. Negro ministers, as a rule, take it for granted that a company union in which Negro workers are forced to be members, is a form of a beneficent economic philanthropy, which is to be accepted with gratitude instead of rejected with condemnation.

Because the Negro preachers regarded the industrial paternalism of the Pullman Company, manifested in its Employee Representation Plan and the Pullman Porters Benefit Association, as a generous concession to the race, they viewed the rise of the Brotherhood of Sleeping Car Porters in August, 1925, with mingled suspicion, distrust and fear. What is true of the attitude of Negro preachers was characteristic of most Negro leaders toward the porters' union.

The outstanding, independent, progressive, intellectual Negro preachers, however, such as Dr. Mordecai Johnson, President, Howard University; the Reverends A. Clayton Powell, of the Abyssinian Baptist Church; W. P. Hayes, of the Mount Olivet Baptist Church; John G. Robinson, of St. Marks Methodist Episcopal Church; A. C. Garner, of the Grace Congregational Church; William Lloyd Imes, of the St. James Presbyterian Church; George Frazier Miller, of St. Augustine Episcopal Church; Shelton Hale Bishop, St. Philips Episcopal Church, of New York; Dr. Prince of Denver; Dr. W. D. Cook, of the Community Church; Dr. Burton, of Chicago; Dr. Griffith of St. Louis; Dr. Cassius A. Ward, of Ebenezer Baptist Church of Boston, Mass.; and Dr. Francis Grimke, of Washington, have consistently supported the Porters' Union.

One of the outstanding instances of a Negro preacher resisting the corrupting influences of the Pullman Company was the flat refusal of Dr. W. D. Cook, of the Community Church of Chicago, to accept a consideration of $500 in order to keep the Brotherhood from holding a meeting in its church which had been extensively advertised throughout the city. Dr. Cook attested to the fact that the offer was made him by a prominent Negro business man, who doubtlessly served as a mediator for the Pullman Company.

In Denver, Colorado, Dr. Prince, pastor of one of the large Baptist churches, refused an offer of $300 to prevent the meeting of the Brotherhood from being held in his church. He publicly expressed, in a church meeting, his sympathy with the Brotherhood and condemned those who attempted to corrupt him against the porters' cause. In the beginning of the movement, every effort was made to close the doors of churches throughout the country to the porters' fight. In every city, however, the organization was able to secure a large prominent church for its meetings, though sometimes it was necessary to pay $50 therefore. In some instances, the use of the churches was given the union without any cost.

Probably the most notorious instance of Negro preachers taking the side of the Pullman Company against the porters' organization, was the occasion of a conference in Washington which was called ostensibly in the interest of fighting race segregation in the Federal Departments at Washington, by Melvin Chisum, self-styled as an efficiency engineer. This conference was presided over by Bishop A. J. Carey, of the African Methodist Episcopal Church; many of the ministers, in his diocese were mobilized by him to attend the conference, the expenses of which, including the cost of transportation to and from the conference, together with hotel bills while at the conference, were defrayed by the Pullman Company through its agent Mr. Chisum. A large number of prominent Negro leaders had been lured into this conference without a complete knowledge of its purpose. The main object was to adopt a resolution endorsing the Pullman Employee Representation Plan, as an expression of the sentiment of the Negro leaders of the country. The assumption was that such a resolution would serve as a condemnation of the Brotherhood of Sleeping Car Porters and cause a stampede of the porters out of the Union. Of course, it did not have the desired effect, because most of the prominent men who attended, upon receiving an explanation of the purpose and significance of the conference by the writer, expressed their disavowal of the conference and their lack of sympathy with its program.

Bishop Reverdy C. Ransom, of the African Methodist Episcopal Church, when approached to lend his name and influence to the above-named conference, definitely refused and sharply condemned its purpose. The Brotherhood counts him among its most powerful champions in the ministry.

In several cities Negro ministerial groups have endorsed the union. An effort was made to secure the endorsement of the General Conference of the

African Methodist Episcopal Church which convened in Chicago, in June, 1928, but to no avail, because of the influence of Bishop A. J. Carey, who dominated the conference.

The Baptist Ministers' Alliance in Chicago, which met in the church of Rev. L. K. Williams, President of the National Baptist Convention, in the summer of 1926, was reported to have endorsed the Brotherhood through a resolution which, however, could never be secured. No minister who was a part of the meeting in which the resolution was supposed to have been adopted, was ever able to give an explanation of the reason why the said resolution could not be secured, or the fact that the Alliance would not permit the Brotherhood to announce that the Union had been endorsed. One reason advanced for the refusal of the Baptist Alliance to come out for the Brotherhood is that the railroads who are interlocked with the Pullman Company give passes, through the President of the Baptist Convention, to the preachers, which enable them to travel throughout the country at half-fare rates.

Since the Negro Church is largely composed of Negro workers there is no good reason why it should not express and champion a proletarian philosophy. There are few men of wealth in the Negro race. Those who possess considerable property do not employ large numbers of Negro workers, and hence could have no economic reason for opposing Negro labor organizations that are concerned with increasing the wage income of its members. Such is not the case with the white ministers. They must preach a Christian doctrine which will not offend their rich communicants.

As to the Negro workers' attitude toward the Church, most of them are members of some Church, although they feel that Negro preachers are not as militant for their cause as they should be.

Negro labor leaders are not anti-Church, though they may not be Church members. All of them feel that the Church can be of constructive social, educational and spiritual service to the Negro workers.

If the Church, white or black, is to express the true philosophy of Jesus Christ, Himself a worker, it will not lend itself to the creed of oppressive capitalism which would deny to the servant his just hire.

Religion and Labor: Then and Now

Msgr. George G. Higgins (1993)

An American Experiment

Cooperation between religion and labor is uniquely American – at least from an historical standpoint. To this day, what many of us would regard as rather ordinary forms of cooperation, such as national church-labor conferences, would come off as spectacular events in most countries. Let me illustrate the point with an example from my own experience.

In November of 1988, I was invited to deliver a paper at an international labor conference sponsored by the Metal Workers Federation of West Germany, the largest union in the world with two and a half million members. It was an extraordinarily interesting and productive gathering. Yet a few weeks before it convened, I learned through the grapevine that the German Catholic bishops' conference (which parallels the U.S. bishops' conference), had sent a telex to our conference in Washington. The Germans were perplexed: they wanted to know who I was and why I would speak at a German labor meeting. By coincidence a German theologian was living at Catholic University and taking his meals with us at Curley Hall, and I mentioned the incident to him. "Well, I'm not surprised," he said. The German visitor said that with the exception of the late Jesuit Father Oswald von Nell-Breuning (the John A. Ryan of Germany), "I can't think of any other priest in my lifetime who has ever addressed a trade union meeting in Germany."

This is a remnant of the very unhappy relationship that existed for many years between religion and labor in Germany and throughout most of Europe – and, especially, between the Roman Catholic Church and Marxist-dominated labor movements. Like our German guest at Curley Hall, I was not surprised by the curiosity of his bishops. It was entirely understandable, given their history.

My first exposure to the church-labor rift in Europe came in 1949 when I spent six months in Germany, working on a study for the U.S. military government there. At the time the need for a united German government was uppermost in the minds of U.S. and British officials. They believed that the deep polarization and factionalism in pre-war German politics had made it possible for a Hitler to rise to power. In light of this, our government and the British had serious concerns about the German labor movement and its unity. Before the war, conflicts between Marxists and Catholics in Germany had produced a divided labor movement, as it had in the rest of Europe: a socialist federation on one side, a Christian federation of Protestants and Catholics on the other. The Allies believed that labor unity would help ensure the future of democracy in Germany.

It was an arguable point, and they asked me to prepare a study of whether a united labor movement – in effect, one without a separate Christian federation – was feasible in post-war Germany. In August of 1949, I submitted a fifty-one page report to the military government, taking a reasonably optimistic view of this prospect. As it turned out, the German Christian Federation of Labor was not resurrected after the war. To some extent, this was a conscious choice on the part of Christian unionists. But some in the movement felt that the Allied governments had placed unwarranted pressure on church authorities to keep the Christian federation out of business.

During my assignment I had ample opportunity to travel in my spare time, and I began developing contacts with labor and church people in Europe. I made my first trip to Rome and, in Switzerland, attended the 1949 meeting of the International Labor Organization (ILO). During the ILO conference I became entwined in a minor instance of the larger disunity between religion and labor in Europe.

I was traveling with the late Father Francis Flanagan, a former AFL-CIO intern who was studying philosophy in Rome, and we ran into George Meany and his wife in the lobby of the hotel near the ILO headquarters. Meany, who was then secretary-treasurer of the old American Federation of Labor, asked if we had anything planned for the evening. We did. But we also wanted to learn all we could about international labor. "Nothing special," I said. He told us, "Well, the Swiss labor movement is having a big dinner for the labor delegates. Why don't the two of you come as our guests?" We arranged to meet in the hotel lobby at six o'clock. A half-hour before that, Meany called on the telephone. "I'm very sorry, very unhappy about this," Meany said. "I've been told by our hosts, the Swiss labor movement, that it would not be proper for them to invite a priest to their dinner."

It was a harmless misunderstanding but indicative of the mood in those days. Then and for many years afterward, there was a cleavage in many parts of Europe between the labor movement and religion. Many of the dominant nineteenth-century labor unions on the continent (and some south of our border) were Marxist in the fullest sense of the word, not only collectivist in their economics, which is less to the point, but all too often vigorously anti-clerical and even at times anti-religious in their official ideology. As a result, many sincere Christians – Catholics, especially, but Protestants as well – found it difficult if not impossible to participate in these unions. Their fear, however well- or ill-founded, was that they would compromise the essentials of their own religious faith. On the other side of the coin, many sincere, militant workers, not only Marxists, looked upon the church and organized religion in general as bastions of reaction.

This may reveal an American bias on my part, but what the Europeans seemed to lack was a concept of labor-union neutrality – that is, neutrality on religious and moral questions that have little to do with trade unionism. Labor unions as well as churches tended to theologize the labor movement. In other words, they seemed unwilling to let unions be unions and keep to the core issues, such as collective bargaining and distribution of property; they also felt called upon to bring in questions of ultimate meaning and reality.

This led to more than a few ridiculous arguments. The polemics between religion and labor became so far-fetched that in some places noisy debates erupted over the question of cremation. Some of the socialist unions saw it as a symbolic issue. At the time, the Catholic Church was speaking out against cremation, so the unions decided that they would draw public attention to the cremations of some of their members as a way of sticking it to the church. (As usual, the church went for the bait.) Of course, outlandish debates of this kind had nothing to do with the trade union problem and only brought on further division.

In Holland, any Catholic who belonged to any union except the Catholic union did so under pain of excommunication. The Dutch labor movement had split along both denominational and ideological lines, with separate trade union federations for Protestants, Catholics, socialists and communists. There, as in other parts of Europe, the church's feelings toward the labor movement were more or less .the same as they were toward the wider culture. That is to say, they were dis-

tant, and Holland had the most ghettoized Catholic Church in all of Europe. If you were a Dutch Catholic, you went to a Catholic doctor, read a Catholic newspaper, listened to a Catholic radio station – and you joined a Catholic trade union.

Today the situation of the Catholic Church in Holland appears to have shifted to the other extreme. There is no Christian trade union in Holland nor, for that matter, no overwhelming presence of Catholic institutions of any other kind. The Dutch church is in disarray, at least from an institutional standpoint. The change is striking. When I arrived in Holland, a first order of business was to acquire a copy of the so-called "Mandatum," the document in which the Dutch bishops decreed that Catholics should belong to Catholic unions and no others. One of the signers of the decree was the young Bishop Bernard Jan Alfrink. Less than two decades later, at the Second Vatican Council, Cardinal Alfrink emerged as a leading liberal voice for the church's opening to the modern world.

In more recent years, church-labor relations have taken a significant turn for the better on the Continent, although the German inquiry as to why a priest would go to a labor gathering, in 1988, showed the lingering bad will between the two groups. (If the bishops of Germany think the metalworkers are radical, they haven't looked recently at the number of banks and other capitalist enterprises owned by the union.) Still, the European experience tells us much about the uniqueness of the American situation. There has long been a good working relationship between organized labor and organized religion in our country – so much so that European labor representatives who visit for the first time often point to this as one of the most striking characteristics of our national tradition.

A Belgian labor leader passing through Washington in 1989 asked the very question: How did labor and religion get on such good terms in the United States? This fellow is an officer of the Christian federation of labor in Belgium, one of several European countries that still have divided labor movements. I started off by telling him a story about a nineteenth-century cardinal from Baltimore who intervened with the Vatican at a critical moment in the history of church-labor relations.

* * *

When I go to Rome, I try, if possible, to visit the fourth-century Basilica of Santa Maria in Trastevere. I do so not for aesthetic but for nostalgic historical reasons. It was in that basilica that James Gibbons of

Baltimore, upon his elevation to the rank of cardinal in 1887, spoke in defense of religious liberty in the United States. This was generations before Rome would come around to endorsing the concept of religious liberty as a universal value. Gibbons' faith in the American experiment and openness toward American institutions would, within a few years, lead him to head off a Vatican condemnation of the labor movement in this country.

"For myself, as a citizen of the United States, without closing my eyes to our defects as a nation," he said in the basilica, "I proclaim, with a deep sense of pride and gratitude, and in this great capital of Christendom, that I belong to a country where the civil government holds over us the aegis of its protection without interfering in the legitimate exercise of our sublime mission as ministers of the gospel of Jesus Christ." For the great progress which the church in the United States has made "under God and the fostering care of the Holy See, we are indebted in no small degree," he added, "to the civil liberty we enjoy in our enlightened republic."

Gibbons was not the first American bishop to voice these sentiments, not the first to display an openness to what the modern world, within reason, had to offer. Seven years before the principle of religious freedom was legally guaranteed by the First Amendment to the Constitution, the first bishop of the United States, John Carroll of Baltimore, declared: "We have all smarted heretofore under the lash of an established church and shall be on our guard against every approach toward it." He made this declaration despite the fact that the twenty-five thousand Catholics committed to his pastoral care suffered under severe legal disabilities. Such was the state of the church in all of the original colonies except Pennsylvania – even in Catholic-founded Maryland, where Catholics were disenfranchised in 1654. But, in 1776, Maryland followed Virginia's lead with a grant of religious freedom, and Pennsylvania reiterated its standing promise of religious liberty. Thereafter the Declaration's inalienable right of "liberty and the pursuit of happiness" became meaningful for Catholics.

Carroll was thus prompted to say that "the United States has banished intolerance from its system of government. Freedom and independence, acquired by the united efforts and cemented by the mingled blood of Protestant and Catholic fellow citizens, should be equally enjoyed by all." Bishop Carroll's guarded optimism proved somewhat premature. Intolerance toward Catholics persisted, in varying degrees, for many gen-

erations. And yet the American Catholic community never muted its applause for the political system of our country and never hesitated in its belief in the promise of American democracy.

In the latter part of the nineteenth century, it was the American labor movement that held out hope of advancing the American experiment. The only organization at the time that even remotely resembled what we would today recognize as a union was the Knights of Labor. By modern standards, it was not much of a labor movement. It was, however, all we had, and many of the new Catholic immigrants rallied behind it. The Knights were unlike trade unions of today in that they welcomed, as the saying had it, "everyone but bankers and bartenders." In other words, the Knights took in non-salaried workers such as self-employed craftsmen and shopkeepers. They did as much fraternizing as collective bargaining. And the Knights shrouded themselves in secrecy, having all the paraphernalia of a secret society – passwords, ceremonial vows of secrecy, and the like.

This was the rub for the Catholic Church, which harbored a deep suspicion of secret societies, mainly as a result of the church's experience with the Masons and other societies with anti-religious overtones. It was inevitable, then, that the Knights would become a point of contention in the church. In Quebec, the French Canadian bishops had prevailed upon the Vatican to condemn the Knights in Canada and, for all practical purposes, forbade Catholics to belong to the union. In Rome, church leaders were ready to extend the ruling to the United States.

The prospects of condemnation alarmed Gibbons and the American bishops, particularly the liberal-minded "Americanists," as they were known. Unlike their Canadian counterparts, the U.S. bishops did not look upon the Knights of Labor as a danger to the faith of their people. They knew that the secret nature of the organization pertained not to religion or ideology but to the need for protection against enemies. Aside from this, the bishops were shrewd enough to know that the idiosyncratic Knights would not become the permanent labor movement in the United States. Indeed the organization would soon fade away, setting the stage for Samuel Gompers and the American Federation of Labor.

The bishops chose not to sit around and wait for word from the Holy See. In 1886 they drafted a memorandum signed by Gibbons, who, as the only cardinal and spokesman for the Catholic Church in the United

States, sailed off to Rome to make their case. In their memorandum, the bishops argued that at a time when American workers were struggling for their rights, an organization such as the Knights of Labor was indispensable. They told Rome that a condemnation would lead to disaffection among Catholic workers, at least some of whom, they warned, would leave the church. In short, the bishops urged the Holy See to drop the matter, and they prevailed. There was no condemnation of the Knights of Labor in the United States.

The Gibbons memorandum is one of the neglected classics in the histories of American religion and labor. Certainly it is required reading for anyone who would hope to understand the tradition of church-labor cooperation in this country. Perhaps the following excerpt from the memorandum will suggest the flavor of the cardinal's thinking:

> Since it is acknowledged by all that the great questions of the future . . . [are] the social questions, the questions which concern the improvement of the condition of the great masses of the people, and especially of the working people, it is evidently of supreme importance that the church should always be found on the side of humanity, of justice toward the multitudes who compose the body of the human family. . . . In our country, especially, this is the inevitable program of the future, and the position which the church must hold toward the solution is sufficiently obvious.

My friend, the late Msgr. John Tracy Ellis, a first-rate historian, viewed the cardinal's memorandum as perhaps the single most important document ever issued by the American bishops. For had the Vatican gone the other way and condemned the Knights of Labor, as the French Canadian bishops had urged, a split would have occurred in the American labor movement, as it had in Europe. In that case, some Catholics would have remained loyal to the church and joined an inconsequential Catholic union, while others would have fallen away from the church to one degree or another. This would have proved disastrous for not only the church but the workers, who needed solidarity. But the American labor movement was never divided along religious lines, and there has never been a serious attempt to organize a national Catholic or Christian or Protestant union.

Although the American bishops stood up for the Knights and rejected the sectarian option, they did not extend the argument by saying their European counterparts should do the same. To do so would have been not only unwise from a tactical point of view but, perhaps, bad sociology as well. The Americans knew that whatever social and political conditions had prompted the European church to cultivate a separate Christian labor movement, those conditions did not exist in the United States.

For one thing, in contrast to Europe, no atheistic or anti-religious or anti-clerical movement had ever and would ever take hold in the American trade union movement. The United States, like most European countries, did embrace the concept of separation of church and state. But our variety of church-state separation differed fundamentally from theirs.

As it developed from the French Revolution, the European doctrine of separation of church and state aimed at keeping religion out of the social realm. In the United States, on the other hand, the founders who drafted the First Amendment wanted to keep the government out of religion. So, unlike the case in Western Europe after the French Revolution and up until fairly recent times, our government never took an anti-religious stand. This gave the Catholic Church some breathing space in the secular order. And as a result, Catholics could join the labor movement with the full blessing of their church, and, in fact, they became extraordinarily active in the movement, more so than any other religious or ethnic group. Despite the many changes in religious, cultural, social, ethnic and political life, that still holds true today.

Closing Ranks

The Gibbons intervention might have made for a good start in American Catholic social action, but no movement of any consequence appeared for at least a generation afterward. The church had other things on its mind. In those years, millions of immigrants arrived on the shores of the United States, and the larger burden fell on the Catholic Church to settle and assimilate these new Americans. Bishop Carroll's scattered band of twenty-five thousand Catholics was augmented by the influx of millions of Europeans during the second half of the nineteenth century and the first quarter of the twentieth century. This massive movement of impoverished people from the Old World to the New confronted the church with a pastoral problem of staggering proportions.

During the early waves of immigration, the institution of American Catholicism, as we know it today, began to take shape. The church went about the business of building schools, parishes, hospitals, orphanages and homes for unwed mothers, assimilating millions of poor and penniless workers. This became a total preoccupation, and little time remained for serious consideration of the larger issues of social justice (although individual Catholics labored in the social field). The church, as an institution, had yet to make social reform an integral part of its mission.

This hardly means, however, that the Catholic Church was irrelevant to the processes of social change in America. The church's response to the immigration problem, with all its strengths and weaknesses, has only recently begun to receive the degree of scholarly attention it so richly deserves. In any event, it is clear even now, as the distinguished (non-Catholic) historian Henry Steele Commager has written, that the Catholic Church was during the immigration period "one of the most effective of all agencies for democracy and Americanization. Representing as it did a vast cross section of the American people, it could ignore class, section, and race; peculiarly the Church of the newcomers, of those who all too often were regarded as aliens, it could give them not only spiritual refuge but social security."

It is easy by hindsight to criticize the church's manner of dealing with the problem of mass immigration (some historians believe the church should have been more critical of the "melting-pot" process of assimilation). Yet it can hardly be denied that the church helped millions of immigrants become acclimated to their new and strange surroundings and adapt to American social and political institutions – on their own terms. One of these institutions, in due course, would be the labor movement. Underlying the church's response to the new Americans was a communitarian ethos that would help sustain the very notion of collective bargaining.

During the early immigration period, the Social Gospel movement in American Protestantism provided leadership in the arena of religious social action. The movement worked to apply biblical teachings to the economic realm. (One of its more memorable battle cries was against "economic atheism," that is, economics as if God and moral principles did not exist.) I think many of my Protestant friends, however, would agree that the Social Gospel movement amounted to little more than a sideshow in American Protestantism. It caught the interest of intellectuals and some socially minded people in the upper classes. But the movement, partly due to its elitist character, never reached deeply into the grass roots. It had little connection to working people and organized labor.

Nonetheless, Social Gospelers helped awaken the consciences of certain elite segments in America, forming the soul of a Progressive movement that achieved early victories in the area of legislative reform. And the movement came to exert an indirect influence on American Catholicism in the person of John A. Ryan, born and bred on progressivist soil in Minnesota. Ryan, one of those moved by the preaching of Midwestern Social Gospelers, believed that the American experiment (particularly its reformist strands) and Catholic tradition could be reconciled. The enduring testimony to this belief is the bishops' *Program of Social Reconstruction*, issued in 1919 and drafted by Ryan. The *Program* served as the vehicle of American Catholicism's formal entry into the social arena, at once embracing and going beyond the progressive agenda of social reform.

Those who believe today's church leaders go too hard on business should listen to the words of the bishops in 1919. After pointing out that laborers should put in an honest day's work for an honest day's pay, the *Program* ended with these words:

> The capitalist must likewise get a new viewpoint. He needs to learn the long-forgotten truth that wealth is stewardship, that profit-making is not the basic justification of business enterprise, and that there are such things as fair profits, fair interest, and fair prices. Above all, he must cultivate and strengthen within his mind the truth . . . that the laborer is a human being, not merely an instrument of production; and that the laborer's right to a decent livelihood is the first moral charge upon industry. The employer has a right to get a reasonable living out of his business, but he has no right to interest on his investment until his employees have obtained at least living wages. This is the human and Christian, in contrast to the purely commercial and pagan, ethics of industry.

The *Program* marked a turning point for the Catholic Church in this country, signaling a new desire by the church's hierarchy to compete in the marketplace of social ideas. (The bishops even enlisted the services of a public relations specialist in New York to promote the document, which drew extensive notice when first released.) In terms of official Catholic social action, the statement helped set a progressive tone for the bishops' national organization, which came into existence a few months later, in November.

It was hardly pre-ordained that the bishops' Social Action Department (from its beginning, under the leadership of John Ryan) would push a basically progressive agenda. Nor, for that matter, was it so ordained that the bishops' conference itself would amount to much more than a paper organization. On both counts, a large part of the credit (or blame, depending on one's viewpoint) goes to a Paulist priest who served as the conference's first general secretary. By most Vatican II standards, Paulist Msgr. John Burke was admittedly conservative or, at best, very moderate in his approach to a number of theological and secular issues. But by the standards of his own generation he was significantly ahead of his time across the board.

The bishops' conference, a significant element of any Catholic social action movement, almost died on the vine. For those accustomed to having an activist organization representing the bishops at the national level, it may be difficult to understand how unique and controversial it was at the beginning. Previously, during the First World War, there was an organization called the National Catholic War Council, set up to oversee war-related activities in the church. The agency coordinated, among other things, assignments of Catholic chaplains and what later became known as U.S.O. work among Catholic soldiers. As a voluntary organization, the bishops did not have to belong to it, much less follow its lead on social issues. With the close of World War I, the bishops decided that their experiment with a national coordinating body had been reasonably successful, and they decided to form a permanent organization called the National Catholic Welfare Council.

The new organization came under fierce attack from a small but vocal group of bishops who feared that it might come to exert authority over them and their dioceses. They saw a kind of legislative authority implied in the very word "Council." The Vatican agreed and ordered that it be dissolved, not only suppressing the young organization but banning annual meetings of bishops as well. Yet as they had done a generation earlier with regard to the Knights of Labor, the bishops rallied together. Burke played an important, behind-the-scenes role in arranging for Bishop Joseph Schrembs of Cleveland to argue the conference's case in cliff-hanger negotiations with Vatican authorities in Rome.

In the end, the bishops succeeded in their effort to reverse the Holy See's ill-advised suppression of the organization. Rome's only demand was that the bishops drop "Council" from their name, and with this minor concession, the National Catholic Welfare "Conference" (NCWC) was born in 1922. (Today, once again, this debate is being played out in the back-and-forth arguments between U.S. Catholic leaders and Rome over the status of national bishops' conferences. Much like the curia of Burke's day, Vatican officials such as Cardinal Joseph Ratzinger have questioned the teaching authority of national organizations of bishops.)

With the bishops' conference firmly in place, Father Burke's never-failing support of progressive social action programs made it possible for John Ryan's agenda to become the NCWC's. Msgr. Burke was the right man in the right place at the right time; for this the Catholic Church in the United States has every reason to honor his legacy. One shudders to think of what might have happened, what direction the NCWC might have taken, if its first general secretary had come from a more hidebound or conservative theological and political tradition. Be that as it may, the only thing that matters now is that the conference – whose uniqueness, in its time, has yet to be fully appreciated – got off to a basically progressive start under Msgr. Burke's farsighted and resourceful leadership.

Notwithstanding Burke's support and Ryan's renown, the Social Action Department might have labored in relative obscurity if not for its assistant director, Father Raymond McGowan. Working deliberately in the shadow of his illustrious superior, McGowan gave the department its distinctive character. For all practical purposes, he directed the department while Ryan pursued his apostolate of writing and lecturing on social concerns.

In 1922 McGowan spawned, from the side of the Social Action Department, the Catholic Conference on Industrial Problems, which he once described as "a kind of traveling show of Catholic social teaching." Assisted by Linna Bresette, the department's field secretary, McGowan staged conferences around the country, bringing together labor leaders, government officials, employers and exponents of Catholic social teaching to discuss industrial issues. McGowan's organizational activities were a prototype of his industrial vision – that of genuine cooperation between labor, management and government. In McGowan's vision of a cooperative society, employees worked as full partners in business enterprises; unions participated in decisions not only about wages and work conditions but about prices and profits as well.

McGowan's efforts at reform came during a dry period of social action in the church and wider society. In her advance field work for the conferences on industrial problems, Bresette encountered a recurring skepticism (notably among employers and well-to-do Catholics) about the need for such an organization during a supposedly prosperous era. Furthermore, after early advances in the organization of skilled workers, the labor movement went into a period of steep decline during the 1920s, in large part because of renewed resistance by employers. In this conservative climate, McGowan promoted such reforms as a mandatory minimum wage, recognition of labor unions and the right to strike, and the establishment of consumer cooperatives. The labor-management-government conferences, while lasting into the 1950s, made their most distinctive contribution by sounding an industrial wake-up call during the complacent 1920s.

In the 1930s, when social action was still of questionable centrality in the church, the bishops' conference quietly nurtured a constituency of priests dedicated to social ministry. My predecessor at the Social Action Department, Father John Mayes of Chicago, had begun to circulate *Social Action Notes for Priests*, written for what was intended to be, at most, a few hundred priests with an interest in social problems. The newsletter paid special attention to the labor problem. It reported on the activities of priests and lay people in this field and carried excerpts from some of the more useful articles and documents that touched on organized labor. Its distribution was based purely on demand in the sense that every priest who received the newsletter had specifically asked to be placed on the mailing list. By the time it went out of publication, approximately six thousand priests had written in for subscriptions.

When Father Hayes took sick and had to leave the conference (in what turned out to be only a brief interruption of his long and fruitful ministry of social action), this part of the department's work fell to me. The assignment put me in contact with thousands of priests, some of whom would later become leading social-minded bishops of the 1960s and 1970s. In those fluid and formative years of Catholic social action, I seldom knew what I would be doing from one day to the next. I would arrive at my desk in the morning and find a stack of letters from priests with questions about the Taft-Hartley Labor Act of 1947 (which outlawed such union practices as the closed shop and secondary boycotts) or any other aspect of the labor problem. As the one whose job it was to involve clergy, I answered every one of them.

In the front ranks stood the so-called labor priests, those who made the working person their apostolate. In many places where workers struggled to organize, the priests opened "schools" for the rank and file,

sometimes as an extension of colleges and universities run by the Jesuits. Numbering in excess of one hundred at their peak in the 1940s and 1950s, the labor schools represented an early and somewhat raucous form of what we know today as "adult education." They arose in a context of struggle and confrontation, a time when millions of workers asserted their rights of free association in the workplace. After quitting time, many of these workers (who tended to know as little about unions as former Soviet citizens today know about free markets) would come together for basic education in the workings of labor. One of the more ambitious undertakings was in Connecticut, where Msgr. Joseph Donnelly oversaw the establishment of nearly two dozen labor schools. He went on to become chairman of the state's labor mediation board, a post that he held for twenty years before being named auxiliary bishop of Hartford.

One of those who remain active in local affairs is Msgr. Charles Owen Rice, a well-known figure in Pittsburgh who emerged as the industrial city's leading labor priest during the Depression. In 1936 he and Father Carl Hensler formed the Catholic Radical Alliance, which had its roots in the Catholic Worker movement. "I am a radical, a Catholic radical," Rice said on many occasions. "I believe that the present social and economic system is a mess and should be changed from top to bottom." A native of New York City who spent seven years of his boyhood in Ireland, living among relatives after his mother died, Rice was never one to run from a fight. In fact, he deliberately and almost gleefully started many a good fight himself. Rice personally took part in strikes by the Congress of Industrial Organizations. He joined with workers on the picket line during such actions as the 1937 strike against the Pittsburgh-based Heinz Corporation. He spoke to many an overflow crowd in churches, union halls and immigrant meeting houses.

Unlike most other labor priests, Rice plunged himself into the internal politics of the labor movement, fighting communists in the leadership ranks of CIO unions, especially during the late 1940s and early 1950s. He became one of the leaders of an anti-communist movement in the United Electrical Workers, then a communist-controlled union with a big local in Pittsburgh, home of Westinghouse Corporation. (On this point, Rice has openly voiced some regrets in recent years, a matter to which I will return presently.) Yet during the CIO's formative years in the 1930s, Rice's name was virtually synonymous with the movement of industrial unions, so much so that he became known as "the chaplain of the CIO."

Although labor priests generally kept to matters of local concern, there is at least one whose name and cause became known all across the country. John "Pete" Corridan, a Jesuit priest, was one of the most colorful and effective opponents of labor racketeering. A rough-and-tumble New Yorker, Corridan inspired author and screenwriter Budd Schulberg's 1953 movie, *On the Waterfront*, based on events during the 1940s and 1950s, when Corridan led a crusade against racketeering in New York's maritime industry. The "waterfront priest," as he was known, worked through the Xavier Labor School, headed by his fellow Jesuit, the late Rev. Philip Carey.

In the early 1940s the school directed its attention to unions controlled and influenced by communists, including the Transit Workers of New York City. Carey believed that the communists did not have the interests of the unions at heart and, unless opposed, would hijack the unions for their own ideological ends. His strategy, he always said, was to train workers in "union democracy," with a view toward fair union elections. When Corridan came on board in the late 1940s, the focus turned to racketeering, and the two Jesuits made for an ideal combination. Gentle, though shrewd, Carey was the man on the inside, overseeing the day-to-day work of the labor school, which trained longshoremen who wanted to clean up their union. Corridan, tough and street-smart, was the man out on the docks, going up against the triple alliance of crooked union leaders, employers, and politicians who looked the other way.

Corridan's swashbuckling manner was hardly the usual style of labor priests, and yet he was typical in the sense that he sought to apply the universals of social ethics to the particulars of concrete reality. The harsh, day-to-day reality on the waterfront was its outmoded hiring system. They called it the "Shape-Up" – the notorious system that required stevedores to line up or "shape up" for work twice a day before a hiring agent, who had the power to determine their economic life or death. Getting a favorable nod from the hiring boss often meant having to go see the loan shark, who lent money at the usurious rate of twenty percent a week. This form of extortion came with a union seal of approval.

To those workers struggling against the system of the Shape Up, Corridan held out a deep and lively spirituality, a blessed assurance that they were not alone. "I suppose some people would smirk at the thought of Christ in the Shape. It's about as absurd as the fact that he carried carpenter's tools in his hands and earned his bread and butter by the sweat of his brow," he once said. "As absurd as the fact that Christ redeemed all men irrespective of their race, color or station in life."

Corridan was revered by the dockworkers. When they staged a wild-cat strike on the morning of November 8, 1948 (which quickly spread up and down the Atlantic Coast, lasting eighteen days) the Waterfront Priest was catapulted onto the national stage. His presence in the rebel movement required a shift of tactics on the part of the top union boss, Joe Ryan, president of the International Longshoremen's Association. Up until this point, Ryan could garner a certain amount of public sympathy by labeling the rebel dockworkers' movement and its underground publication, *The Crusader*, "a Communist production." But after Corridan's responsibility for the newspaper became known, Ryan began calling it "the work of a religious fanatic." Somehow the new scare words did not pack the same punch.

While excellent in many respects, the motion picture *On the Waterfront* could easily give a simplistic impression of good guys vs. bad guys. This may be expected of Hollywood, and yet it would have probably taken little more than a few lines to get across the bigger picture that Corridan always kept in view. He was more than a Jesuit gangbuster; he had a social critique. The problem, as he saw it, was not just a few crooks but an economic system driven purely by profit. Like other labor priests of his time, Corridan knew that individual moral reform alone was not enough. There had to be reform of economic institutions and structures, whether it was of the Shape Up on the docks or the Shake Down by any others who would deny workers a living wage.

Extremely affable, but fearless and tough as nails, Corridan risked his life to bring about needed labor-management reforms. But for the grace of God, he might have well ended up in the East River for challenging the gangster-controlled hiring system on the docks. In the end, Pete's efforts led to congressional hearings, labor-law reforms and the formation of the New York/New Jersey Watchdog Waterfront Commission. In a fitting tribute at the time of his death in 1984, Budd Schulberg said Corridan was about the "closest I ever came to feeling what true Christianity was about."

The labor school which served as Corridan's base would turn out to be one of the very last in the Catholic Church. At one time church-sponsored labor schools provided a source of hope for workers battling against great odds. If the schools accomplished nothing else, they lent a certain respectability to the union movement in an era of extreme resistance toward its campaigns. With representatives of Roman Catholicism teaching workers how to organize themselves and build institutions, labor's enemies found it harder to portray the movement as a wholly owned subsidiary of the Soviet Union. Yet many of them would keep on trying.

In New York ten thousand union members passed through the Xavier Labor School, which Carey operated for fifty years in Lower Manhattan. But when the Jesuit passed away in July 1989, so did the labor school. As Carey admitted to the *National Catholic Reporter* in 1988, his work at the labor school was not what it was when fifty thousand longshoremen worked New York's bustling ports. Today, only one thousand union members staff the docks, but Carey said he thought he still had a contribution to make. His death, at the age of eighty, signaled the end of an era of Catholic social action. In his time Catholic labor schools dotted the industrial landscape; now they have all but disappeared. As of this writing, the late Father Ed Boyle's Boston Catholic Labor Institute was the only one left. Yet as I will discuss later in this chapter, new circumstances have given rise to new efforts toward collaboration between religion and labor.

* * *

Since the heyday of church-labor cooperation, revisionist historians have looked for dark and cynical motives behind the Catholic Church's involvement in the labor movement. A common thesis is that if not for the Catholic Church's intervention, there might have been a socialist labor movement in the United States. It is worth clearing the air on this point, if for no other reason than that the ghosts of past quarrels appear now and then in dialogues between religion and labor.

Much of the revisionism has dealt with the now-defunct Association of Catholic Trade Unionists (ACTU). That's "unionists," not unions; the difference is between separate Catholic unions of the European variety and parallel organizations of Catholic union members – the ACTU model. Launched in New York City by former members of the Catholic Worker (notably John Cort, a Catholic convert and early organizer of the International Ladies Garment Workers Union), ACTU defined its mission as spreading the church's teachings on labor. The movement drew part of its mandate from Pope Pius XI's 1931 encyclical

which encouraged Christian workers to form parallel (though not necessarily competing) associations of Catholic workers.

In practically no time, the movement branched out from New York and spawned independent chapters across the map of urban industrial America. ACTU published a number of first-rate newspapers. In Detroit, for example, *The Wage Earner* took an active role in promoting the legitimacy of industrial unions as ACTU leaders worked closely with Walter Reuther of the United Auto Workers. For better or worse, ACTU had no national coordination. So while in many places the movement rallied support for striking workers, in others it knocked heads with communists in the labor movement or tried to root out organized crime. It is the brush with Bolshevism that has driven so much of the historical investigation.

A fairly typical work of this genre is Douglas P. Seaton's *Catholics and Radicals: The Association of Catholic Trade Unionists and the American Labor Movement from Depression to Cold War*. In his 1981 book, Seaton argues tendentiously – almost ad nauseam – that "the partisans of the church" and specifically ACTU were a, if not the, crucial factor in determining the "conservative" direction taken by the industrial unions during the period between 1937 and 1950.

Undergirding this sweeping generalization is Seaton's recurrent charge, tinged with a note of personal pique and hostility, that Catholic social teaching (which ACTU, however effectively or otherwise, tried to put into practice) is hopelessly "conservative." In a telltale footnote, Seaton gives his hand away by defining his loaded terms. In short, "radicals" (the good guys) are those committed to class struggle and a socialist order. "Conservatives" (the bad guys) are, conversely, those who reject the philosophy of class struggle and do not belong to any formal school of socialism.

With his basic code words so defined Seaton has no trouble proving, at least to his own satisfaction, that the Catholic Church in general and ACTU in particular were conservative. Even John A. Ryan, in the author's mind, was only a half-hearted progressive. On the other hand, he locates the "radicals" more often than not in the communist leaderships of some of the old CIO unions. All this begs the question of whether the program pushed by these so-called "radicals" in labor's communist ranks represented the best interests of labor and the nation as a whole. It's not as if we're talking about Mikhail Gorbachev-style communists, much less democratic socialists of the Michael Harrington variety. These were Stalinists, and their virtually absolute allegiance to the Communist Party was regarded by many, not unreasonably, as contrary to the idea of an independent labor movement.

Be that as it may, Seaton argues that ACTU's commitment to "conservative" Catholic social teaching and its reluctance to break with the church made it inevitable that an obsessive anti-communism would become "virtually the sole issue which occupied the organization." Seaton and other historians of his ilk are not alone in thinking that ACTU (or, more precisely, some local chapters of ACTU) went overboard with its anti-communism. One who has looked back on that period is Msgr. Charles Owen Rice, whose penitent reflections are captured in the title of his summer 1989 article, "Confessions of an Anti-Communist," published in *Labor History*.

Rice, who worked closely with ACTU through his Catholic Radical Alliance in Pittsburgh, says he is not proud of the crusades to remove communists from positions of influence in the labor movement. He still holds, quite rightly, that the primary loyalty of communists was to the Communist Party, not to the labor movement, and that their triumph would have been labor's disaster. In retrospect, however, he believes that the communists never had a chance. Most of all, he regrets that he (and other "actists," as they were known) at times employed tactics as ruthless and merciless, in his view, as those of their adversaries.

"Most of us ACTU people had been influenced by Dorothy Day in the direction of enthusiastic support for organized labor, but we lost Dorothy's serenity and positive spirit along the way," he wrote in Commonweal in 1984. "We were pro-labor and not merely anti-communist, but I for one wish there had been far less emphasis on the negative."

Misgivings about anti-communist crusades in labor have not only come after the fact. At the height of labor's cold war, the communist question provoked heated debates, pro and con, in ACTU circles around the country. The failure of many historians to report adequately on the ins and outs of this intramural ACTU debate is but one indication of their ideological bias. In Seaton's case the oversight stems not only from the apparently limited scope of his research (he appears to have relied much too heavily on the extant files of the New York ACTU, which, in the opinion of some, took its anti-communism too far). It also grows out of an almost compulsive desire to nail down his central thesis.

Other revisionists have attributed even darker motives to the church's interest in the labor problem. In his 1989 critical biography, *Rev. Charles Owen Rice: Apostle of Contradiction*, Patrick McGeever gives credence to charges that Rice and ACTU were primarily concerned not with social justice (nor even, for that matter, with anti-communism) but rather with having Catholicism prevail over all other religious groups. "Of particular note in this line of criticism," McGeever writes, "was the interest that the ACTU and its 'labor leaders' were at that time expressing in having the CIO establish relations in Europe not with the socialist trade union federation, the World Federation of Trade Unions, but with its Catholic rival, the International Confederation of Free Trade Unions."

While McGeever does not actually say he agrees with this "criticism," he does tailor the evidence to fit the thesis. In fact, the example that he relates is simply untrue. The World Federation of Trade Unions was then and up until its demise in 1990 a communist, not a socialist, federation; the International Confederation of Trade Unions was and still is a social-democratic federation and by no means a Catholic rival to the world federation. This spurious example betrays yet another flaw in many of these studies – the blurring of any distinction between "socialist" and "communist." At several points McGeever uses the two words interchangeably, as if to suggest that anti-communist equals anti-socialist (and therefore anti-progressive). In fact, not only is there a huge difference between the two, but ACTU and other Catholic activists often teamed up with democratic socialists in opposing labor's communist forces.

Still other revisionists have described ACTU as a plot on the part of the church's hierarchy to influence the labor movement. In other words, the bishops pulled ACTU's strings. This charge rankles in particular because it raises, once again, the myth of the monolithic church. During those years I happened to be the bishops' liaison to groups such as ACTU. I would have sooner attempted to infiltrate the Politburo or General Motors than insinuate myself into the politics of ACTU. The actists were fiercely jealous of their autonomy, guarding it against church authorities as well as other chapters of the organization.

More often than not, in a given city, ACTU got off the ground without any Episcopal blessing and in some cases against the better judgment of the bishop. It would be hard to imagine that the New York ACTU was even remotely started up by the archbishop there. As it turned out, during a 1949 gravediggers' strike against cemeteries owned by the archdiocese of New York, ACTU sided squarely with the cemetery workers and opposed the archbishop. This could not have pleased Francis Spellman.

Did ACTU as well as other Catholic activists make mistakes in their dealings with labor? Undoubtedly. But being in a position to travel around at the time, I was about as close to ACTU as anyone else; and while I did not always like what I saw, the decisions were made, for better or worse, by actists on their own. They did not take their cue from the bishops. One exception to this determined autonomy was the situation in Detroit, where ACTU worked hand in hand with Archbishop Edward Mooney. Mooney, though, was a progressive, and it would be, at the very least, gross overstatement to call him a union red-baiter. Mooney's alliance with ACTU and organized labor eventually led him into a confrontation with his best-known priest, one that illustrates the church's encounter with the labor problem.

Father Charles Coughlin, the powerful priest of the nation's airwaves, was closely identified with the cause of organized labor because of his early support of the movement. But when the Congress of Industrial Unions arrived on the scene in the late 1930s, he turned into one of its bitter detractors. In radio sermon after radio sermon, Coughlin charged that the CIO – and its affiliate, the auto workers – had fallen into the hands of communists. John L. Lewis, the illustrious founder of the CIO, came in for especially harsh criticism for not expelling communists from CIO ranks. Coughlin went so far as to help organize a separate union of Ford workers that would be more agreeable to management, although this quixotic venture was short-lived.

At the time, ACTU chapters in Detroit and elsewhere were urging its members to rebut the anti-union broadcasts of Coughlin and his diatribes against the CIO in particular. While Mooney, too, lent his support to the CIO, he was more cautious in his handling of Coughlin, a pastor in the Detroit archdiocese. For one thing, the archbishop realized that he could make a martyr out of Coughlin by coming down too hard on him. Furthermore, no one knew how the unsteady Coughlin, with his enormous and dedicated following, would react to a move against him by Mooney. (Douglas Fraser, former president of the United Auto Workers, once mentioned to me that when he was a boy, Coughlin's Sunday broadcasts were sacred in his family. When the radio priest came on, everything in his home came to a stop. Fraser recalls that this was

true of his entire neighborhood.) The idea of Coughlin, directly or indirectly, stirring up a public outcry against his own archbishop was not unthinkable.

Mooney, however, found an opening at the time of a nationwide strike by Chrysler workers in 1939. Coughlin, who called for Chrysler workers to go back to work, made the mistake of quoting from *Quadragesimo Anno* – out of context. In describing the fascist system in Italy, the encyclical by Pius XI stated that strikes are forbidden. The encyclical did not say that strikes should be forbidden; it simply said that under the fascist system, they are forbidden. It was a declarative statement. Coughlin, however, took it as an admonitory statement – that workers should never strike – and he turned it against the United Auto Workers. This gave Mooney an opening because the matter involved not mere political judgment but church teaching, which he had to uphold as archbishop.

Mooney instructed Father Raymond Clancy, his social-action vicar, and Paul Weber, editor of the *Wage Earner*, to buy radio time to respond to Coughlin's attacks on the striking Chrysler workers. In his broadcast Father Clancy adopted ACTU's argument that Coughlin had repeatedly misrepresented Catholic social teaching. The message of disapproval sent by Coughlin's own archbishop amounted to one large step in the radio priest's eventual downfall.

Such an episode in the Catholic engagement with labor would be hard to find in the volumes of revisionist history. It does not fit neatly into the thesis of a "conservative" church that joined the labor struggle merely to oppose communism or, worse yet, to serve narrow, institutional interests. And yet, action for the genuine progress of labor was the rule rather than the exception in the Catholic social action movement. It defined the church's relationship to organized labor during the movement's formative battles for recognition.

A Tapering Off and Falling Out

During the days of the Mooneys, Corridans and Rices, religion and labor faced a relatively simple, moral issue – the right to organize. When the Congress of Industrial Organizations came on the scene, only a handful of independent labor unions had opened up in the major industries. With the masses of industrial workers unorganized, religious friends of labor could take a simple approach. Those in Catholic social action would say: unions are a good thing, the papal encyclicals say so, and the church ought to help this movement. The labor schools, in this respect, were unique to a period in which industrial unions conducted massive drives to organize the unorganized.

But with the great campaigns mostly behind them, religious leaders had considerably less to say about labor problems. Unions turned their attention to technical matters: negotiating and drawing up contracts and building their institutions. The tasks were somewhat removed from the basic principle of the right to organize, which provided the religious community's natural point of entry into the labor debate. From then on, collective bargaining became more and more complex. This is reflected in the union contract itself, originally little more than a statement of principle.

For instance, the first contract between General Motors and the United Auto Workers amounted to a page or two, in recognition of the union's right to represent the workers. These days the UAW contract runs about five hundred pages, with several volumes of supplementary material. After helping the UAW win its original contract, religious groups had no business telling the union how to write the fine print; and any cleric who presumed to do so would have looked rather foolish. The UAW's Walter Reuther (who benefited from church support as much as any other labor leader) did not need Cardinal Mooney's advice on how to run his union.

Not surprisingly, in the 1950s labor problems began to recede into the background of Catholic social concerns. Once the auto workers, for example, became a highly complex institution with a million and a half members, what was there for the church to do? By the same token, it makes sense that in more recent years, church involvement in the labor causes gravitated toward areas left untouched by the earlier industrial organizing campaigns. In the 1970s it was the agriculture and textile industries that demanded a religious response.

With the farm workers, the Catholic Church returned to first principles. The U.S. Catholic Conference and other church-related organizations became deeply involved in the farm labor problem. But we did not enter the dispute to tell Cesar Chavez or the growers how they should write their contracts. What we did tell the growers (and I think to some extent we helped the farm workers, merely through the respectability that comes with church backing) was that they had to recognize the right of these men and women to organize and bargain collectively. If the United Farm Workers had developed along the lines of the United Auto Workers, religious organizations would have long

since moved out of the farm labor field. Unfortunately, however, the UFW has signed and held on to very few contracts. Chavez still has to call on church groups to endorse his boycotts and other union campaigns; he still struggles to organize the farm workers.

Likewise, simple moral principle drew religious organizations into one of the longest and hardest-fought labor disputes in recent American history. Throughout the 1970s, the name of the J. P. Stevens Company, one of the nation's leading textile manufacturing firms, was synonymous with flagrant anti-unionism. Most of its competitors also opposed unions, but Stevens almost seemed to glory in its notoriety. At the time the company refused to recognize the right of its employees to bargain collectively through their union, the Amalgamated Clothing and Textile Workers. This was reason enough for intervention by the Catholic bishops of the southeast and other religious leaders. Their message to Stevens: We don't know how to run your business, but we do know these people have a right to organize. With this show of solidarity, church leaders bolstered the labor movement's boycott of Stevens products. They helped bring about eventual recognition of the Amalgamated union.

Religion and labor, however, were a coalition only for special occasions in the post-CIO era. When things started going fairly well for organized labor, after its major organizing drives, the movement began to lose interest in establishing coalitions with other organizations, churches included. For their part, many religious activists – who might have stepped into the labor arena a generation earlier – went off to fight other battles. During the 1960s they found new causes in the rise of the civil rights and anti-war movements.

How much did the tapering off of cooperation between labor and the Catholic Church, in particular, have to do with shifting demographics among Catholics in the United States? I will leave this question to the sociologists, except to note that in the past few decades, Catholics have moved rather rapidly up the economic ladder. Let me suggest one possible implication of this with an example from my own experience.

During this writing I received a letter from a frustrated labor leader. The letter seemed to bear out what some observers have seen as a disappearance of the working class from the consciousness of middle-class professionals, Catholic or otherwise. In the late 1980s my correspondent's local union in Connecticut decided that, because of a great lack of library materials pertaining to the labor movement in the senior high schools of his city, the union would fully fund the establishment of labor libraries in those three schools, one of which is under Catholic auspices. The union had already donated approximately fifty labor titles to each of the schools. It also provided the schools with a bibliography of four hundred and fifty titles to simplify the process of selecting new ones. (The union would periodically update the bibliography so as to make available to schools any newly published works.)

In negotiating with the three schools, the union discovered that not only students but the teachers themselves were sorely lacking in basic knowledge of labor studies. They were even uncomfortable with teaching from the materials on labor already in their regular curriculum. So the union decided to do something else. Together with the labor education center of a local university, the union put together a twenty-hour labor education course providing a certain number of required continuing education credits for teachers in the three schools.

The point of my correspondent's letter was that the principal of the Catholic high school refused to cooperate with the program. He explained to the union leader that his school was basically a college preparatory school and therefore he did not see any reason to teach about unions. The union leader, quite understandably, was dumbfounded. To him, the principal was taking a rather elitist view, out of character for a professedly "Catholic" school. In his letter the union leader said he hadn't realized that Catholics have come so far from their origins as blue-collar workers and the backbone of the labor movement. They had come so far that they no longer wanted to remember or reflect on the struggles of their forebears (struggles, I might add, that made it possible for their offspring to attend college preparatory schools).

I, too, was dumbfounded. Here was a Catholic principal unwilling to even consider the possibility of cooperating, at no cost to his school, with a labor education program. I could conceive of a high school principal declining the union's offer on strictly technical grounds and for arguably good professional reasons. But to do so on grounds that labor history has no place in a college preparatory school is something else again. It is evidence, unfortunately, of what social critic Barbara Ehrenreich has described as the growing provincialism of the professional class – living in its own social and restricted enclaves, hearing only the opinions of its own members (or, of course, the truly rich) and cut off from the lives and struggles and insights of the American majority.

If Gallup polls are any indication, the Catholic principal was not alone in his seemingly distant feelings toward working people. In their 1987 book *The American Catholic People: Their Beliefs, Practices and Values*, George Gallup and Jim Castelli report on the opinions and attitudes of Catholics toward a variety of subjects, including trade unionism. "While the new Catholic affluence has not caused a callousness toward the poor, it has contributed to a distancing of American Catholics from the labor movement – despite the fact that 23 percent of Catholics live in families with a member who belongs to a labor union and that 34 percent of all union members are Catholics," says the Gallup-Castelli book. "While Catholics remain more supportive of unions than do Protestants, the gap is narrowing."

This is mainly due, I suspect, to the thinking of many upwardly mobile Catholics. Many of them have bought into the idea that while unions may have served a useful purpose when their fathers, grandfathers, or great-grandfathers struggled to make ends meet, that is no longer the case. They seem to think, in other words, that in a society as affluent as our own, workers can readily fend for themselves in the so-called free market; workers have no need to organize.

Sad to say, they are wrong about that. Their own relative affluence has blinded them to the fact that, like their immigrant forebears, millions of today's workers struggle to maintain a minimum standard of living. Many of these workers are themselves recent immigrants, but not all by any means. A growing number of second, third and fourth generation American workers, who thought that they, too, were climbing up the economic ladder, now find themselves slipping back into poverty or near-poverty. All this, however, seems to have escaped the notice of many affluent Americans, Catholics included. During the 1980s they made much of the fact that millions of new jobs had appeared every year in the United States. They seem not to know, or at least not to care, that a sizeable percentage of these jobs paid poverty-level wages. For too many workers, economic growth meant twice the jobs at half the pay.

* * *

The loosening of ties between religion and labor had to do with more than just changing times and shifting priorities. With the tumult of the 1960s came a new cynicism toward unions. Many reform-minded people began to look upon organized labor as much less a movement than an institution (which, of course, is what all successful movements become). The image of the stodgy, conservative labor leader, embodying an "establishment" out of touch with the times, entered into the consciousness of social activists. These included the "new breed" of church activists. In the midst of the anti-war struggle, critics took a look around and noticed few labor unions on the battlefield (or at least on their side of it). And in the 1960s, if you weren't part of the solution, you were part of the problem.

In the religion-labor relationship, there came not only a tapering off but a falling out. The arguments, then and for a generation following, usually turned on international affairs in general and American labor movement's antagonism toward communism in particular. In the view of some critics, this anti-communism was so extreme that it blinded labor to the true causes of revolt, namely, oppressive poverty and underdevelopment. The critics argued that in pursuing its foreign-policy goals, the American labor movement sometimes worked too closely with unsavory governments simply because of their stated anti-communism.

Religious activists had good reason to raise these issues with the labor movement, which at times made mistakes in its dealings overseas. Yet the issues were always more involved and less black-and-white than church critics were willing to admit. This appeared evident in the fractious debates between religion and labor during the 1980s.

At the time, Central America and Nicaragua in particular provided many of the sparks for religion-labor conflict. Church activists took special aim at the AFL-CIO's Latin American arm, the American Institute for Free Labor Development, known by its acronym, AIFLD ("A-field"). In some respects, the AFL-CIO and religious activists found themselves at opposite ends of the Nicaragua debate. The federation and AIFLD relentlessly bombarded Nicaragua's Sandinista government with criticism of its treatment of trade unions. Meanwhile, many religious activists sang an unending hymn of praise to the Sandinistas.

I heard the choir perform on many occasions, including once in Los Angeles, during a large Catholic social action gathering in 1985. At several points my remarks were interrupted with cheers and applause, once for condemning Chile's Pinochet regime for its suppression of labor, another time for praising the Solidarity labor union in Poland. Then I rather mildly criticized the Sandinista regime for restricting the freedom of certain Nicaraguan unions which had refused to affiliate with the official government-sponsored labor fed-

erations. Applause turned to dead silence. Afterward several people walked up to me to say I was playing into the hands of the Reagan administration.

This did not surprise me. Others before had taken exception with my comments on the matter. "Reverend: I am one of those dumbfounded by your remarks about Nicaragua and the Sandinistas," one correspondent had told me. "Certainly did not expect you to contradict the ideas of Maryknollers and Jesuits and the nuns, etc., who have gone to Nicaragua. I thought you were a liberated priest who understood that there are issues on which we do not break ranks. Shame." I would write back to the dumbfounded and assure them: "Yes, I oppose the Reagan policies in Nicaragua. Yes, I'm against aid to the contras. And yes, I think the U.S. economic embargo is a bad idea – but I also think that harassing free trade unions is inexcusable." That last point never went down well with the followers of Sandino.

It was this almost mystical attraction to the Sandinistas that helped set up a collision course between religion and organized labor in the 1980s. I never thought that the church critics fully understood the situation in Nicaragua or labor's position toward the Sandinista government. For labor, the critical issue was free trade unions, which were not free in Nicaragua under Sandinista leadership. Some church critics, however, were reluctant to admit this or simply allergic to any discussion of the matter.

When I visited the country, I met with officials of all of the country's trade union groups, including the ones under government control. It became clear to me that a number of non-government unions had to contend with constant harassment from the government. The Sandinistas tried to force the independent unions out of business by arresting, detaining and otherwise harassing their leaders. One conversation with the head of a major non-government union in Managua had shed particular light on the problem with some church activists.

I told this labor leader, whose union is affiliated with the International Confederation of Free Trade Unions, that church people made regular trips to Nicaragua. "Do they ever come to see you?" I asked. He said, "Never. You're the first one." It is not surprising, then, that a number of religious activists, hearing only one side of the story, knew or cared little about the situation of trade unions in Nicaragua.

Church activists tended more to excuse than categorically deny the suppression of free trade unions in Nicaragua. Some blamed it on the United States – the

U.S.-financed war against Nicaragua (even though, in fact, the Sandinistas cracked down on labor before the arrival of Ronald Reagan in Washington). Others blamed it on the non-Sandinista unions themselves – allegedly "American-dominated" or "counter-revolutionary" (labels that the Sandinistas applied to everyone who disagreed with them). But in truth, too many of labor's critics simply placed little importance on freedom of trade union association. This accounted for at least part of the conflict between labor and religious activists, on Nicaragua and other international issues.

The question of labor's foreign policy is a ghost that haunted religion-labor coalitions until the last gasps of the cold war, and has so even since. I still hear complaints that George Meany, the late AFL-CIO president, and the people around him were so obsessed with anti-communism that it was the only issue on their minds. According to this view, Meany's obsession revealed itself in the AFL-CIO's adamant refusal to deal with government-run labor unions in communist countries. The AFL-CIO steered clear of the unions not because they were communist but because they were controlled by governments. Whatever one might think of this policy, the fact is that the federation applied it with equal force to government unions in anti-communist countries. Indeed, up until the death of General Francisco Franco, the AFL-CIO had a special antipathy toward the Franco unions in Spain.

During my years at the Catholic Conference, the labor attaché to Spain's embassy in Washington would occasionally drop by my office and tell of his frustrated attempts to get a foot in the door at the AFL-CIO. This Spanish official could not even get past the front desk there. I heard labor representatives of other countries express similar disappointment. One of them was the labor attaché to the Polish embassy (prior to the fall of the communist government there), a friend of mine with whom I had lunch every couple of months. When he first arrived in Washington, he asked me if I could assist him in making contacts at the AFL-CIO. I did not want to give him any false illusions. "Look, you haven't got a chance," I said. "You are never going to get inside the AFL-CIO building. If they see you coming, they'll tell the switchboard operator, 'Sorry, we're not in. We don't talk to people from government unions.'"

So even when exerting poor judgment in some areas of international policy, the labor movement has held to the principle of free trade unionism. What does this say about the debate over labor's international posi-

tion? It suggests, at the very least, that the arguments are not all on one side, the issue not as simple as so-called progressives have framed it. Labor's foreign policy was not simply an anti-communist policy.

Yet even when labor's liberal critics in the churches were right, they were wrong about one thing: the nature of cooperation between different groups and institutions. They failed to draw a crucial line between mistakes by an institution and the essential purpose of that institution. Church critics could have dealt with mistakes by honestly and openly debating the issues while realizing that disagreements will happen. Mistakes and differences of opinion need not lead to disaffection, and yet this is precisely what happened in many areas of the relationship between religion and labor.

In the mid-1980s, officials of the AFL-CIO and national religious organizations began working toward a revival of religion-labor cooperation. This ambitious project had as its goal the formation of a national religion-labor organization, with representation by the major Protestant, Catholic and Jewish agencies. The effort, however, ran aground when some of the religious members of the dialogue started in with demands having to do with the AFL-CIO's foreign policies.

These church representatives (who, in this case, happened to be the liberal Protestant ones) wanted a quid pro quo. They wanted the AFL-CIO to formally condemn the Institute on Religion and Democracy (IRD), a small, neo-conservative group that was slamming liberal Protestant denominations because of their left-leaning stands on international affairs. The church participants also pressed the federation to discipline an AFL-CIO staff member who, as a Methodist layman, helped found the IRD. These liberal Protestant representatives were unyielding in their demands. And in the background lurked the whole issue of labor's foreign policy and Central America in particular.

While I had no particular affection for the IRD, I also had no desire to enter into a coalition on the basis of quid pro quo demands. It seemed to me that this way was doomed to failure, one reason being that two can play at that game. Suppose that the AFL-CIO had entered the dialogue saying, "Look, we can't deal with you. Look at the wage rates in your church office. Do you have a union there?" I would guess that the clerical staff in agencies represented by these church officials were not organized. In the game of quid pro quos, I could picture a hard-headed unionist telling his religious counterparts, "Well then, get out. When your people are organized, we can talk." That would be ridiculous, of course, but perhaps no more so than the demands issued by some on the religious side of the table.

Soon enough, I lost all interest in this religion-labor initiative. Shortly after another one of those insufferable quid pro quo sessions, I traveled to Miami to address the annual convention of the AFL-CIO's Industrial Union Department. Several of these church people sat at the table next to mine, so I went over to say hello. At that point I was told, rather frostily, that they weren't planning to stay for the dinner. "Why is that?" I asked. "Because Lane Kirkland is going to give the main address," was the reason – and they did leave before Kirkland spoke. As they left I thought to myself: What is wrong with this picture? These people want a coalition with a particular organization, and here they are walking out of a talk given by the elected leader of that organization. About then I decided that my life was too short to play along with this sort of dialogue between religion and labor.

Toward a New Solidarity

In 1965 a fledgling columnist for the National Catholic Reporter came up with what he considered a sure-fire way of telling "the older generation of Catholic liberals from the younger." Older liberals, said Garry Wills, who has since deservedly gained a national reputation as a distinguished author and scholar, "still think of labor unions as a sacred cause. Placidly mellowing monsignori, if they hear criticisms of the unions, still get red hot under their white Roman collars, and begin to froth the rhetoric of the 30s. The cause of labor was, for many of them, the Great Fight; and, like all victorious veterans, they get a bit misty-eyed and prosey on the subject."

That was a simple litmus test that one would have thought even a monsignor could apply without advance training. Try as I would, however, I couldn't get the hang of it. "Labor priests" aside, very few monsignori I knew personally had anything to say in public about unions; fewer still seemed to fit Wills' caricature. (Incredibly, one still hears this complaint – that priests have gone overboard with their support of organized labor – despite the fact that the number of labor priests has declined almost to a vanishing point.)

But time marches on and, behold, the labor problem which Wills apparently thought was old hat in 1965 is still with us today. In the mid-1960s, nearly a third of American workers were organized into unions. By 1992 that figure had shrunk to approximately seventeen percent – the lowest in any of the industrialized countries. (Union representation in the private sector stands at around twelve percent.)

As we near the final laps of a century that made great strides in the labor field, the labor movement is clearly on the defensive, and the right to organize is, once again, a live issue. The right itself is seldom explicitly or directly challenged as a matter of principle or theory. But in everyday practice, the right to organize faces a huge assault. Hundreds of thousands of workers struggle against great odds to achieve or hold on to the basic protection and benefits of collective bargaining shared by their fellow workers in other industries and other countries.

In their efforts to form new unions or hold on to ones that exist, workers have met with widespread and increasing employer opposition – which frequently violates the spirit and all too often the letter of the law. This led the American bishops in their 1986 pastoral letter on Catholic social teaching and the American economy to state that they "firmly oppose organized efforts, such as those regrettably now seen in our country, to break existing unions and prevent workers from organizing."

As the fortunes of organized labor have waned, so have those of America's working people. At the height of the so-called boom of the 1980s, economists Barry Bluestone and Bennett Harrison dealt with this problem very graphically in an article entitled "A Low-Wage Explosion: The Grim Truth About the Job 'Miracle.'" Their findings clearly demonstrated that those affluent Americans who look upon the labor problem in the United States as a matter of ancient history were, and still are, living in a dream world. Bluestone and Harrison reported, for instance, that since the early 1970s average wage and salary incomes adjusted for inflation had declined for nearly all groups within the population and in most industries. "Even more disturbing," they point out, "is the proliferation of low-wage employment. Between 1979 and 1985 – the most recent years for which Government data are available – 44 percent of the net new jobs created paid poverty-level wages."

There is no easy solution – surely no single solution – to this disturbing problem, but Bluestone and Harrison hit the mark when they concluded that "in the absence of a new wave of labor organizing in services and of government policies to expand high-value-added production, wage standards for a substantial fraction of American working people will likely continue to erode." (From the standpoint of Catholic social teaching, unions would remain essential – Pope John Paul II calls them "indispensable" – even if the vast majority of workers had adequate wages. For one thing, unions have an irreplaceable part in any credible system of labor-management cooperation, an idea that has gained currency during the age of lagging American competitiveness. Later on I will say more about this role – the representative and coordinating function of organized labor.)

Stirred by such harsh reality, many social-minded people in the religious community have rediscovered the labor problem. Religious activists may have had problems with unions, but few of them ever entertained the notion that we would be better off without a strong labor movement. This feeling of labor decline has led to renewed interest in union struggles on the part of some in the Catholic social action movement and its various counterparts in the ecumenical and interreligious communities. In my own reading of the situation, the danger is not that the labor movement may go out of business (although this is the prognosis of some labor-management experts), but that it would be rendered so weak as to be ineffectual.

Labor, too, is confronting this reality. For a long time labor leaders seemed uninterested in coalitions with religious and civic groups that lent the movement so much of its moral credibility in the early years. All this has changed. More and more the labor movement is calling on old friends, initiating coalitions and soliciting direct church involvement in labor-related causes. The new cooperation found dramatic expression in the 1989-1990 strike by mineworkers against the Pittston coal company in Virginia. The strike generated extraordinary solidarity, among unions as well as between labor and the churches. Leaders of the United Mine Workers gave the churches a large part of the credit for what could have been a union debacle but turned into one of labor's most dramatic victories in recent times.

For their part, religious organizations have looked more and more to the labor movement for help in pushing their social agenda. This amounts to an acknowledgment on the part of many church activists that they have seriously overestimated what they could accomplish on their own in the way of social reform. In the wake of the 1960s, a kind of euphoria took hold of liberal Christian activists. They managed to convince themselves that with enough position statements

and "justice-and-peace" projects, they could change the world. By now, most of them know this is nonsense.

On the issue of health care, for instance, church activists would delude themselves by thinking they could lead the way in a movement for national health insurance. Such a step forward for America's working people will never happen without the active participation of working people themselves and their representatives in the labor movement. In other words, religious groups and organized labor need each another.

Furthermore, some of the pitfalls along the way to religion-labor cooperation have been covered up, happily, by the passing of cold war antagonism. This is not to say that quarrels over international affairs will go the way of the Stalinists and cold warriors. As two separate institutions with diverging interests and ultimate purposes, religion and labor will not always see eye to eye. Yet churches and unions find themselves drawing closer together around global concerns. Labor leaders debate the issues more seriously than they had in the past; church people recognize that some of their opinions may have been a little simplistic. In the future, differences over foreign policy are unlikely to be so great as to hinder serious efforts toward cooperation.

Indeed, mainstream religion and labor may be more likely in coming years to close rather than break ranks on international affairs. In the year following the demise of communism in eastern Europe, the nation's major unions and mainline religious denominations joined in opposition to high levels of American aid to El Salvador's military. Their common efforts contributed to a collapse of the Reagan doctrine as it applied to that country. It was but one indication of the new paths to cooperation opened up by shifting geo-political ground.

All this, however, does not add up to a new relationship between religion and labor. A revival of church-labor cooperation will require effort and determination on the part of many people. For those interested in forging this solidarity, I offer a handful of tentative but pointed suggestions on how and how not to go about it.

• Both labor and the churches and synagogues have much to learn about each other's organizational structure, mode of operation, chain of command, and so forth. My own experience leads me to suggest, and indeed to insist, that we both have a lot of homework to do in this regard. Ignorance of this kind can lead to false expectations and even disillusionment. I would suggest, therefore, that both sides start off by getting to know one another in our local and regional communities and by listening to one another before we plunge precipitously into programmatic cooperation. Find out what each side can and cannot do, and at what level. I know from experience that many labor leaders haven't the faintest idea of the structure of the Catholic Church. Now and then I hear from a labor leader whose local has been tussling with a Catholic institution – very often, a hospital – over union organizing in the institution. One would think, from their attitude, that I was the pope. "Call the bishop; get him to take care of this," I've been told by more than a few labor leaders in these situations. More often than not, though, the bishop has no direct influence over the Catholic hospital. It is often the sisters who are in charge, and chances are that a bishop poking his nose into their business would be put in his place right away. "Go take a walk, Bishop. This is our hospital," sisters have been known to say.

In some cases, a little knowledge about church structure can be dangerous. Most labor leaders do have a very rough idea of the levels of leadership in the Catholic Church, so they definitely know what they want when they come looking for a statement of support for a labor cause. They always want a cardinal, because a cardinal is presumably better than an archbishop, and an archbishop is better than a bishop, all of whom, of course, are better than simple priests. While this temptation to always "go to the top" may be understandable, it really doesn't go very far in the way of effective action. Usually it delivers only a superficial kind of support.

Yet this was precisely the kind that one labor leader tried to get when he met with a group of bishops in a Washington hotel at the time of the J. P. Stevens boycott. He wanted to leave the meeting with an official statement by members of the Catholic hierarchy on the Stevens dispute – but I threw a monkey wrench into the plan. As an individual, I had already endorsed the nationwide boycott of Stevens products. But I said that as long as I chaired the meeting, the bishops would not put out a statement on a matter about which they knew nothing.

What does the bishop of Rockford, Illinois, for example, know about the textile industry in the southeast? We decided that the bishops of the southeast should pick up the ball on this one, and they did. The southeastern bishops undertook a serious study of the issue, meeting with people on all sides. They wound up putting out a strong state-ment that proved quite effective, far more so than if the labor leader had gotten his way at the meeting in Washington. Their appeal rang out through the region, counteracting the anti-union rhetoric of industry leaders and bolstering the case of the workers.

- Labor and religion, no matter how united, are two very different institutions. While labor and the religious community have much in common, they may at times, inevitably, have conflicting agendas. Neither side should expect the other to agree on everything. By definition a coalition means that we agree to work on those things that we can work on, and quietly and in good humor go our own way on other issues.

- Don't try to convert the other party to your own agenda. This has been an unfortunate part of the relationship between religion and labor, much of it, in recent years, touching on matters of international policy. As earlier noted, organized labor has a somewhat different approach to some of these questions than do a number of church groups. This is a fact of life, and the changing geo-political climate, while lessening the problem, will not make it go away. I think we need to learn to live with these disagreements and talk about them amicably. To do otherwise would be to hold church-labor cooperation – and ultimately, the needs of working people – hostage to our own agenda.

Those in the churches, especially, need to keep this in mind. The labor movement has a long and unhappy history of outside groups trying to reform it or, worse, use it for their own ideological purposes. (I know of more than a few instances involving church people, stretching back to day one.) In light of this, church people should respect the internal procedures of the labor movement. We should keep in mind that unions are democratic organizations, however imperfect their structures may be. Much as I may disagree with the unions on certain aspects of international relations, I would have to admit that they are far more democratic than we in the churches. Their policy decisions are hammered out within the movement, and reform, if needed, must come from within the movement, democratically. It cannot come from church activists who claim to have the answers that the rank-and-file members are not smart enough to know.

Church people have found this lesson particularly hard to learn. Over the years a few bishops have asked how I could so strongly support the labor movement when it has refused to support Catholics on the issue of federal aid to parents with children in parochial schools. "What are you going to do about it?" one bishop called to ask. I said, "I'm not going to do anything about it. If somebody wants my opinion on the issue, I'll give it. But if you want the labor movement to change its position on federal aid to education, the way you start is to get people in the labor movement to bring it up on the floor. But don't call on a national representative like myself to go to a labor convention and try to change policies. That's not the way it works."

- Avoid like the plague anything that smacks of a quid pro quo approach. This is what derailed the initiative in the mid-1980s when some church representatives set forth demands relating to labor's foreign policy. On this and other matters, some church groups have refused to cooperate with the labor movement "unless" – whatever "unless" may be. That's the quid pro quo approach, and it's fatal. It will inevitably doom any attempt at church-labor cooperation in the future.

- Both as a practitioner and to a very limited extent as a teacher, I have noticed an appalling lack of knowledge in church circles (and U.S. society in general) about the history of the American labor movement. My own students, most of them seminarians, appear to suffer from a general amnesia with respect to the labor movement and its origins in the United States.

  I would go so far as to say there ought to be a law against any church person getting involved in religion-labor cooperation unless he or she can certify as having read at least a few good books on labor history. A knowledge of labor history will help us to understand why and how the American labor movement has developed differently from the way others have – not necessarily better but, by the same token, not necessarily worse. In this regard, my experience in this and other countries has made me allergic to the more radical rhetoric of some labor movements, the ones admired by certain church people as more militant and more radical than the allegedly conservative American movement.

  To these church people, I would recommend a trip to Latin America and a front-row seat at any one of the ideological sermons by certain so-called militant labor leaders. They would find that much of it is froth. In the mid-1980s I had an experi-

ence of this kind with a small American delegation that spent a few weeks in Brazil, visiting at one point with a young bishop in the part of Sao Paulo where the auto industry is based. He gave a great spiel about the conservativism of the American labor movement and seemed to think that the United Auto Workers, God help us, was somehow an agent of Wall Street.

I consider this bishop a great and wonderful man, a truly militant defender of the labor movement. But I had to say, "Bishop, I could cite some failures on the part of the Auto Workers, but I can say without fear of contradiction that you do not have a labor movement anywhere in all of Latin America that can even remotely compare to the Auto Workers in effectiveness in promoting the interest of workers." I could have said the same about the Steelworkers and some other international unions in the United States.

- Beware of stereotypes. Church and labor people come in all shapes and sizes, and so do their organizations.

  That is the moral of a story told by Doug Fraser, former president of the United Auto Workers. In 1988 he gave a series of lectures at Columbia University's business school. After Fraser finished one of these lectures, a young man stood up and said, "Mr. Fraser, I owe you an apology." Fraser said, "Well, I don't know why. I've never laid eyes on you." The student said, "My stereotype of a labor leader of your rank is a man who is grossly overweight, who is wearing a very expensive but vulgarly flashy suit, who has big vulgar diamonds on his pinkies, who is smoking a very expensive and big cigar, and who is very vulgar and profane." Fraser said, "Young man, you have just given a perfect description of my good friend Lee Iacocca."

  I would suggest to our friends in the labor movement that they probably have some of their own stereotypes – about "conservative" prelates, for one. So I think we ought to take people as we find them. There is no monolithic group on either side.

- Go slow in dreaming about a national religion-labor organization. This was the goal of those conversations in the 1980s that foundered on the quid pro quo demands. Although I went along with these discussions, up to a point, my feeling was, and still is, that cooperation between religion and labor should start at the bottom, at the local and regional levels. Plow the fields and do the preparatory spadework that needs to be done. Then, eventually, if the need arises, a national organization will grow naturally and organically.

- Build relationships, and the issues will follow. The first order of business is to get to know and trust one another, and once this is done, someone from a church group may feel comfortable in asking, "Hey, can you tell us about the situation of race relations in your building trade unions?" Or a labor leader might say, "Look, you've got a labor problem in a number of your Catholic hospitals. Is there anything we can do together on this?" Once they have sufficient competence and structures of cooperation, religion-labor groups might also want to address the organization of women workers. This is a new frontier.

  It seems that the time is long overdue for church-related groups interested in the labor field to begin concentrating heavily on women in the workplace. Women make up nearly half of all workers, yet only a minuscule percentage of them are organized into unions. In all honesty, I must say – speaking only of my own tradition – that relatively few Catholic women take part in the Coalition of Labor Union Women and in other associations dedicated to the organization of women workers and protection of their economic rights. Similarly, any working coalition of religion and labor will have to pay significant attention to the problems of immigrant workers, the lowest paid of our increasingly low-paid workforce. Without female and immigrant workers, the labor movement has no future in this country.

* * *

Some might ask: Is it all worth it? One school of thought says that in standing up for labor's right to organize, those of us in the church-labor movement are beating a dead horse, or that, alternatively, the labor movement is passé. No one doubts that labor has fallen on hard times. But as for myself, I have stopped counting the number of times the labor movement has been buried in my lifetime. I am glad I didn't waste time going to its funerals.

The labor problem is not a matter of ancient history. It is an ongoing problem that calls for active involvement on the part of those who believe in social justice. While organized labor is undoubtedly far from perfect – I even have intimations at times that my own church is far from perfect – no other movement in sight would enable American workers to protect their legitimate economic interests. No other movement would enable American workers to play an effective and responsible role in helping to promote the general economic welfare both at home and abroad.

At the height of the Great Depression, in one of his many books on industrial ethics, Msgr. John A. Ryan wrote two sentences that sum up his views on labor. This is my credo, as well as his:

> "Effective labor unions are still by far the most powerful force in society for the protection of the laborer's rights and the improvement of his or her condition. No amount of employer benevolence, no diffusion of a sympathetic attitude on the part of the public, no increase of beneficial legislation, can adequately supply for the lack of organization among the workers themselves."

I have spent my life saying this, in one way or another. I believe it remains true, and I hope the religion-labor dialogue will help us see the relevance of Ryan's words to the problems of today.

At Work in the Vineyard: The Jesuit Labor Apostolate

Edward F. Boyle, SJ (2000)

To priests in a special way we recommend anew the oft-repeated counsel of Our Predecessor Leo XIII to go to the working man. We make this advice our own and thus complete it, 'Go to the working man, especially where he is poor; and in general go to the poor' ... So we must act in today's crisis ... Let our parish priests, therefore, while providing of course for the normal needs of the faithful, dedicate the better part of their endeavors and their zeal to winning back the laboring masses to Christ and to his church.

This passage from the 1937 encyclical "Atheistic Communism" (*Divini Redemptoris*) by Pius XI is perhaps the most direct appeal of any social encyclical on what would become the apostolate of the "Catholic labor schools." The urgency cited in the papal writing carries a human face in the reflection of Father Philip Carey SJ of the Xavier Institute:

It was the winter of 1936. The Great Depression was ravaging the country. Idle freight cars were parked along the rails for 75 miles to Poughkeepsie and the Pennsylvania Road to Baltimore was lined with bleak factory skeletons. The effects upon the working people of the nation were devastating. It wasn't only that they were cold and hungry and idle. People staggered about in a hopeless daze. Father Francis P. LeBuffe gathered a group of teachers and lawyers. 'Can we do anything to give some hope, some meaning to living?'

The fruit of this meeting was a simple eight line letter from the dean of the high school to the Cardinal Archbishop requesting to start a worker education program, and a similarly brief, uncluttered, six line approval both indicative of the felt need for this ministry.

This article describes the Jesuit involvement in the tradition of Catholic labor schools. The Jesuit labor schools (which almost universally preferred the title "Institute of Industrial Relations") constituted the first major Assistancy-wide social justice initiative in this nation. Three points can be made regarding the initiative. First, this was truly a work of the church, insofar as it was a response to papal pleadings extending back to *Rerum Novarum* in 1891 and was in collaboration with diocesan and other religious institutions. Second, it represented a bold leap into the unknown:

an insertion into the secular world in a new way in competition with other players, principally leftists of socialist-communist bent, but with a strong spiritual base. Finally, it testified to the social and economic malaise created by the Depression, which served as the catalyst for the first federal labor relations statute, the National Labor Relations Act (the so-called Wagner Act), while also facilitating the church's intervention into secular life.

Ecclesial Background

The call for reform of the economic values and practices of the early industrialized world started with Leo XIII's *Rerum Novarum*. In that document the Pope proposed a middle path between the class-struggle doctrine and statism of socialist-communism on the left, and the laissez-faire, free market liberalism on the right. This middle path incorporated a prominent role for voluntary associations, such as worker organizations, as well as limited state oversight. These ideas would be ratified and expanded in *Quadragesimo Anno* (1931), including the introduction of a new economic model of shared business and labor governance known as "industrial councils."

In 1919, the American church hierarchy through the National Catholic Welfare Conference (NCWC) had already promulgated in 1919 a remarkable social program entitled "The Bishops' Program of Social Reconstruction." Combining the most progressive features of the papal documents and the writings of European social ethicists and progressive Bishops, this Program called for such elements as:

- the curbing of excessive profit-taking through regulation of the rates of return to ownership of public utilities;

- progressive taxation;

- participation of labor in management decisions, and a wider distribution of ownership through cooperative enterprises, and worker ownership in the stock of corporations;

- legal enforcement of the right of labor to organize.

Although this social vision was opposed by many members of the American hierarchy as well as by the broader church community, it nevertheless provided some legitimacy for future social justice initiatives including the labor schools. At that time the Bishops established the Social Action Department (SAD) of the NCWC to serve as its educational and advocacy arm on social matters, now the Department of Social Development and World Peace. In the early 1920s, this office began to sponsor the Catholic Conference on Industrial Problems in summer meetings across the country. Soon thereafter, the office started a bimonthly newsletter, Social Action Notes For Priests. All these national efforts, combined with the Roman papal documents, created the climate that would undergird the labor school apostolate. This ecclesial context, in turn, determined the central place that social ethics and such concepts as industry council plans, rights and duties of private property, and the living wage would have in the core labor school curriculum.

The Catholic Labor School Tradition

At the peak, there were 100-150 labor schools in the nation with several of them sponsoring multiple satellite schools: the Detroit chapter of the Association of Catholic Trade Unionists (ACTU) with more than 30, the Hartford Diocesan Center coordinating 12. Two principal institutions, the ACTU and the U.S. Jesuits, as well as grassroots programs of individual parishes and diocesan-based schools, sponsored the activity. ACTU was an independent organization of Catholic trade unionists with lay officers, but under the sponsorship of local bishops. At its height, there were ACTU chapters in Chicago, Detroit, Denver, New Orleans, New York, Pittsburgh and San Francisco, with many sponsoring schools at several different sites. There were at least 20 Jesuit Institutes scattered across the nation.

The flyers from these labor schools – Jesuit, ACTU, or diocesan – reveal remarkably similar formats: one or two nights per week for eight to ten weeks; classes running one hour, with two to three class periods per night; a set of core courses consisting of ethics, public speaking, parliamentary procedure and labor problems. The faculty consisted of largely lay practitioners: union leaders, labor attorneys, school teachers, all of whom volunteered their services. Clergy or religious normally handled the ethics course. Classes were usually held in church basements or parish halls, save those programs allied with colleges or universities such as the Jesuit efforts. The cost was minimal ($1- $5) or, at times, free. Sometimes enrollment was restricted to Catholics or unionists, but in the case of the Jesuit programs, open to all.

Into New Terrain

Until this initiative, the energies of the church were almost totally devoted to sacramental worship, corporal works of mercy and parochial school education. With this project the church entered into adult education in the secular world of economic activity. The basic school format was the product of a trial and error entry into a new world with each school adding its own unique elements to the basic pattern. For many, this would include at least a simple newsletter distributed each class night.

The Jesuit contribution to this labor school movement distinguished itself by its core spirituality, the diversity and quantity of supporting educational programs, and the specialized personal ministries of the Institute directors. Common to all was the theme of bipartisanship rather than a union-only focus to their efforts, as evidenced by the preference for the neutral title of "Institute of Industrial Relations" rather than "Labor School." The joint labor-management focus represented both respect for the rejection of class-war ideology of the social encyclicals, as well as sensitivity to the social ties of the alumni of its high schools and colleges and universities.

Bipartisanship however, was addressed in different ways. At some schools, there were separate programs for union and management representatives, often on different evenings. This pattern prevailed at Holy Cross College in Worcester, Massachusetts; Loyola University in Los Angeles; and St. Peter's College, Jersey City, New Jersey. Other Jesuit institutes offered a joint labor-management curriculum such as Loyola University, New Orleans, and St. Joseph's College, Philadelphia. Still others, such as Crown Heights School in Brooklyn and Xavier Institute in New York City, as well as St. Peter's College, sponsored numerous forums addressing broader issues such as the criminal justice system, public education, communism, etc., appealing to the entire community. They also offered workshops or extended courses tailored to special occupational groups such as lawyers, public school teachers and senior labor relations management staff.

The outside work of the Jesuit directors ranged widely, from mediating/arbitrating labor management disputes, to lecturing to church, business or civic organizations, to service on government boards overseeing employee relations. In addition they labored intensively in spiritual ministry. Such activities were made possible by the assignment of a full-time priest, the more extended academic training of our men, and their linkage to institutions of higher education with substantial academic and physical resources.

Not surprisingly these Jesuit Institutes developed distinctive "personalities" through the influence of their charismatic individual Jesuits. Under the aegis of Fr. Lou Twomey, SJ, the Loyola University Institute in New Orleans moved into the racial issue in the late 1940s well in advance of the decisive court cases and early protest marches of the mid-1950s. He also authored the newsletter "Christ's Blueprint of the South" which for almost two decades served as basic social justice reading for all the seminarians of the assistancy. The St. Joseph's Institute in Philadelphia, led by Dennis Comey, SJ, staked out an image of a sophisticated, academically demanding, labor-management program, while Comey himself became known as the Waterfront Peacemaker through his extensive arbitration work. Fr. Willie Smith, SJ, after starting the Crown Heights School in Brooklyn in the late 1930s, moved to St. Peter's College in Jersey City where he introduced the most diverse range of educational programs of any Jesuit Institute. Along with Fr. Richard McKeon of LeMoyne, Smith was about the only Institute Director who published articles for the national media on this labor school tradition.

The Xavier Institute in New York City developed a high profile for the work on the waterfront of the Assistant Director John "Pete" Corridan. His activism among dockworkers became the subject of the book and movie "On The Waterfront." Also noteworthy was the more controversial involvement of the Director Phil Carey in seeking to eliminate the Communist influence in the New York City Transit Workers Union. Finally, the Massachusetts labor scene was greatly influenced by the presence of Fr. Mortimer Gavin, SJ. After completing doctoral studies in economics, working with the Institute of Social Order, and a career as a labor arbitrator and university professor, Gavin joined the Boston Archdiocesan Labor School (the Labor Guild). He helped fashion a blend of advocacy and bipartisan programs that injected new life into the Guild, a pattern which is still proving effective today in one of the few remaining Jesuit guided programs.

Anti-Communism

It is worth assessing the relative priority given to the three major motivating forces of the movement:

- improving the material and social well-being of the largely impoverished American working class;

- overcoming the growing Communist presence and influence in the United States;

- deepening the faith-life of the American Catholic worker in an increasingly secular culture.

Simultaneous with the 1937 encyclical "Atheistic Communism," the SAD began to use its summer regional educational conferences to survey the activities and institutional structures of local communists in major urban areas. From these surveys, the office fashioned a "Program of Action" that would both goad and guide church efforts in the 1940s and '50s. Although not rejecting direct attacks on Communists, it held that only major reform of key American economic policies and practices would keep the workers from Communist activities and goals. It is Steven Rosswurm's contention that the anti-communist concern gradually received increasing attention, until by 1945 it had become almost all-encompassing, particularly in its relationship with the CIO branch of the American labor movement. The anti-communist campaign actively involved many Bishops, pastors, Chancery officers, and the whole range of labor schools Jesuit, ACTU, and others. Their efforts would be manifest in the purging of regional and national labor unions, such as that in the United Electrical Union, during World War II and the immediate post-war years.

A glance at the curriculum of the typical labor school provides telling evidence of the urgency of this concern, for alongside the social ethics and industrial problems courses, there would always be found courses on parliamentary procedure and public speaking. Only Catholic unionists, so trained, were judged able to effectively counter the maneuverings of a minority Communist caucus at local union meetings. Some of the labor priests who established strong anti-communist credentials were the Jesuit Fr. Philip Carey, Monsignor Charles Owen Rice of Pittsburgh and Sulpician John Cronin.

Spirituality

Perusal of the correspondence and the appointment schedules of several Jesuit labor priests reveals the high priority given to the spiritual or religious dimension of this labor school movement. Thanks to an article, "The Church Is Not for the Cells and the Caves: The Working Class Spirituality of the Jesuit Labor Priests," by Joseph McShane in the *U.S. Catholic Historian* (1990, vol. 9, 289-304), we have some valuable details on this key matter. He breaks down their work in the spiritual vineyard into three categories: workers' retreats, an array of devotional writings and the labor school programs. McShane writes that:

> Although the vast majority of the students who attended the labor schools did so because the technical courses offered there enabled them to rise to positions of leadership in their respective unions, the Jesuits did not believe that the schools existed solely or even primarily to assist the upward mobility of unionists. Quite contrary, they felt that the schools had a bigger and more specifically religious mission. Conscious of the fact that the modern world tended to divorce religion from economic life (and thus turned a deaf ear to clerics who spoke on industrial issues), they realized that the church needed lay agents to bring about 'the ultimate Christian reconstruction of (industrial) society.'

Via their retreat activities and their devotional writings the labor priests sought to provide both a theological framework and role models that might inspire and guide the everyday life of workers, including their involvement in union-management relations. Through the development of certain doctrinal themes, they sought to encourage an active involvement in efforts to improve conditions in both the workplace and the unions.

In order to put flesh and blood on these ideals, much attention was given to the study of the life of Christ, the Holy Family and individual saints. It was Jesus, the Carpenter of Nazareth, who was explored: His birth into a poor, unsophisticated, working family; his own life as a carpenter; and his decision to choose ordinary workers, with only rudimentary formal education, as his disciples. In that same perspective, attention was directed to the Holy Family, with its unpredictable vicissitudes mirroring the vagaries in the lives of so many American workers in the Depression, war and post-war years. Occasionally attention was given to individual saints with whom the priest director had some affinity

The best vehicles to disseminate the spirituality were the annual weekend retreats and intermittent days of recollection sponsored by these Jesuit institutes. Many institutes appear to have been quite faithful to this annual retreat program, and even more sponsored occasional days of recollection either to supplement or to substitute for the weekend retreat experience. In addition the practice of an annual Communion breakfast, often around Labor Day, took hold in many, if not most, institutes.

The devotional writings of some Jesuits were a second approach for this spiritual ministry. Fathers Smith, McKeon, and John Delaney were most zealous in applying this tool. As the first director of the Institute on Social Order, Delaney was closely allied with the labor ministry and produced several spiritual brochures for workers including, "What, Me a Saint?" The devotional writing of most of the Jesuit labor priests was intended to incorporate a spiritual tone into the newsletter published each week of school. This consisted of quotations from papal writings and ascetical works, events in the lives of saints and pious stories around workplace life.

The school program itself provided an interesting and quite varied third vehicle. There was great latitude for the instructor in the standard social ethics course to introduce various religious themes. There was also the widespread practice of opening and closing the class night with a prayer such as the following:

Prayer of the Worker

Lord Jesus, Carpenter of Nazareth, you were a worker as I am. Give to me and all workers of the world the privilege to work as you did, so that everything we do may be to the benefit of our fellow men and the greater glory of God the Father. Thy Kingdom come into the factories and into the shops, into our homes and into our streets. Give us this day our daily bread. May we receive it without envy or injustice. To us who labor and are heavily burdened, send speedily the refreshment of thy love. May we never sin against thee. Show us Thy way to work, and when it is done, may we with all our fellow workers rest in peace. Amen.

A fourth dimension to this spiritual ministry was something that might be termed "presence." The labor priests would often deliver invocations at various labor management events, preside at a special Eucharist for delegates to labor conventions, or deliver talks on church social teaching at Communion breakfasts or professional gatherings. At other times this ministry was manifest in the priest's availability for informal talk with drop-in visitors or special counseling sessions for troubled workers. Whatever forum, the message was that God cares about the events and conditions of the working life of his sons and daughters. In a time when so many of those on the union side were frequently called "Communists," or on the management side singled out as "traitors" to the rights of business, such affirmation by the church was very important.

Phasing Out

In the late 1940s and '50s, several changes in the conditions that had initially generated the demand for the labor school ministry prompted the closing of many programs. Two surveys conducted by the National Catholic Social Action Conference in 1956 and 1962, show how dramatically the decline was in this apostolate. In 1956, only 49 of the original 100 plus schools were still operating; in 1962 there were only 15, of which 10 were Jesuit.

First, in the 20 or so years after the Depression and the enactment of the National Labor Relations Act, there was substantial growth in the size and sophistication of the American labor movement, enabling it to provide its own training. Second, the worries about Communist infiltration in America had substantially subsided, in part because of the purging efforts in the 1940s and early '50s of various sectors of the community including unions. Further, the economy had exhibited relative vitality since the outbreak of World War II, somewhat stabilizing the psyche of the American worker and undercutting, in turn, interest in unionism with its perceived anti-business animus. The economic prosperity, coupled with the GI Bill, brought about the gradual emergence of an upwardly mobile Catholic managerial class. This shift tended to reduce the pro-worker, pro-union rhetoric from church pulpits and journals. Finally, the federal and state government hearings on corruption in certain unions made many justice activists averse to identifying with unions, while at the same time there was the attraction of the emerging new justice causes of racial discrimination and urban or rural poverty.

Amidst such changes, roughly half of the Jesuit programs continued into the 1960s, '70s and '80s. Their bipartisan spirit enabled them to better endure the deterioration of the union image, and the greater variety and more sophisticated nature of their educational programs were a better fit with an upwardly mobile Catholic populace and the demands of an increasingly complex labor-management interface. The linkage of these programs with prestigious colleges and universities also provided a kind of status to the labor schools. Thus, some Jesuit institutes survived in modest form into the 1980s, several being incorporated into an Associate's Degree Program in Human Resources or Industrial Relations. At least one institute (St. Joseph's College) has recently revived its non-degree adult training program.

Impact

It is difficult to gauge the impact of a project that worked for the reform of an economic system in order that workers and management alike might share the joys and burdens, the gains and losses, in some equitable and compassionate way. How does one measure the extent and depth of the spiritual renewal of the workers and the Catholic community sought by these labor priests? Clearly some of these questions defy accurate documentation.

Yet it is possible to make several observations. In less than 20 years, the possibility of the takeover of the American labor movement, and other areas of economic life, by communism was defeated. Additionally, studies such as that by Wesley Allensmith referenced in Betten's book *Catholic Activism and the Catholic Worker* show the participation of Catholics in both union membership and leadership posts since the 1930s has been higher than its share in the total populace would suggest. Along those same lines, the ties between the Catholic hierarchy, the American labor movement, and low-wage workers is singular among American faith communities, as evidenced by the orientation of the Economic Pastoral Letter of 1986 and the practice of semi-annual meetings of a subcommittee of the U.S. Catholic Conference with the national AFL-CIO leadership.

More concretely, from 1935 to 1955 the schools' educational programs and devotional activities were very popular. Records indicate that the complex of ACTU schools in Detroit drew more than 1,000 students a week, while other efforts such as Xavier Institute in New York City, St. Joseph's College, and the Labor Guild in Boston drew 400-500 people per week. Many annual Communion Breakfasts drew 500-1000 attendees, and weekend retreats and days of recollection regularly drew more than 100 per session. Finally, numerous labor priests, including many Jesuits, enjoyed wide respect and held some authoritative posts, such as Fathers Carey, Corridan, Comey, and Twomey, as well as Father Leo Brown, SJ, of the Institute of Social Order, who served for many years on the five-member Dispute Board for the Atomic Energy Commission.

Lessons Learned

- The institutional ties between the church and the union movement established at the pinnacle of the labor schools still exist in some attenuated fashion in the regions where the schools operated, as well as in the national church. As the experience at St. Joseph's College indicates, this relationship can resurrect itself, forming the springboard for new initiatives.

- The growing economic diversity of the Catholic community makes more difficult, yet more important, the task of effectively educating the total church membership about the social justice doctrine of the church.

- The linkages between the performance of the economy and the larger social fabric of the community (family violence and stability, crime, physical and mental health, etc.) indicate that there is a very significant reason for Jesuit involvement in economic justice.

The late Edward F. Boyle, SJ, was the Chaplain/Executive Secretary of the Labor Guild, Archdiocese of Boston. The Labor Guild is a tripartite, interfaith labor relations membership organization.

No Shvitz: Your One-Stop Guide to Fighting Sweatshops

Progressive Jewish Alliance (1993)

Exodus from Eastern Europe

In the 1800s, Jews fled Eastern Europe in massive waves, most of them destined for the United States. Political discrimination, economic hardship and the social quarantine imposed upon them with the institution of the May Laws all contributed to this exodus.

Why the Jews Left

The reign of Russia's Tsar Alexander II ushered in a period of intensified xenophobia and anti-Semitism. After revolutionaries assassinated the Tsar in 1881, the government incited and conducted anti-Jewish pogroms in order to redirect revolutionary fervor away from the regime and toward the Jewish population. The effect: 20,000 Jews were left homeless and destabilized.

In response to a report written by a government commission which claimed that the Jews led the revolutionary movement, Tsar Alexander III enacted emergency regulations called "May Laws." The Laws were in effect from 1882 to 1917 and were applied with increasing severity from year to year.

The May Laws (May 1882): Social Quarantine

Under the May Laws, Jews were barred from purchasing or settling on land in rural areas. In order to maximize the scope of the Laws and to close off as many areas to Jews as possible, thousands of small towns were reclassified as "villages." This led to a massive movement of Jews from countryside to city, a move that thrust them into the economy of the early Russian Industrial Revolution.

Moreover, in 1887 the government instituted laws to preclude Jews from attending universities in pursuit of higher professions such as medicine and law.

Coming to America

The vast majority of new immigrants settled east of the Mississippi. By the end of World War I, 70 percent of American Jews populated the Northeast Corridor, extending from Boston to Baltimore.

The largest number of Jewish immigrants first earned their livelihood in manual labor. But unlike the skilled manual work of the "Old World," the rapidly industrializing "New World" replaced independent craft with machinery and mass production. The 1880s saw the rise of the needle trades. The invention of the steam pressing iron brought on a dramatic production increase in women's garments. Furthermore, the influx of immigrants now provided New York – already the nation's principal port operating as the nucleus of sale and exchange of materials – with substantial human resources.

Triangle Shirtwaist Factory

The Triangle Shirtwaist Company in New York City was the largest manufacturer of the shirtwaist, a style of women's shirts and dresses. Most of the workers were young Jewish women, many of them recent immigrants from Eastern Europe. Employees suffered horrible working conditions and severe exploitation. They had to pay for using the equipment, chairs and lockers, for causing damage to a garment, and even for the slightest tardiness. Unionizing efforts were met with threats of job termination. They were subject to the will of factory supervisors who paid them on a piecework basis. To make matters worse, women were paid less than men and had to get permission to use the bathrooms, located outside.

The Jewish Connection

In the case of the Triangle Shirtwaist Company factory, Jews sat at opposite sides of the same bargaining table; not only were most of the workers Jewish, but factory owners were Jewish too. Before immigrating to the United States, many of the female employees were Bundists (members of the Jewish workers' movement in Eastern Europe). In the U.S., they became part of the women's suffrage movement and the American labor movement. Their efforts eventually led to the historic walkout of Shirtwaist Factory employees, described here.

Uprising of the 20,000

In 1909, after several thwarted attempts to unionize workers at the Triangle Shirtwaist factory, a local chapter of the International Ladies' Garment Workers' Union (ILGWU) – one of the first garment workers unions, and a predominantly Jewish and Yiddish speaking organization – called for a strike against the company. All of the workers responded to the appeal.

As they marched the picket lines with signs in Yiddish and English calling for better working conditions, they were threatened, derided and beaten by company thugs. Some were also arrested. The workers' morale began waning after weeks of striking and as pressure, hunger and physical weakness took their toll.

When the grievances at the Triangle plant were echoed by complaints in other shirtwaist shops, the ILGWU leadership decided to call an emergency meeting of all shirtwaist workers. Three thousand women crowded into the Cooper Union auditorium (appropriately, the same place where Lincoln had criticized the spread of slavery half a century earlier).

Here it was that Clara Lemlich, a 19-year-old worker, rose to speak. She described the humiliation of factory labor and appealed for united action against all shirtwaist manufacturers. Her impassioned speech brought the crowd to its feet and inspired thousands of shirtwaist workers to rise up against the injustice. Also known as the "uprising of the 20,000," the 1909 walkout was the largest documented strike to have occurred up until that time in American history. It also inspired sizeable walkouts in various other garment industry sectors.

Strength in Numbers

After months of mounting public support for the strikers, the factory owners decided it was time to negotiate. Weeks later, management agreed to reduce the workweek, raise wages, improve sanitary conditions in the factory, provide workers with equipment (rather than make them bring their own) and to establish a joint grievance committee through which complaints would be settled. Of even greater significance was the establishment of a labor union in the factory, as well as a newfound respect for female strikers.

Tragedy

Sadly, however, not enough was done to improve working conditions at the factory. Less than two years later, someone on the eighth floor of the Triangle Shirtwaist Factory building carelessly dropped a cigarette into a pile of material and the building went up in flames. The factory's steel doors remained locked (reportedly to keep union organizers out as well as to prevent workers from stealing clothes), thereby sealing the fate of the hundreds trapped inside. Some workers burned or suffocated on the spot. Others linked arms and leaped to their death. Those who survived with critical burns and broken limbs were considered lucky.

The blaze killed 146 workers; 500 more were injured. Sprinkler systems could have prevented the tragedy, but the factory owners weren't willing to incur this expense. Many lives could have also been spared if the factory owners had thought to unlock the doors before they themselves escaped unscathed.

PROFILES
Clara Lemlich, a 19-year-old immigrant worker, made her indelible mark on the labor movement in 1909 when she rose to speak at the Cooper Union meeting of the shirtwaist workers. She described the humiliation of factory labor and appealed for united action against all shirtwaist manufacturers. Her emotional plea brought the crowd to its feet and inspired thousands of shirtwaist workers to join the walkout. Thus began the "uprising of the 20,000."

Fast Forward: Injustice Prevails

Almost 100 years after the Triangle Shirtwaist Factory fire, garment workers are still dying under similar conditions.

In August 2001, a fire alarm sounded at an eight-story factory building in Bangladesh. The workers were locked inside. Twenty-three were crushed to death as people tried desperately to escape. It turned out to be a false alarm.

In June 2002, a factory fire in India claimed 42 lives. At the time of the accident the only door at the entrance of the factory was locked.

PROFILES
Rose Freedman was the last survivor of the 1911 Triangle Shirtwaist Factory fire. She died in 2000 at the age of 107. She was fluent in six languages, and was learning a seventh. Born in Vienna, Austria, in 1893, Freedman later immigrated to the United States where, at age 16, she found a job at the Triangle Shirtwaist Factory. Like her fellow workers, she was severely exploited.

When a fire broke out in the factory on March 25, 1911, the company executives showed little concern for their employees. Rather than unlocking the doors so that their workers could escape, they fled the building unscathed while flames consumed 146 lives.

Rose escaped by counter-intuitively going up to the roof, figuring (correctly) that the management must have survived by doing exactly that. She went on to graduate from college, worked until 79, and was a tireless champion of the labor movement.

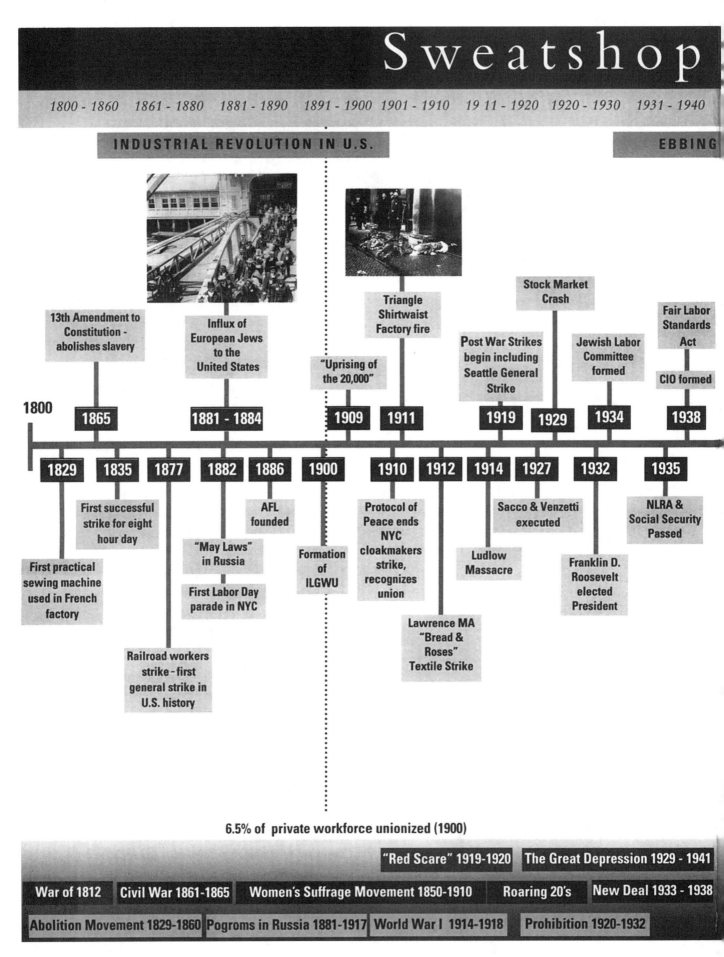

Sweatshop

| 1800 - 1860 | 1861 - 1880 | 1881 - 1890 | 1891 - 1900 | 1901 - 1910 | 19 11 - 1920 | 1920 - 1930 | 1931 - 1940 |

INDUSTRIAL REVOLUTION IN U.S.

EBBING

13th Amendment to Constitution - abolishes slavery

Influx of European Jews to the United States

"Uprising of the 20,000"

Triangle Shirtwaist Factory fire

Post War Strikes begin including Seattle General Strike

Stock Market Crash

Jewish Labor Committee formed

Fair Labor Standards Act

CIO formed

1800

1865 **1881 - 1884** **1909** **1911** **1919** **1929** **1934** **1938**

1829 **1835** **1877** **1882** **1886** **1900** **1910** **1912** **1914** **1927** **1932** **1935**

First successful strike for eight hour day

AFL founded

Protocol of Peace ends NYC cloakmakers strike, recognizes union

Sacco & Venzetti executed

NLRA & Social Security Passed

First practical sewing machine used in French factory

"May Laws" in Russia

Formation of ILGWU

Ludlow Massacre

Franklin D. Roosevelt elected President

First Labor Day parade in NYC

Railroad workers strike - first general strike in U.S. history

Lawrence MA "Bread & Roses" Textile Strike

6.5% of private workforce unionized (1900)

| "Red Scare" 1919-1920 | The Great Depression 1929 - 1941 |

| War of 1812 | Civil War 1861-1865 | Women's Suffrage Movement 1850-1910 | Roaring 20's | New Deal 1933 - 1938 |

| Abolition Movement 1829-1860 | Pogroms in Russia 1881-1917 | World War I 1914-1918 | Prohibition 1920-1932 |

Timeline

| 1941 - 1950 | 1951 - 1960 | 1961 - 1965 | 1966 - 1970 | 1971 - 1990 | 1991 - 2000 | 2001 - present |

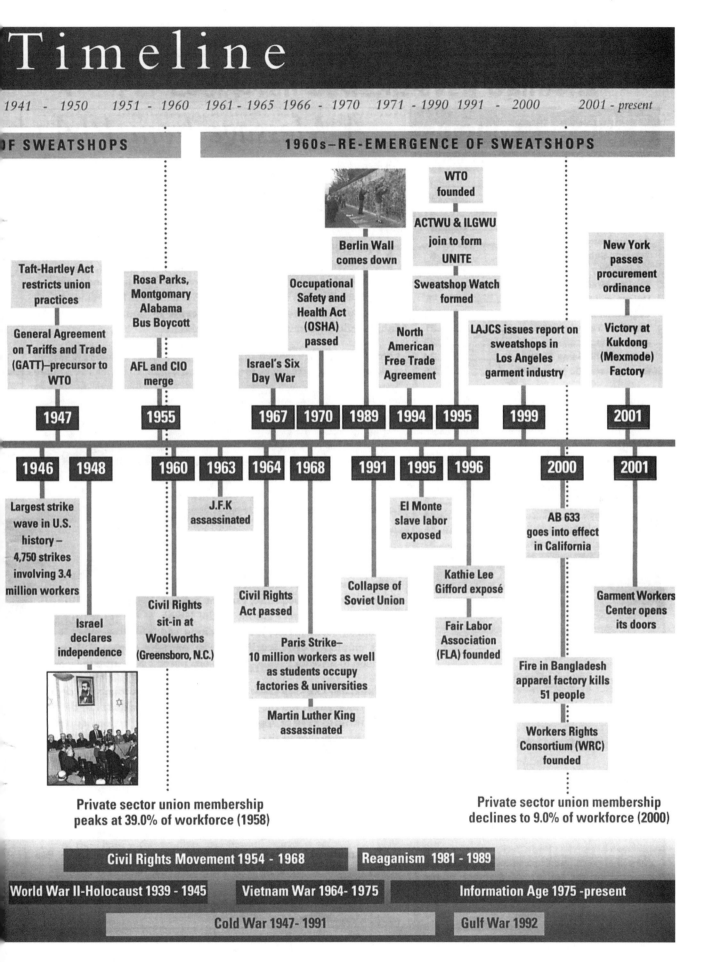

OF SWEATSHOPS

1960s–RE-EMERGENCE OF SWEATSHOPS

WTO founded

ACTWU & ILGWU join to form UNITE

New York passes procurement ordinance

Taft-Hartley Act restricts union practices

Rosa Parks, Montgomary Alabama Bus Boycott

Berlin Wall comes down

Occupational Safety and Health Act (OSHA) passed

Sweatshop Watch formed

General Agreement on Tariffs and Trade (GATT)–precursor to WTO

AFL and CIO merge

Israel's Six Day War

North American Free Trade Agreement

LAJCS issues report on sweatshops in Los Angeles garment industry

Victory at Kukdong (Mexmode) Factory

1947 — **1955** — **1967** **1970** **1989** **1994** **1995** — **1999** — **2001**

1946 **1948** — **1960** **1963** **1964** **1968** — **1991** **1995** **1996** — **2000** — **2001**

Largest strike wave in U.S. history – 4,750 strikes involving 3.4 million workers

J.F.K assassinated

El Monte slave labor exposed

AB 633 goes into effect in California

Israel declares independence

Civil Rights sit-in at Woolworths (Greensboro, N.C.)

Civil Rights Act passed

Collapse of Soviet Union

Kathie Lee Gifford exposé

Garment Workers Center opens its doors

Paris Strike– 10 million workers as well as students occupy factories & universities

Fair Labor Association (FLA) founded

Fire in Bangladesh apparel factory kills 51 people

Martin Luther King assassinated

Workers Rights Consortium (WRC) founded

Private sector union membership peaks at 39.0% of workforce (1958)

Private sector union membership declines to 9.0% of workforce (2000)

Civil Rights Movement 1954 - 1968   **Reaganism 1981 - 1989**

World War II-Holocaust 1939 - 1945   **Vietnam War 1964- 1975**   **Information Age 1975 -present**

Cold War 1947- 1991   **Gulf War 1992**

Charles Stelzle and the Workingmen's Department

Richard P. Poethig (2003)

Charles Stelzle was a man of his time. Though the Presbyterian Church historically had paid little attention to working people, Stelzle saw the need to change that. His early ministry had taken him from New York's East Side to the Markham Mission Chapel, a working class congregation in St. Louis, where he developed a Sunday School of 1400 people, the largest west of the Mississippi.

On the occasion of the 250th anniversary of the adoption of the Westminster Confession, Stelzle was asked to address a meeting of Presbyterian clergy in Joplin, Missouri, on the theme, "The Workingman and the Westminster Confession of Faith." Stelzle confronted the audience with the fact that most workingmen didn't *know* there was a Westminster Confession – and those who did know it existed cared little about it. The streets of Joplin, he proclaimed, were filled with working men, very few of whom attended the Presbyterian churches of the city.

Someone in the audience challenged Stelzle to conduct a service in the streets of Joplin that very night … and Stelzle agreed.

That evening, as hundreds of miners were gathered by the music of a cornet, Stelzle stood on the seat of a carriage and gathered his thoughts. As he was about to address the crowd, his eye fell on the sign of a clothing dealer named Gottlieb. Pointing to the sign, Stelzle told his audience that "Gottlieb, the love of God," was to be the text of his sermon. The Jewish shopkeeper, standing in the doorway, nodded with approval.[1]

Among the crowd of miners and ministers on the streets of Joplin that night was Dr. John Dixon from the Presbyterian Board of Home Missions in New York City. As he watched Charles Stelzle interact with the crowd in the streets, he knew instinctively that Stelzle was the man for the job he and Charles Thompson, head of the Board, had in mind.

On his return to New York City, Dixon reported to Thompson that he had met a man with a vision for reaching workingmen in the United States. Charles Stelzle, he said, was a workingman's preacher. Thompson quickly issued an invitation for Stelzle to come to New York to discuss the Presbyterian Church's ministry to working people.

Thompson, a New York City pastor, was concerned about the exploding working class population that was crowding into U.S. cities at the turn of the 20th century. Everywhere he turned, Presbyterian congregations were abandoning their neighborhoods in the face of a tide of new immigrants. Stelzle impressed Thompson with his grasp of the problems of working people and his aspirations for meeting their spiritual needs. After the meeting, Thompson, with the approval of the Board of Home Missions, organized the Workingmen's Department and put Stelzle in charge.

The creation of the Workingmen's Department in 1903 was the first such effort of any Protestant denomination. Stelzle, the first secretary of the new department, set in motion a stream of ministries that were to challenge the Presbyterian Church in its responsibility to an expanding industrial society for decades to come. In many ways, the directions for our continuing patterns of social ministry were set in those years, as this issue of *Church & Society* will try to demonstrate.

Like Charles Stelzle, Richard Poethig, the grandson of German immigrants, spent his early years in the tenements of New York's East Side. In his youth he attended a camp sponsored by the Labor Temple founded by Stelzle and the GoodWill Sunday School, an East Side mission of the Madison Avenue Presbyterian Church. A graduate of Wooster College and Union Theological Seminary (NYC), he was a participant in the first summer Ministers-In-Industry Program of the Presbyterian Institute of Industrial Relations (PIIR), then located in Pittsburgh. Following ordination as a Presbyterian minister, he did new church development work in the industrial suburbs of Buffalo-Niagara Presbytery and then served with the Urban-Industrial Mission program of the United Church of Christ in the Philippines. He returned to the U.S. to become Dean of PIIR (1972-75) and Director of the Institute on the Church in Urban-Industrial Society (1972-82). He served as Co-Content Editor of this issue of Church & Society.

---

1. Charles Stelzle, *A Son of the Bowery: The Life Story of an East Side American* (George H. Doran Co., 1926), p. 67.

Stelzle's Early Life

Stelzle came to his work as a pioneer. In 1903, few Protestant ministers had the background or experience to engage directly with working people, but Stelzle was different. Having grown up in the working class tenements of the lower East Side of New York, he went to work at the age of eight, stripping tobacco leaves in a sweatshop across the street from his family's apartment. He left school at the age of eleven to help his widowed mother as a "cutter" in a shop that made artificial flowers. When he was 15, a relative got him a job at R. Hoe, one of the city's largest printing press manufacturers. In nine years he rose to the position of machinist and was promised a supervisory position.[2]

During his teenage years, Stelzle had attended a number of East Side chapels, but he was particularly attracted to the "warm and sympathetic" environment of Hope Chapel, a Presbyterian mission led by Dr. W.J. McKittrick. It was under McKittrick's tutelage that Stelzle studied English grammar, plane geometry and mathematics three nights a week. In his hunger for knowledge, he studied Latin with a Jewish peddler, Greek with a Brooklyn lawyer, and Hebrew through an extension course. But it was his early involvement in the Presbyterian Church that led him ultimately to commit himself to the Christian ministry.

Bridging the Gap between the Church and Labor

Under Stelzle, the Workingmen's Department[3] brought the Presbyterian Church into direct engagement with workers and their unions. Stelzle's primary advantage was that he had been a skilled machinist and carried an International Association of Machinists' (IAM) union card. In his writings and speeches he used illustrations from the workplace; this gave him an entree into the worker's world. From the beginning he said that his main task was to interpret the church to working people, to interpret working people to the church, and to interpret employers and employees to each other.

In 1901, even before taking up his work at the Board of Home Missions, Stelzle had conducted a survey of 200 labor leaders about their attitudes toward the church and church life. The survey reflected the critical view that labor leaders had of the churches as "rich men's clubs." Stelzle had begun his work with the view that the worker was sympathetic to the person and teachings of Jesus Christ. This was confirmed in a second survey that he sent to workers in 1903 soon after he began his national work. The survey showed that workers distinguished between the church of the early 1900s and the church of Jesus Christ. Working people, in fact, held orthodox beliefs about Christianity, but the surveys clearly showed that they were repelled by the class nature of the contemporary church.

Breaking down this barrier became Stelzle's goal. To Stelzle, pastors had a primary role in interpreting the problems of the new industrial working class to church members. The issue was not one of winning over workers who were bitter against the church, but one of reaching those who were indifferent. Stelzle felt that worker indifference was deepened by the fact that most pastors had little to say to industrial workers.

To bridge this gap, Stelzle organized workshop floor meetings as a means of bringing local pastors and workers together. By 1906, his efforts had generated over 1000 such shop meetings in six cities, reaching an audience of 200,000 working people. Stelzle also set in motion a plan for an exchange of fraternal delegates between central labor bodies and local ministerial associations. By 1910, 157 ministers were serving as fraternal delegates to trade unions in 117 cities.

The unique work being carried out by Charles Stelzle was noted with interest by Samuel Gompers, head of the American Federation of Labor, the major body of organized labor in the U.S at the turn of the 20th century. In Stelzle, Gompers saw a useful spokesperson for the goals of the trade union movement. Stelzle had raised the cause of unionism to a moral level. This appealed to those trade unionists who saw the labor movement as more than a matter of monetary goals. It was, in fact, the reality of the moral commitments of laboring people in the early part of the century that provided Stelzle with his most effective base for reaching them.

Stelzle's primary means for speaking to trade unionists came through a weekly syndicated column that appeared in over 300 labor newspapers. Stelzle remembered the religious importance of his column:

---

2. Information on the life of Charles Stelzle is drawn largely from his autobiography, *A Son of the Bowery*, cited above.

3. The title was changed to the Department of Church and Labor in 1906.

The articles which contained the most Scripture and the most frequent reference to Bible stories were always given the biggest headlines. Here again was demonstration of the fact that working-men responded more eagerly to the religious appeal.

Ever sensitive to those in the church who were critical of his work, Stelzle pointed out that if the church had had to bear the cost of printing this material in pamphlet form and distributing it among individual workers, "it would have cost more each week than the entire annual budget of the Department."[4] Instead, the labor press provided an effective system for reaching thousands of workers with no cost to the church other than support for Stelzle's work.

In 1906, in order to win wider recognition of the importance of industrial work among church members, Stelzle introduced the concept of Labor Sunday. Pastors were asked to use the Sunday before Labor Day as an opportunity to explore the biblical theme of work as it related to the U.S. industrial system. The American Federation of Labor immediately seized upon the celebration of Labor Sunday and urged unions to work with local ministers to make the day a success. The Board of Home Missions' Report to the 1906 General Assembly proclaimed that more workingmen had attended church that day than on any previous Sunday and that many pastors had written to say that the men were still attending.

The high point of Stelzle's ability to attract working-men to a church sponsored function occurred at the 1908 General Assembly meeting in Kansas City. Stelzle's presence attracted 15,000 workingmen to a mass meeting at the Coliseum, at which he spoke on the theme of "A Square Deal ... for the boss, for the workingman, for the Church and for Jesus."

Ministry to Immigrant Neighborhoods

Stelzle's effectiveness, however, went far beyond developing programs to reach working people. Coming from German immigrant parentage, he had a special concern for new immigrants. In 1908, recognizing the strong link between "working people" and the streams of immigrants filling the cities of the northeastern United States, the Board of Home Missions asked Stelzle to assume direction of the newly created Department of Immigration. Stelzle later wrote that the work was given to him because "practically all immigrants were working men and ... for the most part

the immigrant was a city 'problem' and practically all of my activities were centered in the city."[5]

In pursuit of this new work, Stelzle immediately conducted four one-day conferences among specific immigrant groups in New York – Hungarians, Italians, Ruthenians and Jews. Out of these conferences he prepared sociological surveys of the religious and social conditions of immigrant peoples on Manhattan Island. So thorough were Stelzle's charts and statistics that the New York State Commission for the Study of the Immigrant Problem, as well as the Russell Sage Foundation and the Young Women's Christian Association, used them for developing their own programs. In 1909, in following up on Stelzle's work, the General Assembly asked the Departments of Church and Labor and Immigration "in so far as may be practicable, upon application of any local church, Presbytery or Synod, (to) study such problems in the locality to which the application relates, outline plans for local work, and aid in making such work efficient."[6] Thus began the art of consultation and strategic planning in the Presbyterian Church.

Stelzle's social analysis had documented the continual flight of downtown congregations from the neighborhoods into which the immigrant working class had been moving. Charles Thompson, having been called from his position as minister of Madison Avenue Presbyterian Church to head the Board of Home Missions, knew this situation first hand. Thompson had held the line and refused to allow the Madison Avenue congregation to move to a new location. Instead, he called for the development of church programs to meet the needs of the church's new immigrant neighbors. Stelzle also believed it was the churches' responsibility to continue to minister in these areas and to develop ways to serve the new inhabitants' social needs.

The Labor Temple

The ideal opportunity arose in 1910. The facilities of the Second Presbyterian Church at 14th Street and Second Avenue, a church that had been abandoned by its congregation, were not being used. Stelzle saw the site as the ideal point from which to carry out a major social program in the largely immigrant lower East Side neighborhood of 400,000 people. Labor historian

---

4. Stelzle, *A Son of the Bowery*, p. 89ff.

5. Ibid., p. 147.

6. *GA Minutes*, Presbyterian Church in the USA, 1909, pp. 60-61.

George Nash described the neighborhood of Second Presbyterian Church in this way:

> In 1910 this section of New York City was the most forbidding ground for Protestantism in the United States. The "new immigration" – predominantly Jewish and Roman Catholic – had virtually overwhelmed the city missions and churches, many of which had simply retreated to more congenial neighborhoods. "Monk" Eastman the gangster, rebellious Wobblies, and Leon Trotsky were active in the area. Even Dwight L. Moody, who had once conducted a month long revival at the Presbyterian Church on Fourteenth Street and Second Avenue, had been unable to surmount the indifference of the masses.[7]

But this was Stelzle's old neighborhood, and he presented the Church Extension Committee of New York Presbytery with a proposal: purchase the Second Church building and allow him to develop a program for the people of the neighborhood. The Church Extension Committee agreed, with the stipulation that the program would be experimental for a two-year period.

Stelzle was jubilant. He later wrote:

> I was about to realize a dream which I had since my machinist days – of organizing and conducting a church such as I felt would appeal to the average workingman. It was to be a real workingman's church in every particular. Avowedly it was to be run by workingmen, the men who actually lived in the community. So I called it the "Labor Temple."[8]

Labor Temple soon developed a worldwide reputation as a unique experiment in ministry among working people, most of them from immigrant backgrounds. It was not long before the auditorium of the former Second Presbyterian Church was filled with the people who lived in the four- and five-story tenements of the neighborhood.

The highlight of Labor Temple's programs was the open forum. Stelzle's reputation provided him access to a wide range of speakers, and he invited everyone – socialists, radicals of all stripes, labor leaders, and social gospel preachers – to address the crowds. On Sundays, the program went from 2:30 in the after-

noon to 10:00 at night. It included a children's hour, Bible class, organ recital, reading of a literary masterpiece, concert or lecture, and sermon. In 1910, a denominational journal reported:

> After the meetings the superintendent and the pastor are surrounded by working men, young and old, some seeking advice and other proffering it on the affairs of the Temple. One and all receive the same kindly attention, but these are the pillars of the Labor Temple. They are made to feel that the responsibility for the success or failure rests upon them alone. In the near future will be formed a Brotherhood of the men which will largely direct its affairs.[9]

The experimental program at Labor Temple extended beyond Stelzle's initial leadership and continued its work in the lower East Side for over forty years. It stood alongside the many other neighborhood houses and community centers that the Presbyterian Church developed during the years of immigrant growth in urban centers.[10] As immigration subsided during and after World War I, the programs of the neighborhood houses responded to the social and economic problems of the ethnic and racial groups that made up the community. As neighborhoods changed so did the programs serving the residents.

The Presbyterian Institute of Industrial Relations

The life of Labor Temple continued into the fifth decade of the 20th century. After World War II, it was apparent that dramatic changes would be occurring in the U.S. economy. As the war was ending, Jacob A. Long, Secretary for City and Industrial Work of the Board of National Missions, called for a program to prepare pastors and laity for possible management/labor conflicts. The proper location for such a program, Long suggested, was Labor Temple. Thus in January 1945, the Presbyterian Institute of Industrial Relations (PIIR) began its work at the Labor Temple under the leadership of Marshal L. Scott.

7. George Nash III, "Charles Stelzle: Apostle to Labor," *Labor History*, II:2, Spring 1970.

8. James Armstrong, *The Labor Temple, 1910 – 1957: A Social Gospel in Action in the Presbyterian Church* (Doctoral Dissertation, University of Wisconsin, Madison, 1974).

9. George J. Anderson, "The Church of the Heavy Laden," *The Congregationalist and the Christian World*, 4, June 1910, 772ff.

10. Many such programs were directly involved in communities with major industries: Gary Neighborhood House served the immigrants working in the steel industry of northwest Indiana; Dodge Community Center was in the midst of the growing automobile industry in Detroit.

As Dean of the PIIR program, Scott initiated a model of immersion in the city and in industry. Over the thirty years of the program's existence, PIIR was the means by which more than three thousand seminarians, pastors and lay leaders came into direct contact with the growing complexity of the industrial economy and its impact in the U.S. and the world. In 1952, the program moved to the McCormick Seminary campus in Chicago. There it became even more directly involved in shaping the choices of seminarians in their ministries. As participants in the program, they worked in industry and were directly involved in working-class neighborhoods. Through these experiences, increasing numbers of seminarians were drawn into inner city ministries as well as industrial mission programs in the U.S. and throughout the world.

Over the years, PIIR's involvement with scores of international clergy and seminarians led the World Council of Churches to invite PIIR to provide the foundation for the Institute on the Church in Urban-Industrial Society (ICUIS), a documentation and information-sharing program they envisioned to connect the urban-industrial mission practitioners of the worldwide church.[11]

The Social Creed

At the beginning of the 20th century, like many others in the social gospel movement, Stelzle was aware of the larger forces at work in the economy. He recognized the impact that industry was having on the lives of families and the conditions under which men, women and children worked. He himself had experienced these conditions. He also knew that change would require cooperation. Looking beyond the exclusivity of denominationally focused work, Stelzle was one of the Presbyterian representatives at the founding meeting of the Federal Council of Churches in 1908.

At that meeting, Dr. Frank Mason North, a Methodist, gave a major speech entitled "The Church and Modern Industry." In one particular paragraph, North called for the churches' support of social principles on behalf of "the toilers of America." North asked Stelzle to give the supporting statement on behalf of the principles. It was the only supporting statement given. Following Stelzle's speech, the resolution on behalf of the principles was unanimously adopted by the

Council. Later, a statement of social principles, which Stelzle lifted from North's speech, became "The Social Creed of the Churches."

The "Creed" centered on the rights and the conditions of working people in an industrial society. It was to become the first among many such social statements adopted by church bodies. In its initial form, the Creed focused directly on practical industrial problems:

- the need for workers to be protected "against the hardships often resulting from the swift crises of industrial change";
- the need for conciliation and arbitration in times of industrial conflict;
- the protection of workers from dangerous machinery, occupational disease, injuries and mortality;
- the abolition of child labor;
- "such regulation of the conditions of toil of women as shall safeguard the physical and moral health of the community";
- the suppression of the "sweating system";
- the "gradual and reasonable reduction of the hours of labor to the lowest practicable point and for that degree of leisure for all which is a condition of the highest human life";
- relief from the seven day work week;
- a living wage (defined as "a minimum in every industry" and "the highest wage that each industry can afford");
- "the most equitable division of the products of industry that can ultimately be devised";
- "suitable provision" for elderly and disabled workers; and
- the "abatement of poverty."

The Bethlehem Steel Strike

In 1910, with the Social Creed as background, the Commission on the Church and Social Service of the Federal Council of Churches investigated a steel strike at Bethlehem Steel, where the strikers were protesting Sunday work.

The Council appointed Stelzle to chair the investigating committee, which produced a 21 page report, the first such study of an industrial conflict by a church-related organization. The issue of Sunday work, how-

---

11. In 1967, Scott invited Bobbi Wells to become the Documentation Director of ICUIS. Richard Poethig was named Director of the program in 1972 following service in the Philippines.

ever, pointed to a larger problem in the steel industry: that of long hours and low wages. More than half of the Bethlehem workers worked twelve-hour shifts and 61 percent of them received less than 18 cents an hour. A considerable number, the committee discovered, received only 12.5 cents an hour – 12 hours a day, seven days a week. In reviewing the larger issues in the Bethlehem strike, Stelzle saw that the strike:

> … *Not only raised issues which concerned the nine thousand men employed in the steel works, but brought to the attention of the American public certain industrial problems which could not be settled by capital and labor alone.*[12]

"… Therefore, be it resolved …"

In 1910, the Presbyterian General Assembly issued its first social pronouncement, which was essentially drawn from "The Social Creed of the Churches." The social statements passed by subsequent General Assemblies became a primary means for calling the church's attention to the major social issues confronting the United States. The social thinking embodied in these statements became especially important during the Depression years, when they provided the basis for study documents and publications of the Social Education and Action Committee of the Board of Christian Education. These study documents were used in the educational programs of local congregations and became the means for encouraging action by local congregations and presbyteries. *Social Progress,* a monthly publication of the Social Education and Action Committee, provided regular information and exposition on current issues for the education of church members.[13]

---

12. Stelzle, *A Son of the Bowery,* p. 161. See also, Richard Poethig, "Charles Stelzle and the Roots of Presbyterian Industrial Mission," *Journal of Presbyterian History,* 77:1, Spring 1999.

13. From 1970 onward, its successor, *Church & Society,* became the major instrument for promoting dialogue and involvement in the changing social issues of the day.

Summary

In 1903, the Workingmen's Department was a symbol of the awakening commitment of the Presbyterian Church to ministries of social justice. As the stream moved on from this early action, the following decades saw the development of new expressions of social ministry. Each new generation found encouragement in the stories of those who had responded to the social inequities of their own time.

As Presbyterians have moved through this century since 1903, the witness of these early social justice pioneers has become incorporated directly into the heart of our church's life and witness. *The Directory of Worship* tells us that doing justice calls for:

a. dealing honestly in personal and public business,

b. exercising power for the common good,

c. supporting people who seek the dignity, freedom and respect they have been denied,

d. working for fair laws and just administration of the law ….

e. seeking to overcome the disparity between rich and poor,

f. bearing witness against political oppression and exploitation,

g. redressing wrongs against individuals, groups, and peoples in the church, in the nation, and in the whole world. (Book of Order, W-7.4002)

As Labor Temple responded to the struggles of immigrant peoples on the lower East Side of New York, so the church has continued to respond to issues of degradation in inner-city neighborhoods, unequal treatment of minorities in housing, jobs and education, struggles to achieve equality for women in the economy, working and living conditions of migrant workers in the vineyards and truck farms of rural America, and hazardous conditions facing *maquiladora* workers on the Texas/Mexico border. The line stretches back to the initial response of the church in 1903 and moves forward as we continue to engage inequity in our society in its new manifestations.

3 What Our Religious Traditions Say about Work

Introduction

The sacred scriptures and denominational statements of Christians, Muslims and Jews speak of labor, work, justice and economics throughout history. These scriptures and denominational statements are rich with language about dignity, human creation, just wages and respect for laborers. This section offers the voices of various religious perspectives on work and labor.

The first statement is taken from the chapter "The Christian Vision of Economic Life," from the pastoral letter, "Economic Justice for All," written in 1997 by the National Conference of Catholic Bishops. The Catholic Church has the most extensive social teaching on labor unions of all the Christian bodies.

The next pieces are a compilation of religious social statements on worker and economic justice issues developed by religious denominations. Students and faculty have found these helpful in classrooms and congregations.

"The Qur'an and Worker Justice," focuses on Muslim perspectives on work and labor. It was written by Muslim staff and board members of Interfaith Worker Justice.

The Christian Vision of Economic Life

U.S. Conference of Catholic Bishops (1986)

The basis for all that the Church believes about the moral dimensions of economic life is its vision of the transcendent worth – the sacredness – of human beings. *The dignity of the human person, realized in community with others, is the criterion against which all aspects of economic life must be measured.* All human beings, therefore, are ends to be served by the institutions that make up the economy, not means to be exploited for more narrowly defined goals. Human personhood must be respected with a reverence that is religious. When we deal with each other, we should do so with the sense of awe that arises in the presence of something holy and sacred. For that is what human beings are: we are created in the image of God (Gn 1:27). Similarly, all economic institutions must support the bonds of community and solidarity that are essential to the dignity of persons. Wherever our economic arrangements fail to conform to the demands of human dignity lived in community, they must be questioned and transformed. These convictions have a biblical basis. They are also supported by a long tradition of theological and philosophical reflection and through the reasoned analysis of human experience by contemporary men and women.

In presenting the Christian moral vision, we turn first to the Scriptures for guidance. Though our comments are necessarily selective, we hope that pastors and other church members will become personally engaged with the biblical texts. The Scriptures contain many passages that speak directly of economic life. We must also attend to the Bible's deeper vision of God, of the purpose of creation, and of the dignity of human life in society. Along with other churches and ecclesial communities who are "strengthened by the grace of Baptism and the hearing of God's Word," we strive to become faithful hearers and doers of the word. We also claim the Hebrew Scriptures as common heritage with our Jewish brothers and sisters, and we join with them in the quest for an economic life worthy of the divine revelation we share.

A. Biblical Perspectives

The fundamental conviction of our faith is that human life is fulfilled in the knowledge and love of the living God in communion with others. The Sacred Scriptures offer guidance so that men and women may enter into full communion with God and with each other, and witness to God's saving acts. We discover there is a God who is creator of heaven and earth, and of the human family. Though our first parents reject the God who created them, God does not abandon them, but from Abraham and Sarah forms a people of promise. When people are enslaved in an alien land, God delivers them and makes a covenant with them in which they are summoned to be faithful to the torah or sacred teaching. The focal points of Israel's faith – creation, covenant, and community – provide a foundation for reflection on issues of economic and social justice.

1. Created in God's Image

After the exile, when Israel combined its traditions into a written torah, it prefaced its history as a people with the story of the creation of all peoples and of the whole world by the same God who created them as a nation (Gn 1-11). God is the creator of heaven and earth (Gn 14:19-22; Is 40:28; 45:18); creation proclaims God's glory (Ps 89:6-12) and is "very good" (Gn 1:31). Fruitful harvests, bountiful flocks, a loving family are God's blessings on those who heed God's word. Such is the joyful refrain that echoes throughout the Bible. One legacy of this theology of creation is the conviction that no dimension of human creation lies beyond God's care and concern. God is present to creation, and creative engagement with God's handiwork is itself reverence for God.

At the summit of creation stands the creation of man and woman, made in God's image (Gn 1:26-27). *As such every human being possesses an inalienable dignity that stamps human existence prior to any division into races or nations and prior to human labor and human achievement* (Gn 4-11). Men and women are also to share in the creative activity of God. They are to be fruitful, to care for the earth (Gn 2:15), and to have "dominion" over it (Gn 1:28), which means they are "to govern the world in holiness and justice and to render judgment in integrity of heart" (Wis 9:3). Creation is a gift; women and men are to be faithful stewards in caring for the earth. They can justly consider that by their labor they are unfolding the Creator's work.

The narratives of Genesis 1-11 also portray the origin of the strife and suffering that mar the world. Though created to enjoy intimacy with God and the fruits of the earth, Adam and Eve disrupted God's design by trying to live independently of God through a denial of their status as creatures. They turned away from God and gave to God's creation the obedience due to God alone. For this reason the prime sin in so much of the biblical tradition is idolatry: service of the creature rather than of the creator (Rom 1:25), and the attempt to overturn creation by making Do in human likeness. The Bible castigates not only the worship of idols, but also manifestations of idolatry, such as the quest for unrestrained power and the desire for great wealth (Is 40:12-20; 44:1-20; Wis 13:1-14:31; Col 3:5, "the greed that is idolatry"). The sin of our first parents had other consequences as well. Alienation from God pits brother against brother (Gn 4:8-16), in a cycle of war and vengeance (Gn 4:22-23). Sin and evil abound, and the primeval history culminates with another assault on the heavens, this time ending in a babble of tongues scattered over the face of the earth (Gn 11:1-9). Sin simultaneously alienates human beings from God and shatters the solidarity of the human community. Yet this reign of sin is not the final word. The primeval history is followed by the call of Abraham, a man of faith, who was to be the bearer of the promise to many nations (Gn 12:1-4). Throughout the Bible we find this struggle between sin and repentance. God's judgment on evil is followed by God's seeking out a sinful people.

The biblical vision of creation has provided one of the most enduring legacies of Church teaching. To stand before God as the creator is to respect God's creation, both the world of nature and of human history. *From the patristic period to the present, the church has affirmed that misuse of the world's resources or appropriation of them by a minority of the world's population betrays the gift of creation since "whatever belongs to God belongs to all."*

2. A People of Covenant

When the people of Israel, our forerunners in faith, gathered in thanksgiving to renew their covenant (Jos 24:1-15), they recalled the gracious deeds of God (Dt 6:20-25; 26:5-11). When they lived as aliens in a strange land and experienced oppression and slavery, they cried out. The Lord, the God of their ancestors, heard their cries, knew their afflictions, and came to deliver them (Ex 3:7-8). By leading them out of Egypt, God created a people that was to be the Lord's very own (Jer 24:7; Hos 2:25). They were to imitate God by treating the alien and the slave in their midst as God had treated them (Ex 22:20-22; Jer 34:8-14).

In the midst of this saving history stands the covenant at Sinai (Ex 19-24). It begins with an account of what God has done for the people (Ex 19:1-6; cf Jos 24:1-13) and includes from God's side a promise of steadfast love (hesed) and faithfulness ('emeth, Ex 34:5-7). The people are summoned to ratify this covenant by faithfully worshiping God alone and by directing their lives according to God's will, which was made explicit in Israel's great legal codes such as the Decalogue (Ex 20:1-17) and the Book of the Covenant (Ex 20:22-23:33). Far from being an arbitrary restriction on the life of the people, these codes made life in community possible. The specific laws of the covenant protect human life and property, demand respect for parents and the spouses and children of one's neighbor, and manifest a special concern for the vulnerable members of the community: widows, orphans, the poor, and strangers in the land. Laws such as that for the Sabbath year when the land was left fallow (Ex 23:11; Lv 25:1-7) and for the year of release of debts (Dt 15:1-11) summoned people to respect the land as God's gift and reminded Israel that as a people freed by God from bondage they were to be concerned for the poor and oppressed in their midst. Every fiftieth year a jubilee was proclaimed as a year of "liberty throughout the land" and property was to be restored to its original owners (Lv 25:8-17, cf Is 61:1-2; Lk 4:18-19). The codes of Israel reflect the norms of the covenant: reciprocal responsibility, mercy, and truthfulness. They embody a life in freedom from oppression: worship of the One God, rejection of idolatry, mutual respect among people, care and protection for every member of the social body. Being free and being a co-responsible community are God's intentions for us.

When the people turn away from the living God to serve idols and no longer heed the commands of the covenant, God sends prophets to recall his saving deeds and to summon them to return to the one who betrothed them "in right and in justice, in love and in mercy" (Hos 2:21). The substance of prophetic faith is proclaimed by Micah: "to do justice, and to love kindness, and to walk humbly with your God" (Mi 6:8, RSV). Biblical faith in general, and prophetic faith especially, insist that fidelity to the covenant joins obedience to God with reverence and concern for the neighbor. The biblical terms which best summarize this double dimension of Israel's faith are sedaqah, justice (also translated as righteousness), and mishpat (right judgment or justice embodied in a concrete act or deed). The biblical understanding of justice gives a fundamental perspective to our reflections on social and economic justice.

God is described as a "God of justice" (Is 30:18) who loves justice (Is 61:8, cf. Ps 11:7; 33:5; 37:28: 99:4) and delights in it (Jer 9:23). God demands justice from the whole people (Dt 16:20) and executes justice for the needy (Ps 140:13). Central to the biblical presentation of justice is that the justice of a community is measured by its treatment of the powerless in society, most often described as the widow, the orphan, the poor, and the stranger (non-Israelite) in the land. The Law, the Prophets, and the Wisdom literature of the Old Testament all show deep concern for the proper treatment of such people. What these groups of people have in common is their vulnerability and lack of power. They are often alone and have no protector or advocate. Therefore, it is God who hears their cries (Ps 109:21; 113:7), and the king who is God's anointed is commanded to have special concern for them.

Justice has many nuances. Fundamentally, it suggests a sense of what is right or of what should happen. For example, paths are just when they bring you to your destination (Gn 24:48; Ps 23:3), and laws are just when they create harmony within the community, as Isaiah says: "Justice will bring about peace; right will produce calm and security" (Is 32:17). God is "just" by acting as God should, coming to the people's aid and summoning them to conversion when they stray. People are summoned to be "just," that is, to be in a proper relation to God, by observing God's laws which form them into a faithful community. Biblical justice is more comprehensive than subsequent philosophical definitions. It is not concerned with a strict definition of rights and duties, but with the rightness of the human condition before God and within society. Nor is justice opposed to love; rather, it is both a manifestation of love and a condition for love to grow. Because God loves Israel, he rescues them from oppression and summons them to be a people that "does justice" and loves kindness. The quest for justice arises from loving gratitude for the saving acts of God and manifests itself in wholehearted love of God and neighbor.

These perspectives provide the foundation for a biblical vision of economic justice. Every human person is created as an image of God, and the denial of dignity to a person is a blot on this image. Creation is a gift to all men and women, not to be appropriated for the benefit of a few; its beauty is an object of joy and reverence. The same God who came to the aid of an oppressed people and formed them into a covenant community continues to hear the cries of the oppressed and to create communities which are responsive to God's word. God's love and life are present when people can live in a community of faith and hope. These cardinal points of faith of Israel also furnish the religious context for understanding the saving action of God in the life and teachings of Jesus.

3. The Reign of God and Justice

Jesus enters human history as God's anointed son who announces the nearness of the reign of God (Mk 1:9-14). This proclamation summons us to acknowledge God as creator and covenant partner and challenges us to seek ways in which God's revelation of the dignity and destiny of all creation might become incarnate in history. It is not simply the promise of the future victory of God over sin and evil, but that this victory has already begun – in the life and teaching of Jesus.

What Jesus proclaims by word, he enacts in his ministry. He resists temptations of power and prestige, follows his Father's will, and teaches us to pray that it be accomplished on earth. He warns against attempts to "lay up treasures on earth" (Mt 6:19) and exhorts his followers not to be anxious about material goods but rather to seek first God's reign and God's justice (Mt 6:25-33). His mighty works symbolize that the reign of God is more powerful than evil, sickness, and the hardness of the human heart. He offers God's loving mercy to sinners (Mk 2:17), takes up the cause of those who suffered religious and social discrimination (Lk 7:36-50; 15:1-2), and attacks the use of religion to avoid the demands of charity and justice (Mk 7:9-13; Mt 23:23).

When asked what was the greatest commandment, Jesus quoted the age-old Jewish affirmation of faith that God alone is One and to be loved with the whole heart, mind, and soul (Dt 6:4-5) and immediately adds: "You shall love your neighbor as yourself" (Lv 19:18, Mk 12:28-34). This dual command of love that is at the basis of all Christian morality is illustrated in the Gospel of Luke by the parable of a Samaritan who interrupts his journey to come to the aid of a dying man (Lk 10:29-37). Unlike the other wayfarers who look on the man and pass by, the Samaritan "was moved with compassion at the sight"; he stops, tends the wounded man, and takes him to a place of safety. In this parable compassion is the bridge between mere seeing and action: love is made real through effective action.

Near the end of his life, Jesus offers a vivid picture of the last judgment (Mt 25:31-46). All the nations of the world will be assembled and will be divided into those blessed who are welcomed into God's kingdom or those cursed who are sent to eternal punishment.

The blessed are those who fed the hungry, gave drink to the thirsty, welcomed the stranger, clothed the naked, and visited the sick and imprisoned; the cursed are those who neglected these works of mercy and love. Neither the blessed nor the cursed are astounded that they are judged by the Son of Man, nor that the judgment is rendered according to the works of charity. The shock comes when they find that in neglecting the poor, the outcast, and the oppressed, they were rejecting Jesus himself. Jesus who came as "Emmanuel" (God with us, Mt 1:23) and who promises to be with his people until the end of the age (Mt 28:20) is hidden in those most in need; to reject them is to reject God made manifest in history.

4. Called to Be Disciples in Community

Jesus summoned his first followers to a change of heart and to take on the yoke of God's reign (Mk 1:14-15; Mt 11:29). They are to be the nucleus of the community which will continue the work of proclaiming and building God's kingdom through the centuries. As Jesus called the first disciples in the midst of their everyday occupations of fishing and tax collecting; so he again calls people in every age in the home, in the workplace, and in the marketplace.

The Church is, as Pope John Paul II reminded us, "a community of disciples" in which "we must see first and foremost Christ saying to each member of the community: follow me." To be a Christian is to join with others in responding to this personal call and in learning the meaning of Christ's life. It is to be sustained by that loving intimacy with the Father that Jesus experienced in his work, in his prayer, and in his suffering.

Discipleship involves imitating the pattern of Jesus' life by openness to God's will in the service of others (Mk 10:42-45). Disciples are also called to follow him on the way of the cross, and to heed his call that those who lose their lives for the sake of the Gospel will save them (Mk 8:34-35). Jesus' death is an example of that greater love which lays down one's life for others (cf. Jn 15:12-18). It is a model for those who suffer persecution for the sake of justice (Mt 5:10). The death of Jesus was not the end of his power and presence, for he was raised up by the power of God. Nor did it mark the end of the disciples' union with him. After Jesus had appeared to them and when they received the gift of the Spirit (Acts 2:1-12), they became apostles of the good news to the ends of the earth. In the face of poverty and persecution they transformed human lives and formed communities which became signs of the power and presence of God. Sharing in this same resurrection faith, contemporary followers of Christ can face the struggles and challenges that await those who bring the gospel vision to bear on our complex economic and social world.

5. Poverty, Riches and the Challenge of Discipleship

The pattern of Christian life as presented in the Gospel of Luke has special relevance today. In her Magnificat, Mary rejoices in a God who scatters the proud, brings down the mighty, and raises up the poor and lowly (Lk 1:51-53). The first public utterance of Jesus is "The Spirit of the Lord is upon me, because he has anointed me to preach good news to the poor" (Lk 4:18 cf. Is 61:1-2). Jesus adds to the blessing on the poor a warning, "Woe to you who are rich, for you have received your consolation" (Lk 6:24). He warns his followers against greed and reliance on abundant possessions and underscores this by the parable of the man whose life is snatched away at the very moment he tries to secure his wealth (Lk 12:13-21). In Luke alone, Jesus tells the parable of the rich man who does not see the poor and suffering Lazarus at his gate (Lk 16:19-31). When the rich man finally "sees" Lazarus, it is from the place of torment and the opportunity for conversion has passed. Pope John Paul II has often recalled this parable to warn the prosperous not to be blind to the great poverty that exists beside great wealth.

Jesus, especially in Luke, lives as a poor man, like the prophets takes the side of the poor, and warns of the dangers of wealth. The terms used for the poor, while primarily describing lack of material goods, also suggest dependence and powerlessness. The poor are also an exiled and oppressed people whom God will rescue (Is 51:21-23) as well as a faithful remnant who will take refuge in God (Zep 3:12-13). Throughout the Bible, material poverty is a misfortune and a cause of sadness. A constant biblical refrain is that the poor must be cared for and protected and that when they are exploited, God hears their cries (Prv 22:22-23). Conversely, even though the goods of the earth are to be enjoyed and people are to thank God for material blessings, wealth is a constant danger. The rich are wise in their own eyes (Prv 28:11), and are prone to apostasy and idolatry (Am 5:4-13; Is 2:6-8), as well as to violence and oppression (Jas 2:6-7). Since they are neither blinded by wealth nor make it into an idol, the poor can be open to God's presence; throughout Israel's history and in early Christianity the poor are agents of God's transforming power.

The poor are often related to the lowly (Mt 5:3, 5) to whom God reveals what was hidden from the wise (Mt 11:25-30). When Jesus calls the poor "blessed," he is not praising their condition of poverty, but their openness to God. When he states that the reign of God is theirs, he voices God's special concern for them, and promises that they are to be the beneficiaries of God's mercy, and justice. When he summons disciples to leave all and follow him, he is calling them to share his own radical trust in the Father and his freedom from care and anxiety (cf. Mt 6:25-34). The practice of evangelical poverty in the Church has always been a living witness to the power of that trust and to the joy that comes with that freedom.

Early Christianity saw the poor as an object of God's special love, but it neither canonized material poverty nor accepted deprivation as an inevitable fact of life. Though few early Christians possessed wealth or power (1 Cor 1:26-28; Jas 2:5), their communities had well-off members (Acts 16:14; 18:8). Jesus' concern for the poor was continued in different forms in the early Church. The early community at Jerusalem distributed its possessions so that "there was no needy person among them," and held "all things in common" – a phrase that suggests not only shared material possessions, but more fundamentally, friendship and mutual concern among all its members (Acts 4:32-34; 2:44). While recognizing the dangers of wealth, the early Church proposed the proper use of possessions to alleviate need and suffering, rather than universal dispossession. Beginning in the first century, and throughout history, Christian communities have developed varied structures to support and sustain the weak and powerless in societies that were often brutally unconcerned about human suffering.

Such perspectives provide a basis today for what is called the "preferential option for the poor." Though the Gospels and in the New Testament as a whole the offer of salvation is extended to all peoples, Jesus takes the side of the most in need, physically and spiritually. The example of Jesus poses a number of challenges to the contemporary Church. It imposes a prophetic mandate to speak for those who have no one to speak for them, to be a defender of the defenseless, who in biblical terms are the poor. It also demands a compassionate vision that enables the Church to see things from the side of the poor and powerless and to assess lifestyle, policies, and social institutions in terms of their impact on the poor. It summons the Church also to be an instrument in assisting people to experience the liberating power of God in their own lives so that they may respond to the Gospel in freedom and in dignity. Finally, and most radically, it calls for an emptying of self, both individually and corporately, that allows the Church to experience the power of God in the midst of poverty and powerlessness.

6. A Community of Hope

The biblical vision of creation, covenant, and community, as well as the summons to discipleship, unfolds under the tension between promise and fulfillment. The whole Bible is spanned by narratives of the first creation (Gn 1-3) and the vision of a restored creation at the end of history (Rv 21:1-4). Just as creation tells us that God's desire was one of wholeness and unity between God and the human family and within this family itself, the images of a new creation give hope that enmity and hatred will cease and justice and peace will reign (Is 11:4-6; 25:1-8). Human life unfolds "between the times," the time of the first creation and that of a restored creation (Rom 8:18-25). Although the ultimate realization of God's plan lies in the future, Christians in union with all people of good will are summed to shape history in the image of God's creative design, and in response to the reign of God proclaimed and embodied by Jesus.

A Christian is a member of a new community, "God's own people" (1 Pt 2:9-10), who, like the people of Exodus, owes its existence to the gracious gift of God and is summoned to respond to God's will made manifest in the life and teaching of Jesus. A Christian walks in the newness of life (Rom 6:4), and is "a new creation; the old has passed away, the new has come" (2 Cor 5:17). This new creation in Christ proclaims that God's creative love is constantly at work, offers sinners forgiveness, and reconciles a broken world. Our action on behalf of justice in our world proceeds from the conviction that, despite the power of injustice and violence, life has been fundamentally changed by the entry of the Word made flesh into human history.

Christian communities that commit themselves to solidarity with those suffering and to confrontation with those attitudes and ways of acting which institutionalize injustice, will themselves experience the power and presence of Christ. They will embody in their lives the values of the new creation while they labor under the old. The quest for economic and social justice will always combine hope and realism, and must be renewed by every generation. It involves diagnosing those situations that continue to alienate the world from God's creative love as well as presenting hopeful alternatives that arise from living in a renewed creation. This quest arises from faith and is sustained by hope as it seeks to speak to a broken world of God's justice and loving kindness.

7. A Living Tradition

Our reflection on U.S. economic life today must be rooted in this biblical vision of the kingdom and discipleship, but it must also be shaped by the rich and complex tradition of Catholic life and thought. Throughout its history, the Christian community has listened to the words of Scripture and sought to enact them in the midst of daily life in very different historical and cultural contexts.

In the first centuries, when Christians were a minority in a hostile society, they cared for one another through generous almsgiving. In the patristic era, the church fathers repeatedly stressed that the goods of the earth were created by God for the benefit of every person without exception, and that all have special duties toward those in need. The monasteries of the Middle Ages were centers of prayer, learning, and education. They contributed greatly to the cultural and economic life of the towns and cities that sprang up around them. In the twelfth century the new mendicant orders dedicated themselves to following Christ in poverty and to the proclamation of the good news to the poor.

These same religious communities also nurtured some of the greatest theologians of the Church's tradition, thinkers who synthesized the call of Christ with the philosophical learning Greek, Roman, Jewish, and Arab worlds. Thomas Aquinas and the other scholastics devoted rigorous intellectual energy to clarifying the meaning of both personal virtue and justice in society. In more recent centuries Christians began to build a large network of hospitals, orphanages, and schools, to serve the poor and society at large. And beginning with Leo XIII's *Rerum Novarum*, down to the writings and speeches of John Paul II, the popes have more systematically addressed the rapid change of modern society in a series of social encyclicals. These teachings of the modern popes and of the Second Vatican Council are especially significant for efforts to respond to the problems facing society today.

We also have much to learn from the strong emphasis in Protestant traditions on the vocation of lay people in the world and from ecumenical efforts to develop an economic ethic that addresses newly emergent problems. And in a special way our fellow Catholics in developing countries have much to teach us about the Christian response to an ever more interdependent world.

Christians today are called by God to carry on this tradition through active love of neighbor, a love that responds to the special challenges of this moment in human history. The world is wounded by sin and injustice, in need of conversion and of the transformation that comes when persons enter more deeply into the mystery of the death and Resurrection of Christ. The concerns of this pastoral letter are not at all peripheral to the central mystery at the heart of the Church. They are integral to the proclamation of the Gospel and part of the vocation of every Christian today.

B. Ethical Norms for Economic Life

These biblical and theological themes shape the overall Christian perspective on economic ethics. This perspective is also subscribed to by many who do not share Christian religious convictions. Human understanding and religious belief are complementary, not contradictory. For human beings are created in God's image, and their dignity is manifest in the ability to reason and understand, in their freedom to shape their own lives and the life of their communities, and in the capacity for love and friendship. In proposing ethical norms, therefore, we appeal both to Christians and to all in our pluralist society to show that respect and reverence owed to the dignity of every person. Intelligent reflection on the social and economic realities of today is also indispensable in the effort to respond to economic circumstances never envisioned in biblical times. Therefore, we now want to propose an ethical framework that can guide economic life today in ways that are both faithful to the Gospel and shaped by human experience and reason.

First we outline the *duties* all people have to each other and to the whole community: love of neighbor, the basic requirements of justice, and the special obligation to those who are poor or vulnerable. Corresponding to these duties are the "human rights" of every person; the obligation to protect the dignity of all demands respect for these rights. Finally these duties and rights entail several *priorities* that should guide the economic choices of individuals, communities, and the nation as a whole.

1. The Responsibilities of Social Living

Human life is life in community. Catholic social teaching proposes several complementary perspectives that show how moral responsibilities and duties in the economic sphere are rooted in this call to community.

a. Love and Solidarity

The commandments to love God with all one's heart and to love one's neighbor as oneself are the heart and soul of Christian morality. Jesus offers himself as the model of this all-inclusive love: "… love one another as I have loved you" (Jn 15:12). These commands point out the path toward true human fulfillment and happiness. They are not arbitrary restrictions on human freedom. Only active love of God and neighbor makes the fullness of community happen. Christians look forward in hope to a true communion among all persons with each other and with God. The Spirit of Christ labors in history to build up the bonds of solidarity among all persons until that day on which their union is brought to perfection in the Kingdom of God. Indeed Christian theological reflection on the very reality of God as a trinitarian unity of persons – Father, Son, and Holy Spirit – shows that being a person means being united to other persons in mutual love.

What the Bible and Christian tradition teach, human wisdom confirms. Centuries before Christ, the Greeks and Romans spoke of the human person as a "social animal" made for friendship, community, and public life. These insights show that human beings achieve self-realization not in isolation, but in interaction with others.

The virtues of citizenship are an expression of Christian love more crucial in today's interdependent world than ever before. These virtues grow out of a lively sense of one's dependence on the commonweal and obligations to it. This civic commitment must also guide the economic institutions of society. In the absence of a vital sense of citizenship among the businesses, corporations, labor unions, and other groups that shape economic life, society as a whole is endangered. Solidarity is another name for this social friendship and civic commitment that make human moral and economic life possible.

The Christian tradition recognizes, of course, that the fullness of love and community will be achieved only when God's work in Christ comes to completion in the kingdom of God. This kingdom has been inaugurated among us, but God's redeeming and transforming work is not yet complete. Within history, knowledge of how to achieve the goal of social unity is limited. Human sin continues to wound the lives of both individuals and larger social bodies and places obstacles in the path toward greater social solidarity. If efforts to protect human dignity are to be effective, they must take these limits on knowledge and love

into account. Nevertheless, sober realism should not be confused with resigned or cynical pessimism. It is a challenge to develop a courageous hope that can sustain efforts that will sometimes be arduous and protracted.

b. Justice and Participation

Biblical justice is the goal we strive for. This rich biblical understanding portrays a just society as one marked by the fullness of love, compassion, holiness, and peace. On their path through history, however, sinful human beings need more specific guidance on how to move toward the realization of this great vision of God's Kingdom. This guidance is contained in the norms of basic or minimal justice. These norms state the minimum levels of mutual care and respect that all persons owe to each other in an imperfect world. Catholic social teaching, like must philosophical reflection, distinguishes three dimensions of basic justice: commutative justice, distributive justice, and social justice.

Commutative justice calls for fundamental fairness in all agreements and exchanges between individuals or private social groups. It demands respect for the equal human dignity of all persons in economic transactions, contracts, or promises. For example, workers owe their employers diligent work in exchange for their wages. Employers are obligated to treat their employees as persons, paying them fair wages in exchange for the work done and establishing conditions and patterns of work that are truly human.

Distributive justice requires that the allocation of income, wealth, and power in society be evaluated in light of its effects on persons whose basic material needs are unmet. The Second Vatican Council stated: "The right to have a share of earthly goods sufficient for oneself and one's family belongs to everyone. The fathers and doctors of the Church held this view, teaching that we are obliged to come to the relief of the poor and to do so not merely out of our superfluous goods." Minimum material resources are an absolute necessity for human life. If persons are to be recognized as members of the human community, then the community has an obligation to help fulfill these basic needs unless an absolute scarcity of resources makes this strictly impossible. No such scarcity exists in the United States today.

Justice also has implications for the way the larger social, economic, and political institutions of society are organized. *Social justice implies that persons have an obligation to be active and productive participants in the life of society and that society has a duty to enable them to participate in this way.* This form of justice can also be called "contributive," for it stresses the duty of all who are able to help create the goods, services, and other nonmaterial or spiritual values necessary for the welfare of the whole community. In the words of Pius XI, "It is of the very essence of social justice to demand from each individual all that is necessary for the common good." Productivity is essential if the community is to have the resources to serve the well-being of all. Productivity, however, cannot be measured solely by its output in goods and services. Patterns of production must also be measured in light of their impact on the fulfillment of basic needs, employment levels, patterns of discrimination, environmental quality, and sense of community.

The meaning of social justice also includes a duty to organize economic and social institutions so that people can contribute to society in ways that respect their freedom and the dignity of their labor. Work should enable the working person to become "more a human being," more capable of acting intelligently, freely, and in ways that lead to self-realization.

Economic conditions that leave large numbers of able people unemployed, underemployed, or employed in dehumanizing conditions fail to meet the converging demands of these three forms of basic justice. Work with adequate pay for all who seek it is the primary means of achieving basic justice in our society. Discrimination in job opportunities or income levels on the basis of race, sex, or other arbitrary standards can never be justified. It is a scandal that such discrimination continues in the United States today. Where the effects of past discrimination persist, society has an obligation to take positive steps to overcome the legacy of injustice. Judiciously administered affirmative action programs in education and employment can be important expressions of the drive for solidarity and participation that is at the heart of true justice. Social harm calls for social relief.

Basic justice also calls for the establishment of a floor of material well-being on which all can stand. This is a duty of the whole of society and it creates particular obligations for those with greater resources. This duty calls into question extreme inequalities of income and consumption when so many lack basic necessities. Catholic social teaching does not maintain that a flat, arithmetical equality of income and wealth is a demand of justice, but it does challenge economic arrangements that leave large numbers of people impoverished. Further, it sees extreme inequality as a threat to the solidarity of the human community, for great

disparities lead to deep social divisions and conflict.

This means that all of us must examine our way of living in the light of the needs of the poor. Christian faith and the norms of justice impose distinct limits on what we consume and how we view material goods. The great wealth of the United States can easily blind us to the poverty that exists in this nation and the destitution of hundreds of millions of people in other parts of the world. Americans are challenged today as never before to develop the inner freedom to resist the temptation constantly to seek more. Only in this way will the nation avoid what Paul VI called "the most evident form of moral underdevelopment," namely greed.

These duties call not only for individual charitable giving but also for a more systematic approach by businesses, labor unions, and the many other groups that shape economic life – as well as government. The concentration of privilege that exists today results far more from institutional relationships that distribute power and wealth inequitably than from differences in talent or lack of desire to work. These institutional patterns must be examined and revised if we are to meet the demands of basic justice. For example, a system of taxation based on assessment according to ability to pay is a prime necessity for the fulfillment of these social obligations.

c. Overcoming Marginalization and Powerlessness

These fundamental duties can be summarized this way: *basic justice demands the establishment of minimum levels of participation in the life of the human community for all persons.* The ultimate injustice is for a person or group to be treated actively or abandoned passively as if they were nonmembers of the human race. To treat people this way is effectively to say they simply do not count as human beings. This can take many forms, all of which can be described as varieties of marginalization, or exclusion from social life. This exclusion can occur in the political sphere: restriction of free speech, concentration of power in the hands of a few, or outright repression by the state. It can also take economic forms that are equally harmful. Within the United States, individuals, families, and local communities fall victim to a downward cycle of poverty generated by economic forces they are powerless to influence. The poor, the disabled, and the unemployed too often are simply left behind. This pattern is even more severe beyond our borders in the least-developed countries. Whole nations are prevented from fully participating in the international economic order because they lack the power to change their disadvantaged position.

Many people within the less developed countries are excluded from sharing in the meager resources available in their homelands by unjust elites and unjust governments. These patterns of exclusion are created by free human beings. In this sense they can be called forms of social sin. Acquiescence in them or the failure to correct them when it is possible to do so is a sinful dereliction of Christian duty.

Recent Catholic social thought regards the task of overcoming these patterns of exclusion and powerlessness as a most basic demand of justice. Stated positively, justice demands that social institutions be ordered in a way that guarantees all persons the ability to participate actively in the economic, political, and cultural life of society. The level of participation may be legitimately greater for some persons than for others, but there is a basic level of access that must be made available for all. Such participation is an essential expression of the social nature of human beings and of their communitarian vocation.

2. Human Rights: The Minimum Conditions for Life in Community

Catholic social teaching spells out the basic demands of justice in greater detail in the human rights of every person. These fundamental rights are prerequisites for a dignified life in community. The Bible vigorously affirms the sacredness of every person as a creature formed in the image and likeness of God. The biblical emphasis on covenant and community also shows that human dignity can only be realized and protected in solidarity with others. In Catholic social thought, therefore, respect for human rights and a strong sense of both personal and community responsibility are linked, not opposed. Vatican II described the common good as "the sum of those conditions of social life which allow social groups and their individual members relatively thorough and ready access to their own fulfillment." These conditions include the right to fulfillment of material needs, a guarantee of fundamental freedoms, and the protection of relationships that are essential to participation in the life of society. These rights are bestowed on human beings by God and grounded in the nature and dignity of human persons. They are not created by society. Indeed society has a duty to secure and protect them.

The full range of human rights has been systematically outlined by John XXIII in his encyclical Peace on Earth (*Pacem in Terris*). His discussion echoes the United Nations Universal Declaration of Human Rights and implies that internationally accepted human rights standards are strongly supported by Catholic teaching. These rights include the civil and political rights to freedom of speech, worship, and assembly. A number of human rights also concern human welfare and are of a specifically economic nature. First among these are the rights to life, food, clothing, shelter, rest, medical care, and basic education. These are indispensable to the protection of human dignity. In order to ensure these necessities, all persons have a right to earn a living, which for most people in our economy is through remunerative employment. All persons also have a right to security in the event of sickness, unemployment, and old age. Participation in the life of the community calls for the protection of this same right to employment, as well as the right to healthful working conditions, to wages, and other benefits sufficient to provide individuals and their families with a standard of living in keeping with human dignity, and to the possibility of property ownership. These fundamental personal rights – civil and political as well as social and economic – state the minimum conditions for social institutions that respect human dignity, social solidarity, and justice. They are all essential to human dignity and to the integral development of both individuals and society, and are thus moral issues. Any denial of these rights harms persons and wounds the human community. Their serious and sustained denial violates individuals and destroys solidarity among persons.

Social and economic rights call for a mode of implementation different from that required to secure civil and political rights. Freedom of worship and of speech imply immunity from interference on the part of both other persons and the government. The rights to education, employment, and social security, for example, are empowerments that call for positive action by individuals and society at large.

However, both kinds of rights call for positive action to create social and political institutions that enable all persons to become active members of society. Civil and political rights allow persons to participate freely in the public life of the community, for example, through free speech, assembly, and the vote. In democratic countries these rights have been secured through a long and vigorous history of creating the institutions of constitutional government. In seeking to secure the full range of social and economic rights today, a similar effort to shape new economic arrangements will be necessary.

The first step in such an effort is the development of a new cultural consensus that the basic economic conditions of human welfare are essential to human dignity and are due persons by right. Second, the securing of these rights will make demands on all members of society, on all private sector institutions, and on government. A concerted effort on all levels in our society is needed to meet these basic demands of justice and solidarity. Indeed political democracy and a commitment to secure economic rights are mutually reinforcing.

Securing economic rights for all will be an arduous task. There are a number of precedents in the U.S. history, however, which show that the work has already begun. The country needs a serious dialogue about the appropriate levels of private and public sector involvement that are needed to move forward. There is certainly room for diversity of opinion in the Church and in U.S. society on *how* to protect the human dignity and economic rights of all our brothers and sisters. In our view, however, there can be no legitimate disagreement on the basic moral objectives.

3. Moral Priorities for the Nation

The common good demands justice for all, the protection of the human rights for all. Making cultural and economic institutions more supportive of the freedom, power, and security of individuals and families must be a central, long-range objective for the nation. Every person has a duty to contribute to building up the commonweal. All have a responsibility to develop their talents through education. Adults must contribute to society through their individual vocations and talents. Parents are called to guide their children to the maturity of Christian adulthood and responsible citizenship. Everyone has special duties toward the poor and marginalized. Living up to these responsibilities, however, is often made difficult by the social and economic patterns of society. Schools and educational policies both public and private often serve the privileged exceedingly well, while the children of the poor are effectively abandoned as second-class citizens. Great stresses are created in family life by the way work is organized and scheduled, and by the social and cultural values communicated on TV. Many in the lower middle class are barely getting by and fear becoming victims of economic forces over which they have no control.

The obligation to provide justice for all means that the poor have the single most urgent economic claim on the conscience of the nation. Poverty can take many forms, spiritual as well as material. All people face struggles of the spirit as they ask deep questions about their purpose in life. Many have serious problems in mar-

riage and family life at some time in their lives, and all of us face the certain reality of sickness and death. The Gospel of Christ proclaims that God's love is stronger than all these forms of diminishment. Material deprivation, however, seriously compounds such sufferings of the spirit and heart. To see a loved one sick is bad enough, but to have no possibility of obtaining health care is worse. To face family problems, such as death of a spouse or a divorce, can be devastating, but to have these lead to the loss of one's home and end with living on the streets is something no one should have to endure in a country as rich as ours. In developing countries these human problems are even more greatly intensified by extreme material deprivation. This form of human suffering can be reduced if our own country, so rich in resources, chooses to increase its assistance.

As individuals and as a nation, therefore, we are called to make a fundamental "option for the poor." The obligation to evaluate social and economic activity from the viewpoint of the poor and the powerless arises from the radical command to love one's neighbor as one's self. Those who are marginalized and whose rights are denied have privileged claims if society is to provide justice for *all*. This obligation is deeply rooted in Christian belief. As Paul VI stated:

"In teaching us charity, the Gospel instructs us in the preferential respect due to the poor and the special situation they have in society: the more fortunate should renounce some of their rights so as to place their goods more generously at the service of others."

John Paul II has described this special obligation to the poor as "a call to have a special openness with the small and the weak, those that suffer and weep, those that are humiliated and left on the margin of society, so as to help them win their dignity as human persons and children of God."

The primary purpose of this special commitment to the poor is to enable them to become active participants in the life of society. It is to enable all persons to share in and contribute to the common good . The "option for the poor," therefore, is not an adversarial slogan that pits one group or class against another. Rather it states that the deprivation and powerlessness of the poor wounds the whole community. The extent of their suffering is a measure of how far we are from being a true community of persons. These wounds will be healed only by greater solidarity with the poor and among the poor themselves.

In summary, the norms of love, basic justice, and human rights imply that personal decisions, social policies, and economic institutions should be governed by several key priorities. These priorities do not specify everything that must be considered in economic decision making. They do indicate the most fundamental and urgent objectives.

a. The fulfillment of the basic needs of the poor is of the highest priority. Personal decisions, policies of private and public bodies, and power relationships must be all evaluated by their effects on those who lack the minimum necessities of nutrition, housing, education, and health care. In particular, this principle recognizes that meeting fundamental human needs must come before the fulfillment of desires for luxury consumer goods, for profits not conducive to the common good, and for unnecessary military hardware.

b. Increasing active participation in economic life by those who are presently excluded or vulnerable is a high social priority. The human dignity of all is realized when people gain the power to work together to improve their lives, strengthen their families, and contribute to society. Basic justice calls for more than providing help to the poor and other vulnerable members of society. It recognizes the priority of policies and programs that support family life and enhance economic participation through employment and widespread ownership of property. It challenges privileged economic power in favor of the well-being of all. It points to the need to improve the present situation of those unjustly discriminated against in the past. And it has very important implications for both the domestic and the international distribution of power.

c. The investment of wealth, talent, and human energy should be specially directed to benefit those who are poor or economically insecure. Achieving a more just economy in the United States and the world depends in part on increasing economic resources and productivity. In addition, the ways these resources are invested and managed must be scrutinized in light of their effects on non-monetary values. Investment and management decisions have crucial moral dimensions: they create jobs or eliminate them; they can push vulnerable families over the edge into poverty or give them new hope for the future; they help or hinder the building of a more equitable society. They can have either positive or negative influence on the fairness of the global economy. Therefore, this priority presents a strong moral challenge to policies that put large amounts of talent and capital into the production of luxury consumer goods and military technology while failing to invest sufficiently in education, health, the basic infrastructure of our society and economic

sectors that produce urgently needed jobs, goods and services.

d. Economic and social policies as well as organization of the work world should be continually evaluated in light of their impact on the strength and stability of family life. The long-range future of this nation is intimately linked with the well-being of families, for the family is the most basic form of human community. Efficiency and competition in the marketplace must be moderated by greater concern for the way work schedules and compensation support or threaten the bonds between spouses and between parents and children. Health, education and social service programs should be scrutinized in light of how well they ensure both individual dignity and family integrity.

These priorities are not policies. They are norms that should guide the economic choices of all and shape economic institutions. They can help the United States move forward to fulfill the duties of justice and protect economic rights. They were strongly affirmed as implications of Catholic social teaching by Pope John Paul II during his visit to Canada in 1984: "The needs of the poor take priority over the desires of the rich; the rights of workers over the maximization of profits; the preservation of the environment over uncontrolled industrial expansion; the production to meet social needs over production for military purposes." There will undoubtedly be disputes about the concrete applications of these priorities in our complex world. We do not seek to foreclose discussion about them. However, we believe that an effort to move in the direction they indicate is urgently needed.

The economic challenge of today has many parallels with the political challenge that confronted the founders of our nation. In order to create a new form of political democracy they were compelled to develop ways of thinking and political institutions that had never existed before. Their efforts were arduous and their goals imperfectly realized, but they launched an experiment in the protection of civil and political rights that has prospered through the efforts of those who came after them. *We believe the time has come for a similar experiment in securing economic rights: the creation of an order that guarantees the minimum conditions of human dignity in the economic sphere for every person.* By drawing on the resources of the Catholic moral-religious tradition, we hope to make a contribution through this letter to such a new "American Experiment": a new venture to secure economic justice for all.

C. Working for Greater Justice: Persons and Institutions

The economy of this nation has been built by the labor of human hands and minds. Its future will be forged by the ways persons direct all this work toward greater justice. The economy in not a machine that operates according to its own inexorable laws, and persons are not mere objects tossed about by economic forces. Pope John Paul II has stated that "human work is a key, probably the essential key, to the whole social question." The Pope's understanding of work includes virtually all forms of productive human activity: agriculture, entrepreneurship, industry, the care of children, the sustaining of family life, politics, medical care, and scientific research. Leisure, prayer, celebration, and the arts are also central to the realization of human dignity and to the development of a rich cultural life. It is in their daily work, however, that persons become the subjects and creators of the economic life of the nation. Thus, it is primarily through their daily labor that people make their most important contributions to economic justice.

All work has a threefold moral significance. First, it is a principal way that people exercise the distinctive human capacity for self-expression and self-realization. Second, it is the ordinary way for human beings to fulfill their material needs. Finally, work enables people to contribute to the well-being of the larger community. Work is not only for one's self. It is for one's family, for the nation, and indeed for the benefit of the entire human family .

These three moral concerns should be visible in the work of all, no matter what their role in the economy: blue collar workers, managers, homemakers, politicians, and others. They should also govern the activities of the many different, overlapping communities and institutions that make up society: families, neighborhoods, small businesses, giant corporations, trade unions, the various levels of government, international organizations, and a host of other human associations including communities of faith.

Catholic social teaching calls for respect for the full richness of social life. The need for vital contributions from different human associations – ranging in size from the family to government – has been classically expressed in Catholic social teaching in the "principle of subsidiarity":

"Just as it is gravely wrong to take from individuals what they can accomplish by their own initiative and industry and give it to the community, so also it is an injustice and at the same time a grave evil and disturbance of right order to assign a greater and higher association what lesser and subordinate organizations can do. For every social activity ought of its very nature to furnish help (subsidium) to the members of the body social, and never destroy and absorb them."

This principle guarantees institutional pluralism. It provides space for freedom, initiative, and creativity on the part of many social agents. At the same time, it insists that all these agents should work in ways that help build up the social body. Therefore, in all their activities these groups should be working in ways that express their distinctive capacities for action, that help meet human needs, and that make true contributions to the common good of the human community. The task of creating a more just U.S. economy is a vocation of all and depends on strengthening the virtues of public service and responsible citizenship in personal life and on all levels of institutional life.

Without attempting to describe the tasks of all the different groups that make up society, we want to point to the specific rights and duties of some of the persons and institutions whose work for justice will be particularly important to the future of the United States economy. These rights and duties are among the concrete implications of the principle of subsidiarity. Further implications will be discussed in Chapter IV of this letter.

1. Working People and Labor Unions

Though John Paul II's understanding of work is a very inclusive one, it fully applies to those customarily called "workers" or "labor" in the United States. Labor has a great dignity, so great that all who are able to work are obligated to do so. The duty to work derives both from God's command and from a responsibility to one's own humanity and to the common good. The virtue of industriousness is also an expression of a person's dignity and solidarity with others. All working people are called to contribute to the common good by seeking excellence in production and service.

Because work is this important, people have a right to employment. In return for their labor, workers have a right to wages and other benefits sufficient to sustain life in dignity. As Pope Leo XIII stated, every working person has "the right of securing things to sustain life." The way power is distributed in a free market economy frequently gives employers greater bargaining power than employees in the negotiation of labor contracts. Such unequal power may press workers into a choice between an inadequate wage or no wage at all. But justice, not charity, demands certain minimum wage guarantees. The provision of wages and other benefits sufficient to support a family in dignity is a basic necessity to prevent this exploitation of workers. The dignity of workers also requires adequate health care, security for old age or disability, unemployment compensation, healthful working conditions, weekly rest, periodic holidays for recreation and leisure, and reasonable security against arbitrary dismissal. These provisions are all essential if workers are to be treated as persons rather than simply a "factor of production."

The Church fully supports the right of workers to form unions or other associations to secure their rights to fair wages and working conditions. This is a specific application of the more general right to associate. In the words of Pope John Paul II, "The experience of history teaches that organizations of this type are an indispensable element of social life, especially in modern industrial societies." Unions may also legitimately resort to strikes where this is the only available means to the justice owed to workers. No one may deny the right to organize without attacking human dignity itself. Therefore, we firmly oppose organized efforts, such as those regrettably now seen in this country, to break existing unions and prevent workers from organizing. Migrant agricultural workers today are particularly in need of the protection, including the right to organize and bargain collectively. U.S. labor law reform is needed to meet these problems as well as to provide more timely and effective remedies for unfair labor practices.

Denial of the right to organize has been pursued ruthlessly in many countries beyond our borders. We vehemently oppose violations of the freedom to associate, wherever they occur, for they are an intolerable attack on social solidarity.

Along with the rights of workers and unions go a number of important responsibilities. Individual workers have obligations to their employers, and trade unions also have duties to society as a whole. Union management in particular carries a strong responsibility for the good name of the entire union movement. Workers must use their collective power to contribute to the well-being of the whole community and should avoid pressing demands whose fulfillment would damage the common good and the rights of more vulnerable members of society. It should be noted, however, that wages paid to workers are but one of the factors affecting the competitiveness of industries. Thus, it is unfair to expect unions to make concessions if managers and shareholders do not make at least equal sacrifices.

Many U.S. unions have exercised leadership in the struggle for justice for minorities and women. Racial and sexual discrimination, however, have blotted the record of some unions. Organized labor has a responsibility to work positively toward eliminating the injustice this discrimination has caused.

Perhaps the greatest challenge facing United States workers and unions today is that of developing a new vision of their role in the United States economy of the future. The labor movement in the United States stands at a crucial moment. The dynamism of the unions that led to their rapid growth in the middle decades of this century has been replaced by a decrease in the percentage of U.S. workers who are organized. American workers are under heave pressures today that threaten their jobs. The restrictions on the right to organize in many countries abroad make labor costs lower there, threaten American workers and their jobs, and lead to the exploitation of workers in these countries. In these difficult circumstances, guaranteeing the rights of U.S. workers calls for imaginative vision and creative new steps, not reactive or simply defensive strategies. For example, organized labor can play a very important role in helping provide the education and training needed to help keep workers employable. Unions can also help both their own members and workers in developing countries by increasing their international efforts. A vital labor movement will be one that looks to the future with a deepened sense of global interdependence.

There are many signs that these challenges are being discussed by creative labor leaders today. Deeper and broader discussions of this sort are needed. This does not mean that only organized labor faces these new problems. All other sectors and institutions in the U.S. economy need similar vision and imagination. Indeed new forms of cooperation among labor, management, government, and other social groups are essential, and will be discussed in Chapter VI of this letter.

2. Owners and Managers

The economy's success in fulfilling the demands of justice will depend on how its vast resources and wealth are managed. Property owners, managers, and investors of financial capital must all contribute to creating a more just society. Securing economic justice depends heavily on the leadership of men and women in business and on wise investment by private enterprises. Pope John Paul II has pointed out, "The degree of well-being which society today enjoys would be unthinkable without the dynamic figure of the business person, whose function consists of organizing human labor and the means of production so as to give rise to the goods and services necessary for the prosperity and progress of the community." The freedom of entrepreneurship, business, and finance should be protected, but the accountability of this freedom to the common good and the norms of justice must be assured.

Persons in management face many hard choices each day, choices on which the well-being of many others depends. Commitment to the public good and not simply the private good of their firms is at the heart of what it means to call their work a vocation and not simply a career or a job. We believe that the norms and priorities discussed in this letter can be of help as they pursue their important tasks. The duties of individuals in the business world, however, do not exhaust the ethical dimensions of business and finance. The size of a firm or bank is in many cases an indicator of relative power. Large corporations and large financial institutions have considerable power to help shape economic institutions within the United States and throughout the world. With this power goes responsibility and the need for those who manage it to be held to moral and institutional accountability.

Business and finance have the duty to be faithful trustees of the resources at their disposal. No one can ever own capital resources absolutely or control their use without regard for others and society as a whole. This applies first of all to land and natural resources. Short-term profits reaped at the cost of depletion of natural resources or the pollution of the environment violate this trust.

Resources created by human industry are also held in trust. Owners and managers have not created this capital on their own. They have benefited from the work of many others and from the local communities that support their endeavors. They are accountable to these workers and communities when making decisions. For example, reinvestment in technological innovation is often considered crucial for the long-term viability of a firm. The use of financial resources solely in pursuit of short-term profits can stunt the production of needed goods and services; a broader vision of managerial responsibility is needed.

The Catholic tradition has long defended the right to private ownership of productive property. This right is an important element in a just economic policy. It enlarges our capacity for creativity and initiative. Small and medium-sized farms, businesses, and entrepreneurial enterprises are among the most creative and efficient sectors of our economy. They should be highly valued by the people of the United States, as are land ownership and home ownership. Widespread distribution of property can help avoid excessive concentration of economic and political power. For these reasons ownership should be made possible for a broad sector of our population.

The common good may sometimes demand that the right to own be limited by public involvement in the planning or ownership of certain sectors of the economy. Support of private ownership does not mean that anyone has the right to unlimited accumulation of wealth. "Private property does not constitute for anyone an absolute or unconditional right. No one is justified in keeping for his exclusive use what he does not need, when others lack necessities." Pope John Paul II has referred to limits placed on ownership by the duty to serve the common good as a "social mortgage" on private property. For example, these limits are the basis of society's exercise of eminent domain over privately owned land needed for roads or other essential public goods. The Church's teaching opposes collectivist and statist economic approaches. But it also rejects the notion that a free market automatically produces justice. Therefore, as Pope John Paul II has argued, "One cannot exclude the socialization, in suitable conditions, of certain means of production." The determination of when such conditions exist must be made on a case by case basis in light of the demands of the common good.

United States business and financial enterprises can also help determine the justice or injustice of the world economy. They are not all-powerful, but their real power is unquestionable. Transnational corporations and financial institutions can make positive contributions to development and global solidarity. Pope John Paul II has pointed out, however, that the desire to maximize profits and reduce cost of natural resources and labor has often tempted these transnational enterprises to behavior that increases inequality and decreases the stability of the international order. By collaborating with those national governments that serve their citizens justly and with intergovernmental agencies, these corporations can contribute to overcoming the desperate plight of many persons throughout the world.

Business people, managers, investors, and financiers follow a vital Christian vocation when they act responsibly and seek the common good. We encourage and support a renewed sense of vocation in the business community. We also recognize that the way business people serve society is governed and limited by the incentives which flow from tax policies, and availability of credit, and other public policies.

Businesses have a right to an institutional framework that does not penalize enterprises that act responsibly. Governments must provide regulations and a system of taxation which encourage firms to preserve the environment, employ disadvantaged workers, and create jobs in depressed areas. Managers and stockholders should not be torn between their responsibilities to their organizations and their responsibilities toward society as a whole.

3. Citizens and Government

In addition to rights and duties related to specific roles in the economy, everyone has obligations based simply on membership in the social community. By fulfilling these duties, we create a true commonwealth. Volunteering time, talent, and money to work for greater justice is a fundamental expression of Christian love and social solidarity. All who have more than they need must come to the aid of the poor. People with professional or technical skills needed to enhance the lives of others have a duty to share them. And the poor have similar obligations: to work together as individuals and families to build up their communities by acts of social solidarity and justice. These voluntary efforts to overcome injustice are part of the Christian vocation.

Every citizen also has the responsibility to work to secure justice and human rights through an organized social response. In the words of Pius XI, "Charity will never be true charity unless it takes justice into account … Let no one attempt with small gifts of charity to exempt himself from the great duties imposed by justice." The guaranteeing of basic justice for all is not an optional expression of largesse but an inescapable duty for the whole of society.

The traditional distinction between society and the state in Catholic social teaching provides the basic framework for such organized public efforts. The Church opposes all statist and totalitarian approaches to socioeconomic questions. Social life is richer than governmental power can encompass. All groups that compose society have responsibilities to respond to the demands of justice. We have just outlined some of the duties of labor unions and business and financial enterprises. These must be supplemented by initiatives by local community groups, professional associations, educational institutions, churches, and synagogues. All the groups that give life to this society have important roles to play in pursuit of economic justice.

For this reason, it is all the more significant that the teachings of the Church insist that *government has a moral function: protecting human rights and securing basic justice for all members of the commonwealth*. Society as a whole and in all its diversity is responsible for building up the common good. But it is the government's role to guarantee the minimum conditions that make this rich social activity possible, namely, human rights and justice. This obligation also falls on individual citizens as they choose their representatives and participate in shaping public opinion.

More specifically, it is the responsibility of all citizens, acting through their government, to assist and empower the poor, the disadvantaged, the handicapped, and the unemployed. Government should assume a positive role in generating employment and establishing fair labor practices, in guaranteeing the provision and maintenance of the economy's infrastructure, such as roads, bridges, harbors, public means of communication, and transport. It should regulate trade and commerce in the interest of fairness. Government may levy the taxes necessary to meet these responsibilities, and citizens have a moral obligation to pay those taxes. The way society responds to the needs of the poor through its public policies is the litmus test of its justice or injustice. The political debate about these policies is the indispensable forum for dealing with the conflicts and tradeoffs that will always be present in the pursuit of a more just economy.

The primary norm for determining the scope and limits of governmental intervention is the "principle of subsidiarity" cited above. This principle states that, in order to protect basic justice, government should undertake only those initiatives which exceed the capacities of individuals or private groups acting independently. Government should not replace or destroy smaller communities and individual initiative. Rather it should help them contribute more effectively to social well-being and supplement their activity when the demands of justice exceed their capacities. This does not mean, however, that the government that governs least, governs best. Rather it defines good government intervention as that which truly "helps" other social groups contribute to the common good by directing, urging, restraining, and regulating economic activity as "the occasion requires and necessity demands." This calls for cooperation and consensus building among the diverse agents in our economic life, including government. The precise form of government involvement in this process cannot be determined in the abstract. It will depend on an assessment of specific needs and the most effective ways to address them.

D. Christian Hope and the Courage to Act

The Christian vision is based on the conviction that God has destined the human race and all creation for "a kingdom of truth and life, of holiness and grace, of justice, love and peace." This conviction gives Christians strong hope as they face the economic struggles of the world today. This hope is not a naive optimism that imagines that simple formulas for creating a fully just society are ready at hand. The Church's experience through history and in nations throughout the world today has made it wary of all ideologies that claim to have the final answer to humanity's problems. Christian hope has a much stronger foundation than such ideologies, for it rests on the knowledge that God is at work in the world, "preparing a new dwelling place and a new earth where justice will abide."

This hope stimulates and strengthens Christian efforts to create a more just economic order in spite of difficulties and setbacks. Christian hope is strong and resilient, for it is rooted in a faith that knows that the fullness of life comes to those who follow Christ in the way of the Cross. In pursuit of concrete solutions, all members of the Christian community are called to an ever finer discernment of the hurts and opportunities in the world around them, in order to respond to the most pressing needs and thus build up a more just society. This is a communal task calling for dialogue, experimentation, and imagination. It also calls for deep faith and a courageous love.

Unitarian Universalist Economic Justice Statements

Working for a Just Economic Community

1997 General Resolution

BECAUSE Unitarian Universalists covenant to affirm and promote justice, equity and compassion in human relations;

WHEREAS current global economic, social and political developments have brought about greater concentration of wealth and economic power in the hands of major corporations and wealthy individuals while resulting in a lower standard of living and growing lack of opportunity for many people;

WHEREAS in the United States there is increasing disparity between the wealthiest ten percent and the remainder of the population;

WHEREAS democracy is at risk as wealthy individuals and corporations continue to dominate the United States' political process;

WHEREAS many corporations benefit from preferential treatment in the form of grants, subsidies and tax deductions, frequently referred to as "corporate welfare," while increasingly neglecting their moral obligation to the welfare of their employees, communities, and the global ecosystem;

WHEREAS government funding for social programs is declining while spending for penal institutions is escalating;

WHEREAS access to legal recourse has been reduced and restricted at the same time that public assistance is being administered through state block grants with the likelihood that such funds will be reduced or diverted to other uses;

WHEREAS we now see massive numbers of people who are homeless, children who are impoverished, people working for below poverty-level pay, environmental degradation, lack of adequate health care and erosion of workers' rights; and

WHEREAS the poor, immigrants, racial minorities, unemployed and aged are unjustly blamed for the perceived decline in the quality of life of upper and middle income groups;

THEREFORE BE IT RESOLVED that the Unitarian Universalist Association urges its member congregations and individual Unitarian Universalists in the United States to work in cooperation with Unitarian Universalists for a Just Economic Community, other public-spirited organizations and individuals in support of a more just economic community, and toward that objective to implement practices in our own congregations which are congruent with the intent of this resolution, and to work specifically in favor of mechanisms such as:

1. A true single minimum wage, applicable to all workers, that provides an adequate standard of living;

2. A full employment policy, utilizing public works, if necessary, to supplement employment levels achieved by private enterprise;

3. Government restrictions and consumer boycotts, where appropriate, on the import of goods produced under substandard conditions, forced labor, child labor, very low wages, or conditions that contribute to environmental degradation;

4. A more equitable federal tax system, including more progressive income tax rates, with fewer preferential provisions for high income corporations and individuals, greater earned income credits for low-wage earners, and fair exemptions for middle-income taxpayers;

5. More effective limits on the concentration of ownership of major businesses, particularly in the fields of banking, insurance, utilities, communications, pharmaceuticals and health organizations, accompanied by effective price controls where no substantial competition exists;

6. A universal health plan, covering the basic needs of all individuals, with adequate freedom of choice, and with a "single payer" system to reduce administrative costs and inequities in treatment;

7. Reform of labor legislation and employment standards to provide greater protection for workers, including the right to organize and bargain collectively, protection from unsafe working conditions and protection from unjust dismissal;

8. Reform of labor legislation and employment standards to provide greater protection for workers, including "workfare" recipients and prison inmates;

9. Periodic review, renewal, or, if necessary, revocation of corporate charters, depending on assessment of

performance consistent with the public interest;

10. Fair access to fully funded legal aid for the poor;

11. Equitable funding of public education, without regard to local economic conditions.

Economic Injustice, Poverty, and Racism: We Can Make a Difference!

2000 Statement of Conscience

We, the member congregations of the Unitarian Universalist Association, hereby rededicate ourselves to the pursuit of economic justice, an end to racism, and an end to poverty. We recognize that racism is a major contributor toward economic injustice. We pledge ourselves to strive to understand how racism and classism perpetuate poverty and to work for the systemic changes needed to promote a more just economy and compassionate society. Together, we can make a difference.

Economic injustice persists in spite of the longest period of economic prosperity in our history. The gap between the rich and the poor continues to widen. Tens of millions, particularly children, women, and the elderly live in poverty, a disproportionate share of whom are ethnic and racial minorities.

Working for a just society is central to our Unitarian Universalist faith. An economically just society is one in which 1) government and private institutions promote the common economic good and are held accountable; 2) all people have equal opportunity to care for themselves and their families; and 3) individuals take responsibility for the effects of their actions on their own and others' lives. Conversely, racism encourages people to perpetuate a system of privileges and economic rewards that opens the door of opportunity much wider for some than for others. This should not be tolerated.

We must look both inward and outward as we organize ourselves for action within our congregations and beyond. Looking inward, the 1997 General Assembly of the Unitarian Universalist Association urged Unitarian Universalists to examine carefully our own conscious and unconscious racism and to work toward our transformation to an anti-racist, multi-cultural institution. The Unitarian Universalist community has only begun its soul-searching toward the goal of becoming more inclusive and affirming. We acknowledge the lack of racial and economic diversity within most of our congregations. However, having diverse congregations is not the only way to understand injustice in our society. Looking outward, our 1997 General Assembly also called upon Unitarian Universalists to work for a more just economic community. We can learn much and accomplish much by joining and creating community organizations in which diverse groups of people work together on economic justice issues, hold community leaders accountable, and monitor those leaders' efforts toward achieving systemic improvements. Our work for economic justice must include support for:

- fair wages and benefits;

- access to adequate housing, social services, child care, adult daycare, education, health care, legal services, financial services, and transportation;

- the removal of environmental and occupational hazards that disproportionately affect low-income people;

- respect for treaty rights of First Nations and Native American Tribes;

- government and corporate policies that promote economic investment in the urban core and rural communities;

- a more equitable criminal justice system;

- tax systems that prevent affluent individuals and corporations from sheltering assets and income at the expense of those less privileged; and

- campaign reforms that ensure equal access to the electoral process regardless of wealth.

As Unitarian Universalists, we have a religious and moral obligation to challenge complacency in ourselves and in our communities. We commit to fighting injustice wherever we find it. We acknowledge that this may disturb our own comfort and require us to broaden our interest to include the greater good of an economically just and compassionate community. We will learn much as we do this work.

Historically, Unitarians and Universalists have often been in the forefront of social reform. Our history teaches that social change does not come easily and is not without risk. Nevertheless, at the beginning of this new century, let us recommit to justice, equity, and compassion in human relations. Let us embrace our responsibility to help create a more just world. Let us continue to reflect and organize for action within our congregations and beyond our doors. Let us not concede that economic injustice, poverty, and racism are tolerable.

Resolution on Workers' Rights in the United States

Union for Reform Judaism (2005)

Submitted by the Commission on Social Action of Reform Judaism to the 68th Union for Reform Judaism General Assembly

Passed – Houston, November 2005

Background

In 1935, Congress enacted the National Labor Relations Act (NLRA), also known as the Wagner Act. The act codified the basic rights of most workers to bargain collectively through representatives of their own choosing and sanctioned activities, including strikes, designed to protect their bargaining rights. The NLRA also set up an enforcement body, the National Labor Relations Board, to administer the act and provide federal oversight over union representation elections.

In recent years, workers' rights to organize and bargain collectively have come under increasing attack, and gaps in existing law provide insufficient protection for many workers. For example, the NLRA has never offered protections to certain categories of workers, including agricultural workers. Furthermore, since 1935, changes in both U.S. labor law and in the workforce have weakened the ability of workers to organize unions.

Current penalties for unfair labor practices, particularly the discriminatory discharge of union supporters, are not strong enough to be a deterrent to employers that are fighting organizing drives. The current remedy for an employer's unfair labor practices is to require reinstatement of workers with back pay, reduced by any interim earnings. That penalty, however, may take up to two years before it is imposed and is too easily written off as just another business expense.

Employees seeking union representation face an election process that favors opponents of unionization and allows employers a disproportionate role. Increasing penalties for unfair labor violations only partially addresses the current power imbalance in the election process. In "Free and Fair: How Labor Law Fails U.S. Democratic Election Standards," University of Oregon Professor Gordon Lafer evaluated the rules surrounding union elections according to six democratic elections standards (equal access to information, freedom of speech, equal access to the voters, absence of voter coercion, timely implementation of the voters'

will and campaign finance regulation) and found that union elections fail all six tests.

For example, while employers have access to employees throughout the work day, union representatives have access to employees only after work hours when and if they can find them. Specifically, during a representation election campaign, employers frequently require employees to attend "captive audience" meetings, in which company representatives attempt to deter employees from voting in favor of unionization. At the same time, employers routinely prevent employees from discussing their union activities on the job through rules against solicitation. Furthermore, union representatives are often barred from distributing information in publicly accessible parking lots in which employees park their cars while at work.

These inequities are exacerbated by delays in processing representation petitions and directing an election, often because of disagreements over who belongs in the appropriate bargaining unit. During a delay, an election can be made to seem futile; the impending petition freezes most changes and delay thus becomes a tool to discourage employee support for representation. Furthermore, delay increases the opportunity for an employer who chooses to use unlawful tactics to defeat an election campaign to do so. In addition, delay can increase the acrimony that makes negotiating a first contract following a successful representation election difficult.

Delay and lack of access are both matters that can be dealt with by procedural reform. Prospective employee representatives should be provided equal access to employees within the workplace and elections should be conducted early, allowing employees whose status is at issue to vote subject to challenge and impounding ballots until other issues are resolved.

Though the NLRA, along with the Fair Labor Standards Act (FLSA), provides protections for most American workers, state labor laws also play an important role in guaranteeing U.S. workers' ability to exercise their right to organize. State laws govern labor relations for all workplaces not engaged in interstate commerce.

Some states, like New York and California, have created model labor relations legislation. These states not only protect the organizing rights of both public sector and private employees, but they also provide this protection to agricultural workers who, though frequently engaged in the work of interstate commerce, have never been protected by the NLRA. Other states have been less proactive in enacting legislation that protects worker rights. In many states, state employees are not provided with legal protections to ensure their right to organize, and recent decisions by Missouri and Indiana governors to rescind collective bargaining agreements with state employees suggest that there is a movement at the state level to roll back worker rights protections.

In many states, "right-to-work" laws create an impediment to effective union representation. Although the National Labor Relations Act authorizes employers and unions to enter into collective bargaining agreements that require employees to pay union dues after they become employed, such agreements are not permitted in states with right-to-work laws. Advocates of right-to-work laws argue that this legislation allows individuals who disagree with their union's political activities to avoid supporting positions that violate their conscience, and that employees who do not wish to pay dues should not be required to do so. Those who oppose right-to-work laws point out that union security agreements require employees to pay only core dues – dues that cover the expenses for negotiating and enforcing collective bargaining agreements – and not expenses for political activities or organizing other employees. Because unions are obligated to bargain on behalf of all members of the bargaining unit and to represent all bargaining unit members in grievance proceedings – whether or not they pay dues – right-to-work laws make it financially more difficult for unions to effectively represent workers.

The ability to organize and to engage in collective bargaining can make a significant difference in the lives of American workers. According to the Economic Policy Institute, the union wage premium – the degree to which union wages exceed non-union wages – is 15.5 percent when adjusted for comparable experience, education, region, industry, occupation and marital status. For minorities, this premium is even greater: 20.9 percent for African Americans and 23.2 percent for Hispanics.

But the right to organize is not only an economic issue; it is also a human rights issue. The 1948 Universal Declaration of Human Rights asserts that "[E]veryone has the right to form and to join trade unions for the protection of his interests." As employers are increasingly able to move their capital across international borders, ensuring that workers' rights are protected both domestically and abroad is a critical part of the fight against human rights abuses and global poverty. In its 2001 study on organizing rights in the United States, Human Rights Watch found that "workers' freedom of association is under sustained attack in the United States, and the government is often failing its responsibility under international human rights standards to deter such attacks and protect workers' rights."

Worker health and safety also remains a serious concern. Currently, willful violations of safety regulations that result in a fatality are only misdemeanors, and the Occupational Safety and Health Administration (OSHA) rarely recommends cases to the Justice Department for prosecution.

Judaism has a strong tradition of supporting the right to employment with dignity. We are taught in the Torah, "You shall not abuse a needy and destitute laborer, whether a fellow Israelite or a stranger in one of the communities of your land. You must pay out the wages due on the same day, before the sun sets, for the worker is needy and urgently depends on it; else a cry to the Eternal will be issued against you and you will incur guilt" (Deut. 24:14–15). Later tradition expands on this teaching by addressing not only wages but also working conditions. The rabbis of the Talmud taught in the case in which an employer says to workers, "I raised your wages in order that you would begin early and stay late," they may reply, "You raised our wages in order that we would do better work" (Bava M'tzia 83a).

While Jewish law traditionally assumed that an individual contract between an employer and an employee regulates workplace relationships, with the rise of the industrial economy in the nineteenth century, many Jewish workers in Europe and in North America realized that their livelihood and safety depended on collective action. In the United States, Jewish immigrants played a dominant role in the founding of several unions, including the International Ladies' Garment Workers Union and the Amalgamated Clothing Workers of America, and in 1935, Jewish activists joined with fellow members of the labor movement to support the passage of the NLRA.

Both the Union for Reform Judaism and the Central Conference of American Rabbis have been active supporters of workers' rights, and the Union's own administrative and maintenance staff are unionized.

In a series of resolutions beginning in the early 1960s, the Union and the CCAR extended their support to agricultural workers seeking better working conditions and union recognition. In 1997, the Union and the CCAR affirmed their support for worker dignity, speaking out forcefully against sweatshops and child labor both at home and abroad in their resolutions on "Sweatshops and Child Labor." These resolutions also called upon the U.S., Canadian, state and provincial governments to "provide for adequate staffing and funding to enforce existing workers' protection statutes." In 1999, the Union adopted a resolution supporting living wage campaigns, which would "require that to qualify for government contracts or assistance, service providers must pay their employees living wages, often defined as no less than the poverty line for a family of four." In 2003, the Commission on Social Action of Reform Judaism passed a resolution in support of the rights of federal employees to bargain collectively. There is, however, no general resolution that deals more broadly with workers' rights to organize and bargain collectively.

THEREFORE, the Union for Reform Judaism resolves to:

1. Support the rights of workers to organize and bargain collectively;

2. Call upon employers to:

   a. Recognize the rights of those who work for them either directly or indirectly, under contractual arrangements for services, to be treated with dignity, to be paid a living wage and to work in a healthy, safe and secure workplace;

   b. Allow their employees to choose freely whether to unionize or not, without intimidation or coercion;

   c. Abide by their employees' decision when a majority indicates that it supports union representation;

   d. Refrain from abusing National Labor Relations Board elections and appeals by using them as means for delaying or avoiding representation for their employees;

3. Call upon the U.S. government to amend the National Labor Relations Act to:

   a. Cover agricultural workers;

   b. Provide for increased penalties for the commission of unfair labor practices;

   c. Ensure timely conduct of elections following the filing of representation petitions by relegating issues to postelection proceedings whenever possible;

   d. Ensure that employers and labor organization representatives have equal access to potential members of a bargaining unit during representation election campaigns.

4. Call upon the U.S. government to enforce existing OSHA regulations and increase penalties for OSHA violations;

5. Address specific labor issues on the state level by:

   a. Opposing adoption by states of "right-to-work" laws;

   b. Supporting enactment of state labor laws to provide organizing and collective bargaining rights for agriculture workers;

   c. Affirming support for the organizing and collective bargaining rights of state employees.

Sufficient Sustainable Livelihood for All

Evangelical Lutheran Church in America (1999)

Social Statements: Economic Life

Adopted by a more than two-thirds majority vote (872-124) as a social statement of the Evangelical Lutheran Church in America by its sixth Churchwide Assembly on August 20, 1999, in Denver, Colorado.

Economic life pervades our lives, the work we do, the income we receive, how much we consume and save, what we value, and how we view one another. An economy (*oikonomia* or "management of the household") is meant to meet people's material needs. The current market-based economy does that to an amazing degree; many are prospering as never before. At the same time, others continue to lack what they need for basic subsistence. Out of deep concern for those affected adversely, we of the Evangelical Lutheran Church in America here assess economic life today in light of the moral imperative to seek *sufficient, sustainable livelihood for all.* *

To an unprecedented degree, today's market economy has become global in scope, intensity, and impact. Common brand names appear throughout the world. Many companies based in the United States generate most of their revenues and profits abroad. Daily foreign exchange trading has increased a hundredfold over the past quarter century. Billions of dollars of capital can flow out of one country and into another with a few computer keystrokes. This economic globalization has brought new kinds of businesses, opportunities, and a better life for many. It also has resulted in increasing misery for others. Intensive global competition can force a company to relocate if it is to survive, generating jobs elsewhere, while leaving behind many workers who lose their jobs. Sudden shifts in globalized capital and financial markets can dramatically affect the economic well-being of millions of people, for good or for ill.

Human beings are responsible and accountable for economic life, but people often feel powerless in the face of what occurs. Market-based thought and practices dominate our world today in ways that seem to eclipse other economic, social, political and religious perspectives. To many people, the global market economy feels like a free-running system that is reordering the world with few external checks or little accountability to values other than profit. Economic mandates often demand sacrifices from those least able to afford them. When any economic system and its effects are accepted without question, when it becomes a "god-like" power reigning over people, communities, and creation, then we face a central issue of faith.

The Church confesses

If the economic arena becomes a reigning power for us, the question arises: in what or whom shall we place our trust and hope? The First Commandment is clear: "You shall have no other gods before me" (Exodus 20:3). Or as Jesus said, "You cannot serve God and wealth" (Matthew 6:24c; Luke 16:13). To place our trust in something other than God is the essence of sin. It disrupts our relationships with God, one another, and the rest of creation, resulting in injustices and exploitation: "For from the least to the greatest of them, everyone is greedy for unjust gain" (Jeremiah 6:13).

As a church, we confess that we are in bondage to sin and submit too readily to the idols and injustices of economic life. We often rely on wealth and material goods more than God and close ourselves off from the needs of others. Too uncritically, we accept assumptions, policies and practices that do not serve the good of all.

Our primary and lasting identity, trust and hope are rooted in the God we know in Jesus Christ. Baptized into Christ's life, death, and resurrection, we receive a new identity and freedom, rather than being defined and held captive by economic success or failure. In the gathered community of Christ's Body, the Church, we hear the Word and partake of the Supper, a foretaste of the fullness of life promised by Jesus, "the bread of life" (John 6:35). Through the cross of Christ, God forgives our sin and frees us from bondage to false gods. Faith in Christ fulfills the First Commandment. We are called to love the neighbor and be stewards in economic life, which, distorted by sin, is still God's good creation.

God who "executes justice for the oppressed, who gives food to the hungry" (Psalm 146:7) is revealed in Jesus, whose mission was "to bring good news to the poor … release to the captives and recovery of sight to the blind, to let the oppressed go free, to proclaim the year of the Lord's favor" (Luke 4: 18-19). The kingdom of God he proclaimed became real through concrete acts of justice: feeding people, freeing them from various forms of bondage, embracing those excluded by the systems of his day, and calling his followers to a life of faithfulness to God.

God's reign is not a new system, a set of prescriptive laws, or a plan of action that depends on what we do. Nor is it a spiritual realm removed from this world. In Jesus Christ, God's reign intersects earthly life, transforming us and how we view the systems of this world. Our faith in God provides a vantage point for critiquing any and every system of this world, all of which fall short of what God intends. Human impoverishment, excessive accumulation and consumerism driven by greed, gross economic disparities, and the degradation of nature are incompatible with this reign of God.

Through human decisions and actions, God is at work in economic life. Economic life is intended to be a means through which God's purposes for humankind and creation are to be served. When this does not occur, as a church we cannot remain silent because of who and whose we are.

Our obligation and ongoing tensions

Based on this vantage point of faith, *"sufficient, sustainable livelihood for all"* is a benchmark for affirming, opposing and seeking changes in economic life. Because of sin we fall short of these obligations in this world, but we live in light of God's promised future that ultimately there will be no hunger and injustice. This promise makes us restless with less than what God intends for the world. In economic matters, this draws attention to:

- the scope of God's concern – "for all,"

- the means by which life is sustained – "livelihood,"

- what is needed – "sufficiency," and

- a long-term perspective – "sustainability."

These criteria often are in tension with one another. What benefits people in one area, sector or country may harm those elsewhere. What is sufficient in one context is not in another. What is economically sufficient is not necessarily sustainable. There are difficult and complex trade-offs and ambiguities in the dynamic processes of economic life. As believers, we are both impelled by God's promises and confronted with the practical realities of economic life. We often must choose among competing claims, conscious of our incomplete knowledge, of the sin that clouds all human judgments and actions *and* of the grace and forgiveness given by Christ.

Economic assumptions can conflict with what we as a church confess. Who we are in Christ places us in tension with priorities given to money, consumption, competition and profit in our economic system.

- While autonomy and self-sufficiency are highly valued in our society, as people of faith we confess that we depend on God and are interdependent with one another. Through these relationships we are nurtured, sustained, and held accountable.

- While succeeding or making something of themselves is what matters to many in economic life, we confess that in Christ we are freely justified by grace through faith rather than by what we do.

- While a market economy emphasizes what individuals want and are willing and able to buy, as people of faith we realize that what human beings want is not necessarily what they need for the sake of life.

- While a market economy assumes people will act to maximize their own interests, we acknowledge that what is in our interest must be placed in the context of what is good for the neighbor.

- While competitiveness is key to economic success, we recognize that intense competitiveness can destroy relationships and work against the reconciliation and cooperation God desires among people.

- While economic reasoning assumes that resources are scarce relative to people's wants, we affirm that God promises a world where there is enough for everyone, if only we would learn how to use and share what God has given for the sake of all.

- While economic growth often is considered an unconditional good, we insist that such growth must be evaluated by its direct, indirect, short-term and long-term effects on the well-being of all creation and people, especially those who are poor.

When we pray in the Lord's Prayer, *"Give us this day our daily bread,"* we place ourselves in tension with economic assumptions of our society. Rather than being self-sufficient, we need and depend on what God gives or provides through people, practices, and systems. *"Daily bread"* is not earned by efforts of individuals alone, but is made possible through a variety of relationships and institutions.[1] God gives in ways that expand our notions of who "us" includes, from people close at hand to those around the globe. In stark contrast to those who seek unchecked accumulation and profit, our attention is drawn to those who are desperate for what will sustain their lives for just *this day*.

For all: especially those living in poverty

"For all" refers to the whole household of God, all people and creation throughout the world. We should assess economic activities in terms of how they affect "all," especially people living in poverty.

We tend to view economic life by how it affects us personally. The cross of Christ challenges Christians to view this arena through the experience of those of us who are impoverished, suffering, broken, betrayed, left out, without hope. Through those who are "despised" and "held of no account" (Isaiah 53:3) we see the crucified Christ (Matthew 25:31-46), through whom God's righteousness and justice are revealed. The power of God's suffering, self-giving love transforms and challenges the Church to stand with all who are overlooked for the sake of economic progress or greed. Confession of faith ought to flow into acts of justice for the sake of the most vulnerable.

Outrage over the plight of people living in poverty is a theme throughout the Bible. At the heart of Jesus' ministry and central to the message of the Old Testament prophets was God's partiality toward the poor and powerless. The poor are those who live precariously between subsistence and utter deprivation. It is not poor people themselves who are the problem, but their lack of access to the basic necessities of life. Without such, they cannot maintain their human dignity. Strong themes in Scripture indicate that people are poor because of circumstances that have afflicted them (such as "aliens, orphans, widows"), or because of the greed and unjust practices of those who "trample on the poor" (Amos 5:11). The basic contrast is between the weak and the greedy. The psalmist decries that "the wicked draw the sword and bend their bows to bring down the poor and needy" (Psalm 37:14). The prophet rails against those "who write oppressive statutes to turn aside the needy from justice" (Isaiah 10:1-2). Their moral problem is that they have followed greed rather than God. As a result, the poor lose their basic productive resource (their land), and fall into cycles of indebtedness. Poverty is a problem of the whole human community, not only of those who are poor or vulnerable.

In relation to those who are poor, Martin Luther's insights into the meaning of the commandments against killing, stealing and coveting are sobering. We violate "you shall not kill" when we do not help and support others to meet their basic needs. As Luther explained, "If you see anyone suffer hunger and do not feed [them], you have let [them] starve."[2] "To steal" can include "taking advantage of our neighbor in any sort of dealing that results in loss to him [or her] . . . wherever business is transacted and money is exchanged for goods or labor."[3] "You shall not covet" means "God does not wish you to deprive your neighbor of anything that is [theirs], letting [them] suffer loss while you gratify your greed."[4] Related Hebraic laws called for leaving produce in the fields for the poor (Deuteronomy 24:21), a periodic cancellation of debts (Deuteronomy 15:1), and a jubilee year in which property was to be redistributed or restored to those who had lost it, so that they might again have a means of livelihood (Leviticus 25).

Today, well over a billion people in the world are deprived of what they need to meet their basic needs. Far more lack clean water, adequate sanitation, housing, or health services. They use whatever limited options are available to them in their daily struggle to survive. Thousands die daily. Millions pursue economic activities that are part of the underground or informal economy, and are not counted in economic statistics. Children often have no option but to labor under unjust conditions to provide for themselves and their families. Political struggles, militarism, and warfare add to this travesty, displacing masses of people from their homes.[5] In many of the poorest countries, incomes continue to decline, and people subsist on less and less. Although most of the impoverished live in developing countries, where their numbers continue to grow at alarming rates, many millions are in the industrialized countries. Millions of poor people live in communities in the United States and the Caribbean where the Evangelical Lutheran Church in America is present.

Developing countries that have opened their economies to global markets have generally reduced poverty over time more than those that have not, but the terms of trade often work to the disadvantage of developing countries. Seeking more just exchanges "for all" through investment and trade is a significant challenge. The danger is that less developed parts of the world, or less powerful groups within a country, will be exploited or excluded from participation in global markets.

When a developing country becomes heavily indebted, the poorest are usually the most adversely affected. A huge share of a country's income must be used to pay off debt, which may have been incurred unjustly or under corrupt rulers. Structural adjustment programs to pay off debt typically divert funds from much needed educational, health and environmental efforts, and from infrastructures for economic development.

God stands in judgment of those in authority who fall short of their responsibility, and is moved with compassion to deliver the impoverished from all that oppresses them: "Give justice to the weak and the orphan; maintain the right of the lowly and the destitute" (Psalm 82:3). The rich are expected to use wealth to benefit their neighbors who live in poverty here and throughout the world.

In light of these realities, *we commit ourselves* as a church[6] and urge members to:

- address creatively and courageously the complex causes of poverty;

- provide opportunities for dialogue, learning, and strategizing among people of different economic situations and from different regions who are harmed by global economic changes;

- give more to relieve conditions of poverty, and invest more in initiatives to reduce poverty.

We call for:

- scrutiny of how specific policies and practices affect people and nations that are the poorest, and changes to make policies of economic growth, trade, and investment more beneficial to those who are poor;

- efforts to increase the participation of low-income people in political and civic life, and citizen vigilance and action that challenge governments and other sectors when they become captive to narrow economic interests that do not represent the good of all;

- shifts throughout the world from military expenditures to purposes that serve the needs of low-income people;

- support for family planning and enhanced opportunities for women so that population pressures might be eased; [7]

- reduction of overwhelming international debt burdens in ways that do not impose further deprivations on the poor and cancellation of some or all debt where severe indebtedness immobilizes a country's economy;

- investments, loan funds, hiring practices, skill training and funding of micro-enterprises and other community development projects that can empower low-income people economically.

Livelihood: vocation, work and human dignity

Vocation: Our calling from God begins in the waters of Baptism and is lived out in a wide array of settings and relationships. Freed through the Gospel, we are to serve others through arenas of responsibility such as family, work and community life. Although we continue to be ensnared in the ambiguities and sin of this world, our vocation is to seek what is good for people and the rest of creation in ways that glorify God and anticipate God's promised future.

"Livelihood" designates our means of subsistence or how we are supported economically. This occurs through paid jobs, self-employment, business ownership and accumulated wealth, as well as through support of family, community networks and government assistance.

Strong families, neighborhoods and schools should support and help prepare persons for livelihood. Churches, businesses, financial institutions, government and civil society also play key roles. Through these relationships people can be enabled and obligated to pursue their livelihoods as they are able. When these infrastructures for livelihood are absent, weak or threatened (as they are for many today), people are more likely to be impoverished materially, emotionally or spiritually.

Through these relationships and structures, individuals can learn important virtues, such as:

- trust, accountability and fidelity in relationships;

- discipline, honesty, diligence and responsibility in work;

- frugality, prudence and temperance in the use of resources;

- compassion and justice toward other people and the rest of creation.

These virtues, along with perspectives and skills acquired through education and training, make it more likely that individuals will be able to flourish in their livelihood.

We commit ourselves as a church and urge members to:

- develop God-given capacities and provide stable,

holistic, loving development of children and youth through families, neighborhoods, congregations and other institutions;

- support and encourage one another as we live out our vocation in ways that serve the neighbor and contribute to family and community vitality;

- pray and act to provide livelihood for ourselves and others through the institutions of our day, trusting in God's providential care for all.

We call for:

- policies that promote stable families, strong schools and safe neighborhoods;

- addressing the barriers individuals face in preparing for and sustaining a livelihood (such as lack of education, transportation, child care and health care).

Work: In Genesis, work is to be a means through which basic needs might be met, as human beings "till and keep" the garden in which God has placed them (Genesis 2:15). Work is seen not as an end in itself, but as a means for sustaining humans and the rest of creation. Due to sin, the work God gives to humans also becomes toil and anguish (Genesis 3:17,19). Injustice often deprives people of the fruits of their work (Proverbs 13:23), which benefits others instead.

God calls people to use their freedom and responsibility, their capacities and know-how to participate productively in God's world. As stewards of what God has entrusted to us, we should use available resources to generate jobs for the livelihood of more people, as well as to create capital for the growth needed to meet basic needs. Wealth should serve or benefit others so that they also might live productively.

What matters in many jobs today, rather than a sense of vocation, is the satisfaction of wants or desires that the pay from work makes possible. Work becomes a means toward increased consumerism. Many also feel a constant sense of being judged, having to measure up according to an unrelenting bottom line of productivity or profit. We are freed from such economic captivity by the forgiveness, new life and dignity that is ours in Christ.

Competitive economic forces, as well as changing technologies and consumer demands, significantly affect the kinds of jobs available and the nature of work. Increased productivity and technological innovation continue to make some jobs obsolete, while creating others. A growing proportion of jobs are part-time,

temporary or contractual, without the longevity and security assumed in the past. Workers in the United States increasingly produce services rather than tangible goods. Many people choose to be self-employed. A large number lose their jobs when companies merge, downsize or move to areas with lower labor costs.

Job transitions can be enriching, but also painful. Feeling invested in one's job as a calling or being able to count on a future livelihood can be difficult when work is continually in flux. Many workers feel treated as if they are dispensable. Amid these changes, our faith reminds us that our security and livelihood rest ultimately on God. Our hope is grounded in God's promise that people "shall long enjoy the work of their hands" (Isaiah 65:21). This gives us courage to ask why changes are occurring, to challenge forces of greed and injustice when they deny some people what they need to live, and, when necessary, to seek new possibilities for livelihood.

Therefore, *we commit ourselves* as a church and urge members to:

- deliberate together about the challenges people face in their work;

- counsel and support those who are unemployed, underemployed and undergoing job transitions;

- provide skill and language enhancement training that will enable the most vulnerable (including new immigrants) to become better prepared for jobs.

We call for:

- public and private sector partnerships to create jobs and job retention programs;

- national economic policies that support and advance the goal of low unemployment.

Human dignity: Human beings are created "in God's image" (Genesis 1:27) as social beings whose dignity, worth and value are conferred by God. Although our identity does not depend on what we do, through our work we should be able to express this God-given dignity as persons of integrity, worth and meaning. Yet work does not constitute the whole of our life. When we are viewed and treated only as workers, we tend to be exploited.

Employers have a responsibility to treat employees with dignity and respect. This should be reflected in employees' remuneration, benefits, work conditions, job security and ongoing job training. Employees have a responsibility to work to the best of their potential in a reliable and responsible manner. This includes work habits, attitudes toward employers and co-workers, and a willingness to adapt and prepare for new work situations. No one should be coerced to work under conditions that violate their dignity or freedom, jeopardize their health or safety, result in neglect of their family's well-being, or provide unjust compensation for their labor.

Our God-given dignity in community means that we are to participate actively in decisions that impact our lives, rather than only passively accept decisions others make for us. People should be involved in decision making that directly affects their work. They should also be free to determine their lives independent of particular jobs. Public policy can provide economic and other conditions that protect human freedom and dignity in relation to work.

Power disparities and competing interests are present in most employment situations. Employers need competent, committed workers, but this does not necessarily presume respect for the personal lives and needs of individual workers. Individual workers depend on the organization for employment as their means of livelihood, but this does not necessarily presume respect for the organization's interest and goals. Management and employees move toward justice as they seek cooperative ways of negotiating these interests when they conflict. Because employees often are vulnerable and lack power in such negotiations, they may need to organize in their quest for human dignity and justice. When this occurs, accurate information and fair tactics are expected of all parties involved.

We commit ourselves as a church to:

- hire without discriminating on the basis of race, ethnicity, gender, age, disabilities, sexual orientation or genetic factors;

- compensate all people we call or employ at an amount sufficient for them to live in dignity;

- provide adequate pension and health benefits, safe and healthy work conditions, sufficient periods of rest, vacation, and sabbatical and family-friendly work schedules;

- cultivate workplaces of participatory decision-making;

- honor the right of employees to organize for the sake of better working conditions and for workers to make free and informed decisions; encourage

those who engage in collective bargaining to commit themselves to negotiated settlements, especially when participatory attempts at just working conditions fail;** and discourage the permanent replacement of striking workers.

We call for:

- other employers to engage in similar practices;

- government enforcement of regulations against discrimination, exploitative work conditions and labor practices (including child labor), and for the right of workers to organize and bargain collectively;

- public policies that ensure adequate social security, unemployment insurance and health care coverage;

- a minimum wage level that balances employees' need for sufficient income with what would be significant negative effects on overall employment;

- tax credits and other means of supplementing the insufficient income of low-paid workers in order to move them out of poverty.

Sufficiency: enough, but not too much

"Sufficiency" means adequate access to income and other resources that enable people to meet their basic needs, including nutrition, clothing, housing, health care, personal development and participation in community with dignity. God has created a world of sufficiency for all, providing us daily and abundantly with all the necessities of life.[8] In many countries, the problem is not the lack of resources, but how they are shared, distributed and made accessible within society. Justice seeks fairness in how goods, services, income and wealth are allocated among people so that they can acquire what they need to live.

Human need and the right to ownership often are in tension with each other. The biblical understanding of stewardship is that what we have does not ultimately belong to us. We are called to be stewards of what God has given for the sake of all. This stewardship includes holding economic, political and social processes and institutions responsible for producing and distributing what is needed for sufficiency for all. Private property is affirmed insofar as it serves as a useful, yet imperfect means to meet the basic needs of individuals, households and communities.

Government is intended to serve God's purposes by limiting or countering narrow economic interests and promoting the common good. Paying taxes to enable government to carry out these and other purposes is an appropriate expression of our stewardship in society, rather than something to be avoided. Government often falls short of these responsibilities. Its policies can harm the common good and especially the most vulnerable in society. Governing leaders are to be held accountable to God's purposes: "May [they] judge your people with righteousness, and your poor with justice. . . . May [they] defend the cause of the poor of the people" (Psalm 72:2).

The lack of material sufficiency for some within the human community is itself a spiritual problem. "How does God's love abide in anyone who has the world's goods and sees a brother or sister in need and yet refuses to help?" (1 John. 3:17). Sin disrupts our bonds with and our sense of responsibility for one another. We live separated from others on the basis of income and wealth and resent what others have. Huge disparities in income and wealth, such as those we face in this country, threaten the integrity of the human community.

Those who are rich and those who are poor are called into relationships of generosity from which each can benefit. Within the Church, those in need and those with abundance are brought together in Christ. On this basis and in the face of disparities in the church of his day, Paul calls for "a fair balance between your present abundance and their need, so that their abundance may be for your need." In so doing, "the one who had much did not have too much, and the one who had little did not have too little" (2 Corinthians 8:9, 13-15).

God's mandate is clear. "Is not this the fast that I choose: to loose the bonds of injustice … and to break every yoke? Is it not to share your bread with the hungry, and bring the homeless poor into your house; when you see the naked to cover them, and not to hide yourself from your own kin?" (Isaiah 58:6-7). God's lavish, justifying grace frees us from self-serving preoccupations and calls us to a life of mutual generosity as we relate to all who are our neighbors. Faith becomes active through personal relationships, direct assistance and wider policy changes in society.

Not enough: In the United States, tens of millions of people live in poverty, although many refuse to think of themselves as "poor." Some make daily choices as to which necessities they will have to live without. Many work part- or full-time, but on that basis, are still unable to lift their families out of poverty. Others are physically or mentally unable to work. Many lack the family, educational and community support important for making good choices in their lives. Although those living in poverty are particularly visible in cities, their more hidden reality in suburban, small town and rural areas can be just as painful. A greater proportion of people of color live in conditions of poverty. The poor are disproportionately women with their children.[9] Systemic racism and sexism continue to be evident in the incidence of poverty.

In light of these realities, *we commit ourselves* as a church and urge members to:

- provide counsel, food, clothing, shelter and money for people in need, in ways that respect their dignity;

- develop mutual, face-to-face, empowering relationships between people who have enough and people living in poverty, especially through congregational and synodical partnerships;

- advocate for public and private policies that effectively address the causes of poverty;

- generously support organizations and community-based efforts that enable low-income people to obtain more sufficient, sustainable livelihoods;

- continue working to eradicate racism and sexism.

We call for:

- government to provide adequate income assistance and related services for citizens, documented immigrants and refugees who are unable to provide for their livelihood through employment;

- adequate, consistent public funding for the various low-income services non-profit organizations provide for the common good of all;

- scrutiny to ensure that new ways of providing low-income people with assistance and services (such as through the private sector) do not sacrifice the most vulnerable for the sake of economic efficiency and profit;

- correction of regressive tax systems, so that people are taxed progressively in relation to their ability to pay;

- opposition to lotteries and other state-sponsored gambling because of how these regressive means of raising state revenues adversely affect those who are poor.[10]

Too much: Because most of us in the United States have far more than we need, we can easily fall into bondage to what we have. We then become like the young man Jesus encountered, whose bondage to his possessions kept him from following Jesus (Matthew 19:16-22; Mark 10:17-22; Luke 18:18-25).

We consume goods and use services to meet our needs. To increase consumption and expand sales, businesses stimulate ever new *wants*. Rather than human need shaping consumption, advertising and media promotion both shape and expand wants. Our very being becomes expressed through what we have or desire to possess. When consuming to meet basic needs turns into consumerism as an end in itself, we face a serious crisis of faith.

Endless accumulation of possessions and pursuit of wealth can become our god as we yearn for a life without limits. "Ah, you who join house to house, who add field to field, until there is room for no one but you" (Isaiah 5:8). Many look to material possessions and money as the means for participating in the "fullness of life," and thus become ever more dependent on economic transactions. But Jesus asks, "What does it profit them if they gain the whole world, but lose or forfeit themselves?" (Luke 9:25).

In the United States, people's worth and value tend to be measured by the size of their income and wealth. If judged by their multimillion dollar compensations, top corporate officers and sports superstars would seem to be the most highly valued in our society. Enormous disparities between their compensations and the average wages of workers are scandalous.

The economic power of large transnational corporations continues to grow, making some of them larger than many national economies. Along with this financial strength comes an inordinate potential to influence political decisions, local and regional economies and democratic processes in society. The power they wield, enhanced through mergers and buyouts, can have positive effects, but it can also hold others captive to transnational corporate interests. The global community must continue to seek effective ways to hold these and other powerful economic actors more accountable for the sake of sufficient, sustainable livelihood for all.

In light of these realities, *we commit ourselves* as a church and urge members to:

- examine how we are in bondage to our possessions and can be freed to be faithful stewards of them;

- serious and ongoing consideration in our families and congregations of how to resist the allure of

consumerism and live lives less oriented toward the accumulation of goods and financial assets;

- educate one another, beginning with the young, on how to deal responsibly with money, credit and spending within one's means;

- give generously of our wealth (for example, through tithing and planned giving), especially for purposes that serve the needs of others.

We call for:

- corporate policies that lessen the disparities between compensations of top corporate executives and that of the workers throughout an organization;

- corporate governance that is accountable for the effects of a company's practices on workers, communities and the environment here and throughout the world;

- scrutiny of the tax breaks, subsidies and incentives many companies receive, to assure that they serve the common good;

- enforcement of laws to prevent the exercise of inordinate market power by large corporations;

- appropriate government regulatory reform so that governments can monitor private sector practices more effectively and efficiently in an ever-changing global economy.

Sustainability: of the environment, agriculture and low-income communities

"Sustainability" is the capacity of natural and social systems to survive and thrive together over the long term. What is sufficient in providing for people's wants often is in tension with what can be sustained over time. Sustainability has implications for how we evaluate economic activity in terms of its ongoing effects on the well-being of both nature and human communities. Economic life should help sustain humans and the rest of creation now and in the future.

Efforts to provide a sufficient livelihood must be sustainable economically. Individuals and families should not borrow*** more than they are able to pay back and still meet their future needs. Governments should not finance their spending by excessive borrowing or money creation that reduces national income and production and threatens the livelihood of future generations. Tax rates and government regulations must not be so burdensome as to stifle the production of the very goods and services people need to live.

"The earth is the Lord's and all that is in it, the world, and those who live in it" (Psalm 24:1). As God created, so God also sustains: "When you send forth your spirit … you renew the face of the ground" (Psalm 104:30). God makes a covenant with Noah, his descendants, and every living creature that they will not be destroyed (Genesis 9:8-17). In God's promise of "new heavens and a new earth … they shall build houses and inhabit them; they shall plant vineyards and eat their fruit" (Isaiah 65:17, 21). The vantage point of the kingdom of God motivates us to focus on more than short-term gains. Humans, called to be stewards of God's creation, are to respect the integrity and limits of the earth and its resources.

Sustaining the environment: The growth of economic activity during the twentieth century, and the industrialization and consumerism that fueled it, radically changed the relationship between humans and the earth. Too often the earth has been treated as a waste receptacle and a limitless storehouse of raw materials to be used up for the sake of economic growth, rather than as a finite, fragile ecological system upon which human and all other life depends.

Instead of being stewards who care for the long-term well-being of creation, we confess that we have depleted non-renewable resources, eroded topsoil, and polluted the air, ground and water. Without appropriate environmental care, economic growth cannot be sustained. Caring for creation means that economic processes should respect environmental limits. "When we act interdependently and in solidarity with creation, we *do* justice. We serve and keep the earth, trusting its bounty can be sufficient for all and sustainable."[11]

We commit ourselves as a church and urge members to:

- use less, re-use, recycle and restore natural resources;
- plan for careful land use of church property and receive and manage gifts of land and real estate in sustainable ways.

We call for:

- appropriate policies and regulations that help reverse environmental destruction;
- planning that accounts for the impact of regional growth on communities and ecosystems;
- ending subsidies for economic activities that use up non-renewable natural resources;
- companies to pay more fully for the wider social

and environmental costs of what they produce;

- the development and use of more energy-efficient technologies.

Sustaining agriculture: Agriculture is basic to the survival and security of people throughout the world. Through the calling of agriculture, farmers produce the grain for our daily bread and the rest of our food supply. Without a bountiful and low-cost food supply, most Americans would not enjoy the livelihood they do. Farmers face the challenge of producing this food in ways that contribute to the regeneration of the land and the vitality of rural communities. At the same time, society as a whole must address the high levels of risk farmers face and the low prices they often receive. Changing agricultural policies and the growing power of large agribusiness corporations make this even more challenging.

We commit ourselves as a church and urge members to:

- pray for and support those who farm the land;
- pursue new ways for consumers to partner with small farmers in sharing the risks and yields of farming.

We call for:

- changes to assure that farmers will receive a greater proportion of the retail food dollar;
- adequate prices for agricultural products so that farmers can be compensated fairly for their labor and production costs;
- sustainable agricultural practices that protect and restore the regenerative capacities of the land, rather than practices that deplete the land (for example, by measuring productivity only by short-term agricultural yields);
- more just work conditions for farm workers, especially immigrants, and opportunities for them to acquire their own land;
- greater entry-level opportunities for the next generation of family farmers.

Sustainable development of low-income communities: In many low-income communities, disinvestment and neglect have taken their toll. In contrast to this are examples of sustainable community economic development that take into account the overall health and welfare of people, the environment and the local economy. Such an approach creates jobs, prepares people for work, generates income that is re-circulated several times in the community and sustains and renews environmental resources, all for the sake of a community's long-term viability.

Instead of a top-down approach focused on a community's deprivation and its lack of economic growth, effective community development draws upon its assets and emphasizes quality and diverse production. Effective policies build and enhance a community's social relationships, values and institutions, which together can further economic development. Local residents determine the future of their community by initiating, supporting, and sustaining new projects. Their capacities, skills and assets help shape the vision and plan for the community.

Through broad-based community organizing people can be mobilized to address economic and other issues that directly impact them. Government and the private sector also must invest in health, education and infrastructures necessary for sustainable development. When people and resources are connected in ways that multiply their power and effectiveness, this will help bring about productive results and meaningful participation in community and economic life.

Therefore, *we commit ourselves* as a church and urge members to:

- learn about, participate in, and provide financial support for community economic development and organizing strategies that enhance the current and future well-being of communities and the environment;

- support community development corporations and locally-owned or producer-owned cooperatives;

- integrate social values into our investment decisions, and invest more in socially responsible companies and funds that sustain businesses as well as workers, consumers, the environment and low-income communities.

We call for:

- support of the above strategies by governments, financial institutions and the wider society;

- alternatives to gambling as a means of community economic development;

- grants and low-interest loans that enable small companies and farms to get started, develop and expand in order to provide livelihood for more people in low-income communities.

In conclusion, a vision renewed

Pursuing policies and practices that will lead to "sufficient, sustainable livelihood for all" is such a formidable challenge that to many it seems unrealistic or not worth the effort. The Church as an employer, property owner, consumer, investor and community of believers can be as caught up in the reigning economic assumptions as the rest of society. But despite the Church's failings, through the Word and the sacraments, we are forgiven, renewed and nourished. At the Table, we together receive the same bread and drink of the same cup. What we receive is sufficient; it *does* sustain us. We are strengthened to persist in the struggle for justice as we look forward to the coming of God's kingdom in all its fullness.

We are sent forth *into the world* to bear witness to God's promised reign. The world is the whole household of God that economic life is intended to serve. The Spirit of God expands our vision and transforms our priorities. We realize that we do not eat alone; everyone needs to eat. The multitudes present around God's global table become our neighbors rather than competitors or strangers. Empowered by God, we continue to act, pray and hope that through economic life there truly will be *sufficient, sustainable livelihood for all.*

Endnotes

1. See Martin Luther's discussion of this in "The Large Catechism," *The Book of Concord,* Theodore G. Tappert, transl. and ed. (Fortress Press, 1959), 430-431.

2. The Fifth Commandment as discussed in "The Large Catechism," 391.

3. The Seventh Commandment as discussed in "The Large Catechism," 395.

4. The Ninth and Tenth commandments as discussed in "The Large Catechism," 406.

5. See the ELCA Message on Immigration (1998), online at www.elca.org/socialstatements/immigration; and the ELCA Social Statement "For Peace in God's World" (1995), online at www.elca.org/socialstatements/peace.

6. In this and subsequent "we commit" sections, "church" includes congregations, synods, the churchwide organization, and where relevant, this calls upon affiliated organizations such as seminaries, schools, colleges and universities, and social ministry organizations to adjust their policies and practices accordingly.

7. "Global population growth, for example, relates to the lack of access by women to family planning and health care, quality education, fulfilling employment, and equal rights." ELCA Social Statement, "Caring for Creation: Vision, Hope, and Justice" (1993), 3-4.

8. See how Luther explains the First Article of the Creed in the Small Catechism.

9. See the Women and Children Living in Poverty Strategy of the Evangelical Lutheran Church in America (800-638-3522 extension 2863).

10. See "Gambling: A Study for Congregations" (Division for Church in Society, 1998), 20-22.

11. "Caring for Creation …" (1993).

Addendum

This social statement has been adopted in accordance with "Policies and Procedures of the Evangelical Lutheran Church in America for Addressing Social Concerns" (1997), which calls for an addendum to be added to indicate amendments that received significant support but not enough for adoption (see the asterisks in the text).

* It should be noted at the outset that the economy and economic life of a people in a Christian sense must serve the whole of the human spirit and of human life. Economic goals are not ends in themselves but must serve to enrich the spiritual life of humans in a just and caring way. The ends of human existence should not be directed to material and power enrichment but to spiritual growth and blessings. However, the material needs of the poor and disenfranchised must not be overlooked; rather they must be emphasized.

** to refrain from intentionally undercutting union organizing activities.

*** should not borrow irresponsibly [with the remainder of this sentence deleted].

Ethical Guidelines for Labor Relations in United Church of Christ Organizations and Related Organizations

United Church of Christ (1995)

A Resolution Adopted by the XX General Synod of the United Church of Christ (1995)

Whereas the General Synod, Board for Homeland Ministries, Office for Church in Society and other bodies of the United Church of Christ (UCC) have affirmed that all workers covered under the National Labor Relations Act have the legal right to organize for the purpose of bargaining collectively with their employers;

Whereas UCC congregations, institutions, judicatories and instrumentalities are widely expected to exercise compassion, decency and respect toward their employees who are, in turn, expected to exercise compassion, decency and respect toward those whom their employing body serves and respect to their employers;

Whereas it is important to formally reaffirm commonly accepted standards of compassion, decency and respect which can inform the labor relations policies of UCC organizations and related organizations;

Therefore, be it resolved that the Twentieth General Synod:

Adopts the following Statement of *Ethical Guidelines for Labor Relations in UCC Organizations and Related Organizations,* commends them to all employers who operate in official relationship to the UCC and are subject to the provisions of the National Labor Relations Act, and urges their formal consideration and adoption by such organizations.

Be it further resolved that the Twentieth General Synod of the UCC directs the Executive Council to communicate this action along with the guidelines to all UCC employers and related employers and to annually prepare a list of those organizations which have adopted these guidelines, or through other organizational policies and practices have demonstrated substantial compliance with the substance and intent of these guidelines.

I. Treat Employees as You Would Like to be Treated

A. Unambiguously affirm that employees do *not* forfeit their right to organize and bargain collectively when they go to work for a UCC organization or related organization.

B. Refrain from any actions, legal or illegal, which exercise the power of the employer in an abusive or coercive fashion, including, but not limited to, the following:

1. Conducting "closed door" or "captive audience" meetings with employees.

2. Subtle or overt threats to employee job security as a result of any involvement in union organizing activity.

3. In the event of a strike, hiring of permanent replacement workers.

II. Resolve Differences Quickly

A. Immediately recognize the self-determination of employees expressed through an affirmative majority vote to be represented by a union. Refrain from engaging in challenges to election results unless there is unambiguous evidence that elections were unfairly conducted.

B. If a union is recognized, make every effort to negotiate a fair contract quickly. Specifically, refrain from engaging in any delaying tactics which might be perceived as an effort to overturn the original result in a recertification election.

C. Consider allowing card-check recognition as an alternative to the standard union election procedure.

III. Seek Win-Win Solutions

A. If a union representation is established, retain labor relations counsel with a reputation and record of fair and timely negotiation of labor contracts.

B. Openly affirm that employees can be loyal to both the union and the employer. Avoid statements or materials which imply that union participation is anti-employer behavior.

C. Expect to work with the union as a partner and resource in the pursuit of the organization's mission to those it, and by extension its employees, serves.

Covenanting for Justice in the Economy and the Earth

World Alliance of Reformed Churches (in the U.S. this includes the UCC, Presbyterian Church [USA], Reformed Church of America, and Christian Reform Church) (2004)

This document is a report from the WARC 24th General Council Proceedings and is presented here by permission of the World Alliance of Reformed Churches (WARC).

24th General Council, Accra, Ghana
July 30 – August 13, 2004
Document GC 23-e
English
(As agreed by General Council)

Introduction

1. In response to the urgent call of the Southern African constituency which met in Kitwe in 1995 and in recognition of the increasing urgency of global economic injustice and ecological destruction, the 23rd General Council (Debrecen, Hungary, 1997) invited the member churches of the World Alliance of Reformed Churches to enter into a process of "recognition, education, and confession (*processus confessionis*)." The churches reflected on the text of Isaiah 58:6 "… break the chains of oppression and the yoke of injustice, and let the oppressed go free," as they heard the cries of brothers and sisters around the world and witnessed God's gift of creation under threat.

2. Since then, nine member churches have committed themselves to a faith stance; some are in the process of covenanting; and others have studied the issues and come to a recognition of the depth of the crisis. Further, in partnership with the World Council of Churches, the Lutheran World Federation and regional ecumenical organizations, the World Alliance of Reformed Churches has engaged in consultations in all regions of the world, from Seoul/Bangkok (1999) to Stony Point (2004). Additional consultations took place with churches from the South in Buenos Aires (2003) and with churches from South and North in London Colney (2004).

3. Gathered in Accra, Ghana, for the General Council of the World Alliance of Reformed Churches, we visited the slave dungeons of Elmina and Cape Coast where millions of Africans were commodified, sold and subjected to the horrors of repression and death. The cries of "never again" are put to the lie by the ongoing realities of human trafficking and the oppression of the global economic system.

4. Today we come to take a decision of faith commitment.

Reading the Signs of the Times

5. We have heard that creation continues to groan, in bondage, waiting for its liberation (Romans 8:22). We are challenged by the cries of the people who suffer and by the woundedness of creation itself. We see a dramatic convergence between the suffering of the people and the damage done to the rest of creation.

6. The signs of the times have become more alarming and must be interpreted. The root causes of massive threats to life are above all the product of an unjust economic system defended and protected by political and military might. Economic systems are a matter of life or death.

7. We live in a scandalous world that denies God's call to life for all. The annual income of the richest 1 percent is equal to that of the poorest 57 percent, and 24,000 people die each day from poverty and malnutrition. The debt of poor countries continues to increase despite paying back their original borrowing many times over. Resource-driven wars claim the lives of millions, while millions more die of preventable diseases. The HIV and AIDS global pandemic afflicts life in all parts of the world, affecting the poorest where generic drugs are not available. The majority of those in poverty are women and children and the number of people living in absolute poverty on less than one US dollar per day continues to increase.

8. The policy of unlimited growth among industrialized countries and the drive for profit of transnational corporations have plundered the earth and severely damaged the environment. In 1989, one species disappeared each day, and by 2000 it was one every hour. Climate change, the depletion of fish stocks, deforestation, soil erosion and threats to fresh water are among the devastating consequences. Communities are disrupted, livelihoods are lost, coastal regions and Pacific islands are threatened with inundation, and storms increase. High levels of radioactivity threaten health and ecology. Life forms and cultural knowledge are being patented for financial gain.

9. This crisis is directly related to the development of

neoliberal economic globalization, which is based on the following beliefs:

- unrestrained competition, consumerism and the unlimited economic growth and accumulation of wealth is the best for the whole world;

- the ownership of private property has no social obligation;

- capital speculation, liberalization and deregulation of the market, privatization of public utilities and national resources, unrestricted access for foreign investments and imports, lower taxes, and the unrestricted movement of capital will achieve wealth for all;

- social obligations, protection of the poor and the weak, trade unions, and relationships between people, are subordinate to the processes of economic growth and capital accumulation.

10. This is an ideology that claims to be without alternative, demanding an endless flow of sacrifices from the poor and creation. It makes the false promise that it can save the world through the creation of wealth and prosperity, claiming sovereignty over life and demanding total allegiance, which amounts to idolatry.

11. We recognize the enormity and complexity of the situation. We do not seek simple answers. As seekers of truth and justice and looking through the eyes of powerless and suffering people, we see that the current world (dis)order is rooted in an extremely complex and immoral economic system defended by empire. In using the term "empire" we mean the coming together of economic, cultural, political and military power that constitutes a system of domination led by powerful nations to protect and defend their own interests.

12. In classical liberal economics, the state exists to protect private property and contracts in the competitive market. Through the struggles of the labor movement, states began to regulate markets and provide for the welfare of people. Since the 1980s, through the transnationalization of capital, neoliberalism has set out to dismantle the welfare functions of the state. Under neoliberalism the purpose of the economy is to increase profits and return for the owners of production and financial capital, while excluding the majority of the people and treating nature as a commodity.

13. As markets have become global, so have the political and legal institutions which protect them. The government of the United States of America and its allies, together with international finance and trade institutions (International Monetary Fund, World Bank, World Trade Organization) use political, economic, or military alliances to protect and advance the interest of capital owners.

14. We see the dramatic convergence of the economic crisis with the integration of economic globalization and geopolitics backed by neoliberal ideology. This is a global system that defends and protects the interests of the powerful. It affects and captivates us all. Further, in biblical terms such a system of wealth accumulation at the expense of the poor is seen as unfaithful to God and responsible for preventable human suffering and is called Mammon. Jesus has told us that we cannot serve both God and Mammon (Lk 16:13).

Confession of Faith in the Face of Economic Injustice and Ecological Destruction

15. Faith commitment may be expressed in various ways according to regional and theological traditions: as confession, as confessing together, as faith stance, as being faithful to the covenant of God. We choose confession, not meaning a classical doctrinal confession, because the World Alliance of Reformed Churches cannot make such a confession, but to show the necessity and urgency of an active response to the challenges of our time and the call of Debrecen. We invite member churches to receive and respond to our common witness.

16. Speaking from our Reformed tradition and having read the signs of the times, the General Council of the World Alliance of Reformed Churches affirms that global economic justice is essential to the integrity of our faith in God and our discipleship as Christians. We believe that the integrity of our faith is at stake if we remain silent or refuse to act in the face of the current system of neoliberal economic globalization and therefore **we confess** before God and one another.

17. **We believe** in God, Creator and Sustainer of all life, who calls us as partners in the creation and redemption of the world. We live under the promise that Jesus Christ came so that all might have life in fullness (Jn 10:10). Guided and upheld by the Holy Spirit we open ourselves to the reality of our world.

18. **We believe** that God is sovereign over all creation. "The earth is the Lord's and the fullness thereof" (Psalm 24:1).

19. **Therefore, we reject** the current world economic order imposed by global neoliberal capitalism and any other economic system, including absolute planned economies, which defy God's covenant by excluding the poor, the vulnerable and the whole of creation from the fullness of life. We reject any claim of economic, political, and military empire which subverts God's sovereignty over life and acts contrary to God's just rule.

20. **We believe** that God has made a covenant with all of creation (Gen 9:8-12). God has brought into being an earth community based on the vision of justice and peace. The covenant is a gift of grace that is not for sale in the market place (Is 55:1). It is an economy of grace for the household of all of creation. Jesus shows that this is an inclusive covenant in which the poor and marginalized are preferential partners, and calls us to put justice for the "least of these" (Mt 25:40) at the centre of the community of life. All creation is blessed and included in this covenant (Hos 2:18ff).

21. **Therefore we reject** the culture of rampant consumerism and the competitive greed and selfishness of the neoliberal global market system, or any other system, which claims there is no alternative.

22. **We believe** that any economy of the household of life, given to us by God's covenant to sustain life, is accountable to God. We believe the economy exists to serve the dignity and well being of people in community, within the bounds of the sustainability of creation. We believe that human beings are called to choose God over Mammon and that confessing our faith is an act of obedience.

23. **Therefore we reject** the unregulated accumulation of wealth and limitless growth that has already cost the lives of millions and destroyed much of God's creation.

24. **We believe** that God is a God of justice. In a world of corruption, exploitation and greed, God is in a special way the God of the destitute, the poor, the exploited, the wronged, and the abused (Psalm 146:7-9). God calls for just relationships with all creation.

25. **Therefore we reject** any ideology or economic regime that puts profits before people, does not care for all creation, and privatizes those gifts of God meant for all. We reject any teaching which justifies those who support, or fail to resist, such an ideology in the name of the gospel.

26. **We believe** that God calls us to stand with those who are victims of injustice. We know what the Lord requires of us: to do justice, love kindness and walk in God's way (Micah 6:8). We are called to stand against any form of injustice in the economy and the destruction of the environment, "so that justice may roll down like waters, and righteousness like an ever-flowing stream" (Amos 5:24).

27. **Therefore we reject** any theology that claims that God is only with the rich and that poverty is the fault of the poor. We reject any form of injustice which destroys right relations – gender, race, class, disability, or caste. We reject any theology which affirms that human interests dominate nature.

28. **We believe** that God calls us to hear the cries of the poor and the groaning of creation and to follow the public mission of Jesus Christ who came so that all may have life and have it in fullness (Jn 10:10). Jesus brings justice to the oppressed and gives bread to the hungry; he frees the prisoner and restores sight to the blind (Lk 4:18); he supports and protects the downtrodden, the stranger, the orphans and the widows.

29. **Therefore we reject** any church practice or teaching which excludes the poor and care for creation, in its mission; giving comfort to those who come to "steal, kill and destroy" (Jn 10:10) rather than following the "Good Shepherd" who has come for life for all (Jn 10:11).

30. **We believe** that God calls men, women and children from every place together, rich and poor, to uphold the unity of the church and its mission, so that the reconciliation to which Christ calls can become visible.

31. **Therefore we reject** any attempt in the life of the church to separate justice and unity.

32. **We believe** that we are called in the Spirit to account for the hope that is within us through Jesus Christ, and believe that justice shall prevail and peace shall reign.

33. **We commit ourselves** to seek a global covenant for justice in the economy and the earth in the household of God.

34. **We humbly confess** this hope, knowing that we, too, stand under the judgment of God's justice.

- We acknowledge the complicity and guilt of those who consciously or unconsciously benefit from the current neoliberal economic global system; we recognize that this includes both churches and members of our own Reformed family and therefore we call for confession of sin.

- We acknowledge that we have become captivated by the culture of consumerism, and the competitive greed and selfishness of the current economic system. This has all too often permeated our very spirituality.

- We confess our sin in misusing creation and failing to play our role as stewards and companions of nature.

- We confess our sin that our disunity within the Reformed family has impaired our ability to serve God's mission in fullness.

35. **We believe**, in obedience to Jesus Christ, that the church is called to confess, witness and act, even though the authorities and human law might forbid them, and punishment and suffering be the consequence (Acts 4:18ff). Jesus is Lord.

36. **We join in praise** to God, Creator, Redeemer, Spirit, who has "brought down the mighty from their thrones, lifted up the lowly, filled the hungry with good things and sent the rich away with empty hands" (Lk 1:52f).

Covenanting for Justice

37. By confessing our faith together, we covenant in obedience to God's will as an act of faithfulness in mutual solidarity and in accountable relationships. This binds us together to work for justice in the economy and the earth both in our common global context as well as our various regional and local settings.

38. On this common journey, some churches have already expressed their commitment in a confession of faith. We urge them to continue to translate this confession into concrete actions both regionally and locally. Other churches have already begun to engage in this process, including taking actions, and we urge them to engage further, through education, confession and action. To those other churches, which are still in the process of recognition, we urge them on the basis of our mutual covenanting accountability, to deepen their education and move forward towards confession.

39. The General Council calls upon member churches, on the basis of this covenanting relationship, to undertake the difficult and prophetic task of interpreting this confession to their local congregations.

40. The General Council urges member churches to implement this confession by following up the Public Issues Committee's recommendations on economic justice and ecological issues.

41. The General Council commits the World Alliance of Reformed Churches to work together with other communions, the ecumenical community, the community of other faiths, civil movements and people's movements for a just economy and the integrity of creation and calls upon our member churches to do the same.

42. Now we proclaim with passion that we will commit ourselves, our time and our energy to changing, renewing, and restoring the economy and the earth, choosing life, so that we and our descendants might live (Deuteronomy 30:19).

The Economic Community

United Methodist Church (2004)

We claim all economic systems to be under the judgment of God no less than other facets of the created order. Therefore, we recognize the responsibility of governments to develop and implement sound fiscal and monetary policies that provide for the economic life of individuals and corporate entities and that ensure full employment and adequate incomes with a minimum of inflation. We believe private and public economic enterprises are responsible for the social costs of doing business, such as employment and environmental pollution, and that they should be held accountable for these costs. We support measures that would reduce the concentration of wealth in the hands of a few. We further support efforts to revise tax structures and to eliminate governmental support programs that now benefit the wealthy at the expense of other persons.

A) Property – We believe private ownership of property is a trusteeship under God, both in those societies where it is encouraged and where it is discouraged, but is limited by the overriding needs of society. We believe that Christian faith denies to any person or group of persons exclusive and arbitrary control of any other part of the created universe. Socially and culturally conditioned ownership of property is, therefore, to be considered a responsibility to God. We believe, therefore, governments have the responsibility, in the pursuit of justice and order under law, to provide procedures that protect the rights of the whole society as well as those of private ownership.

B) Collective Bargaining – We support the right of public and private (including farm, government, institutional, and domestic) employees and employers to organize for collective bargaining into unions and other groups of their own choosing. Further, we support the right of both parties to protection in so doing and their responsibility to bargain in good faith within the framework of the public interest. In order that the rights of all members of society may be maintained and promoted, we support innovative bargaining procedures that include representatives of the public interest in negotiation and settlement of labor-management contracts, including some that may lead to forms of judicial resolution of issues. We reject the use of violence by either party during collective bargaining or any labor/management disagreement. We likewise reject the permanent replacement of a worker who engages in a lawful strike.

C) Work and Leisure – Every person has the right to a job at a living wage. Where the private sector cannot or does not provide jobs for all who seek and need them, it is the responsibility of government to provide for the creation of such jobs. We support social measures that ensure the physical and mental safety of workers, that provide for the equitable division of products and services, and that encourage an increasing freedom in the way individuals may use their leisure time. We recognize the opportunity leisure provides for creative contributions to society and encourage methods that allow workers additional blocks of discretionary time. We support educational, cultural, and recreational outlets that enhance the use of such time. We believe that persons come before profits. We deplore the selfish spirit that often pervades our economic life. We support policies that encourage the sharing of ideas in the workplace, cooperative and collective work arrangements. We support rights of workers to refuse to work in situations that endanger health and/or life without jeopardy to their jobs. We support policies that would reverse the increasing concentration of business and industry into monopolies.

D) Consumption – Consumers should exercise their economic power to encourage the manufacture of goods that are necessary and beneficial to humanity while avoiding the desecration of the environment in either production or consumption. Consumers should avoid purchasing products made in conditions where workers are being exploited because of their age, gender, or economic status. And while the limited options available to consumers make this extremely difficult to accomplish, buying "Fair Trade Certified" products is one sure way consumers can use their purchasing power to make a contribution to the common good. The International Standards of Fair Trade are based on ensuring livable wages for small farmers and their families, working with democratically run farming cooperatives, buying direct so that the benefits and profits from trade actually reach the farmers and their communities, providing vitally important advance credit, and encouraging ecologically sustainable farming practices. Consumers should not only seek out companies whose product lines reflect a strong commitment to these standards, but should also encourage expanded corporate participation in the Fair Trade market. Consumers should evaluate their consumption of goods and services in the light of the need for enhanced quality of life rather than unlimited production of material goods. We call upon consumers, including local congregations and Church-related institutions, to organize to achieve these goals and to express dissatisfaction with harmful economic, social, or ecological practices through such appropriate methods as boycott, letter writing, corporate resolution, and advertisement. For example, these methods can be used to influence better television and radio programming.

E) Poverty – In spite of general affluence in the industrialized nations, the majority of persons in the world live in poverty. In order to provide basic needs such as food, clothing, shelter, education, health care, and other necessities, ways must be found to share more equitably the resources of the world. Increasing technology, when accompanied by exploitative economic practices, impoverishes many persons and makes poverty self-perpetuating. Therefore, we do not hold poor people morally responsible for their economic state. To begin to alleviate poverty, we support such policies as: adequate income maintenance, quality education, decent housing, job training, meaningful employment opportunities, adequate medical and hospital care, and humanization and radical revisions of welfare programs. Since low wages are often a cause of poverty, employers should pay their employees a wage that does not require them to depend upon government subsidies such as food stamps or welfare for their livelihood.

F) Migrant Workers – Migratory and other farm workers, who have long been a special concern of the Church's ministry, are by the nature of their way of life excluded from many of the economic and social benefits enjoyed by other workers. Many of the migrant laborers' situations are aggravated because they are racial and ethnic persons who have been oppressed with numerous other inequities within the society. We advocate for the rights of all migrants and applaud their efforts toward responsible self-organization and self-determination. We call upon governments and all employers to ensure for migratory workers the same economic, educational, and social benefits enjoyed by other citizens. We call upon our churches to seek to develop programs of service to such migrant people who come within their parish and support their efforts to organize for collective bargaining.

G) Gambling – Gambling is a menace to society, deadly to the best interests of moral, social, economic, and spiritual life, and destructive of good government. As an act of faith and concern, Christians should abstain from gambling and should strive to minister

to those victimized by the practice. Where gambling has become addictive, the Church will encourage such individuals to receive therapeutic assistance so that the individual's energies may be redirected into positive and constructive ends. The Church should promote standards and personal lifestyles that would make unnecessary and undesirable the resort to commercial gambling – including public lotteries – as a recreation, as an escape, or as a means of producing public revenue or funds for support of charities or government.

H) Family Farms – The value of family farms has long been affirmed as a significant foundation for free and democratic societies. In recent years, the survival of independent farmers worldwide has been threatened by various factors, including the increasing concentration of all phases of agriculture into the hands of a limited number of transnational corporations. The concentration of the food supply for the many into the hands of the few raises global questions of justice that cry out for vigilance and action. We call upon the agribusiness sector to conduct itself with respect for human rights primarily in the responsible stewardship of daily bread for the world, and secondarily in responsible corporate citizenship that respects the rights of all farmers, small and large, to receive a fair return for honest labor. We advocate for the rights of people to possess property and to earn a living by tilling the soil. We call upon our churches to do all in their power to speak prophetically to the matters of food supply and the people who grow the food for the world.

I) Corporate Responsibility – Corporations are responsible not only to their stockholders, but also to other stakeholders: their workers, suppliers, vendors, customers, the communities in which they do business, and for the earth, which supports them. We support the public's right to know what impact corporations have in these various arenas, so that people can make informed choices about which corporations to support. We applaud corporations that voluntarily comply with standards that promote human well-being and protect the environment.

J) Trade and Investment – We affirm the importance of international trade and investment in an interdependent world. Trade and investment should be based on rules that support the dignity of the human person, a clean environment and our common humanity. Trade agreements must include mechanisms to enforce labor rights and human rights as well as environmental standards. Broad-based citizen advocacy and participation in trade negotiations must be ensured through democratic mechanisms of consultation and participation.

THE QUR'AN *and* WORKER JUSTICE

Interfaith Worker Justice (2002)

The Muslim community and the labor movement share the common goals of social justice, economic fairness, and fair treatment in the workplace. In fact, the history of Islam is rooted in a firm stand against economic exploitation. When Prophet Muhammad ibn (son of) Abdullah, *may Allah be pleased with Him,* began teaching Islam in Mecca, it shook up an unjust economic structure that allowed the rich to take advantage of the poor. Before Prophet Muhammad departed, he left behind The Holy Qur'an, a book filled with guidance on how men and women should treat each other in various situations, including the workplace.

The Holy Qur'an urges the proper treatment and respect of workers. Several Muslim leaders discussed the relevance of the Holy Qur'an to the struggle for dignity in the workplace with union leaders and other religious leaders during the "Islam and Labor: Forging Partnerships Conference," held Nov. 10, 2001, in Washington, D.C. Co-convened by the National Interfaith Committee for Worker Justice and the Muslim Public Affairs Council, the conference sought to build relationships between the Muslims, interfaith committees and labor communities.

Referencing heavily from the Holy Qur'an and the life of Prophet Muhammad, several Muslim Imams (leaders) discussed worker justice, the connection between faith and works, class and gender equality, and the responsibility of employers. The essence of their remarks can be summed up in one sentence uttered by Prophet Muhammad to his companions about 1400 years ago:

"None of you has faith unless you love for your brother what you love for yourself."

The Imams pledged to work with organized labor to secure economic justice for low-wage workers in America. This booklet is a result of the dialogue and highlights key themes discussed during the conference.

Standing Together for Worker Justice

In Islam, it is neither a person's wealth, gender, or ethnicity that makes them a better person. "Islam teaches that the best in God's sight are those that stand for righteousness," said Imam Mahdi Bray of the Muslim Public Affairs Council. "To me, that signals a commonality of the human spirit regardless of our faith tradition, ethnicity, social status." The Holy Qur'an calls on all of humanity to stand for justice and to work together to ensure that people are treated fairly. "This alliance that we're working to build, reinforcing a traditional relationship between labor and religion, is needed now probably more than ever," said Imam Johari Abdul-Malik, the Muslim chaplain at Howard University in Washington, D.C. "Workers being laid off are looking to the traditional sources of support – labor unions, the church, the synagogue, the mosque and other community service organizations – to fill the gap that's being created by some of these (corporations). We have to be together with labor. We have to be on the picket line. We have to be before Congress and organizing workers around the country to fight against this consolidation of wealth."

This statement reflects a core teaching of Islam. Muslims are told to strive for justice – even "against your own self" and to establish justice coalitions that transcend faith. Prophet Muhammad discussed this very idea.

"One day a trader came to do business in Mecca (a major place of trade at the time), but was wronged by a businessman who didn't pay him his money. The trader stood on a mountain and he cried out for justice. When he cried out, people of Mecca decided to create an alliance that transcended tribal and religious barriers to fight for the rights of those wronged. Before Muhammad Ibn Abdullah received revelation and became a prophet, he joined this coalition and after becoming a prophet, he said to one of his companions, 'I was called to this coalition before I became a prophet and if somebody called me today to stand for what is just and address issues of equality and fairness with people of different backgrounds, I would respond,'" said Imam Mohamed Magid of the Washington, D.C.-based ADAMS Center. "One of the missions of a Muslim is to work with those who work for justice."

- O you who believe! Stand out firmly for justice, as witnesses to Allah, even as against yourselves, or your parents, or your kin, and whether it be (against) rich or poor…. *Holy Qur'an 4:135*
- The Messenger of Allah said, "Help thy brother whether he is the doer of wrong or wrong is done to him." His companions said, "O Messenger! We can help a man to whom wrong is done, but how could we help him when he is the doer of wrong?" He said: "Take hold of his hand from doing wrong." *Manual of Hadith*

Qur'an – (kə-ran′, -rän′ also spelled Koran, Quran, Alkoran) is the holy scripture revealed by Allah (God) to Muhammad ibn Abdullah. The word Qur'an literally means readings or recitations. These revelations consist of verses (ayat) grouped into 114 chapters (suras).

Imam Johari Abdul-Malik, Imam Makram El-Amin, and Imam Mohamed Magid

Faith, Works, and Dignity

The idea of "faith and good works" is a theme highlighted often throughout the Holy Qur'an. Though there are some spiritual connotations, it also refers to the duties and responsibilities placed on people to earn a living by contributing to society and taking care of their families. In general, Muslims are encouraged to work hard and be honest.

"With works comes dignity," said Imam Makram El-Amin of Minnesota. "No one enjoys a meal more than a person who actually gives their time, effort, and labor to go out and to provide a way, to take care of themselves and their families." In Islamic tradition, every profession, organization, corporation, and union of service oriented or trade workers should be established with the purpose of serving humanity. Therefore, all are regarded with dignity and honor. This principle is also revealed in the hadith (sayings) of Prophet Muhammad Ibn Abdullah who viewed all professions honorably and taught those who followed him to do the same. Even the humblest of work carries with it dignity, as long as one's worldly pursuit does not take them away from remembrance of God.

- No one eats better food than that which he eats out of the work of his hand. *A Manual of Hadith*
- They believe in Allah and the Last Day; they enjoin what is right, and forbid what is wrong; and they hasten (in emulation) in (all) good works: they are in the ranks of the righteous. *Holy Qur'an 3:114*
- And those who believe and whose seeds follow them in Faith – to them shall We join their families: nor shall We deprive them (of the fruit) of aught of their works: (yet) is each individual in pledge for his deeds. *Holy Qur'an 52:21*
- O ye messengers! Enjoy (all) things good and pure, and work righteousness: for I am well-acquainted with (all) that ye do. *Holy Qur'an 23:51*
- It is these who hasten in every good work, and these who are foremost in them. *Holy Qur'an 23:61*

Hadith – is the record of an individual saying or action or approvals of Muhammad taken as a model of behavior by Muslims. The word *hadith* literally means communication or narrative. The sayings and the traditions of Prophet Muhammad are called *hadith*. These are explanations, interpretations, and the living examples of the Prophet. His sayings are found in books called the *Hadith*, which have been compiled into different books by various authors. Some famous collectors of *hadith* are Imam Al-Bukhari, Imam An-Nasa'i, and Imam Majah.

Equality

One of the tools used by Prophet Muhammad and his companions to end the unjust economic system in Mecca, Arabia, was to teach the concept of equality. During that time in Mecca there was a large underclass of slaves who served the rich. Prophet Muhammad made it clear that all are equal. The same concept is relevant today.

"Prophet Mohammed and his companions ended slavery in Arabia. We now have what some people would call wage slavery," said Imam Abdul-Malik. "The first step of ending slavery (in Arabia) was to say that the slave is equal to the master. Once there is the idea that the slave, or today, the worker, is equal to the master (or employer) that becomes the unraveling of this and other forms of discrimination. We all have rights. No matter whether you are working in the corporate penthouse, or down in the basement sorting the mail, all people have rights. They're equal before their Lord." This principle speaks to class, race and gender differences.

- Men shall have the benefit of what they earn, and women shall have the benefit of what they earn. *Holy Qur'an 4:32*
- I will not waste the work of a worker among you, whether male or female, the one of you being from the other. *Holy Qur'an 3:194*
- O mankind! We created you from a single (pair) of a male and a female, and made you into nations and tribes, that ye may know each other (not that ye may despise each other)....*Holy Qur'an 49:13*

Employer Responsibility

The Holy Qur'an teaches that people should "fulfill all of your obligations," said Imam El-Amin. "An employer is obligated to properly compensate, which is not just about money. We're talking about providing a good atmosphere; good working conditions, benefits, and allowing a person to have time with their families." In Islam, perfect honesty is enjoined in all business transactions, including how an employer treats an employee. Those who are in a better financial position and employ others have more responsibility to ensure that they treat people with fairness, remembering that all humanity is one.

This principle in Islam is displayed during the annual Hajj (pilgrimage) ritual where people from all walks of life come together shedding their traditional ethnic clothing, jewelry, and all other articles that reveal different levels of social status. This helps to demonstrate that God is the God of all, rich and poor.

"Muhammad the Prophet said, 'Pay the worker while the sweat is still on the brow.' This speaks of timely compensation," said Imam Makram El-Amin.

- Give full measure when you measure out and weigh with a fair balance. This is fair and better in the end. *Holy Qur'an 17:35*
- When you hire, compensate the workers and treat them fairly. *A Manual of Hadith*
- Woe to those that deal in fraud. Those who when they have to receive by measure, from men exact full measure, but when they have to give by measure, or weight to men, give less than due. *Holy Qur'an 83:1-3*
- Give just measure, and cause no loss (to others by fraud). *Holy Qur'an 26:181-183*

Labor Statements

Presbyterian Church (USA)

Employment, unemployment, working conditions and labor relations are all subjects that have merited the attention of a variety of Presbyterian General Assemblies. Here are a few of the outstanding examples:

… the church must seek to open the lines of communication for Christian action in the areas of tension between labor and management. … Management, as a governing force, should be called upon to manage fairly for all concerned … and not to be a force only for the few. **1959**

The General Assembly expresses its confidence in collective bargaining as the most responsible and democratic way of resolving issues in labor-management relations … calls upon individual Presbyterian union members to take a responsible part in the activities of their unions. **1959**

Since God has created life and material resources to sustain life, (humanity) does not have the right to deny life by withholding the means of existence to some … justice demands that everyone have the material conditions necessary for their physical and social existence … a guarantee to every American for an income … large enough to provide for basic needs and to sustain every person's participation, with dignity, in society …. **1971**

… we affirm that the Church should espouse for all persons the opportunity and responsibility for productive work … we affirm for all persons the right to be paid adequately and treated with fairness and dignity … we affirm the right of all workers … to join labor organizations and participate in collective bargaining … we affirm the necessity of the church to view economic issues from the side of the lowly and oppressed and for Christians active in our economic system to be concerned for serving the needs of the world …. The Presbyterian Church … will need to engage in a conscious effort to view labor management issues from the perspective of the unskilled, uneducated and underpaid …. The point of the Parable of the Laborers and the Vineyard (Mt. 20:1-16) is that all workers receive a just wage …. The Church affirms the rights of labor organization and collective bargaining as minimum demands of justice … and arrangements which offer opportunities for workers … to share greater economic rewards. **1980**

… employment training (should) be for jobs that will pay a living wage … the focus (should) be on job creation where jobs at a living wage do not exist … continued health benefits for parents and children be made available …. **1987**

Justice demands that social institutions guarantee all persons the opportunity to participate actively in economic decision-making that affects them. All workers – including undocumented, migrant, and farm workers – have the right to choose to organize for the purposes of collective bargaining. **1995**

In **1997**, the 209th General Assembly of the PCUSA resolved to:

- Endorse the Day of Conscience and Holiday Season of Conscience as a public witness to the need to eliminate sweatshops and urge members of the Presbyterian Church (USA) to support and participate in the events.

- Call for the Workplace Code of Conduct and Principles of Monitoring to include provisions that assure wages above subsistence levels and guarantee independent monitoring of compliance.

- Urge the Presbyterian Hunger Program and the Committee on Mission Responsibility Through Investment (MRTI) in collaboration with other offices and networks to give leadership to the education and mobilization effort.

In **2006**, the 217th General Assembly of the PCUSA resolved that "the 217th General Assembly (2006) of the Presbyterian Church (USA), through the Stated Clerk of the PC (USA), communicate to all members of Congress its desire that legislation to increase the minimum wage be swiftly passed and accurately reflect the increase in the cost of living since the last minimum wage increase in 1997. Additionally, middle governing bodies, local congregations, and individuals are encouraged to support efforts to increase the minimum wage at state and local levels as well."

4 Theology and Ethics of Work

Introduction

The majority of academic scholarship on the theology and ethics of work focuses on business ethics and a theology of work that specifically speaks to how to talk about God while at work or how to deal with difficult situations at work as a person of faith. These works are usually written exclusively for businesses or white-collar workers. Too little attention is given to the working class or the power differentials between management and workers.

This section focuses primarily on religious theologies and ethics of work that respect the dignity of workers from Christian and Jewish perspectives. This compilation of scholarly writings also highlights the difference in power dynamics between the poor and wealthy.

Dr. Douglas Meeks has written one of the best-known theological books on economics, *God the Economist: The Doctrine of God and Political Economy* (1989). In the chapter we present here, "God and Work," Meeks begins to develop a theology that respects the dignity, value and meaning of all work.

Dr. Joan Martin is the author of a deeply thought-provoking book titled *More than Chains and Toil: A Christian Work Ethic of Enslaved Women* (2000). The stories she relates are powerful testimonies of enslaved women during the antebellum period. These stories highlight the realities of inhuman treatment of enslaved women and how they managed to survive amidst incredible abuse. The chapter "Whose Work Ethic? A Womanist Reading of 'A Work Ethic' from the Bible to the United States," which we present here, offers new insights in the ethics of work. Martin has served on the Advisory Committee of IWJ's Religious Perspectives on Work project.

In "And Demand Justice," Dr. Aryeh Cohen focuses from a Jewish perspective on the importance of being ethical consumers and the importance of government's involvement in ensuring justice for workers, using Wal-Mart as a case study. Dr. Cohen is an associate professor of Rabbinic Literature at the Ziegler School of Rabbinic Studies, American Jewish University (formerly University of Judaism). He has also served on the Advisory Committee of IWJ's Religious Perspectives on Work project.

Rabbi Jill Jacobs participated in IWJ's Seminary Summer program and has since been one of the leading Jewish writers and teachers engaging in justice for workers and their families. Her article "The Living Wage: A Jewish Approach" focuses on why a living wage matters. It is reprinted from the magazine *Conservative Judaism* (Spring 2003). Rabbi Jacobs recently joined IWJ's Board of Directors.

The final article, focusing on the importance of companies striving to pay a living wage to their employees, is written by Dr. Michael Naughton, director of the John A. Ryan Institute for Catholic Social Thought of the Center for Catholic Studies at the University of St. Thomas. Dr. Naughton has taught for IWJ's summer internship programs.

God and Work

M. Douglas Meeks (1989)

No household will survive without work. Unless what is necessary for human life is made available by human effort we cannot even speak of an economy. Work, moreover, far from being simply the means of producing what is necessary for life, is also a means of access to household and a means of shaping the household. Thus a community constitutes itself in answering the questions, Who gets what kind of work? Who owns the tools and product of work? The way a community understands, distributes, and controls work will decide who will have access to livelihood and how the members of the household will relate to each other. How a community or society views work affects profoundly every person in it.

God concepts, albeit highly secularized in the modern world, have grounded and modeled society's prevailing concepts of work. Work is a central theological issue because nowhere are the relationships of authority and subordination more apparent than in the relationships of work. Work is the most immediate way in which human beings dominate and exploit each other. And those who would control other people through work must be able to control what a society teaches about the value and meaning, the incentives and control, and the distribution of work. The church's teachings about God, full of rationales of authority and subordination, have been available for social understandings of work and for selective use by those who would control work. Richard Baxter recommended employing the godly servant because he would "do all your service in obedience to God, as if God himself had bid him do it." Peter D. Anthony remarks, "The engagement of God as the supreme supervisor was a most convenient device; a great part of the effort of modern management has been aimed at finding a secular but equally omnipotent equivalent in the worker's own psyche."

The Ambiguity of Work

Work, perhaps even more than property, is profoundly ambiguous. For millennia human beings have blessed and cursed each other through work. Positive and negative views of work accompany each other, often in the same person. On the positive side, work has been extolled as the single way in which human beings can find meaning and purpose in life. The promises of work are that it justifies a person's existence, it proves a person's salvation, it gives a person value and dignity, status and security; it guarantees the future; it gives an upper hand over the competitor; it creates the self and the self's world. With such promises work is bound to be extolled. In the United States, especially during election times, political parties vie to elevate work as the reason for America's success in the world. And as for the individual, if he or she is willing to work, there is no reason success will not ensue. Every American, it is assumed, is born with the inclination to work with enthusiasm and devotion.

On the negative side, work has been connected with animal needs and denigrated as a dehumanizing distraction from the higher pursuits of the human soul. Work destroys what is peculiarly human. Work promises nothing but bare survival and that with considerable pain. "In the sweat of your face you shall eat bread . . ." (Gen. 3:19). This is the recognition of those who lead lives of hard work but never expect to find fulfillment in it. It requires only mild objectivity to see the inequities, brutalities, and exploitation of work in the global household. Studs Terkel caught this assessment in the Introduction to his book *Working*: "This book, being about work, is by its very nature, about violence – to the spirit as well as the body."

The paradoxes of work abound. Some say work is the deepest satisfaction of their lives and has made them who they are; others say work has destroyed their health and their family life. Some say technology has overcome backbreaking work; others say machine work and the division of labor have caused social fragmentation and boring and demeaning work. Some say work is the great democratizer; others say workers have had ever less participation in shaping their own work and determining how the resources and product of their work are controlled.

Some say all honest work obtains dignity; others say there is an enormous discrepancy between different kinds of work, not to speak of income from different kinds of work. Some say hard work will allow one to get ahead; others say this is true only for a very few, and often their getting ahead does not have much to do with the quantity and quality of their work. Some say work secures their future; others say their work is the most insecure thing about their future. Some say work has its own built-in assumption of progress;

work will make things better. Others say progress is built on the backs of those who have to work with no prospect of benefiting from progress. Some say work is the way to enjoy the immense benefits of the capitalist society. Others say that working for capitalism spreads the effects of exploitative work relationships like a cancer into every dimension of life.

So there appear to be two deeply opposed views of work. Work, on the one hand, seems to be a curse such that it would be better for people to fold their hands and cease all human activity. On the other hand, work seems to be a blessing associated with the use of work's product and with satisfaction in accomplishment.

While the ambiguities and paradoxes of work are lived out in human relationships hour by hour, what everyone can agree upon is that work has to be done. Whatever value we put on it, human existence is dependent on work, even if some "fortunate" people succeed in escaping from it. But who does it and under what circumstances and with what effect are questions which human beings have always disputed. Only one thing seems fairly certain: There will be a difference in perspective between those who do work and those who control work. The average life span for a migrant farm worker is 49 years, as compared to 72 years for the average American. Work will be regarded differently by those who do hard, dirty, and grueling work and those who do self-determined and satisfying work. And, of course, work will appear differently to those who have no work and those who take their work for granted.

In our time unemployment, underemployment, lack of meaningful work, and inequality in the distribution of hard work lead the list of problems with work, especially in view of the strong ideologies of work that still reign officially in our society. People are told that they are nothing if they do not work, but at the same time they hear that six to eight percent unemployment will be considered normal or desirable in our economy. In recent years one might read front-page headlines declaring the administration's conviction that those who do not work are not "entitled" to what it takes to live and in the next column an announcement that two hundred thousand jobs are being eliminated in the automobile, steel, or other industry. How is it possible for a societal household to say both things: 1) Those in the household who do not work will have no dignity, and yet 2) there is not enough work in the household for everyone to do? It is possible because of ideologies of work.

Ideologies of Work and a Trinitarian View of Work

Historically, there seem to be two choices: coerced work or ideologies of work that convince people to work "voluntarily" or so cover up the dehumanization of work that it can be tolerated. Ideologies of work seek to make hard work, underpaid work, or lack of work seem legitimate in a divided society. Seeking at all costs the cooperation of subordinates, work ideologies keep us from remembering what in the tradition would make us conscious of the suffering of people from work in the present. Their purpose is to make the existing shape of work seem universal or axiomatic, whereas they actually serve specific interests in a historical context. The most successful ideology is one that is not recognized as an ideology. The church's doctrine of God has sometimes aided the camouflage of work ideologies, making them seem common sensical assumptions, generally agreed upon.

To become free from dehumanizing ideologies of work requires that we remember the biblical narratives of God which open up a new praxis of work and criticize the God concepts that shore up the prevalent ideologies of work. Politico-economic theology should seek to detect the theological components of work ideologies and to ask whether they serve the will of God as known in the history of Israel and in Jesus Christ or whether they serve the dehumanization and alienation of human beings through work. To do this, theology should ask about the work of God as known in the triune community's uncovering in the history of Israel and of Jesus. In the biblical traditions work is filled with theological content. It is the epitome of the doctrine of salvation. The human distortion of work makes God's work of redeeming human work necessary. God's work is against domination and exploitation through work. It is against individualistic, noncooperative, falsely motivated, and unjustly distributed work.

The Market View of Work

In our society ideologies have appeared predominantly in connection with the developing market view of work. According to the market view the purpose of work is to produce goods or services in return for money which in turn is spent on goods and services. It is held that people work harder in order to get more. This view assumes that the best way to distribute work is through market mechanisms. That one earns money to buy goods by entering the market distribution of work is basically all the market demands.

But these simple rules of the market are not sufficient to explain the massive suffering that results from work, including being shut out of the work market. For those who have no work or have demoralizing or underpaid work, there must be some justification supplied by ideology. Moreover, as soon as complex industrialism was introduced, such a calculative connection to a job proved insufficient to motivate the kind of skilled work required. Market theory requires a degree of commitment to work that it is incapable of commanding. Thus there was a need for ideologies of work that could support the performance of labor as if it were an absolute end in itself. This is not a "natural state of affairs" and can be achieved only through an "arduous process of education." The problem has been to produce ideologies of work compatible with liberal economic doctrine when in fact imperatives to work that remain within the terms of the market logic prove repellent to subordinates.

Let us consider some principal points of the ideologies of work and set over against them some trinitarian perspectives on work.

Should everyone have a right to humanizing and remunerative work? If labor is made a commodity and distributed according to market rules, then some people will be left out of work. The market view of work will therefore require ideologies that make it appear reasonable that some people do not have work and that some people have degrading work.

Should work be cooperative? Early on, Adam Smith saw that the division of labor at the heart of modern industrialism would make cooperation almost impossible. He did not, however, see the worst consequences: the anomie caused by persons being separated into minute functions and tasks and the alienation caused by the social division of human beings by interest and class. The market view of work will thus require ways of justifying the necessity of alienating and anomic industrial work.

Should work take place in a democratic environment? In the modern workplace efficiency has been the dominant criterion of work. This has led to harsher discipline and bureaucratic control of workers and less participation by workers in the decisions that affect their work and the disposition of the product of their work. Thus ideologies have been constructed that try to motivate workers within a hierarchical situation that robs them of freedom to participate in the shaping of their work.

Should work be motivated by regard for the community? According to Adam Smith, cooperation was to be provided not by a benevolent regard each for the other's welfare but rather through self-interest. The resulting moral principle of selfishness is a process of demoralization unprecedented in history. When fear of losing one's job is the whip with which employers extract greater work effort, work destroys community rather than supporting it. This necessitates ideologies exalting the individual at work in isolation.

A Trinitarian Perspective on Work

A trinitarian view of God as the economic community of righteousness will provide us with the hermeneutical keys for understanding biblical perspectives on God's work and human work as well as a critical focus on the ways certain theological emphases on work have been used ideologically in the past and the present. We shall again draw on the focal doctrine of *perichōrēsis*, now applied to God's work. The life of the triune God pictures the economy of work that God is working to bring into being. The Trinity is the church's teaching against domination through work. What is the character of God's work?

The first thing to be said is that each person of the Trinity engages in *distinctive personal work*. Each person of the Trinity is described in the narratives of Jesus/Israel as working. Each makes a specific contribution to the divine economic work in and for the world. On the basis of these narratives we can also speak of the peculiar work of each person within and for the divine community itself.

The tradition has usually identified the work of the Father as creating, the work of the Son as redeeming, and the work of the Holy Spirit as creating anew. Or, more immediately focused in the story of Jesus, we could say that the Father does the work of sending, the Son the work of being sent, and the Holy Spirit the work of empowerment of the mission of the Father and the Son. No person of the divine community is left without distinctive work. Each has a name, a reputation, a dignity, a place within the community of work. The Trinity is a criticism of all systems of work that exclude some people in the household from distinctive personal work.

Second, the Trinity engages in *cooperative work*. Traditional views of the triune persons tend to emphasize the Father as being the exclusively active person and the other two persons as being acted upon or simply doing the bidding of the Father. The work of the Holy Spirit is especially deemphasized. But according to the scriptural narratives the whole community is involved in each work, event, or process of God. The Father does not work as an isolated individual; every work the Father does is in cooperation with the Son and the Holy Spirit. The same is true for the Son and the Holy Spirit. They each contribute their own work to creation, redemption, and new creation. Thus the second hermeneutical key is the *co-work* of the persons of the triune community. God's work is the cooperative work of the three persons of the community of righteousness. Each person's distinctive work coinheres in the work of the other members of the community, that is, each person's work cannot be done without the cooperation of the others. God's work is thoroughly communal or social work. The distinctive work of one member of the Trinity is made possible by the cooperation of the other members. Their freedom is to communicate themselves to each other in love. What of themselves they give up in work they find again in the fullness of the community for whose life they work. The Trinity is a criticism of all structures of work that atomize the worker by separating his or her work from the other members of the community, the worker from the product of his or her work, or working classes from nonworking classes.

The third hermeneutical key is the *equalitarian work* of the triune community. While the three persons of the Trinity have their own work, the work of no one of them elevates that person higher than the others. Traditionally the Father's work has been given ascendancy resulting in a hierarchy or stratification of work within the divine community. This in turn has given justification to an authoritarian order of subordination for human work. The master-slave relationship has found a justification in the notion of the hierarchically arranged work of God. But the fact that the Father initiates the work of the triune community does not mean that the Father's is a higher, more valuable work. The Trinity is a criticism of all forms of work that incur relationships of domination.

The fourth hermeneutical key is the integration of the Triune community's work through the *self-giving* love of each other. The work of each is done for the life of the community. The motivation and incentive of the triune community's work is the fullness of life of the other and the redemption of the creation. God works for the sake of God's faithfulness, for the sake of keeping God's promises and thus showing God to be God. God's work is aimed at the fulfillment of what God has promised. God's work is the expression of God's faithfulness.

This calls into question all human attempts to integrate work through coercive means, such as state laws, or through dehumanizing incentives such as poverty or the drive to unaccountable accumulated wealth. The unity of God's work is not gained by the uniformity of being or a notion of self-possession but by the suffering of each person for the other and for the creation. The work of love is the unifying and integrating of God's work. Life-giving work is suffering love. The Trinity is a criticism of ideologically defined motivations and incentives of work. All ideologies of work stand under judgment by the integration of God's work through suffering love.

God's work is personally distinctive, cooperative, equalitarian, integrated by love, and faithful to God's promises.

We turn now to three major tendencies detectable in modern ideologies of work: the 1) degradation, 2) exaltation, 3) redemption of work.

The Degradation of Work

The first tendency is a negative view of work found in the ancient and modern aristocratic denigration of work, the romantic exaltation of leisure, and the degradation of the worker. Christian teaching abets this ideology when it separates the Holy Spirit from the economic community of the Trinity. The Holy Spirit then becomes a subjective dynamic that can be used to justify, with a view of a God who does not work and suffer, the advantages of some people who do not have to work. Such a narrow pneumatology serves the claim that human life can be filled with meaning only when it can transcend work. This spiritualizing tendency, in turn, plays into the hands of attempts, pervasive in every society, to distribute hard work to degraded people.

Does God work? This is a crucial question, for the denigration of work and the degradation of the worker in both antiquity and modernity are supported by the view that the gods do not have to work. That is what makes them gods. The virtue of the life of the polis is connected with the freedom of the gods from work. Only those who live beyond the realm of the necessity of work can be considered virtuous and hence rulers of the *oikos* and "guardians" of the polis. Thus the *pater familias*, the male householder, is free, like the gods, to leave the realm of necessity and lead a life of decision-making in the polis. Those left behind, slaves, artisans, women, and children, simply reflect the meaninglessness of labor. Not corresponding to such divine virtue, they are merely *metics* or "living instruments" for producing subsistence and reproducing life. To be unfree is to be condemned to work; to work is to become unfree. Work defiles, and whoever is defiled has to work.

Even in our highly developed society this divinely based dichotomy between work and virtue is still enormously influential, especially as regards the question of who will do hard work. Harvesting crops, collecting garbage, mining coal, caring for the sick and aged, cooking, and cleaning are socially necessary, even if we try to hide such work. It is still assumed that degraded work should be assigned to degraded people. As in antiquity, this work is increasingly being done by foreigners. It is impossible to keep completely outside the household people who do such necessary work, without which the household would not survive. But they remain something like strangers in the household, always viewed as lacking in worth. Feminist critiques point to the experience of estrangement through work that many women have in their own homes as well as in their work outside the home.

Christian theology sometimes supports this aristocratic disdain of work and worker by picturing God as resting throughout eternity. God makes the world as a designer makes a machine and then steps back to relax for eternity. It is as if God lives in a permanent Sabbath. Those favored by God should live free from work and enjoy the divinelike leisure that befits their inherent goodness.

This spiritualization of the doctrine of God as the leisured supreme being also lends itself to the modern search for the meaning of life in leisure and against work. Romanticism and idealism maintain that life can be fulfilled only beyond work. These movements are full of nostalgia for the golden age in which work did not kill the human spirit and did not produce inequality. There is a longing for immediate communication with nature, for contemplation, for simple pleasures in noncaste communities. We encounter such views in the utopia of Thomas More, the criticisms of Morris, Ruskin, and Southey, and the Emersonian strains of American literature. Some modern theologies of leisure and play have also echoed to a certain extent the negative view of work. They look upon the human being as a creature of the expression of being in play rather than work. They essay a "life ethic" instead of a "work ethic." They distrust work to produce meaning in life, especially the increasingly narrow sense of work in the industrial society. They also claim that in a society bent against "full employment" it is better to develop an ethic of "full life." Thus they look for positive and creative nonwork alternatives to both employment and unemployment.

A different kind of negative approach to work welcomes technology as the only means to liberation from hard work. By mastering nature technology is supposed to free us from the struggle for survival in nature and increase our leisure for cultural pursuits. Here we encounter the romantic notion that machines and human freedom will be reconciled, at least in the sense that machines will deliver human beings from the work that prevents them from being reconciled with nature. But our modern experience has been that machines save people from only some kinds of hard work and often from work that people actually like to do.

Much is to be gained from these critiques of work and appreciations of leisure and play. But it is a mistake to overlook the consequences of the denigration of work and the exaltation of leisure. Extreme theologies of freedom play into the hands of ideological justifications of unemployment and distorted forms of work. The exaltation of leisure as the meaning of life leaves open the claim that it is permissible for some people not to have meaningful work or for certain people, by their very nature, to deserve dirty work. Leisure is not sufficient compensation for lack of work or meaninglessness in work. Leisure becomes unsatisfying to the extent that society's work systems become unsatisfying, and vice versa.

God the Economist Works

Even if the biblical traditions, as we shall see, have their own negative perspectives toward work, they do not denigrate work and degrade the worker. The reason for this is God's own work. It has to be said, over against every attempt to make God a workless supreme being, that according to the biblical narratives God the Economist works. God the Economist works to bring creation into being, to redeem creation, and to create all things anew. There is also for God no work-free age at the beginning, even though God's work of creation seems relatively effortless. God is not the distant emperor or city-state king living the life of leisure while expecting God's people to do all of God's hard work. Human beings are not made, as in the Sumerian and Babylonian myths, to do the arduous work of the gods. Rather, God is the slave-freeing Economist, the liberator from the household of bondage, and the builder of the household of freedom.

God's work of liberation and creation is the ground of an affirmative view of work. Work is neither condemned nor sacralized. Even after the expulsion from the garden, work itself is not seen as a cursed fate; rather hardship and difficulty that accompany work are the result of sin (Gen. 3:17–19). Work belongs to human existence and is commanded by God (Gen. 2:15). God's work, to be sure, is qualitatively different. Human beings do not do God's work. There is a definite limitation to human work: It must be done within the finitude of the created order. Yet God calls the human being into partnership with God's creative work. Every human being, as the image of God, is called to correspond to God's work as he or she represents God's will to the creation. While human work cannot create something out of nothing, it can with imagination be similar to God's doing a new thing. Work is the power to answer with effort God's call to be God's economist in God's household. That God the Economist works and that human beings are given their own proper work by God means that work in itself is not to be denigrated.

God the Economist Rests

God also rests. God's sabbath rest, however, is justification for neither the hatred of work nor the degradation of the worker. Workday and sabbath are not divided into sacred time and worldly time. The sabbath is not reserved for gods and aristocrats and the workday for slaves and laborers. It is in God's rest that the work of human beings finds its limit. For the human being, a finite creature, sabbath is first of all a limit to the toil, pain, and fatigue of work. "So then, there remains a sabbath rest for the people of God; for whoever enters God's rest also ceases from his labors as God did from his" (Heb. 4:9). The human being, unlike God, needs recuperation. "Sweet is the sleep of the laborer" (Eccles. 5:12). For the majority of people even in our society a Sunday afternoon nap is the margin against physical and mental exhaustion. Only the "surfeit of the rich," as Ecclesiastes says, prevents the sabbath scoffers not only from resting but also from understanding the need for rest among those who labor and are heavy laden. Without sabbath, work will destroy the human being. An economy driven to incessant work by the profit motive is an economy that is driving itself mad. Sabbath is a limit to the presumptions of work.

If God's creative work culminates in rest, it is not because God's energy is depleted but because only joy can fulfill God's creative work. God rejoices in God's work, not in its efficiency or finality but in its goodness: "And God saw everything that he had made, and behold, it was very good" (Gen. 1:31). The joy of the creator makes work meaningful. Joy in being limits work. Joy and glory, not work, have the last word. God yearns for the joy of God's economists in their affirmation of their being and work. Work is connected not only with a productive value but also with a representative, imaginative, and celebrative value of joy in being and festivity. Life is a dialectic between the seriousness of work and the relaxed joy of being.

The relation between arduous work and its fruit is grounded in God's grace, which gives freely both the energy for work and its results (Ps. 65, 104). Thus sabbath is thanksgiving for this gift of the energy of work through which the earth has "yielded its increase" and "God has blessed us" (Ps. 67:6). Work and the benefits of work are to be offered back to God as acts of service and worship (Deut. 14:28–29; 26; Eccles. 38:25–39). Although the human being must work in order to bring forth the fruit of the earth and to keep the community alive, there is no "sexual or ecstatic connection between such work and its results." Work is done for the sake of God's love of the creation. Work is thus demythologized insofar as culture and civilization develop from the creator's joy in work and not from the fire and *techné* given by Prometheus.

Jesus does not do away with the sabbath; he radicalizes it. Jesus announces to the household of Israel that it is called to live by the righteousness of God's sabbath at all times and all places. The sabbath is made for the human being and thus must be removed from every cultic attempt to separate it from the situations in which work destroys human beings.

The Torah and the Gospel grant to the human being sabbath time, redeemed time. The future-giving words of the gospel, "Do not be anxious" or "Do not be afraid," open up time no longer compelled by the drives of work. The sabbath gives time for the generations to remember, tell, reflect on the stories of God's work and rest and thus to create home. The household of God comes to know its past, its future, and its name in sabbath time.

The sabbath, therefore, is not simply a negative zone separated from work. That God commands rest, then, does not mean we can define the church according to modern understandings of leisure as vacation time, the "pause that refreshes." The Sabbath is not "Miller time." The church is not the cult of the private. The church is not the place and time in which one can do anything one pleases. It is the place where sabbath rest transforms work.

The Exaltation of Work

The second ideological tendency is the valuing of work as the means of the ordering and self-justification of life. It is noticeable in the so-called Protestant work ethic and other perceptions of work in the market society. When Christian teaching isolates the Abba/ Father from the economic community with the Son and Holy Spirit, there arises a model of the overbearing task-master who works capriciously to control the work of subordinates. These notions are the mainstay of ideologies of work that attempt to justify master-subordinate relationships. They uphold the "Father God" who works by fiat. This tendency also results in a model of the isolated, self-sufficient worker. The theological view that identifies God with the Father working alone as an absolute subject without feeling with others in the community correlates with the human being as absolute subject working alone.

According to Max Weber, the new economic situation of nascent capitalism required and was partially caused by what he called "the spirit of capitalism," which emerged, he argued, from the Protestant Reformation. When the Christian "call" is secularized, vocation is attached to already existing social privilege, mostly that of civil servants and ministers. Since not everyone has a "position," the "class of the classless" is left out of the vocational ethos. Social stratification appears to be the result of divine will. This results in a hollow ring to the exhortations to work, not unlike those in Proverbs and Ecclesiastes, which assume work relations and conditions will always be as they are. The traditional emphases on work as the means of ordering society and enhancing communal participation thus gave way to increased stratification and individualism in work.

Puritan pastors called their flocks to a life of disciplined work as a way of reducing doubt about their damnation and as a sign to others of their salvation. Work as a necessity for survival or a means of bonding community gave way to work as something positive to do for one's soul. Focusing work on the subjective means of affirming one's calling and election to salvation gave rise to a sense of sovereign individuality and the justification of one's life through proficiency.

The secularization of the doctrines of providence and salvation connects work with the internal laws of progress. Work is good in itself. Work is not fundamentally problematic. It does not need to be redeemed. Work can be affirmed without any dialectic of negation. The new perspective on work produced a radical inversion of the traditional values. People were now individualized and isolated. Each one was set in competitive struggle with everyone else.

The notion of God as Father-taskmaster or as a monadic worker provides justification for (1) *laissez-faire* and libertarian freedom of entrepreneurs to do anything they want without regard to the other's needs and desires in order to realize one's own interests; (2) paternalistic freedom to use the work of others for one's own ends under the disguise of fatherly concern and protection; (3) individualized freedom and power to make one's destiny exclusively by dint of one's own work and denigration of all those who lack the initiative to be competitive in work. These ideologies portray a view of work that coincides with the nature of the market society as accumulation of wealth.

Behind these ideologies is the faith that the mechanisms of the price system, not the state, can best fulfill the utilitarian calculus (pursue pleasure, avoid pain). The "fate" in which the market mechanisms rest can be trusted to motivate the needed work. How? Fate provides poverty as the key to "persuading" people to work. Poverty is the reason for progress, for without the threat of poverty, people would not work. If you do away with the workers' poverty, you remove the workers' incentive to work and thus their sole means of bettering themselves. Since poverty is the motivation for work, it is also the reason for humanity's unhindered happiness and welfare.

The *laissez-faire* ideology of work is the most extreme in its support of hierarchical, individualistic, and egoistic modes of work. Even though entrepreneurs have generally recognized the advantage of moral responsibility inculcated in workers by the church, under the spell of *laissez-faire* they have freed themselves from moral restraint. *Laissez-faire* expressly condemns the interference of do-gooders because their good intentions always harm those they seek to help by ruining their only chance of getting out of poverty: self-restraint. The old evangelical appeal that the poor could be reformed by emulating the upper classes is rejected. *Laissez-faire* ideology even drops out the religious motifs of deferred other-worldly rewards for work. The poor now have to be left to their own attempts to better their lives. Manufacturers gained from *laissez-faire* a sanction to do almost anything as long as it was not benevolent and well-meaning.

In the face of the brutalities of the *laissez-faire* view of work, paternalism seems more humane. Actually, paternalism is a harking back to the medieval network of dependent relationships. It gives to the superior a religious obligation to reward and punish, to care for and dismiss his employees and the right to expect their dutiful service. As does God the isolated Father who rules with an iron will, the owner has the unquestioned right to control the work and life conditions of his workers. For example, George M. Pullman gave a kind of security to his workers while taking away their dignity in their work and family life. He provided his workers with housing and minimal schooling and health care but in exchange expected not only unquestioning obedience in work but also compliance in his own conception as to how necessities of life were to be delivered. The dependent person, who is usually seen as dishonest and irresolute, owes the master work and respect in exchange for keeping him or her housed and generally fit. The motivation to work is the obligation to return the favor of the master. Paternalism has usually protected both servants and masters from the worst aspects of *laissez-faire*. But paternalism, however imperfectly disguised, is the appropriation of one human being's labor power by another.

Laissez-faire and paternalism have been durable ideologies by which entrepreneurs and owners explain their actions to each other, but they convey such bleak and hopeless prospects for workers that they can serve as neither explanation nor motivation for the kind of work needed in a complex industrialized society. They are self-defeating for the purposes of industrialization. They create a dependent person without initiative, high skills, discernment, and ability to survive mobility.

In response to the deadening aspects of *laissez-faire* and paternalism ideologies the most influential and persistent work ethic in the modern world was developed. The success ethic is the individualized theory of progress writ small, in the life of the individual. In its less sophisticated form it is known by the name of Horatio Alger in the United States and by Samuel Smiles' *Self Help* in Britain. But even in its more complex ideological forms the premises are the same, and its essential features continue to appear over and over again in the defense of the advantages of the market household. The success ethic maintains elements from the Protestant work ethic, *laissez-faire*, and paternalism. Its ostensible intention, however, is to give work incentive to the unemployed or underemployed by convincing them that they are in charge of their own fate. In fact, through work they can break any fate under which they may seem to live.

Most notable in the success ethic is its pretension that poverty is no obstacle to the progress of the individual. Far from being connected with wickedness, failure,

and damnation, poverty may even be a blessing and the opulent surroundings of the rich a social disadvantage. For success does not depend on traditional privileges of inherited wealth or even talent. Even the most poverty stricken members of society and the most repressed workers should take hope in what work promises. Positive belief in work and in self are sufficient for overcoming every obstacle. Work allows one to take personal responsibility for one's own wellbeing. Self-made people do not need to cooperate with anyone else. Like *laissez-faire* the success ethic contends that benevolence should be suspended, lest it impede persons from improving themselves through work.

The success work ethic hides the reality of class differences and dampens class conflict. By claiming the common background and common interest of the employer and the worker, it gives the appearance of being democratic and egalitarian. But it envisions no work of justice to redress inequalities. Injustices will be automatically wiped away, if indeed they are real, by work. Even if work brings success to a relatively few persons, this ideology of work offers a double advantage. It promises the prospect of material success and moral virtue for those who succeed by hard work; effort is good in itself, and if one only believes, it will eventually bring material rewards. But at the same time it strengthens the dependency and discipline of those who by hard work will nevertheless fail. Despite the fact that it crops up again and again in our society, the success ethic fails to convince the majority of workers to trust their work or their superiors' values to secure themselves and their families.

Thus, in face of the failures of the ideologies of the work ethic, *laissez-faire*, paternalism, and success through self-help, one might have to draw the conclusion that the market society is not capable of producing an ideology of work that will support the kind of intense work that capitalism requires. For the great majority of people incentives to work based on being taken care of or on success give way to the simple market demand to earn money to buy commodities and services. But as we have seen, this motivation alienates workers from their work and proves constantly insufficient to encourage the work of great energy and discipline required to meet the capitalist's own interests.

Let us summarize the ideologies that attempt to exalt work. Work justifies one's existence. Life is dependent on work and organized around it. Both the self-image and social recognition of the individual depends on his or her work and is measured by the results of his or her work. The meaning of life is dependent on the possibility of work and quality of work. The competitive vocational spirit readily accepts the fragmentation of work as natural and productive so much that it resists any reform of the work situation that would lessen its efficiency and productivity. The meaning of work is fixed ahistorically on the product. The product of work is not shared. Work is understood only as means to an end. This reduces the meaning of work to the working subject and brackets the communal and religious dimensions of work. The result of this view of work is that life becomes meaningless when one is unemployed or does work that is not regarded as valuable. In fact one is not entitled to the basic necessities of life if one does not work.

The Redemption of Work

The third tendency is the distinctively modern ideology of the redemption of work through work. It is found in the thought of Hegel, Saint-Simon, Marx, and Durkheim; it also suffuses much of Western managerialism, which uses psychology and sociology to restructure the worker's attitude and work situation. The Promethean ideologies of work exalt work to the highest conceivable dignity. They draw on the content of Christian eschatological fulfillment and personal redemption as a source to criticize the inadequacies and brutalities of work practices. From the perspective of the Christian doctrine of God this ideological trend distorts the economy of life that God intends by extricating the Son from community with the Father and Holy Spirit. Modern Christology has often helped fill the ideological content of the Promethean ideologies of work. The isolated Son can become the model for *homo faber* and the modern messianism of work.

Hegel, making labor the subject matter of philosophical discourse, reached the opposite conclusion from antiquity. Work is not slavery; rather, it is the means of humanization. For Hegel the dialectic of work is the self-formation and emancipation process of the human spirit. In work human beings create not just something according to an idea, but actually create their world and therefore themselves through work. In work one achieves individual identity by going outside of self and actualizing oneself in the world. I am, because I work. I am what I make out of myself.

According to Marx we express our humanity through artistic, theoretical, and technological work. Work is the revelation of one's hidden, inner self. Our cultural totality is the ongoing labor of men and women in history. Production is the foundation of the relationships, laws, ideas, and institutions of society. Thus the worker is of decisive importance in world history. Only because Marx's estimation of work is so high does he so radically criticize work as it exists in the modern world. People will not recognize their alienation through work until they have been asked to take their work seriously as their self-creation.

Marx argues that workers have become alienated because capital has dehumanized their relationship to work. Human beings have produced their surroundings, but they have been stolen from them. Human beings are important precisely because of their work, but yet work robs and impoverishes them. The market definition of work explained work and its dehumanizing relationships as self-interest. Such cold-blooded and calculated motivations make work meaningless and alienate the worker. In a sense the basic theory of capitalism cannot fathom alienation through work. How can a worker be alienated from work to which he or she has never been committed? The more the bourgeois society emphasizes a work ethic and work-based values, the more this alienation is intensified. The division of labor in machine production turns the worker into a "crippled monstrosity," "riveted to a single, fractional task," "working with the regularity of parts of a machine." The Marxian intention is to redeem work by changing the conditions and relationships of industrialization. How can we make the world a place in which work can be restored and made human? The answer: Remove the obstacles to zealous work which have been erected by capitalism.

Because human beings create themselves, their world, and their future through work, work must be redeemed at all costs. The messianic themes of God's work can be used for this purpose, but only if they are isolated from the creating and sanctifying work of God. When the Trinity is distorted in this way, we are left with the human become Promethean messiah in whose work rests the survival and salvation of the world. The human being takes back all the human excellences which have been projected on God. Now it is up to the human being to go it alone without God. The kingdom of God becomes merely a cipher for human effort or for human agreement with inevitable progress. But how in actuality is work to be redeemed?

In view of the failure of the ideologies designed to overcome alienation in modern work, both capitalism and socialism have turned to managerialism as a way of redeeming work. They agree that the problem is to overcome capitalism's impoverished appeals for work and the bleak picture of the worker's situation in work ideologies. Capitalist managerialism claims that the problem of capitalism is work; socialist managerialism claims that the problem of work is capitalism. The capitalist approach assigns to the manager the Promethean task of saving capitalism by redeeming work. The socialist approach to work assigns to the manager the Promethean task of redeeming work by fulfilling and transcending capitalism.

Managerialism under both capitalism and socialism follows the myth of the objectivity of science as a model for social theory and planning. It attempts to redeem work through the sophisticated applications of psychology and sociology to reconstruct the content of work and its relationships. The older work ideologies failed in their direct ideological appeals for devotion to work. But since they are not owners, it is claimed, managers have a better basis of authority for making appeals for work and cooperation. The impersonal scientific analysis of the situation can take the place of the boss. Furthermore, managers' decisions will never be "wrong" because their decisions are value-free. Managers, social scientists, and administrators can impersonally uncover correct solutions to problems and thus organize social life by organizing work. Management, like politics, becomes something like social physics. It takes on the unquestioned aura of a savior.

Technocratization, rationalization, and efficiency under a managerialist guise, whether capitalist or socialist, do not solve the problem of work. The scientific control of work definitely carries social values. The dominative character of work can be changed only if these social values are submitted to criticism, not just by elites but by people at the grassroots. Work continues to serve the interests of those who control it, unless the relationships of those within the household are changed.

Sin, Evil, and Work

What does the economy of God tell us about why work must be redeemed? One important characteristic of some of the biblical traditions is that they look at work as a worker does. Israel's history with God begins with the stark reality of human bondage through forced labor. Work means "no freedom." In fact, much of Israel's history is lived under the conditions in which the product of one's labor is expropriated by another. One plants and another harvests. One builds and another occupies.

In the midst of societies that practice slavery as the will of the gods Israel stands out in asking why work leads to domination and exploitation. The basic answer is that bondage *through* work is ultimately based in bondage *to* work. Human work becomes destructive because of the sin of the working human being. God gives the human being an infinite capacity for love because God wants another who can love God freely and infinitely. This love of God is meant to be expressed also through the human being's work. The mystery of work is the power given to the human being to love God by serving life in God's creation. But this power for work is turned into the power to enslave. The human being misdirects this infinite capacity for love of God and invests it in self and things, in the power and privilege that will secure oneself. And thus the human being's God-given capacity for work gets caught up in an infinite love of what is not God. Distorted work is misdirected love. The very power God gives for work is also the power by which human beings set themselves over against God, destroy creation, and turn the human community into constant strife, fear, and anxious greed. Were it not for work human beings would not utterly distort life by making their own gods and their own counter-creation. By building their Babels they fool themselves into believing that there is no limit to human work. "Their land is filled with idols; they bow down to the work of their hands, to what their own fingers have made" (Isa. 2:8; cf. Rom. 1:25).

Thus the mystery of work is also its idolatrous service of death. Work, beginning with the work of Cain, is an attempt to escape death, but it ends up serving death. The most normal thing imaginable, work, becomes a threat to the creation because it threatens God's righteousness, which keeps creation in being. Work becomes odious. "What does a man gain by all the toil at which he toils under the sun?" (Eccles. 1:3). Work becomes a burden because the human being's household relationships with God, with each other, and with the creation have been spoiled. Work can no longer be done with innocence. In short, human work produces chaos and therefore work has to deal with the threat of chaos in creation (weeds and brambles) and in one's own heart (sweat and tears).

The human condition is that we depend infinitely on the capacity of our work. We expect that the products of our work will secure us. And yet we have the prevailing awareness that work can never accomplish what we expect of it; work can never finally secure us. Demonic powers gain control over us through our urge to make ourselves through work. Our idolatry gives power and authority over us to the products of our own work. The working human being is an anxious creature. We are neurotically coerced to protect our successes and products with our lives as though they constituted our lives. So we invest our livelihood in awesome weapons which, we wager, have the ultimate power to secure because they have the ultimate power to destroy the world. Nuclear weapons have become in our time the comprehensive symbol of the power of idolatrous human work. They are "the sacrilege set up where it ought not to be" (Mark 13:14).

Sinful work leads to the evil of work. Prideful work leads people to exclude others from their work and its fruits. The work of those who have property and power overwhelms the work of those without property and power. The powerful "work" in order to make the work of others produce riches for themselves. They "abhor justice and pervert all equity." Without even getting out of bed they manipulate the economic instruments for impoverishing others, "because it is in the power of their hand." "They covet fields, and seize them; and houses, and take them away; they oppress a man and his house, a man and his inheritance" (Mic. 2:1–2; cf. Amos 6:3–7). The work that supports the luxurious life of the "cows of Bashan," oppresses the poor and crushes the needy (Amos 4:1). This is a denial of the fundamental truth God's economists know about themselves: Once they were slaves and thus they may never enslave again. It is the abomination of abominations that Solomon builds the house of the Lord with the *corvée*, "forced labor" (1 Kings 9:15).

No one may "own" the labor of another person. But in our society we have become confused about this. When labor was made into a commodity in order to form a market in labor, we developed the simple notion that labor could be bought and sold. This is usually not said publicly, however, since it patently denies the dignity of the human being. Rather it is said that the employer buys the right to command the labor of another for a certain period; or that in exchange for wages the worker agrees to become obedient to the employer for a period of time. How different is this from the notion of owning the labor of another when the employer succeeds in gaining control over the consciousness, values, and family relations of the worker? And then we still have the thorniest question: If one cannot buy the labor of another person, how can it be justified that the employer gains the exclusive right to what the laborer produces?

God the Economist Redeems Work

God's economic work does not simply condemn, criticize, and relativize our work but also redeems the household from the dehumanizing work by which the members of the household want to lord it over each other and the creation. "All the work which the Lord did for Israel" (Josh. 24:31) was the work of redeeming Israel's own work from the power of death and sin.

God's redeeming work begins with God's creating work. God's work of creating has often been construed in tyrannical and mechanical terms. But God's work is not that of a manufacturer who out of raw material "makes" a product by grasping and controlling. God, the single One who has power over the vanity of non-being, calls the creation into being through God's word of righteousness. God's work is not coercive but a passionate evocation of what does not exist to enter into God's grace and thus have being (cf. Rom. 4:17; Ps. 74:12–14; 8:5). Liberating everything that is out of the chaos of nothingness is a costly liberation, just as is that of the exodus and the cross. God's work is a struggle against the power of death (*mot*), the power of nothingness. The presence of night, storm, and sea symbolize the presence of the power of death from the very beginning of creation. Creation is no easy victory. Those who see God's work against death in purely effortless terms are already submitting the biblical narratives to ideological use. God suffers by experiencing the power of nothingness, which wants to hold all things captive to its emptiness. God overcomes the recalcitrance of the *nihil* by embracing it. This work is dangerous and painful. It does not immediately issue in success. God declares that God's work is "very good," but not "perfect." God's work of creation does not end on the "sixth day." Nothing in creation is yet completely safe from death, the last and greatest enemy of God's household. God's work of creation continues every moment in God's liberating struggle against the power of death.

Transformed human work has its source in God's kenosis. "You have burdened me [caused me work] with your sins, you have wearied me with your iniquities" (Isa. 43:24–25). The passion story of Jesus is fashioned after the model of the slave of God in Deutero-Isaiah. Here the language of the work of God refers to suffering, sacrifice, self-giving, emptying, free slaveship, and surrendering self. God's chosen one (*ebed Yahweh*) is a worker who carries our iniquities as a great burden (Isaiah 53). According to John the crucified Jesus speaks of his work being finished and his lordship over the world is pictured as happening in his divine slaveship for all (Philippians 2). God becomes the *metic*, the slave, and we God's free people. God is Lord of the household precisely by being the Economist, servant, of the household. Through the sacrifice of the Son God takes into God's own community the human death-serving work which is sin. This is God's grief work. Having the same mind as Christ, our lives are to be conformed to this self-giving work. Work is self-sacrifice. Love is the power and goal of work (1 Cor. 12, 13).

Our work is useless in creating the righteousness by which we may stand against death and sin. God's work saves us from the attempt to justify and create ourselves through our own effort (Rom. 3:19–31; Galatians 3). The existence of the human being cannot be defined by work or made dependent on work, however necessary work is. God's gracious justification means that no one must justify himself or herself through work nor does anyone have to create or realize himself or herself through work. If that were so, the unemployed would be without rights and the handicapped unreal. We are able to work at our salvation with fear and trembling only because "God is at work in you, both to will and to work for his good pleasure" (Phil. 2:12). Being justified means no longer being dictated to by the demonic powers. Released from work as frenetic self-assertion, the justified person can enter into work as free service of God's grace (Rom. 12:1).

God's redemption of work is the possibility of radical transformation of the work relationships of the household and of its relationship to the Economist. Baptism is the sign of Christian work in God's economy. Those who are baptized enter into the Triune Community's history with the creation and thus are called to cooperate with God's work of building the *basileia* household of justice and peace in which all creatures will find home. Through baptism the Holy Spirit creates a new person with a new name and an open future and makes possible a work that corresponds to and participates in God's work of creation, redemption, and new creation. The primary vocation of the baptized person is to be "in Christ" and "in the Spirit" (1 Cor. 7:17) so that the world can trust in the *basileia* (1 Cor. 14). "All work takes place for the Lord" (1 Thess. 2:12; 4:9–11; 2 Cor. 7:17), "for the sake of Christ" (2 Thess. 3:6; Acts 20:35, Col. 3:17). Abound "in the work of the Lord, knowing that in the Lord your labor is not in vain" (1 Cor. 15:58).

For Paul, being an apostle means being a "fellow worker" for the *basileia* (Col. 4:11). He carries all the marks of the servanthood of Christ (Rom. 1:1). Missionary and congregational work is described as the heaviest and most unpleasant work of a slave (*koros*). Proclaiming the gospel is a necessity (*ananke*) which he cannot escape (1 Cor. 9:16–17). When he claims that he has "worked more" (2 Cor. 11:23–25), he has in mind labors, imprisonment, beatings, mortal danger, persecution, slander, hunger, cold, theft, nakedness, and constant concern about the congregation. All are work for the *basileia*.

Because the *basileia* is present, the household of God can arrange its work relationships according to God's sabbath justice. The sabbath is equalitarian; it is common to all. It can't be purchased. The intention of God's sabbath is not simply to interrupt work or to make work possible again on the old terms; it is to end the injustices that come through work. On the sabbath no one can work, especially not one's manservant or maidservant, especially not one's beast of burden (Exod. 20:9–11). According to the Torah's demands for the Jubilee Year, which is a sabbath year, not even the earth can work (Lev. 25:1–7). Precisely in the here and now in which God's people live the sabbath breaks the exploitation as well as burden of work. God's life-giving justice reigns. The sabbath is a real, if partial, overcoming of the domination and destruction of human work. It is the fragmentary presence under the conditions of history of God's ultimate redemption of work. Every sabbath is a sacramental taste and a glimpse of God's coming triumph when in God's shalom the creation will bloom without the exploitation of work. This does not mean that there will be no work in God's ultimate household of peace. The kingdom of heaven is not a retirement home in which people rock away for eternity. Rather, it is the reign of God's righteousness, in which work will be utterly redeemed and in which God's people will participate in the infinite joy of God's creative work. Thus the sabbath qualifies all work.

Far from eliminating the sabbath, Jesus therefore brings the sabbath into the workday, into everyday life. The sabbath is meant not only for rest but also for the surpassing joy of feeding the hungry, healing the sick, and making home for the homeless.

Redeeming Work

We have detected some theological elements of ideologies that justify dehumanizing practices of work and have criticized them according to the Trinity as the hermeneutic of the biblical narratives of God. Work ideologies make unemployment, underpaid work, isolated work, and degraded work seem tolerable. The work of God as known in the triune community's uncovering in Israel and Jesus Christ cannot be used to justify inhumanity in work.

We now ask what this trinitarian hermeneutic might offer in terms of orientation for new perspectives on work. If any expectation that work can be completely transcended is utopian in character, we can nevertheless speak of ways in which God seeks to redeem work under the conditions of history. What would liberated modes of work look like? How can the congregation as the alternative economy of God envision and demonstrate them? How can it practice "education for good work"?

The Right to Work

Our view of work will not change significantly until we realize that work is not simply a commodity to be defined by workplace efficiency and distributed according to market rules. Work has to do with livelihood, with inclusion in the community, and with a sense of personal dignity and well-being. A humanizing economy depends upon the creation of meaningful work for every person who is able and wants to work. This is necessary for the formation of a community that can realize human rights and redistribute wealth. If work serves the socialization of the person, especially in an increasingly service-oriented society in which work takes place cooperatively, then unemployment threatens people with the loss of community or a kind of social death. Every person has a right to participate in the communal process according to his or her abilities with just compensation and means of deep satisfaction. Work is a way of belonging to, sharing in, and contributing to the life of the community.

The market and its rules, though they are valuable in many respects, are on their own not capable of defining, motivating, and distributing work exhaustively. Other institutions of the community and the state must take responsibility for this as well. This inevitably raises the problem of coercion in work, though we have seen that, despite claims to the contrary, coercion also exists in the labor market. The inalienable right to meaningful work according to one's abilities presup-poses freedom. When the market fails to provide work for all, some proponents of the market seem satisfied to allow state laws to coerce people to work. Workfare programs under the banner of "right to work" retain elements of such coercion. They are often thinly disguised measures to secure cheaper labor by tapping the pool of welfare recipients. It should not be surprising in a society that seeks dignity for all that persons will not accept just any job that is offered.

Without employment security, work is little more rewarding than a painful necessity. When a company lays off workers for the sake of greater technological efficiency or moves its labor market in search of cheaper labor costs, it should be held accountable to provide its share of the cost of creating new jobs and stabilizing the community from which it is removing jobs. Increased profits through automation or through the use of the labor platforms of Third World countries cannot justify the loss of communal cooperation, which is a higher survival value than increased profits.

From the Christian perspective work is fundamentally *diakonia*. Diakonic work is the daily work of Christians in the alternative economy of the household of God. The congregation should be the laboratory where baptismal work is learned. In the congregation part of the world is made into a witness to the power of the Holy Spirit at work and thus a challenge to the way the world organizes work.

The challenge of the congregation is to find diakonic work for all members in the congregation. One of the greatest debilitating factors of our congregations is that there are so many "unemployed" persons in them. Without work the baptized person is robbed of his or her ministry. Within the calling to be in Christ, all are given special ministries, which are their gifts from the Holy Spirit (1 Cor. 12:27–31; 4:11). Almost every person, even the extremely disabled, can contribute some form of work. Prayer and simple testimony are also forms of work irreplaceably necessary to the life of the community. The gifts/tasks of each person are for building the household of God, which exists not for its own sake but for the sake of God's making the world into a home. Perhaps the most important gift we should look for in a pastor is the gift to discern the gifts of others. Pastors should have imagination and courage in discerning the gifts of persons and calling them into the work that is peculiarly theirs.

The alternative economy of the congregation should demonstrate to society how full employment can happen with noncoerced and satisfying work. Of course, incentives for work and reward systems in the church are quite different from those in the market economy. But such alternative incentives and rewards are precisely what the public household needs to see.

Incentive for Work

We have seen that market theory is incapable by itself to motivate humanizing work; the ideological incentives that are used for this purpose enhance domination through work.

In the congregation work can be understood as self-giving for the sake of participation in the fullness of life. Work is service to God and the human being. This is an incentive for work that does not serve the deadly compulsion to work as self-justification. Because God's *basileia* has come in Christ, work for the sake of the Lord receives a meaning that reaches beyond every human grounding of work. Work is a way of practicing patience as we are being formed, not certain of what we shall become. In the time of preparation, maturation, waiting, and anticipation work becomes very significant. If work is done as discipleship in the self-emptying Christ, then it reaches beyond all possible success to participation in the resurrection and the reign of God's righteousness. The true worth of work will be revealed only at the end time with the utter defeat of sin and the realization of God's glory in all things (Eph. 1:3–23; Matt. 7:24–27; 1 Cor. 3:10–15; 2 Cor. 5: 1–10).

The "more than enough" value of the messianic hope results in added effort, self-denial, and self-giving. Work receives a stimulus that moves people to invest more of themselves than is necessary and therefore to expect from work more than the earthly results would justify. The excess of expectations leads to the life of "going the second mile" depicted in Jesus' parables, This is the eschatological logic of the kingdom which market thinking gropes to explain. This is work done not out of market assumptions of scarcity but out of the abundance of God's promise. Only out of such a sense of abundance can work be done in solidarity with and for the sake of the poor and oppressed, those who have been systemically excluded from the household.

Work in Community

The comprehensive meaning of work is active participation in the communal, social process. A new definition of work will have to go beyond the description of work as merely productive, wage earning, business, or professional. When we limit work to these defini-tions, the broader dimensions of work from which society actually lives remain invisible or repressed. Work is falsely defined unless we include reproductive or generative work. This includes all forms of familial and social service. The value of work has to do with increasing relationships among human beings and between human beings and God. Destroying the community of work through relationships of domination and dependence dehumanizes work.

Redeemed work requires a complex participatory consciousness. New technological and organizational demands made on economic life are causing shifts from the production of goods to the production and processing of information and culture. This growing centrality of knowledge at the heart of economic dynamics contains the seeds of new kinds of domination through work. Those who are not given the opportunity to gain expertise in information and culture exchange are left out of the distribution of work. Workers from whom production and organizational information is withheld remain in a constant dependent relationship.

The only nondominative way beyond the destructive struggle of worker and management rights is genuinely shared authority and actual access to power on the part of all who work. Workers should have real influence over workplace relations and decisions. Meaningful participation in decision-making, whether by direct or elected representation, should be consistently available to each member, at least in the area of one's competence and concern. Top decision-makers should be ultimately accountable to and removable by working membership. And discipline of workers should be democratized by an independent appeals system composed of peers as much as possible.

Direct worker involvement in enterprise decisions is the best guarantee against armies of supervisors, producing nothing but grudging effort, and against costly unemployment leading to increased social unrest and crime. A highly democratic culture will not exist for long with highly undemocratic rules. Democratic rules shape actors who are capable of democratic participation. And without such democratic actors the culture and rules of democracy cannot be maintained and renewed. In fact, the future of democracy may be decided by the question of the democratization of the workplace. But there cannot be such democratic involvement without full sharing with employees of management-level information and management-level expertise. Management cannot produce efficiency in work when profits are always put ahead of the community of work.

The Equity of Work

Greed and fear become the work incentives if workers have no equity in working relationships or direct relation to the results of their work. Democratic participation and work security lead to commitment and cooperation. Equity in work depends upon workers having guaranteed individual rights, corresponding to political liberties. In the present-day workplace the problem of equity centers on status, pay, and share in the product of work. If individual return to workers based merely on the surplus they produce is considered the only way to guarantee efficiency, efficiency will always eclipse equity. Equity, however, is in fact the precondition for work that is both communal and efficient. The most momentous problem of equity now, as throughout most of history, is the question of the distribution of work's surplus. Equity in work requires fundamental change in the rules of production and of ownership decisions about capitalization, expansion, and diversification.

It should now be clear that we are not likely to change our praxis of property and work without an accompanying change in our perception and praxis of needs.

Whose Work Ethic? A Womanist Reading of "A Work Ethic" from the Bible to the United States

Joan Martin (2000)

In the preceding chapter, the words and experiences of fugitive enslaved and ex-enslaved women were placed at the center of the work discussion, human meaning, and blackwomen's moral agency as the focus of this womanist ethical investigation. In listening to voices from between 59 and 166 years ago, I have attempted to discover the relationship of enslaved women's moral agency to the meaning of work in their lives. In reflecting on their words and actions, I have constructed four characteristics of an enslaved women's work ethic: 1) a theological and ethical belief in God as the God of life, freedom, and protection; 2) womanish moral authority, instruction, and action as an intergenerational dynamic for communal maintenance, solidarity, and empowerment in the context of oppression; 3) a struggle for self-determination in the use of one's labor, especially sexual and reproductive labor; and 4) a work-related attitude of self-reliance and confidence in one's learned skill and craft. I contend that these characteristics point toward a work ethic that has as its goal the move from survival to the ongoing creation of abundant life, freedom, and human wholeness in the face of and opposition to oppression and evil and the struggle for liberation.

The questions that this chapter takes up ask the meaning of enslaved blackwomen's reality in relation to Christian faith and the work ethic in light of the Christian tradition and in the ethos of the United States. Three issues emerge. One revolves around understanding and interpreting the Protestant social teachings on work and vocation. Biblical perspectives, of course, lay beneath the church's social teachings. Another set addresses the nature of the work ethic in its development in the United States historically. Lastly, there is the interface of these traditions with the lives and experience of enslaved blackwomen.

Biblical and Theological Perspectives on Work

In antiquity, to work was to toil and labor under the yoke of sustaining and reproducing human life itself. In order for human life to exist, persons had to struggle with and/or against nature, depending on whether one saw nature as harmonious or hostile. In the West, one saw nature as harmonious or hostile. In the West, nature was considered hostile to the development of human life and civilization so that work became a precondition of life, not meaningful but necessary. "Freedom" meant freedom from work because work was understood to mean providing the necessities of life. The "free" person did not work because others – women and men slaves and women in the domestic sphere (wives and daughters) – attended to the labors of life. For example, in the Greek city-state, the *polis*, the free person was the citizen who engaged in the public life – politics – and the pursuit of the virtuous or honorable life. Taking their cues from and emulating the gods of their culture, free citizens were patrons of the arts – crafts considered beautiful and more permanent than the work of domestic life or the private sphere. Jürgen Moltmann makes the connection between ethics, work, and slavery in antiquity by asserting that "the separation of virtue and work manifestly reflect[ed] a slaveholding society. . . . In it, not only is labor exploited for the sake of profit. But rather, work itself is understood as enslavement, that is, to 'work means to be a slave of necessity.'"

Decidedly different from the Greek tradition that has shaped one of our conceptualizations of ethics and work are the biblical notions of work. Work is part of the relationship between God and humanity. There are two frameworks within the Bible in which to view work. The first framework has three elements. First there is the work of God – creation and redemption (liberation) – which the Bible attributes to God alone and which consequently encompasses God's covenantal relationships with humanity through Israel and beyond (Gen. 1–2; Ps. 8:3; 33:6; 104:24; 148:5; Isa. 43:24ff. and Isa. 53). Second, there is the realm of human work – that is, all the work that humans do to meet our basic needs and to live socially (Gen. 1–2). Such work is necessary. By *necessary*, I mean work that is for the maintenance and reproduction of human life, mediating between our relationship to nature for the satisfaction of life's basic needs and our relationship as culture-creating building-sustaining beings. Even "at the beginning of creation there was no work-free age ..." and only "after the Fall is work cursed by toil, pain, and uselessness," according to Moltmann. (Of course, it is important to remember that the Church has traditionally read Genesis 3 as justification for the view that Eve's sin is blamed for work becoming "toil.") Third, when the faith community and its members live and work in and for the kin-dom of God (Mark 16:20), such participation in work is a participation "in Christ." This is the metaphorical faith understanding of work, in the sense that the community of faith "works" in the cause of the Gospel or "the work of Christ" (Phil. 2:30).

The second framework consists of the diverse perspectives on work within the varieties of biblical traditions. Work in its several patterns and divisions of labor in this framework is related to the different historical and economic situations of the several biblical traditions and to the ideological commitments present in those traditions. As depicted in the Pentateuch and the "historical books," human labor in Israel's nomadic and agricultural life is seen as self-supporting, communal (in the sense of extended kinship relations and within the context of community), and meaningful. This is true even when work is viewed as toil done "by the sweat of their brow" in such narratives as the story of Cain and Abel, the story of Noah and the Flood, the Abraham and Sarah cycles, and the narratives of the early confederacy period. In Exodus 1–2, the Israelites find themselves in slavery and conscripted for the public work projects by Pharaoh. In 1 Kings 5 and 9, it is clear that King Solomon has created a forced labor system utilizing Israelites or foreigners within Israel's borders to build the Temple and the king's house. Likewise, the Prophetic literature denounces the oppression of the poor through unjust labor systems and their products (Isa. 31:3) and the idle rich (Amos 6:3–6), while the Psalter raises the concern of Israel's faithfulness through its work while the nation is in exile. Ecclesiastes and Proverbs, as examples of the wisdom literature, often commend the proper work attitude as that of diligence and care in one's labor as well as the most fruitful way of securing an identity as God's people (Prov. 6:6–11 and 12:24).

The New Testament – both Synoptic literature and epistolary works – contains multiple meanings and uses of human work. In the Synoptic parables, daily work themes and activities become the context for metaphors of the new reign of God (Matt. 13:1–23, Mark 4:1–20, and Luke 8:4–18; Matt. 20:1–16; and Luke 13:20–21). Pauline and pseudo-Pauline letters stress work and daily living, a cheerful attitude toward work, and the condemnation of idleness (Col. 3:23 and 2 Thess. 3:10–12). Further, the daily work of Christians is addressed in household codes of Paul

(Eph. 6:5–9, Col. 3:22–4:1) and in the letters of 1 Timothy, Titus, and 1 Peter. They pertain to familial relationships, including the master-servant/master-slave relationship. Within the context of daily work, there is the opportunity to see one's work as a response to life rendered to God. Work for the Christian is a vocation – that is, a vehicle through which one is to be obedient to God, who is the Christian's master. In this view of work, Paul in particular is underlining the double use of the term *vocation*, or calling. Persons are "called" into new life by God through repentance and faith and into the life and work of the church. This is the foundation from which Christians become "workers" in whatever they do in daily, "secular" activity.

As such, biblical portraits of work are embedded in the contexts and purposes out of which biblical writers shape their witness to God and the story of the faith community's response to God. In this latter framework, the human activity of work serves as a vehicle to the larger project of the creative purposes of God in human life and the created order. The two frameworks, while distinct, together provide the possible theological meanings of work and also descriptions of human experiences of work that stand under God's judgment and upon which the faith community does theo-ethical reflection.

Womanist Reflections on the Bible, Enslaved Women, and Work

In the Protestant tradition, laity and scholars alike turn to the Bible because it serves as the fundamental source of theological and ethical reflection in two ways. It is the repository for the archetypal, generative, and organizing myths of and for the community of faith in which the community finds its memory and purpose for the past, present, and future. Furthermore, the Bible is the paramount and first source for "doing theology" for most members of the churches – the "textbook" (written and oral/aural) for conversion and faith experiences, church school education at all levels, preaching, and group and individual meditation. This is particularly true of African American Christian women historically, and it still holds true with contemporary blackwomen. Subsequently, African American and feminist liberation biblical interpretation and theologies often ground their hermeneutics of liberation in the Exodus event. But why is this the case given critical studies and interpretations of the Bible from African American liberation scholars that document and demonstrate the use of the Bible as an ideological tool to foster and perpetuate white supremacy, colonialism, and the subjugation of black Americans? Why is this the case when feminist scholars have more than adequately analyzed the prevailing patriarchalism and misogyny of the biblical traditions and texts? Both groups of scholars have drawn upon a formidable array of disciplines and methods in their work. What accounts for blackwomen's allegiance to the biblical witness – an allegiance that has been neither uncritical nor unsophisticated in the face of racism, sexism, and classism in this society?

Womanist biblical scholar Renita Weems has suggested that the answer to this question is very complicated, indeed. Owing to the historical experience of blackwomen's oppression, the Bible ought to speak with existential authority to the experience, identity, and values of blackwomen, and provide a "life guide" that sustains hope and strength in blackwomen's struggle for authentic personhood. For Weems, this complex encounter with the Bible and the Christian God is a matter of understanding and "reading the text" from one's social location. At the same time, blackwomen must be cognizant and critical of the social locations of the biblical narrators in their time and the interpretative voices in the dominant culture historically and currently (including those voices within the black male and white feminist Christian community).

For my purposes here, Weems advocates a blackwomen's biblical hermeneutic grounded in neither solely an African American liberationist perspective nor a white feminist analysis. Simply put, Weems offers a womanist hermeneutic that has three elements. First, it is a hermeneutic that seeks to "uncover whose voice [blackwomen and marginalized people] identify with in the Bible – female as opposed to male, the African as opposed to the non-African, the marginalized as opposed to the dominant. Second, it has equally and more precisely to do with examining the *values* of those readers and the corroboration of those values by the text." Perhaps the third and most important dimension for our reading of blackwomen's slave narratives and womanist reflections on blackwomen's lives, the Bible, and work is what Weems calls the "credibility of the text" in its portrait of how human beings relate to one another. That portrait ought to coincide with the way blackwomen have experienced reality and relationships with other people and, as a text, arouse, manipulate, and harness African American women's deepest yearnings.

Turning to my own blackwoman's "reading" of the Bible in relation to work, what might be said in light of enslaved women's reality and womanist reflections? The passages selected are but possible examples of the interface of enslaved women's work existence and interpretative renderings of the Bible from a womanist perspective. A womanist "voice" or "reading" emerges from the interrelatedness of African American, women, and poor peoples' experiences of oppression, struggles for survival and quality of life, and movements for liberation. As such, one exemplary biblical "portrait" selected for reflection is the narrative of the Hebrew midwives acting in the midst of a continuing and intensifying situation of oppression for the descendants of Abraham and Sarah (Ex. 1:15–22 and 2:1–10).

The major issue confronting the Hebrew midwives is the first, central, and specific issue confronting anyone or group in the narrative – the question of God's identity and authority – that is, whom Israel will worship and serve. Indeed, it is the fundamental question in the book of Exodus. Likewise, it is the major theological and ethical issue for Exodus. For the midwives, authority comes to the fore when Pharaoh commands, "When you act as midwives to the Hebrew women, and see them on the birthstool, if it is a boy, kill him; but if it is a girl, she shall live" (1:16). The first answer given in the narrative is, "But the midwives feared God; they did not do as the king of Egypt commanded them, but they let the boys live" (1:17). The question of God's identity and authority is answered through the action of these women, and then we learn the details. When summoned to account for their actions by Pharaoh, the midwives respond in an ironic twist of midwifery skills: "Because the Hebrew women are not like the Egyptian women; for they are vigorous and give birth before the midwife comes to them" (1:19). Unlike Pharaoh, their knowledge of their clientele is part of their knowledge as midwives. Again we are told of the result, this time a twofold result: "… and the people multiplied and became very strong. And because the midwives feared God, he gave them families" (1:20b–21). Although rewarding positive human action as a response to the will of God is not automatic, it does herald that life and goodness will abound according to God's purpose.

Traditionally, neither African American (male) nor feminist biblical liberation interpretations include the particularity of blackwomen when "blackpeople" and "women" are their respective subjects in relation to the biblical witness in general, or in Exodus specifically. From a womanist reading, this *visible invisibility* is ironic given that Exodus begins with the action of a particularized group of women responding to the oppression of the Egyptian king over Israel. Yet, in the first of the three-part prologue to the Exodus narrative, the midwives are women who can be recognized by ethnicity, by class (that is, work) orientation, and by solidarity with other women. From a blackwoman's reading, they are multiply oppressed people as Hebrews, as Hebrew women, and as "domestic workers." They, like Moses later in the narrative, become deliverers of their people. As Hebrew women, they are by their actions in solidarity with the Hebrew women and their God. By what set of values and hopes do these Hebrew midwives do what they do?

The answer is that Shiphrah and Puah, who in faith, by courage, and perhaps in commitment to their people or in solidarity with others, and with the skill of their craft, positively respond to the God of the Hebrews and thwart the will of Pharaoh. By doing so, they act to maintain the survival of the Hebrew people. And they do so with no stated intention or expectation of receiving a reward. (Survival of the Hebrew people is later placed in the hands of a male hero – Moses – and thus raises thorny sexism issues about women's traditional female and domestic role related to birth, children, and status in patriarchal culture, and the subverting of women's subversive power!) It is their "fear of God" which compels them to risk and act. According to Cheryl Exum, "to 'fear God' does not simply mean to be afraid of God or God's punishment; it is, on the contrary, a far broader theological concept, having at its center the element of *mysterium tremendum* and extending to conduct which is guided by basic ethical principles and in harmony with God's will.'" Exum reminds the reader that in the wisdom literature, it is this sense of awe, "the fear of God," that is the beginning of knowledge, a knowledge that is not the exclusive prerogative of the Israelites. In other words, one needs right knowledge and relationship with God. Such faith and action are not unlike the stance taken by Sojourner Truth in the face of an arrogant proslavery woman, and Harriet Jacobs in opposition to Dr. Flint.

Probing this resonance more deeply with the assistance of a womanist reading of Scripture and enslaved women's narratives can reveal an important insight. It is possible to argue that right knowledge and reflexive action on the part of the Hebrew midwives and enslaved women was more acutely faithful to an understanding of God than that of either Pharaoh or the proslavery "Christian" woman. Pharaoh thought himself to be divine and was worshiped by the Egyptians as god. Over against Pharaoh, the midwives "fear [the] God" of the Israelites. Similarly, the proslavery woman assumed she knew God's intention was the enslavement of African Americans while Truth counters with a different claim about God's identity. As it turns out, Pharaoh is no god at all, at least in comparison with the God of the Israelites, and is in fact a god of oppression and death. Likewise, it turns out that the God of proslavery Christianity is also one of oppression and death in the sensibilities of enslaved women such as Truth and Jacobs.

It is also affirmed that the God who stands in the background behind the Hebrew midwives and the One who stands behind Sojourner Truth is the God and Creator of life. This God is the One who in the creation of the cosmos creates human beings and fashions them after God's own likeness. Moreover, it is the same God who covenants with human beings (Abraham, Sarah, and Hagar's descendants) to make them purposeful people in specific times and in specific ways according to God's expanding purpose. And it is yet again this God who is able to have relationships with the lowliest in life's stations according to the world's standards, and use them for the working of God's purpose. God's work is neither fanciful nor negatively manipulative. It is a working that empowers midwives and enslaved women to act, which aids the growth and multiplication of their people, and which also has an effect on God's own possibilities.

A womanist reading thus uncovers a new dimension of blackwomen's theo-ethical understanding of God. It appears from the dialogue between the biblical and enslaved narratives that the interaction between faithful women and a faithful God makes possible the expansive moral agency of each. Each party calls the other into greater fullness of being in a relationship in which remembrance of the past, faithfulness in the present, and just moral activity combine to affirm, defend, and perpetuate life as the divine purpose of God and the human purpose of women. On one level, the Hebrew midwives "to fear [the] God" of the Israelites is just a contrast of confidence and knowledge between Pharaoh and God. It is more than that, however. On a deeper level, for the midwives to have such a knowledge of God is also to have a knowledge of God's relationship to the ancestors of the Hebrews – Abraham and Sarah, Isaac and Rebekah, and Jacob, Leah, and Rachel. The same is true of Sojourner Truth, and particularly Harriet Jacobs. As we have discovered, both enslaved women, albeit in different ways and at different ages, join their knowledge of God to the knowledge of their ancestors and ancestral ways. For Truth, it is the connection between her mother's name, Mau Mau, and her mother's admonishment to recognize that there is but one Being greater than the then child, Isabella, the God of the universe. For Jacobs, it was the integration of the power of her parents' spirit of freedom and the power of God that launched her on her escape. The blackwomen's theo-ethical insight is that remembrance of the past, faithfulness in the present, and just moral activity by God and persons of faith together restore a degree of moral harmony in the universe.

Returning to the critical nature of the project at hand in reading the narrative of the Hebrew midwives next to narratives of enslaved women, I draw attention to the ethical nature of how women understand the work they do. In the context of Hebrew scriptures and enslaved women's lives, midwifery was itself work that affirmed life and assisted persons and communities through the human life cycle. It was a craft that was viewed as a basic medical support to women in pregnancy and birth – that is, in bringing forth new life. Ex-enslaved woman Aunt Clara Walker recounted for her interviewer, "When I was thirteen years old my ol' mistress put me wid a doctor who learned me how to be a midwife. Dat was cause so many women on the plantation was catchin' babies. I stayed wid that doctor . . . for five years." Yet, midwifery was actually broader in scope. Particularly in traditional societies, midwives served as the "medicine" women of their communities and cultures, often acting as nutritionists, herbalists or rootwomen, physicians, religious ritualists, and counselors. They were teachers, healers, and communicative leaders who sought to empower the health and welfare of their clients and communities. As I implied earlier, one feature of the Hebrew midwives' craft and wisdom was that of knowing their clientele better than Pharaoh. They were women who understood the cultural and countercultural aspects of their work setting and the community. In doing so, they were able to engage in successful subterfuge against Pharaoh.

These too were often the midwife roles of enslaved women. In spite of the fact that slaveholders had a relative self-interest in protecting the health of pregnant women as well as others in one's labor force, they often cut operating expenses by utilizing midwives instead of a doctor. Moreover, midwives served a vital companionship role to pregnant and postpartum women or as instructors to other enslaved women who would support the newborn and its mother on their or neighboring plantations. Especially when attending to health needs on other plantations, midwives served a vital enslaved community communications role, sharing news from one plantation to another in the respective slave quarters. Together, the nature of the work and the moral choices made by the practitioners and clients form the nexus of the moral act or activity in relation to life or death, wellness or sickness.

Given these two dimensions, the work of the midwives and enslaved women offers a critique that counters Pharaoh's understanding of work. The text tells us that military readiness, international competition, and power conditioned Pharaoh's view of work. Work was organized so that taskmasters were set over the Hebrews "to oppress them with forced labor" and to make their lives "bitter with hard service in mortar and brick and in every kind of field labor" (Ex. 1:11, 14). In a sense, the forced labor of the Hebrews was, according to Pharaoh, the appropriate work of the mass of common people (the Hebrews outnumbering the Egyptians) who labored for upper classes, the priests, and god-king. Indeed, large economic enterprises – work supporting empire-building – were connected to the state religion, its cult(s), and its gods in the ancient Near East. In essence, that work maliciously exploited the labor of others, often in a death-dealing fashion. Pharaoh had sought the work of the midwives as part of his exploitative, imperial scheme, but they refused to participate in their own exploitation and that of the Israelites. Instead, they chose to place their labor – its skills and its knowledge – on the side of the Israelite God whose work would be revealed in the redemption of Israel.

As we saw in the Kleckley, Jacobs, and Delaney narratives, slaveholders and the system of slavery appropriated enslaved women's work more often than not. Yet, we also saw how their labor placed in service of enslaved individuals (especially children) and the community affirms and sustains life in the midst of oppression and in the hope of freedom. This latter work, like that of the Hebrew midwives, sought to participate in the purpose of God's work in creation and in redemption – life given by the Creator, life preserved by the Creator, and life enjoyed in the Creator. From the vantage point of the biblical and enslaved narratives in dialogical reading, a womanist understanding of work emerges that connects the work of God and the work of humanity.

Notions of "Work and Calling"

I now turn to the theological and ethical roots that gave rise to the notion of a "work ethic" in Protestant thought. The early Protestant Reformers, Martin Luther and John Calvin, gave Western thought and Christianity the first interpretation of work as a positive social act applicable to all persons in every socio-economic, political, and occupational status. In fact, these respective interpretations were intended to end what the Reformers saw as a false dichotomy between the highly privileged vocation and calling of the religious life and the lesser esteemed life of toil in the everyday world prevalent in Roman Catholic thought. Martin Luther proclaimed the recovery of "the priesthood of all believers" in the Leipzig Disputation of 1519, and in "An Appeal to the Ruling Class of German Nationality . . ." He wrote:

> . . . there is no true, basic difference between laymen and priests, princes and bishops, between religious and secular, except for the sake of the office and work, but not for the sake of status. They are all of the spiritual estate, all are truly priests, bishops, and popes. But they do not all have the same work to do . . . A cobbler, a smith, a peasant – each has the work and office of his trade, and yet they are all alike consecrated priests and bishops. Further, everyone must benefit and serve every other by means of his own work or office so that in this way many kinds of work may be done for the bodily and spiritual welfare of the community, just as all members of the body serve one another [1 Cor. 12:14 – 26].

Theologically and ethically, the godly life of monasticism was posited as the vocation of all people. Labor was part of the human condition, a necessity for individual and collective survival. However, it was affirmed as part of humanity's very vocation. Since God's call comes to every Christian, vocation (call) and work (occupation) now were seen as being a dimension of Christian servanthood in church and society. It was also a vocation for life and, indirectly as an occupation, one that lasts for a lifetime. Any attempt to change even one's indirect vocation (occupation) for Luther was seen as a disloyal, autocratic, or fanatic act.

Agreeing with Luther, and expanding the notion of work as a positive human activity, John Calvin emphasized calling and vocation as demands of the Christian life, entailing obedience to God within one's calling. Calvin wrote:

> . . . the Lord bids each one of us in all life's actions to look to his calling . . . he has appointed duties for every man in his particular way of life. And that no one may thoughtlessly transgress his limits, he has named these various kinds of living "callings." Therefore each individual has his own kind of living assigned to him by the Lord as a sort of sentry post so that he may not heedlessly wander about throughout life.

The first goal of work was obedience to the calling of God who has given each human a calling. To be obedient in and to one's calling is, therefore, a manifestation of glorifying God. However, it was also important to Calvin that a person determine before entering an occupation, craft, or profession one's fitness to undertake it. Calvin also asserted that "Scripture leads us by the hand . . . warns us that whatever benefits we obtain from the Lord have been entrusted to us on this condition: that they be applied to the common good of the church . . . liberally and kindly . . . and are required to render account of our stewardship." This was the second goal of work in Calvin's thought. Given that church and society in Geneva were one, work became a religious "duty" or obligation that enabled glorification of God and living out one's love of neighbor and one's stewardship.

Luther and Calvin believed that Christians were called to serve God and their neighbor in the everyday world, including in and through work. This affirmation gave honor and dignity to all work diligently done. "Neighbors," in Calvin's thought, even included those whom we do not know and those we consider enemies, resulting from the bond that is the human race created by God in God's own image. Calvin further extended his positive valuation of work by stressing its goal – glorification of God and the building up of Christian community.

However, within each theologian's formulation exists an interrelated problem. Luther, in writing to the German nobility, maintained a rather rigid view of hereditary social status. So did Calvin. Relying on the natural law ethics embedded in their respective theologies, each believed that God assigned social and economic stations to all persons that, by implication, defined the nature of work to which one was called. Although in Calvin's thought there existed some guarded latitude in changing one's occupation, generally both he and Luther believed that any attempt to alter one's social position, and therefore one's calling, was sinful. One's calling could be exchanged for another only for the purpose of God's glory. It is this rigidity that is problematic when set in relation to the later development of the notion of the work ethic. Neither Luther's nor Calvin's theology of vocation and calling ever intended to effect a different understanding or critique of the political economies of their situations. In Luther's case spiritual estates, work, temporal authority, and the economy were considered to be ordained by God and not a creation of human society. If this is believed, then not only could all work be meaningful but, by definition, even the most menial work done under the will of and for the profit of another could be just and fair work.

In Calvin's Geneva, two elements were important. First, Calvin's Geneva had been a bustling center of international trade, a site of mercantile capitalist fairs in the previous century and early part of the sixteenth century. When Calvin arrived in 1536, he found a "poor and austere city" which had seen the upheaval of war in its struggle for independence from the House of Savoy. Yet, Reformation refugees from across Europe, and from France and Italy in particular, brought money, skills, and professions to Geneva during the period 1536–1560, increasing its population and reviving its export economic activities as well as its merchant fairs. It thrived on commerce rather than on manufacturing, being totally dependent on its rural peasantry and the neighboring cities of Bern and Savoy for the staples of life. Artisans and retail merchants formed the backbone of the Geneva economy. In such a situation, one was not talking about a community that was dramatically stratified, as were the nobility and peasantry in Luther's Germany. On the contrary, given the rising class status of Geneva in general, Calvin may have been addressing the question of vocation and calling from the perspective of "profession" rather than that of "labor," which may account for his greater flexibility on the matter. Furthermore, he sought to make all citizens politically aware and to instill in them a sense of public responsibility motivated by Protestant religious beliefs.

Second, Calvin's theology evoked the notion of a theocracy – the assumed responsibility to God on the part of secular and ecclesiastical authority alike, and proposing as its end the effectual operation of the will of God. Calvin's conception of human society was as a Christian social organism. Hence, "the Christian society, the society which strives for earthly justice looks to divine law to be reconstituted as just, thus imitating the self's interaction with God's saving grace." Thus, the work one did in the world was commensurate with the calling one did if one labored as a pastor in the church. And he further understood the church to be the model for human social interaction. (In this, he differed from the understanding of the two kingdoms in Luther's thought – that is, the relationship between the church and the state and the respective role of each.) Like that of Luther, Calvin's theology understood the world as a sinful realm. However, to Calvin it was also the place where Christians were called to use their obedience in work, love of neighbor, and stewardship for the transformation of the world and in subordination to the ruling principle of God's law of love. The reality of sin necessitated, for Calvin, proactive opposition. Every member of the church, and therefore of society (a confused and often blurred distinction given the notion of "theocracy"), was to assume a social role for others through subordinating one's self-love for the love of God and others. Therefore, the meaning of work took on the added dimension of the positive effort of the redeemed community to affect the world through coordinated human effort.

A Womanist Reading of the Theology of Vocation and Work

Although we can't believe or act as if the world of enslaved women was parallel or similar to that of the Reformation, a womanist reading which attends to the operations of economic structures, exploitation of work and persons, and theo-ethical critique can raise several issues pertaining to both worlds. Despite the positive affirmation of daily work as part of the Christian vocation and life, work in the theologies of Luther and Calvin is problematic.

Neither wrote from a perspective that seriously understood the economic stratification and the division of labor in which menial work was generally also exploited work. The way in which *economic relations structured economic life and work* was not their interest, and was probably not within their conceptualizations of the way the world operated. Indeed, the Fall was a fracture in society as well as in the individual. In other words, the material conditions of living – shaped by the relationship of people to production and production's role in shaping all areas of human life and structured social relations – were not an issue for theological or ethical scrutiny except as those conditions related to their concepts of the Christian in the world. In this view, poverty was not a matter of whether the economic relations themselves were just or unjust, but whether one was willing to work. Luther commented,

"It is not fitting that one man should live in idleness on another's labor, or be rich and live comfortably at the cost of another's hardship, as it is according to our perverted custom. St. Paul says, 'whoever will not work shall not eat.'" Calvin came closer than did Luther in understanding unjust economic "practices" such as usury and slavery, and in fact his doctrine of Christian freedom understood the Christian as one called to transform the unjust human structures of church and society. Yet both theologians maintained ancient moral ideas: "Economic behavior can be regulated by moral restraint" on the one hand. They also wrestled with the ambivalence of the Christian tradition that had a concern for the plight of the poor and equally a view of the poor as those persons unwilling to work, on the other hand. Luther, a former Augustinian monk, and Calvin, a trained lawyer and academic, were both products of this tradition and history. As a result, neither theologian critiqued the class and social location in which he was embedded as to how that location shaped his notions of work and moral agency, wealth, and poverty. After all, one's class and social location was a result of the divine ordering of the world. Each of these factors seems to have contributed to a notion of work that had little regard for the reality of work as exploitation or "drudgery" and the relationship of exploited work to poverty. Instead, Calvin (and perhaps Luther) distinguished between the deserving and the undeserving poor, and maintained Christianity's traditional mixed view of the poor – that is, as Christ's brethren and as guilty sinners. The morally corrupted were those who, in the eyes of the Christian social organism, refused to work – those who were sturdy but lazy. Social control and social responsibility were commingled in Calvin's Christian social practices in Geneva, reflecting this traditional view of work and the poor. However, "as time went to, business-minded magistrates began to question the traditionalist program of Calvin . . . The poor were described solely as idle and lazy, and relief degenerated to mere social control by the beginning of the seventeenth century."

The coalescing of notions of work and calling as positive goods subordinated for the commonwealth in obedience to the light of God's grace seemed to be only possible in limited periods and geopolitical enclaves such as Geneva. The social theological ideals of Calvin yielded in the next generation to the growing secularization – economically and politically – of European cities such as Geneva and gave way to a new wave of the ideological use of Protestant theology. By placing an unambiguously positive notion on work as calling and vocation, as a theological belief with ethical consequences for obedience and duty without criticizing the social relations of the changing political economy, the tradition was left with no theological or moral recourse for challenging exploitative work. Indeed, because there was virtually no notion of "calling" to social transformation of unjust human structures despite the fact that such institutions were seen as the result of the Fall, little thought was given to the notion of the social structuring of work. This is the incipient danger of abstracting, mystifying, and romanticizing all forms of work as theologically and morally "good." To the extent that work as "vocation" and "calling" remain abstracted from the material conditions of life and systems of exploitation, the legacy of an enslaved woman's work ethic, from a womanist reading, will critically challenge even these theological and ethical doctrinal affirmations.

The Emergence and Convergence of the "Protestant Ethic" and the "Work Ethic"

With the settling of Plymouth, Massachusetts, Bay Colonies and other Puritan enclaves in the British colonies a scant seventy years removed from Calvin's Geneva, a new generation of Calvinism transformed its theological heritage into a New World-building enterprise. Taking its forebears' doctrine of calling and vocation, the discipline and ethic of work was the standard for ruling-class women and men and laboring women and men alike. It was a discourse encompassing a religious ethical code for daily life and communal institutional life stressing the religious and civic virtues of frugality, diligence, postponement of gratification, abstinence, sobriety, moderation, and stewardship. From the writings of English Puritan Richard Baxter, a vivid picture emerges of the co-joined religious and civic nature of vocation:

> The callings most useful to the public good are the magistrates, the pastors, and teachers of the church, the schoolmasters, physicians, lawyers, etc., husbandmen (ploughmen, graziers, and shepherds); and next to them are mariners, clothiers, booksellers, tailors, and such others that are employed about matters most necessary to mankind . . .

This and similar themes run through the writings of Massachusetts Bay Colony Governor John Winthrop; the New England Puritan, the Rev. John Cotton; Emmanuel Downing; and later, Richard Mather.

Another root element in what would become the notion of a work ethic was taking shape roughly in sixteenth-century mercantilist Holland. Many saw this nation's growth as an outcome of its emphasis on its utilization of natural and economic resources, especially its labor force. Human labor in employment, not just capital itself, came to be seen as an important source in the creation of wealth. Further, "by the early seventeenth century, especially new Protestant portions of Holland, England, Scandinavia, Germany, France, and Austria, an overtly positive attitude toward work began to emerge . . . Implicit in this redefinition of work was the assumption that it would foster the disciplines of upward mobility." Thus, at least three dimensions – the religious, the civic, and the economic – served to create gradually a new ethos in the social groups positively affected by the Reformation and mercantile growth.

One group in particular, the emerging new middle class in England, formed the class that would organize the religious, commercial, and adventure-seeking endeavors in the British colonization of North America. In New England, the primary organization for colonization at first was Puritan religious freedom. The southern British colonies, especially Virginia colony, began as business ventures or new life beginnings for the adventure-seekers and the indentured poor. In the former, Reformed theology and ethics were privileged, transformative elements establishing the nature of civil and economic life. This included the Reformers' emphasis on the meaning of work. Later, southern colonies emphasized settlement and the discovery and exploitation of natural resources for English economic development. The introduction of slavery, free wage, and indentured servitude, as well as notions of productivity and the rationalization of time in relation to work, were fledgling elements influencing the drive to colonize North America. Thus, notions of a work ethic grew from the confluence of religious, economic, and social transformation.

According to Mechal Sobel, Scots, Scotch-Irish, Huguenots, and "vexed and troubled Englishmen" brought with them the mixed and changing worldviews of still prevailing Medieval Catholic as well as Protestant, agrarian, and working-class as well as merchant, artisan, and middle-class values. Given that the colonial settlement occurred during a period of intense upheaval – familial, geographic, social, and in some cases, economic – new worldviews, values, and patterns were created and meshed with the persistence of older and traditional ones. In the ensuing religious, economic, and social life of the colonies and later the nation, a notion of a work ethic was shaped. It came to

mean that "hard work, self-control, and dogged persistence" were the virtues necessary in order for most anyone to lead a successful life in America.

For later historical developments of the work ethic in the United States, these religious roots legitimated the same notions of work, now joined with transvalued and transformed social and economic interests – earthly reward, class mobility, and the fulfillment of ambition – in the growing "economic democracy." In this way, the use of the work ethic in the antebellum North was an attempt to acclimate working-class European immigrants into its industrial capitalism. Throughout the nineteenth century, the term *work ethic* became

> synonymous with the idea of social order . . . representing a complex ethical statement of the interrelationship between the individual, what he or she produced, and society. It represented an ideal situation in which individuals received, not just payment, but ethical and aesthetic enrichment for their work as well . . . it is the idealized relationship between individuals and their labor.

Embedded in this ideal work ethic were the notions of work rooted in biblical, Reformation, and Puritan ethos which understood work and labor as manual labor, craft, and mercantile entrepreneurship. According to James B. Gilbert, this "traditional work ethic depended upon the type of environment that existed in a small town or village, where each citizen could learn the values of community through the contribution of his labor." This is the notion of work that Max Weber found intriguing in *The Protestant Ethic and the Spirit of Capitalism.* While the term *Protestant ethic* for Weber meant a worldview – a way of seeing one's work and life as ordered by God's call – the more modern meaning of work ethic was different. According to Ernst Troeltsch, Weber described a secularized calling that gave "rise to that ideal of work for work's sake which forms the intellectual and moral assumption underlying the modern bourgeois [industrial] way of life." Not among the least important elements embedded in the secularization of the work ethic were its assumptions about individual responsibility and autonomy. Secularized as it was in the developing ethos of the United States through the industrial revolution, capitalism, and democratic individualism of the emerging nation, the meaning of work and the work ethic followed more the cultural identity of the nation than formal Protestant theology.

In the antebellum South, slaveholders' Christian ideology attempted to inculcate in the enslaved a sense of obedience to one's slave master or mistress. As for himself, the slaveowner's work ethic is no less a complicated issue than the work ethic of enslaved women. Like their northern counterparts and especially in sectional disputes, the southern planter often appealed to the same values regarding work. The classes of persons settling and planting in the South were drawn from the same English classes as were the Puritans – "pious, hardworking, middleclass, accepting literally and solemnly the tenets of Puritanism – sin, predestination, and election . . ." In that sense, "the work ethic" values upheld the general American ethos about work evident at the time. Yet an attitude also existed that militated against the work ethic as derived from Puritanism. While there was a climate of interest in business and investment in and through plantation economics, that attitude was tempered by one of leisure that defined labor itself as leisurely – that is, "the first end of life is living itself." Eugene Genovese takes this sentiment even further in his Marxist analysis of the "southern ethic." He writes:

> The planters commanded Southern politics and set the tone for social life. Theirs was an aristocratic, anti-bourgeois spirit with values and mores emphasizing family and status, a strong code of honor, and aspirations to luxury, ease, and accomplishment. In the planters' community, paternalism provided the standard of human relationships, and politics and statecraft were the duties and responsibilities of gentlemen. The gentleman lived for politics, not, like the bourgeois politician, off politics.

Enslaved blackwomen were judged by these meanings and held morally accountable under the rubric of "obedience to your master" by the slaveholding community. However, within the enslaved and later emancipated community, ethical values and moral conduct were articulated and lived out relative to the contradictions, circumstances, problems, and possibilities within the larger race, gender, and class structures of society. This ethical construction has neither been "identical with the body of obligations and duties that Anglo-Protestant American society requires of its members," nor always dependent on its basic assumptions.

A Reading of the Notion of a "Work Ethic" through the Lives of Enslaved Women

Having placed a blackwomen's biblical hermeneutic of reading work within the broader biblical notions of work, I now turn to a womanist examination of the "work ethic" and address two issues I see emerging from my reading of enslaved women's narratives. First, I will examine the assumptions embedded in the general notion of a work ethic by discussing social norms that are taken for granted in this notion. Second, I will raise questions about the nature of theological and ethical doctrines concerning work when associated with the learning provided by the lives of enslaved women in the antebellum.

Intrinsic to the idea of the work ethic is the assumption and privileging of labor over leisure and idleness. It implies that human activity and behavior can be understood most fully and systematically organized, or at least directed, toward a positive goal through human labor. Indeed, work itself becomes a positive moral good. In this sense, the work ethic encompasses moral action, ethical reflection, and a social ethos (inclusive of religious beliefs and/or theological views) informing the development of individuals and communities therein. Morally, the work ethic "gives a special nuance to the word 'duty' and creates an infectious model of an industrious life . . . it is not a single or simple idea. Rather, it is a complex of ideas with many roots and branches."

Within these assumptions lie social and economic ones. One such assumption is that the opportunity to work, and the opportunity to achieve through work, creates personal well-being. This "opportunity" is socially and economically assumed to be normative, available, and functional for all persons or members of society at large. I argued in chapter two that a central goal of the New World discovery was exploitation of resources and personal achievement through economic fulfillment. It is plausible to assert that, given favorable conditions of talent, resources, and opportunity, work would lead to self-fulfillment. In such thinking, opportunity inherently means access to resources and power with which to act independently for one's own welfare and that of the common good.

There is nothing in this assumption that admits the existence of social relations of domination, subordination, or power. However, the truth is that by the mature period of the antebellum, slaveholders and the enslaved existed in relationships marked by a complex set of negotiated customs and conventions within the larger framework of domination and subordination. Slaveholders certainly had structured normative positions of dominance and power; generally, enslaved persons were relatively powerless. The enslaved lived in a relationship of enforced and reinforced dependency, in the sense that their reliance on slaveholders was neither of their own choosing nor mutually defined. Considering this situation, enslaved persons' relation to work was not a relationship of opportunity, or potential achievement, or possible personal fulfillment. Their relationship to work did not come with access to the economic, social, legal, and political resources from which further access could be turned into opportunity. Independence and the opportunity to acquire power through knowledge, education, skills, tools, and economic resources are prerequisites for the possibilities of achievement and personal fulfillment attainable through work. The nature of the one-way, enforced dependency in the slaveholder-enslaved relationship (and solidified in objective structures of law, economics, and politics) reveals the near impossibility of "opportunity" as a key concept in the meaning of work in the lives of the enslaved.

A related and deeper manifestation of the notion of "opportunity" is revealed when one considers that the meaning and experience of work are inherited meanings and are experienced not just individually but culturally. As such, inherited meanings are resources – cultural capital – that through their operation as inheritances condition the ethos. These prerequisites to acquisition and use of power should be seen themselves as individual and/or cultural inheritances. Working with this deeper meaning of "opportunity," the notions of opportunity, inheritances, and dependency become more complex.

The slave narratives of Harriet Jacobs and Lucy Delaney speak of such inheritances. Jacobs' father, although enslaved, was considered to be a carpenter of such skill that his owner permitted him to "hire out," and even manage his own affairs with relative freedom. Jacobs' father provided his children with clothing, extra niceties, and, most important, "a feel[ing] that they were human beings." Jacobs' inheritance included a meaning of relative self-esteem related to work from her father (and grandmother); the fulfill-

ment of life's basic needs; and a knowledge of the meaning of freedom.

Lucy Delaney had been born free, and was later kidnapped and sold into slavery. Like Jacobs, she labored as an enslaved child and woman. However, she had not been taught as a child to work – for example, she was not taught the domestic arts of sewing, laundering, cooking, and housekeeping. (As an enslaved child, she had been a nursemaid.) Nevertheless, like Jacobs, she had an inheritance of the meaning of freedom that empowered her in her flight for freedom.

Both these enslaved women inherited different meanings and experiences from their families regarding work, legal, and relative freedom, and knowledge and skills upon which opportunities could be sought and created. Their experiences exemplified the relative maneuverability of the dominated who had access to the resources valued by society (but not intended for the enslaved) that could be used as leverage for opportunities. They were, however, not the norm for most enslaved women. Most enslaved women did not have parents or grandparents who were freeborn or freed. Most enslaved women were not in a context where they could become literate. Indeed, they were forbidden to gain the skills of literacy by law. Moreover, most enslaved women were not in a position to utilize what marketable skills they had to hire themselves out to earn money or to live relatively independent lives. As noted by William Harris, "By confining slaves to unskilled, rural tasks requiring no formal education or training, slavery, it is said, left blacks unprepared for any productive role in the growing cities of the nation."

It would seem, then, that in situations of group dominance and subordination such as slavery, enforced dependency remains the normative structure to thwart truly meaningful work as viewed by the dominant social and economic norm. At the same time, it seems equally true that there did exist those among the enslaved those who gained relative opportunities, knowledge, and skills, and so gained a small measure of distance from the vicissitudes of oppression. This would involve a relative ability to influence the powerful, but rarely the opportunity to exercise consistent power from a structured position so as to be able to represent the enslaved. Such situations gave an individual "influence," and perhaps was a contributing dynamic to the development of intra-group socioeconomic class relations and divisions, as well as the racialized class relations between dominant and subordinate groups.

Another underlying assumption embedded in the work ethic is that no matter what the nature of the work and of the person who does it, all work and all workers are equally valued. But enslaved women's narratives, and related materials, indicate that this assumption is not true. Aunt Sally, the fugitive slave who returned to hire herself out and purchase her freedom when her slave owner was in financial trouble, recalled that hiring oneself out brought the accusation of being uppity and uncontrollable as a slave. She understood that it was not a good thing for a slave to look self-reliant and independent.

It is clear that when work is considered valuable in itself and as a crucial element of positive human identity, it is contradicted in exploitative, objective structures like chattel slavery. According to C. Vann Woodward, an historian of southern culture, notions about the meaning and value of work ranged from subsistence farmers' need to feed and clothe themselves to the middle- and upper-class farmers who associated work with one's hands as indicating a degraded status in society. He writes, "Much [of the] work in early America required of all people was crude and hard, and little of it anywhere could honestly be characterized as stimulating, creative, or inherently enjoyable. Those who wrote of its joys and rewards probably had a larger share of work that could be so characterized than those who failed to record their impressions." Woodward also indicates that "neither the hired man nor the slave (who generally did the same work) shared the dignity and honor conferred by myth on the yeoman." In either case, the contradiction in the value and meaning of work was not lost on enslaved persons. The awareness of this contradiction was captured in a slave song:

> Missus in the big house,
> Mammy in the yard,
> Missus holdin' her white hands, Mammy workin' hard.
> Missus holdin' her white hands, Mammy workin' hard.

This contradiction further unfolds. On the one hand, enslaved women (and men) knew their owners valued their work. On the other hand, the work done by most enslaved people was manual work – work that according to Woodward was "crude and hard." It was work that had historically been done under the will and for the profit of another. Enslaved people knew that they were as valuable as any property owned by a slaveholder. Yet, it was also abundantly clear that as slaves they were instruments of production and were considered tools. They were the "things" that were bought and sold to do the kind of work understood to

be drudgery and toil. They knew that slaveholders generally believed, socially and religiously, that the work slaves did was the work they were created by God to do. Recalling Moltmann's words, "work itself was enslavement . . ." This double meaning of identity and work was not lost on the enslaved. Elizabeth Kleckley records witnessing her first slave auction when she was seven years old, writing, ". . . master had just purchased his hogs for the winter, for which he was unable to pay in full. To escape embarrassment it was necessary to sell one of the slaves. Little Joe . . . was selected as the victim . . . He came in with a bright face, was placed in the scales, and was sold, like the hogs, at so much per pound."

Kleckley's recollection is sobering. It captures the contradiction of slavery and enslavement in an economic and social environment with deeply held biblical, Reformation-Puritan, and democratic foundations. It is no surprise then that the investigations of enslaved peoples' lives have focused not on the meaning of work as exemplified in traditional formulations of "the work ethic" but on how they lived their lives beyond their work. This chapter has placed in perspective the sweep of custom, religious faith and tradition, and historical events in the development of political economy regarding notions of work and calling, and has suggested an interpretation of the work ethic from the perspective of enslaved African Americans. It has called into question the simple historical and theological romanticization of the Reformation (and its later Calvinist-Puritan) notions of work and calling and the secularized "work ethic" in the nineteenth and early twentieth centuries in America. Reading the notion of a work ethic from a womanist perspective on the lives of enslaved women, while maintaining that there existed an enslaved woman's work ethic, is thus at best a historical and theological paradox. At worst, the notion of a work ethic still plagues theological and socioeconomic sensibilities of African American women descendants of the enslaved in our struggle for quality of life, freedom, and liberation. The question that remains for the final chapter is how the current public debate about the need for a renewed work ethic and the clues from the lives of enslaved women stand in tension in our contemporary situation.

"And Demand Justice": A Jewish Response to the Business of Poverty

Aryeh Cohen (2007)

Are you proud of the wages and benefits you provide?

H. Lee Scott (CEO of Wal-Mart): Yes, I'm proud. I think it's very competitive, but I'm particularly proud of the careers we provide. I see associates who like us and appreciate what the company has done for them and who know that the company appreciates what they have done.

("Proud to Be at the Top," By Abigail Goldman, Los Angeles Times, November 23, 2003)

While its workforce has one of the best productivity records of any US corporation, it has kept the compensation of its rank-and-file workers at or barely above the poverty line. As of last spring, the average pay of a sales clerk at Wal-Mart was $8.50 an hour, or about $14,000 a year, $1,000 below the government's definition of the poverty level for a family of three. Despite the implied claims of Wal-Mart's current TV advertising campaign, fewer than half – between 41 and 46 percent – of Wal-Mart employees can afford even the least-expensive health care benefits offered by the company. To keep the growth of productivity and real wages far apart, Wal-Mart has reached back beyond the New Deal to the harsh, abrasive capitalism of the 1920s.

("Inside the Leviathan," by Simon Head, New York Review of Books, Volume 51, Number 20, December 16, 2004)

When asked about the anti-Wal-Mart agitation Alan Zaremberg, president of the California Chamber of Commerce, said: "It's not government's role to interfere with what consumers want" ("Grocery Unions Battle to Stop Invasion of the Giant Stores," by Nancy Cleeland and Abigail Goldman, Times Staff Writers, Los Angeles Times November 25, 2003). This astonishing quote needs to be read, reread and clarified. What is the moral valence of "what consumers want"? What is this class of "consumers" and how does it differ from the class of "workers" or "citizens"? Do "consumers" have special rights vis a vis the government? Other citizens? Is consumer desire an absolute restraint on government power? Is "consumer desire" different than, say, citizen desire? Owner desire? What is it that gives "consumer desire" this more weighty moral presence? What is, after all, government's role?

Deuteronomy 8

[11] Beware that you do not forget the LORD your God by not keeping His commandments and His ordinances and His statutes which I am commanding you today; [12] otherwise, when you have eaten and are satisfied, and have built good houses and lived in them, [13] and when your herds and your flocks multiply, and your silver and gold multiply, and all that you have multiplies, [14] then your heart will become proud and you will forget the LORD your God who brought you out from the land of Egypt, out of the house of slavery. [...] [17] and you say to yourselves, "My own power and the might of my own hand have won this wealth for me."

These verses from Deuteronomy spell out what might be called the spiritual challenge of wealth. The challenge that is articulated in these verses is being able to remember God in times of comfort. In times of adversity it is perhaps easier to remember God. In times of ease and riches, the encroaching danger is that one will forget the God of Egypt and claim wealth as a right: "My own power and the might of my own hand have won this wealth for me." If it is all my power and the strength of my hand then I owe nothing to anybody else. There is no other person who is beyond the power of my ability to acquire, to accumulate. I define the world by my ability to assimilate *it* into *me*. Since there was no reason to break out of the bounds of my self in order to acquire all this wealth – it was I who made this for me – there is no reason to think that there is any reason at all to pay attention to the desires of others. The verses in Deuteronomy suggest that remembering the God of the Exodus would act as a defense against this type of hubris. I want to explore why this might be so.

Who is the God "who brought you out from the land of Egypt, out of the house of slavery"? Why is this aspect of God important in this context?

One of the defining moments of the redemption from slavery in Egypt occurs early on in the book of Exodus. At the end of chapter two, after Moses has escaped to Midian for fear of the Pharaoh, when Israel is deeply mired in slavery, we read the following.

[23] *... The Israelites were groaning under the bondage and cried out; and their cry for help from the bondage rose up to God. [24] God heard their moaning, and God remembered His covenant with*

Abraham and Isaac and Jacob. ²⁵ God looked upon the Isaelites and God took notice of them.

Immediately following this, God commissions Moses to lead the Israelites out of Egypt. This little scene is the precipitating act of redemption and therefore it is important to pay attention to the mechanism which leads to that redemption. The key is verse 24. God *hears* the moaning of the Israelites and then God recalls the covenant with the Patriarchs. *Hearing* the cry of the oppressed leads to God taking notice. Taking notice leads to action.

This causal relation between hearing the cries of the oppressed and taking action for justice is brought into stark relief by its opposite. When Moses first confronts Pharaoh and voices God's demand to let the Israelites go free, Pharaoh famously refuses and increases the burden upon the slaves. The slaves are no longer provided with straw to make bricks, yet they must still make the same number of bricks. The workload of the slaves which until then was "merely" a daily quota of bricks is increased to gathering straw and *then* making the daily quota of bricks.

The Israelite "foremen" come to Pharaoh to advocate on behalf of the slaves.

> **Exodus 5**
> ¹⁵ The foremen of the Israelites came to Pharaoh and cried: "Why do you deal thus with your servants? ¹⁶ No straw is issued to your servants, yet they demand of us: Make bricks! Thus your servants [the Israelites] are being beaten, when the fault is with your own people."

Pharaoh's response to the cries of the foremen is exactly the opposite of God's.

> ¹⁷ He [Pharaoh] replied, "You are shirkers, shirkers! That is why you say 'Let us go and sacrifice to the Lord.' ¹⁸ Be off now to your work! No straw shall be issued to you, but you must produce your quota of bricks!"

Pharaoh does not *hear*. Pharaoh commands. There is no one outside Pharaoh of any significance. "Who is God that I should heed him?" is Pharaoh's response to Moses' demands of freedom. God *hears*, Pharaoh *ignores*.

God's *hearing* is so fundamental that it is memorialized as law.

> **Exodus 22**
> ²⁰ You shall not wrong a stranger or oppress him, for you were strangers in the land of Egypt. ²¹ You shall not ill-treat any widow or orphan. ²² If you do mistreat them, I will heed their outcry as soon as they cry out to Me, ²³ and My anger shall blaze forth and I will put you to the sword, and your own wives shall become widows and your children orphans.

The experience of the Israelite in Egypt is consecrated in law as the experience of God *hearing* the cries of oppression. The law obligates us to choose to be like God – *hearing* the stranger, the widow the orphan, the marginal and unprotected members of society – and at the same time to choose not to be like Pharaoh – *ignoring* the stranger, the widow the orphan, the marginal and unprotected members of society. God premises the obligation to heed the cry of the oppressed on the knowledge that the Israelites have that ultimately, whatever people decide to do, God *will* hear. If you don't hear the cry, and respond to it with acts of justice, and the widow and the orphan are forced to cry out to God, God *will* respond. God's response will, however, include both justice for the oppressed and swift vengeance for the "deaf."

This then is the "God who brought you out from the land of Egypt" – the God who hears the cry of the Other. Hearing the Other forces one out of the self-referential circle of the I. Once one is forced out of this closed circle, one cannot say "My own power and the might of my own hands have won this wealth for me." One is forced to recognize that there are people who are beyond our power to control, to own, to exploit.

This legal and moral obligation to hear the cry of the other person informs what Maimonides (1135–1204), the great Jewish philosopher and jurist, called "ordering the actions of the state and helping its citizens paths succeed" (*Mishneh Torah*, Laws of Sale 14:11). The person who has perfected themselves spiritually, religiously and philosophically, according to Maimonides, recognizes that "those actions [of God's] that ought to be known and imitated are *loving-kindness, justice,* and *righteousness*" (*Guide to the Perplexed* III:54). Imitating God or walking in the ways of God (Deut. 28:9) leads to justice and righteousness and away from the haughty arrogance of "My own power and the might of my own hands."

Once we understand that Jewish law is grounded in an ethic of *loving-kindness, justice* and *righteousness,* it is not surprising to find that the community is mandated to regulate commerce, and assure that there is at least a basic level of resources available to all. We find the following statement in the Talmud:

> The "citizens of a town" are permitted to set parameters for weights, for prices and for workers' wages, and to punish those who abrogate their ordinances.

The "citizens of a town" is some sort of representative body which acts on behalf of the town. Their mandate is to intervene in the market when necessary in order to assure that it operates justly. This means that manufacturers get fair prices and workers get fair salaries and all can afford to eat. This Talmudic statement was accepted as legally binding by the medieval codifiers (*Mishneh Torah,* Laws of Sale 14; *Shulchan Aruch, Choshen Mishpat* 231). There is no right to pay the cheapest price for goods. There is, rather an obligation on the society and its institutions to insure that prices and wages are both fair and just.

This is an important point. Citizenship in a city is defined by Rabbinic law in terms of obligation. Once you live in a city for a certain amount of time you are obligated to contribute to the soup kitchen, the welfare fund, the burial society and the general upkeep of the city. Citizenship is not defined by rights. There is no minimum residency requirement for a person to use the soup kitchen or collect from the welfare fund. A city is a community of obligation. This is often clouded in our large urban areas where the very term "community" is often problematic. However, Rabbinic Judaism – which from its origin was an urban phenomenon – understands the city as a web of obligations between people, some of whom are anonymous to each other, grounded in justice.

Writ large, this prevents us from living with a split consciousness – retreating back into the closed circle of the self when it comes to our role as consumer, then seeing the whole web of community and obligations when we demand justice. The web of obligations that we have toward each other prevents us from muting the voice of justice when we see the smiling face of a greeter as we enter a Wal-Mart.

Rabbi Moshe Feinstein the dean of Orthodox religious decisors/*poskim* in North America in the twentieth century, cited this principle (that the citizens of the town are mandated to regulate prices and wages)

in a responsum written in 1952 deciding that union organizing was obviously sanctioned by *halakhah*/Jewish Law (*Iggeros Moshe, Choshen Mishpat,* 58). Other Rabbis (such as the former Chief Rabbi of the State of Israel, Rabbi Shlomo Goren) cite the sixteenth-century code, the *Shulchan Aruch* (*Choshen Mishpat* 333), which says that a worker has the right to withhold his labor at any time since workers are only slaves to God and not to other slaves of God (based on Leviticus 25:55).

While neither of these pro-union contentions is uncontested, there is a clear understanding in Jewish legal and moral tradition that the aggregation of wealth is neither a right nor necessarily a good thing. The "market" is viewed by the tradition as neutral, and intervention in the market is seen as an obligation of the community in order to insure the just distribution of and access to resources.

In sum, strong voices within the Jewish tradition would definitely say that it is the government's role to interfere with what consumers want when consumer desires creates injustice. My desire to be able to buy a shirt for $7 has no moral standing next to my obligation to make sure that everybody in the community is paid a decent wage and has access to health care and education. When Wal-Mart, whose annual revenues in 2003 were $258 billion (which is 2 percent of US GDP, making it the world's largest corporation ("Inside the Leviathan," by Simon Head, *NYRB,* 51:20, December 16, 2004), claims that it is protecting consumers by keeping its workers under the poverty line, it is the obligation of the community to intervene. It is the obligation of the community to say that they are citizens of communities, not just consumers and workers. All citizens should earn a living wage. Denying this basic principle of justice, as Wal-Mart does, destroys the web of justice-based relationships between people which makes a city into a community of obligation. Wal-Mart uses poverty as a strategic business tool, as one analyst commented. We must hold this practice up to the light of day as the evil that it is and demand justice.

The Living Wage: A Jewish Approach

Rabbi Jill Jacobs (2003)

As of 2003, more than one hundred communities around the country have passed "living wage" ordinances that require businesses holding government contracts to pay their workers enough to be economically self-sufficient. Dozens more communities are considering similar legislation.

The living wage movement, which began in Baltimore approximately ten years ago, responds to the growing disparity between the minimum wage and the earnings necessary to keep a family out of poverty. A person who works full-time at the national minimum wage of $5.15 an hour will earn only $10,712 over the course of the year – less than the national poverty line of $11,610 for a family of two.[1] A minimum wage worker who pays payroll taxes and receives federal and state child and earned income tax credits earns $11,657 a year – barely over the national poverty line.[2] Living wage laws tie wages to the local cost of living or to the national poverty line, in the interest of guaranteeing that even the lowest-paid workers earn enough to be economically self-sufficient.

As many have pointed out, the national poverty line does not accurately reflect the cost of food, clothing, shelter and other necessities. A September 2000 report by the New York State Self-Sufficiency Standard Steering Committee estimates that in Brooklyn, where the cost of living is mid-range for New York City, a single parent with one pre-schooler must earn $35,460 in order to afford adequate housing, food, child care, health care and transportation. The New Jersey Poverty Research Institute estimates that in New Jersey, to be economically self-sufficient, a single adult with one pre-school age child must earn between $25,792 and $35,401 a year, depending on the county.

The nation's first living wage law, which went into effect in Baltimore in July 1995, established an initial minimum wage of $6.10 per hour for workers on city contracts, and stipulated annual increases that, within four years, would raise wages to a level sufficient to lift a family of four over the poverty line.[3] As of July 2003, the living wage in Baltimore will be $8.70 an hour.[4]

The success of the Baltimore living wage ordinance has sparked hundreds of other city, state and campus campaigns, generally spearheaded by coalitions of labor unions, community groups and religious organizations. Current ordinances mandate wages that range from $6.15 an hour in New Orleans to $12.92 an hour in Richmond, California.[5]

The living wage issue has long been controversial, both in America as a whole, and within the Jewish community in particular. Proponents of the living wage consider it an essential tool for lifting workers out of poverty. Opponents argue that market forces should set wages and that the imposition of a living wage will lead to the loss of jobs. In the Jewish community, some argue that living wage laws offer a means of fulfilling the Jewish imperative to eradicate poverty. Others worry that rising wage rates will result in increased costs for Jewish non-profits that rely on minimum wage workers and will thereby impair the ability of these organizations to serve the community.

This Jewish communal tension came to a head in 1999 when the Jewish Community Council of Greater Washington helped to defeat a Montgomery County, Maryland, living wage bill, citing concerns that paying workers the proposed living wage of $10.44 an hour or $9 with benefits would cost Jewish organizations up to $1 million and force the cancellation of some programs.

Other Jewish groups, including Jews United for Justice and a coalition of local rabbis, supported the bill and sponsored a series of community forums to discuss the proposal. Abe Pollin, the majority owner of the Washington Wizards basketball team and father of Robert Pollin, author of a book on the living wage movement, placed ads supporting the legislation in the *Washington Jewish Week*. In the end, two Jewish council members cast the deciding votes in defeating

---

1. Robert Pollin and Stephanie Luce, *The Living Wage: Building a Fair Economy* (The New Press, 1998), p. 2. In Alaska and Hawaii, the poverty line is higher, $14,510 and $13,360 respectively, for a family of two.

2. Diana Pearce with Jennifer Brooks, "The Self Sufficiency Standard for New York" (September, 2000), online at www.sixstrategies.org/files/Resource-StandardReport-NY.pdf.

3. Pollin and Luce, *The Living Wage*, pp. 46–53.

4. Baltimore Wage Commission (www.ci.baltimore.md.us/government/wage/), July 30, 2002.

5. Economic Policy Institute, 2002.

the proposed legislation.[6] During the same time, the Jewish Community Council of Greater Washington led opposition to a resolution in support of living wage laws adopted by the Jewish Council for Public Affairs in February 2000.[7]

In June 2002, the Montgomery County Council approved a compromise living wage ordinance that exempts non-profit organizations from paying the set wages of $10.50 an hour[8] to those working on county contracts. This time, the JCC, whose programs would no longer be affected, encouraged the Jewish council members to support the bill.[9] One of the Jewish members sponsored this compromise bill, and the other voted for it.

This article will propose a Jewish approach to the living wage issue. This will not be a formal teshuvah, but rather, an exploration of the ways in which halakhah governing employer-employee relationships is and is not relevant to the contemporary living wage debate. Given the enormous body of Jewish literature on employer-employee relations, we expect to find direct discussion of appropriate wages within the traditional sources. Our texts, however, pay little attention to this question. We must therefore approach the issue through a more general examination of Jewish assumptions about labor and wages. This paper focuses on three principles of Jewish labor law: the concept of *minhag hamakom* (the legal force of local custom), the responsibilities of an employer to an employee, and the responsibilities of an employee to an employer. Finally, I will discuss the tradition of rabbinic interference in determining and changing local labor laws.

Principles of Jewish Labor Law

Jewish law differentiates between two types of workers – the *poel*, who is paid by the day, and the *kablan*, who is paid by the task. We will focus on the *poel*, whose situation more closely parallels that of the contemporary workers on whom our discussion centers. Though

not the task of this piece, a precise delineation of the distinctions between the *poel* and the *kablan* would be an important topic for further research, particularly as many companies excuse themselves from paying health benefits by classifying certain workers as contractors, rather than as permanent employees.

Most Jewish employment law revolves around the concept of *minhag hamakom* – the idea that the custom of a place determines workers' salaries, as well as other working conditions. This principle is laid out most clearly in Mishnah Bava Metziah 7:1:

> One who hires workers and instructs them to begin work early and to stay late – in a place in which it is not the custom to begin work early and to stay late, the employer may not force them to do so. In a place in which it is the custom to feed the workers, he must do so. In a place in which it is the custom to distribute sweets, he must do so. Everything goes according to the custom of the land.
>
> A story about Rabbi Yohanan ben Matya, who told his son, "Go, hire us workers." His son went and promised them food (without specifying what kind, or how much). When he returned, his father said to him, "My son! Even if you gave them a feast like that of King Solomon, you would not have fulfilled your obligation toward them, for they are the children of Abraham, Isaac and Jacob. However, as they have not yet begun to work, go back and say to them that their employment is conditional on their not demanding more than bread and vegetables." Rabbi Shimon ben Gamliel said, "It is not necessary to make such a stipulation. Everything goes according to the custom of the place."

Many have understood the principle of *minhag hamakom* as evidence of halakhic support for a controlled free market system. According to this understanding, wages, hours and other working conditions are determined primarily by local custom and not by halakhic considerations. No individual employer may depart from the accepted business practice of the area, but there are few halakhic limitations as to what this practice is. While prohibiting employers from forcing employees to work long hours, the mishnah cited above leaves open the possibility that an employer may stipulate long hours in the initial contract. In the Talmud Bavli, the gemara on this mishnah goes on to suggest that Torah law technically permits long hours, but that local custom may be more lenient.[10]

6. Stephen T. Dennis, "Pollins Rally Support for Living Wage Law," *The Gazette*, February 23, 2002.

7. John Rivera, "American Jewish Liberalism Waning," *The Baltimore Sun*, February 26, 2000.

8. Part of these wages may be taken as benefits. Thus, a worker who receives health benefits may actually earn less than $10.50/hour.

9. Eric Fingerhut, "After Opposing Wage Bill, Council to Study Compromise," *Washington Jewish Week*, March 7, 2002.

10. B. Bava Metzia 83b.

The Yerushalmi commentary on the mishnah supports our initial suggestion that rabbinic law prefers a controlled free market system. In the Yerushalmi, Rabbi Hoshea concludes that "the *minhag* overrides the halakhah" – even though the Torah allows employers to insist on long working hours, local *minhag* takes precedence.[11] The Yerushalmi then offers the story of the people of Beit Maon who, unlike the people of Tiberius, were accustomed to starting work early and ending late. According to the Yerushalmi:

> The people of Beit Maon who came down to Tiberius to hire themselves out would hire themselves according to the custom of Tiberius. However, when one went from Tiberius to hire workers in Beit Maon, he could say to them, "Do not think that I could not find workers to hire in Tiberius. Rather, I came here to hire workers because I heard that you will start work early and end late."[12]

From this story we might infer that market forces are the only factor governing working conditions and that employers may demand any conditions that workers will accept. Disturbingly, this story also seems to justify the current practice of employing workers in developing countries at wages that would be illegal in America.

However, a few elements within the mishnah and its accompanying gemara in the Bavli challenge our initial conclusion. We are first struck by the number of apparently superfluous details in the mishnah. Instead of simply offering the concise statement that "everything goes according to the custom of the land," the mishnah offers numerous examples of conditions determined by the accepted *minhag*. We are told, seemingly redundantly, that an employer must follow the *minhag hamakom* in regard to hours, food, and even treats for workers.

The gemara notices the expansive nature of the mishnah and questions the necessity of specifying that an employer may not force workers to begin early and stay late. The Talmud responds that "we need [this statement] for the case in which the employer raises the workers' wages. In the case in which he says to them, 'I raised your wages in order that you would begin work early and stay late,' they may reply, 'you raised our wages in order that we would do better

work.'"[13] With these words, the gemara establishes wages and hours, and presumably other working conditions, as separate categories that do not inherently depend on one another. Raising a worker's salary does not necessarily obligate this worker to work longer hours, or to accept new responsibilities. Employers and workers presumably may stipulate longer hours when they negotiate a contract, but an employer who fails to make such a stipulation before raising wages may not, post facto, demand a longer workday.

The Talmud is surprising in its suggestion that workers may adjust their production rate to salary levels. The gemara implicitly permits an employee who earns low wages to work less hard than one who earns a higher salary. In this allowance, the text calls to mind the common labor tactic of a "work to rule" strike, in which workers refuse to exceed the precise job requirements. In first encountering this talmudic text, I read it as a personal chastisement for the many times I have complained about slow cashiers in grocery stores and other establishments. Instead of blaming cashiers for working slowly, we can perhaps say that these employees perform as well as might be expected of those who earn $6 or $7 an hour. The gemara suggests that increasing production rates and improving work quality requires first raising wages.

In the mishnah's story of Rabbi Yohanan ben Matya, we find a challenge to the idea that the local *minhag* governs all workplace conditions. Rabbi Yohanan assumes not only that the employer must stipulate the exact working conditions, but also that vague statements should be interpreted in favor of the worker. Presumably, no manual worker would expect to receive a feast like that of a king. Still, according to Rabbi Yohanan, a worker who is not told otherwise may expect the best possible meal. With the comment that the workers are "the children of Abraham, Isaac and Jacob," Rabbi Yohanan ben Matya simultaneously asserts the dignity of these workers and emphasizes the lack of distance between himself and his son and those they employ. Many employers fail to recognize the humanity of their workers and, accordingly, show little interest in the workers' history or personal situation. In contrast, Rabbi Yohanan forces his son to confront the humanity of the workers, and to acknowledge the shared narrative of employer and employee. Although the gemara does not eventually accept Rabbi Yohanan ben Matya's demand for clear stipulations regarding food quality and quantity, the inclusion of this aggadah problematizes our acceptance of *minhag hamakom*

---

11. J. Bava Metzia 7:1.

12. Ibid.

13. B. Bava Metzia 83a.

as the sole determinant of worker contracts.

The specification that the workers in Rabbi Yohanan's story are Jewish presents a difficulty, both because our modern sensibilities resist legal separations between ethnic and religious groups, and because most low-wage workers in America are not Jewish. We can read this text either as evidence that the rabbis imagine a separate body of law for Jewish and non-Jewish workers, or as a reflection of the rabbinic inability to conceive of non-Jews working for Jews. The absence of a separate body of rabbinic law for non-Jewish workers supports the latter possibility. However, we acknowledge that biblical law recognizes separate categories for Jewish and Canaanite slaves, and that the rabbis may consider this fact a precedent for creating separate labor laws for Jews. While we are inclined to argue that the rabbis simply cannot imagine a situation in which Jews employ members of other ethnic groups, we admit that the question of the interpretation of this text remains open.

The talmudic texts we have thus examined leave us with questions and paradoxes. On the one hand, some textual evidence points to a bias in favor of workers. On the other hand, the texts assume the principle of *minhag hamakom* to be the basis of all Jewish labor law. Additionally, we have no clear statement about appropriate wage levels, beyond the necessity that these levels conform to the regional *minhag*. Furthermore, it is not clear whether halakhic labor laws apply to non-Jews as well as to Jews. To sort out these issues, we must expand our inquiry and examine the assumptions upon which the relevant halakhah is based.

Two biblical verses provide the foundation for much of Jewish labor law:

> "Do not oppress your neighbor and do not rob him. Do not keep the wages of the worker with you until morning" (Leviticus 19:13).

> "Do not oppress the hired laborer who is poor and needy, whether he is one of your people or one of the sojourners in your land within your gates. Give him his wages in the daytime, and do not let the sun set on them, for he is poor, and his life depends on them, lest he cry out to God about you, for this will be counted as a sin for you" (Deuteronomy 24:14–15).

These verses are significant in their acknowledgment of the essential power and wealth imbalance between employer and employee. The texts understand both the employer's power to rob the employee and the employee's dependence on the wages. From these verses, we understand workers to be a protected category, perhaps similar to widows, orphans and sojourners. The Deuteronomy verses further include sojourners among the protected workers, thereby prohibiting us from distinguishing between Jewish and non-Jewish workers. From the biblical text, we therefore derive a few general principles. First, workers are understood to be poor and deserving of our protection. Second, both Jews and non-Jews are considered to be included in the category of protected workers. Third, the texts assert the need for specific legislation to prevent the oppression of workers.

Still, these biblical verses offer little assistance in determining appropriate wages or other labor conditions. While tardy payment of wages may have been an important labor issue in biblical times, most contemporary labor negotiations focus on wage levels and working conditions. There certainly continue to be instances of employers failing to pay workers, or of workers' checks bouncing, but low-wage workers are generally most concerned about securing higher wages, benefits and safe working conditions.

Two rabbinic texts do explicitly legislate against the gross underpayment of workers. One mishnah forbids an employer from telling an employee paid to handle straw, "take the result of your labor as your wages."[14] The Tosefta considers a case in which an employer hires someone to bring fruit to a sick person. If the employee goes to the home of the sick person and finds that this person has died or recovered, the employer must pay the worker's wages in full and cannot say, "take what you are carrying as payment."[15]

While it might be tempting to compare straw and fruit with today's low wages, we must acknowledge the difference. The current minimum wage of $5.15 an hour may not buy much, but we cannot equate it with straw and fruit, which are not even forms of currency. Furthermore, we assume that the rabbinic texts refer to a case in which the employer originally agreed to reasonable wages and now wishes to break the contract.

As in the biblical verses, these early rabbinic texts are most significant in their understanding of the employer's inherent power over the employee. Because the employee may not have the power to refuse the straw

---

14. B. Bava Metzia 10:5.

15. T. Bava Metzia 6:4.

and fruit and to demand monetary compensation, the texts legislate against the attempt on the part of the employer to take advantage of the employee. Second, while the examples of straw and fruit are extreme, the texts may set a precedent for some sort of minimum wage. Still, we must investigate further to determine whether Jewish law requires anything of the employer beyond complicity with local labor practices.

To understand the biblical and rabbinic texts, we must ask why these texts focus on delayed payment and broken contracts rather than other types of labor concerns. In responding to this question, we are guided by Nahmanides' comment on Deuteronomy 24:15 that "the text speaks in the present." According to Nahmanides, the biblical text addresses the issue of timely payment, because this was the issue most of concern to workers of the time. In singling out one labor law, the text does not imply that delayed payment is the only issue worthy of our consideration. Rather, in addressing the issue most relevant to workers of its own time, the Bible invites us to consider ways to ameliorate the situation of workers in our own time. Paying workers promptly constitutes only one means of fulfilling the more general commandment, "do not oppress the hired laborer." Today, adherence to this commandment may take many other forms.

Rabbinic commentary on the biblical verse further helps us to understand the emphasis on prompt payment of wages, rather than on the amount of the wages themselves. Like Nahmanides after them, the rabbis of the Talmud understand the biblical prohibition against delaying wages to be a general command to respond to the actual needs of workers. Interpreting the phrase, "his life depends on [the wages]," the Talmud explains, "Why does he climb a ladder or hang from a tree or risk death? Is it not for his wages?" Another interpretation: "his life depends on them" indicates that anyone who denies a hired laborer his wages, it is as though he takes his life from him.[16]

This talmudic comment is surprising in its suggestion that the employer assumes responsibility for the health and well-being of his workers. Even more radical is the statement of Jonah Gerondi, the medieval author of the *Sefer HaYirah*:

> *Be careful not to afflict a living creature, whether animal or fowl, and even more so not to afflict a human being, who is created in God's image. If you want to hire workers and you find that they are poor, they should become like poor members of your*

*household (*aniyim b'nei beytekha*). You should not disgrace them, for you are commanded to behave respectfully toward them and to pay their wages.[17]*

Given this emphasis on the employer's responsibilities toward the worker, we are puzzled by the absence of specific legislation about appropriate wages. Even Gerondi assumes that prompt payment will guarantee the workers' well-being. While we still have no clear statement about appropriate wages, this text hints at an assumption that wages, when paid on time, will be sufficient to lift a person out of poverty.

This point becomes even clearer in Nahmanides' commentary to Deuteronomy 24:15, alluded to above. In reference to the hired worker, Nahmanides writes, "For he is poor – like the majority of hired laborers, and he depends on the wages to buy food by which to live . . . if he does not collect the wages right away as he is leaving work, he will go home, and his wages will remain with you until the morning, and he will die of hunger that night." Like Gerondi, Nahmanides holds the employer responsible for the health and sustenance of the worker. If the worker and/or his family die of hunger as a result of non-payment of wages, Nahmanides implies, fault for the death lies with the employer.

With his assertion that a person who does not receive wages on time will "die of hunger that night," Nahmanides takes for granted that a person who *does* receive payment on time *will* be able to provide sufficiently for himself and his family and will not die of hunger. This assumption is also reflected in Maimonides' designation of the highest level of tzedakah as "the one who strengthens the hand of his fellow Jew by giving him a gift or a loan or entering into partnership with him or finding him work in order to strengthen his hand so that he will not need to ask in the future."[18] For Maimonides, a person who has permanent employment or a share in a business will never find it necessary to ask for tzedakah.

The assumption that an employed person will be able to support him or herself and a family may respond to the medieval experience, but does not reflect our current reality. In a time when 22 percent of homeless people and 38 percent of those who apply for emergency food relief are employed, we can no longer

---

16. B. Bava Metzia 112a. cf. *Sefer HaHinukh* 588.

17. *Dibur haMathil,* "*hishamer mil'tzaer.*"

18. *Mishneh Torah, Matanot l'Aniyim,* 10:7.

assume that providing jobs will eradicate poverty.[19] According to Robert Pollin, the original living wage campaign in Baltimore began when a church group noticed an increased number of employed clients in its soup kitchens.[20]

We find ourselves then in a reality that differs from that upon which biblical and rabbinic wage laws are based. The rabbis are familiar with workers who live "check-to-check," but do not imagine that a day's wages might prove insufficient to buy food or other necessities for that day. Our challenge, then, is to determine the appropriate way of applying employment law that assumes one set of conditions to our new reality.

Employees' Obligations

Halakhic discussions of the employees' obligations toward their employers offer additional insight into the assumptions of Jewish labor law. Traditional sources compel employees to work diligently, to be precise in their work and to avoid wasting the employer's time. Workers may even recite abbreviated prayers and excuse themselves from certain religious obligations in order not to detract from their work.[21] According to Maimonides:

> *Just as the employer must be careful not to steal the salary of the poor [worker], so too must the poor person be careful not to steal the work of the owner by wasting a little time here and there until the entire day is filled with trickery. Rather, he should be careful about time. For this reason, the rabbis specified that workers do not need to recite the fourth blessing of* Birkat Hamazon. *Similarly, the worker is obligated to work with all of his strength, for behold, Jacob the righteous said [to Laban,] "I have served your father with all my might."*[22]

Workers are also prohibited from working both a day job and a night job, as working double shifts interferes with one's ability to perform either job well. Furthermore, workers must care for their own health, and are not permitted to starve themselves, as this, too,

is considered stealing work from the employer.[23] An employer, these laws teach us, should know exactly what to expect from his/her workers. If the contract specifies that the workers work eight hours a day, the employer should expect the workers to perform at full capacity for the entire eight hours. Unlike the *kablan*, who is paid for completing a job, the *poel* is paid according to the time worked. If the *poelim* are lazy or unable to complete their jobs, the employer loses money, as s/he will need to employ additional workers, or will need to hire the current workers for additional days. In an agricultural setting, inefficient workers may cause the employer to lose crops, which are potential sources of profit.

The obligations placed on the employee indicate that the relationship between employer and employee is meant to benefit both partners and to favor neither. The employer agrees to pay workers on time and to adhere to the initial contract, and workers agree to work as hard as they can and to refrain from behavior that will impair their ability to work. In theory, the employer receives the best work possible, and the workers receive reasonable compensation for their efforts.

As we found in our discussion of wages, the assumptions that generate laws about employees' obligations do not reflect our current reality. The prohibition against taking multiple jobs assumes that a worker will be able to support him/herself by working a single job, and that this worker takes on a second job only out of greed, or out of a desire to cheat one employer. Today, in contrast, for many Americans, holding multiple jobs is an economic necessity. The Bureau of Labor Statistics estimates that 5.6 percent of Americans (7,556,000) hold multiple jobs, with 300,000 working two full-time jobs.[24] Some have suggested that the actual rate of second jobs may be closer to 15 or 20 percent.[25] As with any labor statistic, the number of undocumented workers and "under-the-table" jobs makes it difficult accurately to determine the frequency of multiple employment, particularly among low-wage workers. Anecdotal evidence suggests that

---

19. U.S. Conference of Mayors, *Report on Hunger and Homelessness* (2002).

20. Pollin and Luce, *The Living Wage*, 9.

21. B. Berakhot 17a; 46a.

22. *Mishneh Torah, Hilkhot Skhirut* 13:7, cf. *Shulhan Arukh, Hoshen Mishpat* 337:20.

23. T. Bava Metzia 8:2, cf. *Shulhan Arukh, Hoshen Mishpat* 337:19.

24. Bureau of Labor Statistics, 2000.

25. Stephen Betts, "An Exploration of Multiple Jobholding (Moonlighting) and an Investigation into the Relationship Between Multiple Jobholding and Work Related Commitment," doctoral dissertation (unpublished), Rutgers University, 2002.

a high percentage of the lowest paid workers supplement their primary jobs with weekend and evening work. When I worked on a campaign to raise wages for office cleaners in New Jersey, virtually all of the workers I encountered held second jobs to supplement the 5-6 dollars an hour they earned as janitors. One living wage organizer reports coming to grips with the frequency of this phenomenon only when he asked a worker in Alexandria, Virginia what he planned to do with his higher wages after the passage of a living wage ordinance. The worker's reply? "Quit my third job."[26]

A strict reading of the *Shulhan Arukh* and other sources might suggest that these workers cheat their employers when accepting second and third jobs. However, given the virtual impossibility of supporting a family on a few hundred dollars a week, we can not reasonably expect low-wage workers to confine themselves to a single, 40-hour a week job. Again, we find ourselves caught between the halakhic ideal and the contemporary reality.

Given the discrepancy between halakhic obligations on workers and the contemporary reality, we find ourselves with two possibilities. We can either reconsider the halakhic prohibition against taking multiple jobs and the requirement that employees work at full capacity, or we can accept the current reality as a challenge to traditional halakhah and, in turn, use halakhah to critique the present-day situation. In his analysis of Jewish labor issues, David Schnall, the dean of Yeshiva University's Azrieli Graduate School of Jewish Education and Administration, takes the former approach. He suggests that in American society, multiple employment may have assumed the status of *minhag hamakom*, and therefore may be acceptable.[27] He also cites evidence that those who work

second jobs "appear no more likely to underperform or to behave in an undesirable fashion [than those who work only one job]." Furthermore, Schnall classifies as "substantial" the argument that permitting multiple employment "is a means of retaining and satisfying talented workers when an employer cannot continue to raise salary or benefits."[28]

Schnall's analysis may appropriately respond to certain instances of multiple employment, including the examples he cites of teachers who tutor after school or during the summer, and professionals who consult in their free time.[29] However, it does not seem reasonable to assume that a low-wage employee working between 60 and 80 hours a week at two or three jobs will be as productive as a person working only one full-time job. Furthermore, other factors, including the lack of access to health care and unreasonable production expectations, make it even more difficult for many workers to perform their assigned tasks adequately.

As we have seen, the traditional obligations placed on the employer and on the employee presuppose a situation that differs significantly from the contemporary work environment. In the halakhic ideal, a person who works full-time and receives wages promptly will be able to buy food and other necessities and maintain his/her health.[30] In return, this person is expected to work efficiently and reliably. In the current situation, then, our halakhah does not work as intended. Our challenge, then, is to create a system that allows halakhah to be operative without violating the fundamental principle of *minhag hamakom*.

Rabbinic Interference

Until this point, we have assumed that the *minhag hamakom* is to create a universally-accepted wage

---

26. Bobbi Murray, "Living Wage Comes of Age: An Increasingly Sophisticated Movement Has Put Opponents on the Defensive," *The Nation* July 23, 2001.

27. David Schnall, *By the Sweat of Your Brow* (Yeshiva University, 2001), p. 141. Schnall's statement assumes an acceptance of the general principle "*haminhag m'vatel et hahalakhah*," suggested by Rav Hoshea in Y. Bava Metzia 7:1. The question of the general applicability of this principle is a matter of much debate. The *Or Zarua* understands this principle to apply only to an accepted *minhag*, certified by a recognized authority (2:393). Similarly, *Masekhet Sofrim* permits only a "*minhag vatikin*" to override halakhah (14:16). The Rashba softens the necessity for earlier precedent, requiring only an "agreed-upon *minhag*" (*She'elot u'Teshuvot*, part II, no. 43). Joseph Caro, however, seems to accept the principle, "*haminhag m'vatel et hahalakhah*" as a general rule (*Beit Yosef* and *Shulh.an Arukh, H. oshen Mishpat* 232:19).

28. Ibid., p. 130.

29. Ibid., pp. 127–143. As Schnall notes, the statistic that teachers are among the most likely to take supplementary jobs corresponds with the fact that most halakhic discussion around multiple employment has concerned teachers. There has been a general halakhic tendency to prohibit teachers from working after hours (pp. 135–136).

30. The definition of "full-time," of course, changes according to the time and place. The rabbis understand the biblical definition of "full-time" to be dawn to dusk, though by talmudic times, the workday appears to be shorter than this (B. Bava Metzia 83a). In America, we can define full-time as approximately forty hours a week, with an appropriate number of sick days and vacation days. In other countries, this definition may be different.

rate, determined primarily by market forces. As we have seen in our time, allowing market forces to set wages creates a situation in which halakhot related to employer-employee relations cannot operate. To restore a workable halakhic system, we must consider the possibility for interference in creating or changing the *minhag hamakom*.

While most texts assume that the *minhag hamakom* develops naturally, a few texts do allow civic and/or religious bodies to determine wages and other working conditions. Tosefta Bava Metzia 11:23 permits the "people of the city" to stipulate workers' wages, as well as prices and measurements.[31] Here, we have an explicit break with the controlled free market system that some other texts seem to describe. In granting individual communities the authority to determine wages, the rabbis indicate an understanding of the failures of a free market system. While certain economic conditions might enable such a system to succeed, other conditions will make this system unworkable. To maintain stability, the local authority must have the power to adjust wage rates according to economic realities.

The Tosefta also extends to groups of artisans permission to make binding stipulations amongst themselves.[32] A number of contemporary halakhic scholars, including Moshe Feinstein and Eliezer Waldenburg (Tzitz Eliezer) have understood this text as a precedent for contemporary labor unions.[33] Medieval halakhic debate about the ability of individual communities or artisans to determine wages and other working conditions primarily concerns the question of whether an "*adam hashuv*" or a "*hakham*" – an important or wise person who holds a position of communal leadership – must approve such stipulations. Rabbi Asher ben Yehiel (the Rosh) defines the "*adam hashuv*" as "a rabbi who is the head and leader of the city" and rules that "when there is such a person, even all of the people of the city together do not have the authority to make stipulations without the consent of this important person."[34] Similarly, Maimonides permits self-regulation only in "a country in which there is no wise authority figure responsible for setting the laws of the country and making its citizens successful."[35] As our own political reality does not include leaders with such unilateral authority, we may assume that the restrictions specified by Maimonides and the Rosh no longer apply.

Other texts similarly emphasize the need to adapt employment laws to current conditions. The laws concerning a worker's right to quit a job in the middle of the day, as enumerated in the Talmud and later codes of law, change according to the availability of other workers. The principle that "the children of Israel are [God's] servants and not servants to servants"[36] grants the worker permission to quit midday without penalty and not to be beholden to his/her employer as a slave is to a master.[37] However, in a case in which the work in question will be lost if not completed immediately and in which no other workers are available, a worker may not be allowed to quit early, or may face penalties for doing so.[38] Here, the texts stipulate one law for an ideal situation, then offer alternate laws for different economic conditions. These laws also suggest a general principle that the law should favor the person in the more precarious position. Most commonly, the law protects the worker, who stands in danger of becoming like a servant to the employer. However, when economic conditions favor the worker, the law benefits the employer.

The texts we have discussed offer us a number of principles of employment law. First, work should allow for the fulfillment of the promises of Maimonides and Nahmanides that a worker should be able to provide for the basic needs of his/her family and lift him/herself out of poverty. Second, employment law must enable employees to fulfill their obligations toward their employers without putting themselves or their families at risk. Third, employment law must change according to the economic reality. Finally, communal authorities have the power to adapt employment law to the needs of the time.

In our day, it is clear that the *minhag hamakom* – the

---

31. Cf. B. Bava Batra 8b. Later halakhic authorities permit the community not only to set wages, but to force community members to comply with the stipulated wages. The Rashbatz even extends the power of *harem* to communities in this regard (*Tashbetz*, part I, no. 159).

32. T. Bava Metzia, 11:24–26.

33. Moshe Feinstein, *Ig'rot Moshe, H.oshen Mishpat*, Part I, nos. 58–59; Eliezer Waldenburg, *She'elot and Teshuvot of the Tzitz Eliezer*, Part II, no. 23.

34. Commentary to B. Bava Batra 9a.

35. *Mishneh Torah, Hilkhot Mekhira* 14:11.

36. Leviticus 25:55, cf. Rashi on Exodus 21:6.

37. B. Bava Kamma 116b.

38. B. Bava Metzia 86b, cf. Maimonides, *Mishneh Torah, Hilkhot Skhirut* 9:4; *Shulh.an Arukh*, Hoshen Mishpat 333:3.

current minimum wage – neither enables workers to lift themselves out of poverty nor allows them to fulfill their responsibilities toward their employers. Our current *minhagim*, therefore, have created a situation in which our halakhic norms cannot operate as intended. Rabbinic sources, understood formalistically, may not mandate the establishment of a living wage, but these sources are predicated on an assumption that even the lowest wages allow for economic self-sufficiency. Instituting a living wage is the first step toward creating a labor situation in which halakhah can work.

Given the emphasis by Maimonides and others on creating sustainable jobs, we cannot conclude without addressing the concerns raised by some opponents of the living wage that such legislation will lead to a loss of low-wage jobs. Without offering an in-depth economic analysis, we will say that these fears generally appear to be unfounded. Extensive studies on the effects of living wage legislation in Baltimore and Detroit, conducted by the Economic Policy Institute and the Wayne State Center for Urban Studies and Labor Studies Center respectively, conclude that living wage legislation in these two cities has not contributed to job loss or to price increases.[39] According to the Wayne State study:

> In terms of contracts alone, approximately 2300 workers would likely benefit from the living wage. Of these 85% would see immediate wage gains whose average ranges from $1,312 to $4,439 a year. Additionally, 50% would gain full family health coverage. These figures do not include the likely large number of workers covered through financial assistance received by their employer. For covered workers, substantial gains in overall income, the proportion of income coming from wages, and family medical coverage are far greater than the small possible losses in public assistance ... The research results are consistent with the findings from studies of Baltimore, Los Angeles, and Miami-Dade County and with the overall record of the living wage laws passed by 35 municipalities. The maximum potential costs to both the city and employers is quite modest. In return, a modest

> number of workers will experience clear wage and health care gains. Concerns of job loss, price increases, or loss of investment or contract bidding do not appear justified. While most non-profit organizations do not receive enough yearly public funds to be covered by the law, the impact for those that are range from small to modest.[40]

In New York City, most owners of commercial buildings have, during the past five years, signed union contracts that have significantly raised salaries for janitors and other service workers, and have not experienced a commensurate loss of profit. Increased salaries instead seem to lead to a reduced employee turnover and a higher level of productivity.[41] If any factor contributes to increased business costs, it is the rise in CEO salaries, which increased by 535 percent in the 1990s, in contrast to average workers' salaries, which increased 32 percent during the same period.[42] We might further wonder whether opponents of the living wage cite the possibility of job loss out of true concern for workers or out of a desire to couch their own economic interests in more altruistic terms.

As we have seen, the underlying assumption of Jewish labor law is that the *minhag hamakom* will create wages that allow workers to afford basic necessities, and that enable workers to do the best work they can. As long as the *minhag hamakom* accomplishes this end, there is no reason to interfere with it. However, in situations such as the one in which we find ourselves, in which the *minhag hamakom* effectively prevents the attainment of other halakhic requirements, there is halakhic permission – and even halakhic imperative – to change the *minhag hamakom* so as to guarantee the viability of the system as a whole.

Jill Jacobs holds rabbinic ordination and an MA in Talmud/ Rabbinics from the Jewish Theological Seminary and an MS in Urban Affairs from Hunter College, CUNY.

39. Christopher Niedt, Greg Ruiters, Dana Wise, and Erica Shoenberger, *The Effects of the Living Wage in Baltimore* (Economic Policy Institute Working Paper 119, February 1999). David Reynolds, Rachel Pearson and Jean Vortkampf, *The Impact of the Detroit Living Wage Ordinance,* Center for Urban Studies and Labor Studies Center (Wayne State University: College of Urban, Labor and Metropolitan Affairs, 1999).

40. Reynolds et al., *The Impact*, p. 2.

41. Jared Bernstein, "Higher wages lead to more efficient service provision" (Economic Policy Institute, August, 2000).

42. Sarah Anderson and John Cavanagh, et al., *Executive Excess* 2000 (Institute for Policy Studies, 2000), p. 5.

Distributors of Justice: A Case for a Just Wage

Michael J. Naughton (2000)

Published in America *June 2000*
*Reprinted with permission of America Press, Inc. © 2000. All
rights reserved. For subscription information, call 1-800-627-
9533 or visit www.americamagazine.org*

In this Jubilee year, the issue of wealth distribution,
especially as it relates to the larger macro issues of
international debt and globalization, has received a
good deal of attention and analysis. For this we should
be thankful. What has not received as much attention, however, are the responsibilities of managers and
entrepreneurs toward wealth distribution in their own
businesses. How should managers and entrepreneurs,
especially those who bear the name Christian, distribute resources, within their limited sphere of influence?
Or to put it more bluntly: How do they become *distributors of justice*, rather than *maximizers of self-inter-
ests?* So as not to be too abstract on this topic, I want
to examine a specific organizational practice that has
specific implications for wealth distribution: *wages*.

Managers will often describe wages as an instrumental
activity that "attracts, rewards, retains, and motivates
employees who best achieve the strategic goals of
the organization." These strategic goals tend to be
exclusively economic in nature: increase productivity
and efficiency, raise customer satisfaction and retention, maximize shareholder wealth and so forth. This
instrumental value of pay, while important, tends to
cloud and even crowd out a Christian insight: *a wage
can never exhaust human labor.* Work is always *more*
than its economic output or instrumental value, precisely because work changes God's creation and we in
turn change ourselves. There is no price to compensate
us for this kind of work.

One company wrestling with integrating this noble
and transcendent vision of human work with the
instrumental reality of wages is Reell Precision
Manufacturing in St. Paul, Minnesota. It is a producer
of hi-tech clutches and hinges for the office machine
and computer industries. The company operates on
the practical application of Judeo-Christian values for
the "growth of people." Based on its mission, Reell
believes that all its workers should at least be paid a
"living wage" or what they call a "target wage." In
1996 their estimate of a living wage in St. Paul was
$11/ hour ($22,000/year). The actual market wage or
"sustainable wage" for assemblers in the company was
$7/hour ($14,000/year).

The $4 discrepancy between a living wage and a
sustainable wage was a tension between two principles
operating in the company: the principle of *need* and
the principle of *economic order*. While the management
of Reell desired to pay its employees not only their
market worth, but also the worth of who they are (persons made in the image of God who deserve at least
a minimum of need), management was all too aware
that customers would only pay for the "instrumental
value" of work. If Reell would pay $11/ hour while
competitors paid $7, Reell's cost disadvantage would
increase their likelihood of losing customers. Realizing
that the *ought* of a living wage always implies the *can*
of a sustainable wage, the company had to seriously
rethink how it was doing business and act creatively.

This rethinking took on several dimensions. First,
Reell's management resisted capitulating their responsibilities to the mechanical force of labor markets.
They saw themselves as moral agents in the market
place and not as mere technicians. Nor were they
simply working toward a "target wage" because they
thought it would "attract and retain" employees who
would make the company more money (although
they certainly welcomed the economic benefits of the
policy when they came). In the words of Aquinas,
Reell's managers were "well disposed towards" their
employees.

Second, they realized that every action has a reaction and that raising wage levels without changing
the work process would have serious consequences
on their cost structure. So in order to raise *labor rates*
to pay a living wage, they would have to reduce their
overall *total costs*. They eventually saw that low wages
were merely a symptom of a much larger problem of
how the company worked. When work is designed to
use $7 of talent, it is difficult to pay people anything
more than that amount.

What concretely enabled the company to pay a living
wage was a whole new way of doing work. Reell rede-
signed their assembly-line from a Command-Direct-
Control style management (CDC) where management and engineers made all the decisions concerning
the conception of the assembly area, to a Teach-
Equip-Trust (TET) style management where employees were taught inspection procedures, equipped with
quality instruments and trusted to do things right on
their own assembly-line. By restructuring the work

process according to the principles of participation and subsidiarity, employees decreased set-up times for new products, reduced the need for quality inspection, increased overall quality and required less supervision. By reducing these costs, the company not only was able to pay a living wage, but also created more humane work.

The living or target wage does not come automatically. For example, the reason the company called it a target wage was that it was something it worked toward. When an employee is hired with no experience and no skills, the company pays the worker the market rate ($7/hour or whatever it is at the time), but then makes a commitment to move that employee to the target or living wage ($11/hour) through training and skill development. So as employees learn the skills and gain experience, which Reell provides for employees, their pay goes up accordingly. Typically, it takes an employee two to three years to reach a target or living wage. I will come back to this issue in a moment.

Interesting enough, Reell did not have to lay anyone off throughout this whole process. The engineers who originally supervised the workers and inspected quality were freed up to focus on things in which they were educated to do – create a better designed product. With a better quality product, Reell was able to gain a premium price for its product and also increase sales, all of which provided adequate revenue to support a living wage and avoid layoffs. While the moral and economic order do not always converge, we should take heed of those cases that do.

There is more to be said about how Reell's mission guided its decision making on wages, but it is important to be clear where the company's responsibilities lie in light of the Christian social tradition. This tradition, especially as it is articulated in Catholic social teaching, does not hold Reell (or any firm) responsible to pay employees in excess of a sustainable wage (a wage consistent with the sound financial management of the firm), even if that wage falls below a living wage. To do so would unjustly place Reell – and all the firm's employees – at risk of economic failure. In a market economy no firm can be obligated to pay without regard to labor costs' effect on its competitive position, since that would amount to the imprudent choice of self-defeating means. Nevertheless, Reell does have an obligation in justice to create right relationships with employees to work toward a living wage. This is why Reell can pay less than a living wage so long as it is working toward correcting the situation through some set of means such as training and skill development.

While at times managers are caught in an irresolvable bind of the market, more often than not managers and entrepreneurs have an area of *discretion* that is usually *larger* than they think. When they fail to see this area of discretion they act like "pawns of market forces" beyond their control, rather than like "distributors of justice" who can contribute to the growth of others. Reell met the strategic demands of efficiency, productivity, and quality, while at the same time satisfying the basic human needs of their employees. The firm's experience underscores an essential insight: the just wage is not a static concept, a flat demand laid upon the firm. It is, rather, a dynamic concept, a goal that is established through a common regard for justice and must be pursued with a prudent regard for concrete possibilities here and now.

Yet, this point of individual and organizational virtue cannot be taken out of context of society's broader responsibility for a just wage. There are times when employers cannot pay a living wage without violating a sustainable wage. For this reason, as John Paul II has explained, employers are not – because they cannot be – solely responsible for achieving living wages. In a real sense, any individual firm's living wage can only be an *instance of a social* achievement founded in cooperation with other employers, employees, unions, government and other "indirect employers." For, apart from a comprehensive commitment – a social commitment – to a living wage, those who decide unqualifiedly to pay living wages in highly competitive, commodity-driven, price-sensitive markets, risk economic disadvantages that cannot long be borne. If the market wage in the industry is below a living wage, and there is no place to reduce labor costs, employers who decide to raise wages unilaterally will price themselves out of the market. Obviously, this constraint becomes increasingly decisive in international markets, a point the protesters in Seattle made quite clear to World Trade Organization participants.

In this age of globalization, a just wage is no doubt a complex problem. Yet, this complexity cannot remove managers' and entrepreneurs' responsibilities as effective *distributors of justice*. To embrace justice, they must realize that an instrumental view of wages, although necessary, is insufficient to help people and themselves grow in their work. It is difficult to believe, for example, that Reell could have developed a living wage policy if they were only concerned about employees' instrumental effect on shareholder value. Rather, the company saw employees as more than "factors of production" or simply "costs" to be reduced. Management saw employees as who they *really* are: persons made to be treated with human dignity because they are created in the image of God destined for glory.

Yet, we should have no illusions here. Justice will not create a blinding flash of "pay nirvana." It will not relieve managers and entrepreneurs of their cost burdens as it relates to pay. In fact, life often gets more complicated for today's managers and entrepreneurs precisely because they are asked to do more than what traditional business practice has done. What Reell seems to have found, however, is some comfort in the reflection that the burdens involved in the quest for just wages are borne for the sake of the common good and God's kingdom, and that success in bearing them is itself growth in virtue.

Michael Naughton is the director of the John A. Ryan Institute for Catholic Social Thought of the Center for Catholic Studies (www.stthomas.edu/cathstudies/cst) at the University of St. Thomas (Minnesota) where he teaches in the theology department and the College of Business. His most recent book (co-authored with Helen Alford O.P.) is Managing as if Faith Mattered: Christian Social Principles in the Modern Organization *(University of Notre Dame Press, 2001). He has collaborated with the chairman of Reell Precision Manufacturing, Robert Wahlstedt, on a variety of projects.*

Exhibit

Some Issues for a Just Wage

1. **A Living Wage: The Principle of Need.** *A living wage is the minimum amount due to every independent wage earner by the mere fact that he or she is a human being with a life to maintain and a personality to develop.*
   Issues: What criteria are used to determine a just wage that serves as a minimum floor? How does one overcome the obstacles of a market wage that falls below this minimum floor? What creative policies are available to implement a living wage? What role does the state have in determining living wages?

2. **An Equitable Wage: The Principle of Contribution.** *An equitable wage is the contribution of an employee's productivity and effort within the context of the existing amount of profits and resources of the organization.*
   Issues: How does one know if they have become too narrow or quantitative or too broad or vague in determining contribution? How does one attract the necessary human talent and maintain internal equity? How does one avoid short-termism, poor morale, and machiavellian politics when instituting incentives?

3. **A Sustainable Wage: The Principle of Economic Order.** *A sustainable wage is the organization's ability to pay wages that are sustainable for the economic health of the organization as a whole.*
   Issues: Sustainable = Livable + Equitable. In light of the unique situation a company finds itself in, what are its constraints and opportunities as it relates to a living and equitable wage? What level of a livable wage is sustainable for the organization? How many people can an organization pay living wages to? What is the role of part-time work? When is it ethical to lay people off because the labor costs are no longer sustainable? When can a company move offshore? What is the role of automation?

5 The Religion-Labor Movement Today

Introduction

There are more than 50 worker centers, interfaith committees and Seminarians for Worker Justice groups affiliated with Interfaith Worker Justice. They are building bridges between the faith and labor communities. The articles and stories in this section focus on their work educating, organizing, and mobilizing the religious community and workers on issues and campaigns that increase wages and benefits and improve conditions for workers.

In "Religion-Labor Partnerships: New Directions, New Opportunities," Kim Bobo, IWJ's Executive and Founding Director, highlights the incredible work people of faith are doing in the religion and labor movement today.

"Struggling for Justice, Sustained by Faith" was transcribed and revised by Will Tanzman, an IWJ organizer, from an interview he did with Cleopatria Kyles, a hotel worker in Chicago who led her colleagues with the support of union organizers, clergy and the community to a second contract victory.

The next two articles, "Faith at Work in Miami," by Rev. C.J. Hawking, and "A New Alliance between Religion and Labor," by Robert Horwitz, provide tangible examples of how the religious community has stood in solidarity with workers, bringing its moral voice to organizing campaigns.

"The Church, the Union and the Trinity" was authored by Rev. Darren Cushman Wood of the Speedway United Methodist Church in Indianapolis. Originally prepared for the Pastor-Theologian Program of the Center of Theological Inquiry, 2007, it is a wide-ranging and thought-provoking meditation on the theological foundations of worker justice.

"Future Religious Leaders Live Their Theology!" is written by Joy Heine, Project Director, Religious Perspectives on Work, IWJ. It focuses on the dynamic work being done in seminaries and religious undergraduate schools in the U.S.

Religion-Labor Partnerships: New Directions, New Opportunities

Kim Bobo (2007)

The existence of strong interfaith religion-labor partnerships and the active engagement of the religious community in fighting for economic justice are critical for the future of the nation.

The United States must be a nation that offers access to opportunity and a sharing of the great wealth of this society. It must be a nation that seeks liberty and justice for all, not liberty for some and wealth for a few. The two institutions most committed to these core values are the religious and labor communities – they are able to influence the political will of the nation, which is why it makes so much sense for these two institutions to partner on shared values.

Despite the strong partnerships forged between religion and labor throughout the first half of the 20th century, the number of such partnerships dwindled to only a handful 10 years ago. In the 1960s and 70s, partnerships between faith bodies and unions either fizzled or were severed for a variety of reasons. As a result of the deteriorating relationship, religious and labor leaders who came into power in the 1980s and 90s no longer knew each other. And although there were some religion-labor partnerships that remained strong in this period, like the religion-labor coalitions in New York state, the Labor Guild in Boston and the ongoing work of the National Farm Worker Ministry, their work tended to be relatively small and mostly unstaffed.

By the mid-1990s, religion-labor partnerships experienced a rebirth: the Pittston Coal Miners strike and the emerging living wage campaigns around the country once again captured the imaginations and the energies of religious leaders. Many unions initiated new aggressive organizing efforts to raise wages and improve benefits for service workers in low-paid jobs. Under the leadership of then newly-elected president John Sweeney, the AFL-CIO worked at reviving important partnerships with traditional allies, particularly the religious community.

Religious communities also started questioning the seemingly permanent nature of faith-based soup kitchens and shelters: clearly, there were not enough good-paying jobs for everyone. Something had to be done.

It was in this context that Interfaith Worker Justice was formed in 1996.

Building upon decades of historic partnerships and the interest and skills of both religious and labor leaders, Interfaith Worker Justice quickly united existing religion-labor groups and set forth to build grassroots structures around the country. Within just a few years, dozens of groups affiliated with Interfaith Worker Justice, and several dozen more new labor-religion labor groups were formed.

At the turn of the 21st century, religion-labor partnerships were once again flush with success and optimism. Local partnerships were winning real improvements in wages, benefits and working conditions for workers in low-paying jobs. Despite the terrible national economic and political environment for workers at that time, groups were passing living wage bills, supporting workers fighting for contracts, helping religious leaders reclaim their activist histories and engaging a future generation of religious leaders.

These new religion-labor partnerships have enormous potential to play a significant role in determining the nation's future. To do so, groups in the network must continually balance efforts to win concrete victories, involve ever-growing numbers of people of faith in the work, and build strong organizations. This combination, known to organizers as the core principles of direct action organizing, builds power and the ability to influence the priorities of the nation. Below are some of the most exciting new directions and opportunities for the work over the next few years.

Improving Wages, Benefits and Working Conditions through Contracts

Getting a union contract is one of the fastest and most effective ways to improve wages, benefits and working conditions for workers in low-wage jobs. (See the section "Why Unions Matter" for more background.) Thus, one of the key things religion-labor partnerships do is support workers in their efforts to get good contracts in a timely fashion. The ways in which this support is expressed have grown and developed over the last few years. Unions are increasingly appreciative of the important role the faith community can play, and religious leaders have more experience working with both unions and employers. Exciting new directions in this work include:

- **Developing Joint Strategies.** When the partnerships were new, labor unions did not appreciate the power of the religious community and at times, did not trust religious leaders. As a result, union staff did most of the strategizing, with religious leaders playing very limited roles (leading prayers at rallies) in campaigns. This "rent-a-collar" approach limited the effectiveness of the religious community and felt disrespectful of the partnerships. Although the tendency to want to "tell" the religious community what to do still exists in many coalitions, unions are recognizing the greater role religious leaders can play. Stronger relationships are developing, which enable creative joint strategy work to emerge in many communities. Having workers, their religious leaders and unions jointly plan strategies for improving wages, benefits and working conditions will unleash much more power and creativity.

- **Coordinating National Campaigns.** More and more contract efforts that will raise wages and improve benefits and working conditions for the largest numbers of workers are national, and not local campaigns. Unions are coordinating across cities; so are faith communities. Increasingly, Interfaith Worker Justice has been convening national planning calls to figure out how multiple groups can be engaged in joint campaigns. This trend of national campaigns and national coordination is likely to continue and expand.

- **Supporting Workers Rights to Organize.** Tens of thousands of workers in this country say they would like to be represented by a union, but are afraid to join one for fear of being fired, harassed or retaliated against. The harsh anti-union behavior of too many employers undermines core religious values and internationally-recognized human rights standards. Although none of the religion-labor partnerships organizes workers – that's what unions do – the religious community actively supports workers' *right* to organize and seeks to help ensure that this right is protected. Religious leaders across the nation are getting quite sophisticated in recognizing employers' anti-union tactics: conducting one-on-one anti-union meetings, distributing anti-union literature and creating a climate of fear in the workplace. A few years ago, few in the religious community had even heard of card check recognition. Today, many religious leaders can explain quite eloquently why workers need card check recognition and other forms of union recognition besides the flawed National Labor Relations Board (NLRB) election process.

Challenging Wage Thievery

Over the years, pastors and religious leaders have referred congregants who are experiencing problems in the workplace to interfaith groups and organizations. In the beginning, the groups did not have the capacity to directly respond to workplace issues; the first response was always to refer workers to unions. Unfortunately, some workplaces are too small, or are in sectors or communities not represented by unions.

As more and more workers sought help, interfaith partnerships saw a void that needed to be filled – a structure for helping those workers not served by unions had to be created. What developed were workers centers, which are safe places for workers to learn about their rights and join with others to improve conditions in their workplace. Workers centers are similar to the farmworker service centers and the Catholic labor schools that operated in the basements of parishes from the mid-1930s through the 1950s. Today there are over 130 workers centers in the nation, with 19 of them affiliated with Interfaith Worker Justice.

The number one problem these workers centers address is wage thievery, which involves cases in which workers are not paid overtime, shorted in their hours, and sometimes are not paid at all. Wage thievery is not a small, isolated problem. It is an epidemic. According to Department of Labor industry surveys, staggering numbers of nursing homes, restaurants, poultry and meatpacking plants, farms, landscaping firms and others are routinely violating wage and hour laws. Wage thievery is a huge problem for workers in low-wage jobs, which is why challenging and addressing it is an emerging direction of interfaith religion-labor partnerships around the nation. Exciting new directions in this work include:

- **Building and Affiliating Workers Centers.** As interfaith groups grow and develop, many more are looking at how they can build workers centers to support workers that are not and will not be served by unions. Still other workers centers that emerged from local congregations or workers themselves are seeking to affiliate with others to share approaches and best practices. These workers centers are important new institutions for challenging wage thievery, protecting workers, and engaging the broader community in the struggles of workers in low-paying jobs.

- **Partnering with Attorneys.** Many workers who seek out workers centers have valid legal cases, but little access to ethical attorneys. Workers centers are partnering with university legal clinics, recruiting attorneys to provide pro-bono services and hiring their own attorneys. Finding ways to expand and broaden these connections will strengthen the work.

- **Partnering with Federal Government Agencies.** Interfaith Worker Justice has been on the forefront of building partnerships with government agencies charged with protecting worker rights. The largest agency, and probably the most important for challenging wage thievery, is the Wage and Hour Division of the Department of Labor. The agency employs approximately 1000 investigators around the country who enforce the most important wage and hour laws. Workers centers' staff members work with these investigators to find ways to help workers understand their rights and file complaints. There are many ways these collaborations could be strengthened and enhanced, particularly with leadership and encouragement from the Secretary of Labor.

- **Partnering with State Government Agencies.** Workers centers usually partner with state, as well as federal government agencies charged with protecting workers. Most state labor agencies, however, are weak and do not have much clout. Over the next few years, workers centers will continue to partner with these agencies, but will work to expand and strengthen the agencies' capacity to address worker issues.

- **Tapping Theft of Services Laws.** The Austin workers center (the Religion and Labor Network of Austin) built a relationship with the local police and got them to begin enforcing a theft of services law, which had previously been used primarily when a customer didn't pay for a service or product. The Chicago workers center has worked with the State Attorney General to enforce Illinois' theft of service law. More workers centers will seek to pass or enforce theft of services laws as one more tool for challenging wage thievery.

Reinventing the Department of Labor

The most significant piece of labor legislation in the last hundred years, the Fair Labor Standards Act, was passed in 1938 by a remarkable coalition of the labor community, the religious community, and social workers. Despite many amendments, it remains the core piece of legislation that protects workers not served by unions. As Secretary of Labor in the 1930s and early 1940s, Episcopalian Frances Perkins put her faith into action by helping usher in this monumental labor legislation. Like her, people of faith recognize that strong labor laws and a strong and active Department of Labor is important to the nation's working men and women.

Interfaith Worker Justice believes in a strong and active Department of Labor. Exciting new directions in strengthening the Department of Labor (DOL) will include:

- **Building Grassroots Partnerships to Reach Out to Workers.** Most workers in low-wage jobs, especially immigrant workers, don't realize that the DOL can help them. Workers centers and interfaith groups have been helping the DOL reach out to workers. More can be done to help broaden the scope of the labor department's outreach. Interfaith Worker Justice and its affiliates will be urging new and creative partnerships.

- **Creating New Educational Resources.** The DOL needs to create new worker-friendly educational resources, written in simple language and available in multiple languages. All the resources should be offered online and promoted at public libraries. Although workers centers are creating some of these resources, as is a special worker rights project of Interfaith Worker Justice, the DOL should take the lead in creating and distributing educational resources to workers.

- **Targeting Egregious Industries.** In the last few years, the DOL Wage and Hour Division has taken a complaint-driven approach to cases. This means that inspectors sit in their offices and respond to complaints filed by workers. Interfaith Worker Justice and its network of workers centers strongly believe this is the wrong approach. Inspectors should target industries with egregious wage violations, investigate them and build large cases against the industries. This kind of high-profile approach would benefit many more workers and would deter employers from stealing wages. Over the next few years, Interfaith Worker Justice will be encouraging the Department of Labor to take a targeted-investigation approach, instead of a complaint-driven approach, to worker issues.

Passing Worker-Friendly Local and State Legislation

Almost all the interfaith groups around the country have been active in supporting worker-friendly legislation. In most cases, the groups have been instrumental in the passage of such local or state legislation. Exciting new directions in this work include:

- **Continuing to Support and Expand Living Wage Laws.** Cities and communities across the country are building upon one another in introducing and passing more creative and more expansive living wage laws. The early living wage bills only included modest wage increases for small numbers of workers. Recent ones covered more workers and tackled related issues like health insurance contributions. Even when the federal minimum wage is increased, it will still be way too low for families to live on, so groups will continue to lift the bottom by passing living wage laws.

- **Setting New Wage and Benefit Standards.** Many workers in low-wage jobs don't have the standard benefits that most middle-class workers expect. Among workers in low-wage jobs, only 39 percent have paid sick leave, 51 percent have paid vacation, and 46 percent have paid holidays. In 2006 the Madison interfaith group (Interfaith Coalition for Worker Justice of South Central Wisconsin) introduced a piece of legislation into the Madison City Council to provide paid sick leave. Even though the legislation failed by one vote, the language was picked up by Young Workers United in San Francisco, who ran an excellent campaign and got it passed. Madison will be trying again on its legislation. Other interfaith groups will be experimenting with ways to set new standards for how all workers should be treated.

- **Supporting State Initiatives on Health Care.** Most workers in low-wage jobs have no health insurance. According to a 2006 survey of benefits from the U.S. Bureau of Labor Statistics (BLS), only 57 percent of workers in jobs paying $15 an hour or less have access to health insurance through their employers; only 38 percent participate in the health benefits offered, usually because of the high costs. Health insurance is becoming a luxury most workers in low-wage jobs don't have or can't afford. Interfaith Worker Justice believes that a national solution to the health care crisis is needed, but until there is sufficient national leadership and will, most of the new initiatives will be coming from the states. Many interfaith groups will be active in supporting state efforts to provide health insurance to all workers and their families.

Passing Worker-Friendly Federal Legislation

The ubiquity of low-wage, low-benefit work is a national crisis demanding national solutions. Interfaith Worker Justice will be building the network's grassroots capacity to better influence national policy debates. Exciting new directions in this work include:

- **Welcoming Immigrants.** All major religious traditions call on people of faith to welcome immigrants. Unfortunately, Congress has been unable to pass fair and comprehensive immigration reform. As the nation debates its immigration policy, Interfaith Worker Justice will join with colleagues to offer sanctuary to immigrants and highlight the need for full labor protections for all workers, regardless of their immigration status.

- **Supporting Efforts to Raise the Minimum Wage and Index it to Inflation.** It has taken 10 years to get an increase in the minimum wage. That means that each year, the value of the minimum wage is less than the year before. Interfaith Worker Justice will work to get the federal minimum wage indexed for inflation.

- **Setting New Wage and Benefit Standards.** As states and communities make progress in setting new wage and benefit standards, it may be possible to pass national legislation on such things as paid sick leave. Interfaith Worker Justice will monitor opportunities and move when openings occur.

- **De-linking Health Insurance from Employment.** As fewer workers in low-wage jobs have access to employer-provided health insurance, it is important for the nation to develop health care structures that are not dependent upon employers. Interfaith Worker Justice will support federal legislation that expands access to all workers in low-wage jobs and that does not link health insurance to employment. There are likely to be at least incremental proposals offered in the next few years.

- **Strengthening Workers' Right to Organize.** Interfaith Worker Justice supports the Employee Free Choice Act, which strengthens workers' right to organize. This has a good chance of passing in the next few years and will be a priority for the network.

- **Updating the Fair Labor Standards Act (FLSA).** In the last few years, there have been too many defensive battles around protecting core provisions of the FLSA, leaving no time to think much about ways to improve and update it. However, Interfaith Worker Justice anticipates there being opportunities to expand and strengthen the FLSA. In particular, it is important to find ways to protect more contingent workers, because increasing numbers of workers are not covered by the FLSA.

- **Recruiting District Organizers.** Interfaith Worker Justice has been structured primarily around its union partnership work. For federal policy work, it is important to also build activist structures in congressional districts, especially in rural and suburban areas. Over the next few years, Interfaith Worker Justice will be experimenting with ways to effectively engage congregations in public policy issues.

Engaging Young Religious Leaders

When Interfaith Worker Justice first began convening religious leaders to work on labor issues, it drew heavily upon those in the religious community who had experience in working closely with labor, such as Monsignor George Higgins, Rev. Addie Wyatt, Rev. Joseph Lowery, Rabbi Robert Marx, Bishop Jesse DeWitt, Rev. James Lawson, and Monsignor Jack Egan. Drawing from their profound depths of knowledge and experience, these leaders provided leadership and wisdom to the development of a new network. They also encouraged Interfaith Worker Justice to focus on engaging young religious leaders in the work. This work is already bearing fruit. Young people engaged while they were in Seminary, Rabbinical school or college are now leading congregations, staffing interfaith groups, or providing leadership at nonprofit organizations. Many have become faithful contributors to the work. Exciting new directions in this work include:

- **Engaging Students through Internship Opportunities.** Almost every interfaith group around the country taps the talent and gifts of student interns. This work will be expanding as groups reach more seminary and rabbinical students, social work students, public policy and law students.

- **Supporting Faculty in Teaching about Worker Justice.** Interfaith Worker Justice has been compil-

ing resources and curricula to support faculty in teaching new classes on worker justice. Most of the resources are available online at www.iwj.org. Hopefully, the number of worker justice courses taught in religious training schools and religiously-affiliated schools will mushroom in the next few years.

- **Organizing and Engaging Seminarians for Worker Justice Groups.** In the last few years, students in communities with clusters of seminaries have organized Seminarians for Worker Justice groups. These activist groups have challenged their schools to become living wage schools, supported workers in contract struggles, organized campus-wide educational events, and mobilized students and faculty to join community rallies, such as the large immigration reform rallies. The groups are critical for the future, because they build relationships between young religious leaders of different backgrounds, push the seminaries to be more relevant to current issues, and help students develop organizing skills. Interfaith Worker Justice will seek additional ways to support and nurture these young leaders.

Let justice roll down like waters and righteousness like an ever-flowing stream. – Amos 5:24

Connecting Workers and Congregations

When Interfaith Worker Justice began organizing, it often began the work by drawing upon the gifts and talents of activists and social justice-oriented clergy. These clergy have provided depth and vision for a growing network. Over the next few years, however, it is important for the groups to experiment with new ways to engage workers in low-wage jobs who are also active people of faith and lay leaders from a range of faith communities. It is also important to reach out intentionally to faith groups and denominations that have not been active in the work, especially those faith traditions with many members in low-wage jobs. Exciting new directions in this work include:

- **Organizing Worker Rights Workshops.** Many of the workers centers are intentionally reaching out to congregations and hosting worker rights workshops. Volunteers and leaders are being recruited from congregations.

- **Creating Democracy Centers.** Interfaith groups in California are experimenting with democracy centers in congregations that help immigrant workers learn about democracy, become citizens and register to vote. These democracy-center approaches will become especially important if there is a wide-scale new immigration program covering many existing residents.

- **Recruiting Congregational Contacts.** Congregational contacts will be sought especially in districts where members of Congress are often undecided on their votes on worker justice issues.

- **Offering Immersion Opportunities.** Because of the economic segregation of many religious congregations, it is important to offer opportunities for more financially secure people of faith to learn from and understand the injustices faced by workers in low-wage jobs. Providing people with immersion-type opportunities stirs up "righteous indignation" that enables people to organize and challenge both unjust structures and wimpy politicians. Interfaith Worker Justice has experimented with seminary immersion opportunities and will be experimenting with ways to offer more opportunities for members of congregations.

Building Diverse Coalitions

In order to build power and effectively improve conditions for workers in low-wage jobs, it is important to strengthen faith involvement and build faith coalitions across different racial and ethnic lines. This is hard to do in a society where most congregations are segregated, few denominations are multiracial, African-Americans still experience the legacies of slavery, many immigrants have no legal status, and employers routinely pit workers of different races and ethnic groups against one another. The social and institutional barriers of racism inhibit and diminish the potential power of the work. Nonetheless, exciting new directions in this work include:

- **Reminding the Nation about New Orleans.** The abominable federal response to Hurricane Katrina in New Orleans exposed the underlying poverty and racism experienced by thousands of workers in that grand city. Interfaith Worker Justice is building a workers center in New Orleans that will not only help workers in the area, but will join with others in continuing to focus the nation's attention on the injustices in New Orleans.

- **Partnering Leaders of Different Backgrounds.** Interfaith Worker Justice seeks to intentionally partner leaders of different faith, racial and ethnic backgrounds in working together to address worker justice issues. Over the coming years, the network of groups will continue to recruit, hire and nurture diverse leadership for board, staff, internship and volunteer positions.

- **Presenting the Diverse Faces of Immigration.** Over the next few years, as the nation struggles with its immigration program, Interfaith Worker Justice will seek to present the diverse faces of immigrants. Although the largest number of immigrants is Latino, there are also many Asian, African, Carribean, and Eastern European immigrants who are undocumented and struggling in low-paying jobs. Immigration reform is for everyone.

- **Building Bridges with the Building Trades.** Historically, many building trades excluded African-Americans, women, and immigrants from the building apprenticeship programs. Today, even though some of the building trades are eager to recruit new members, the historic racism combined with the difficult entrance exams and the confusing entrance requirements of various building trades have prevented many from entering the building trades apprenticeship programs, which offer a pathway to high-paying jobs with good benefits. The Building Bridges program, initiated by the Chicago Interfaith Committee on Worker Issues, offers pre-apprenticeship classes in African-American congregations that help people pass the apprenticeship exams and understand the different opportunities and requirements in the building trades. Interfaith Worker Justice will be working with building trades unions to expand the program to additional cities.

Building Organizational Capacity

In order for the work to grow and develop across the nation, Interfaith Worker Justice and all the local interfaith groups must expand their organizational capacity. Exciting new directions in this work include:

- **Raising More Money through Diverse Sources.** Interfaith Worker Justice believes that raising money is an important ministry. Money enables the work to grow and develop. Fundraising is really friend-raising and requires all leaders to devote organizing skills and time. Additional funds will be sought from individuals, congregations, orders, denominations, unions, foundations, workplace giving and legal *cy-pres* awards.

- **Recruiting and Training Talented Staff.** In small organizations with only a few paid staff, recruiting, training and keeping talented staff will make or break the organizations. Interfaith Worker Justice will be working with groups to strengthen their recruitment, hiring and training capacities. Through its internships and programs, IWJ will seek to spot and recruit potential leaders for organizations.

- **Increasing Leadership Training Opportunities.** Interfaith Worker Justice is stepping up its ongoing training and leadership opportunities through workshops, national gatherings, board retreats and cross-training opportunities.

- **Using Technology in New Ways.** Young leaders will be helping the network discover new ways to use technology to engage and connect people in the work. Training in new approaches will be offered at national and state gatherings.

- **Amplifying the Religious Voice.** All the interfaith groups are learning new ways to access the media and amplify the religious voice on economic justice issues. Both the national office and many local interfaith groups are focusing more staff work on building media contacts, talking with reporters, submitting op-eds, and making sure that the interfaith religious perspective on issues is reflected in the public debate.

The next few years will be critical for the direction of the nation. Will the U.S. continue on the path of growing inequality, with growing numbers of workers in low-wage jobs and a declining middle class, or will it find new ways to rebuild middle-class jobs and boost wages and benefits for workers in low-wage jobs? Will the nation welcome immigrants and celebrate their gifts, or will it build fences and punish those who help immigrants? Will people of faith become active players in creating the directions for the future, or will we sit on the sidelines and bemoan the problems?

These and other critical questions are being tackled by Interfaith Worker Justice and its allied group of interfaith worker justice organizations. To learn more, to join, and to help rebuild the nation, visit www.iwj.org or call (773) 728-8400 and ask to speak with someone in the Organizing Department.

Kim Bobo is the founder and Executive Director of Interfaith Worker Justice.

Struggling for Justice, Sustained by Faith: A Hotel Worker's Words

Cleopatria Kyles (interviewed and edited by Will Tanzman) (2007)

Cleopatria Kyles works at the Chicago Hilton and Towers Hotel and was one of the key leaders in the Chicago religious community's involvement in the 2006 Hotel Workers Rising campaign. She was interviewed by Will Tanzman, an organizer at Interfaith Worker Justice.

Can you tell me a little bit about your background?

I was born in Port Gibson, Mississippi. I came here when I was very young, so you might as well say I'm from Chicago. I've lived here all my life and I love living in Chicago. I live on the South Side, but I was raised on the West Side. I've been living on the South Side, for about 11 years now.

How long have you worked at the Hilton?

I've been working at the Hilton since March 6, 2000.

What church are you part of?

I go to the Apostolic Faith church, that's at 38th and Indiana, and I've been there since September 2004, about the same time I got into the union. And I enjoy it there.

What kind of jobs did you have before working at the Hilton? What path brought you to the Hilton?

Well, surprisingly, I was doing a job that was totally opposite of what I do now. When I was a sophomore in high school, I was in a work program, and they got me a job working at L&B Products. I started off answering the phone, and then I became a typist and from there I was promoted to a purchasing agent, which is what I did for ten years. I did the purchasing of hotel and restaurant furniture, so I think it's quite ironic that I am now on the other end of that. I am working for a hotel. I wash dishes for the restaurants in that hotel.

L&B Products went out of business in 1988, and from there I went to the Archdiocese of Chicago and worked as an Executive Secretary for the Archdiocese of Chicago. I worked on contracts for the four years I was there. From there, I went to work in a hotel as a dishwasher.

So what's it like to work at the hotel?

Well, it's been a struggle. Like I said, I've always done office work, and then to actually have to go to a place where you have to do physical labor, it took some getting used to, and it was a struggle. Because it was totally opposite of what I'd always done. I'd never worked for a hotel (or any place, period) that didn't show any respect or have any regard for its workers. After numerous injuries on the job, it really tested my faith and it was a struggle to continue to work there.

What kind of injuries did you have?

I've had inflammation of the muscle and nerve on my left hand. I've had numerous back injuries. I got a third degree burn on my left wrist. Once, the hospital had to flush lime out of my eyes. I had tissue scarring and cells died. In 2004, I had major surgery because I was injured from lifting up heavy objects. I have to say, the latter was the hardest suffering. That took me out of work for four months. For the first three months, I was literally in pain 24 hours a day. I would try to remember what it was like to be normal, because for those three months, pain was all I knew, and it felt like I would never be normal again. Here is where I feel my faith was tested the most. I remember my first day home from surgery. I walked into the dining room and, in pain, I fell to my knees. I didn't know where else to go, so that is where I stayed. For those three months God had my full undivided attention and I had His. I believe that's when God said, "I got you." I'm reminded of scripture where Moses asks God, "Show me Thy glory." God tells Moses He will place him in a rock and cover him with his hand; He will turn His back, and as He passes by, Moses will "see His Glory." The moral of this story for me is sometimes God has to cover us and then turn his back on us, for us to "see His Glory."

But I feel there is a reason for everything. And perhaps in my suffering and my struggle, God has a script, and He's going to use me to help somebody else. I see this as a light affliction and it's only for a moment. David says, "Let the righteous smite me, it shall be a kindness to me." I understand what he meant by that. So in the end, it's going to be a kindness for me and for others.

How much money did you make before the 2002 union campaign?

When I got there, I started making $7 plus. I came in making the same thing someone who had washed dishes there for 30 years was making. I was fortunate in that respect. In the 2002 contract it's different, it now takes a year to come up to where a person with seniority is making. When the campaign in 2002 started, I was making $8 plus. And then after the union campaign we went up to $9 something. And it was interesting, we were working next to subcontractors. As little as they paid us, they still brought in subcontractors. They said they couldn't find qualified people to hire to wash the dishes so they used a temp agency which used day laborers. How qualified do you have to be to wash dishes? Nobody ever trained me for this job. Interestingly, the temps only spoke Spanish so I couldn't train them if I wanted to. They were getting paid $5.50 an hour and they were doing the same work we were doing. When we were making $11.15 an hour they were making $6.50 an hour. Soon it got to the point that the company brought in subcontractors and some of us were sitting home. As a matter of fact, the union sued the company for that, and we were awarded about $250,000 from 2002 to when they stopped it in 2005. That has since been negotiated down to $180,000 and we are currently waiting for distribution of the money awarded us. That just goes to show where their hearts were. They didn't have to pay them overtime, they didn't have to pay into the pension, they didn't pay the subcontractors vacation time. What was done in the dark has come to light and they're now paying for it.

What was it like when the union campaigned for better wages and benefits in 2002?

Well, for the first time, you really felt that someone was coming in to help you. Someone was coming in to look out for your best interest. They were there on the job. They were people, not just someone who took your money for union dues, but they were actually there. To this day, I know all of the union organizers. They are visible and you can see the big difference. In just four years, our salary has increased from $8 to almost $13 per hour and some departments are well over $13 per hour. I remember in 2002 we got a $1.17 per hour raise right off the top and an additional 35 cents every six months. And that was after 9/11 when the economy went down. We voted for the current union president and staff and when they came in we got a $1.17 raise, so that was quite encouraging.

Henry Tamarin came out of New York and I remember when he came to Chicago the first thing he did was form a negotiating committee made up of actual employees. Henry knows that a unionized city gets the big bucks. We sometimes bump heads but I'm his biggest fan. I was not a part of the 2002 committee but my voice was heard from the sidelines. Not only was this encouraging to me, but to everybody, because all

the years prior to that, we got nickel and dime raises. Prior to that we never had any say in the negotiations. The final year of our contract we got either 10 or 15 cents for that whole year. That 10 or 15 cents was coming from an industry who makes billions of dollars. I can't remember which amount so that tells you it was nothing impressive. The last six months of that year, we didn't even get a raise. It was exciting when we heard the figures, unheard of figures, in our 2002 contract. Simple things like sick days, which we had never gotten before, were negotiated for the first time. We got a four-year contract, and we knew that at the end of that we would now be able to afford health coverage.

Did you feel a sense of collective community with the union, with all the workers coming together? Did that make a difference?

Absolutely it made a difference. For the first time, the union got us involved. We had a voice to speak. When they went to negotiate in 2002, they got together a negotiating committee made up of workers. The union president, Henry Tamarin, wanted the workers' voices to be heard. And when you're a part of that, it does make a difference. It makes you feel that you're worth something, that somebody cares and that you're not in this by yourself. You don't want to feel like you're alone. Everybody wants to feel like someone cares about them and that you're not struggling by yourself. No man is an island. Some people think that they can do it by themselves, but we definitely need each other.

What got you personally more involved in the union?

You know, what got me involved is the fact that there are so many people who were afraid to speak up. The strong have got to help the weak. That's scripture also, "when your brother is weak, strengthen your brother." There has to be somebody who's willing to stand up for those who can't stand up for themselves. God made me a strong person, so that's my job. The union people came to me and said that our department needed a strong leader. It took a minute before I said yes because I knew that once I became a union representative, it would take total commitment. And at that time, I wasn't ready for that kind of commitment. But, I eventually gave in, because there was a need, especially in my department, for stronger leaders. There were all these people who were willing to sit back and take abuse.

I have never been an abused wife, but working in the hotel industry I am learning how someone can be abused and stay in that situation. Because the workers feel that they don't have a choice, and they're limited in their education, and they don't speak the language. However, I find it's a shame that others would take advantage of someone like that. So there was a need. I am a people person and I've always worked around people. Even in my first job, and with the Archdiocese of Chicago, where we did contracts for the home health aides and literacy programs.

What was it like to be a leader in organizing the religious community to support the 2006 Hotel Workers Rising campaign?

I'm reading the fourth chapter of Daniel, and I've been wrestling with that chapter. It's about Nebuchadnezzar, who thinks that he does everything by the power of his might. So in the end, God has him living as a beast. God rules in the kingdom of men, and He's intervening in our hearts to bring about His will. He's not just sitting up there on His throne, unaware and not caring. He's active. He works through the union, the hotel, its workers, Interfaith Worker Justice and the religious leaders.

I have never known so many different faiths to work together in harmony for one cause. The key word here is one, unity. So to be a part of anything that you know God is involved in was great joy for me. Every religious leader and the people that were a part of this campaign were already a reality in the mind of God. I just had to allow Him to use me to bring it to reality here on earth, to bring it to its manifestation. I loved it and love being a part of God's plan. It was an honor to work with so many religious leaders and God made it so easy for me. I'm always so amazed when people give me the credit for organizing the religious leaders and the community. I was never alone in this. We also had a great staff of teachers at various colleges such as Northwestern and the University of Chicago. We also had board members from various companies and just the community itself was very important to us. It was a pleasure to meet and work with so vast a number of people from all walks of life.

There's always a greater call when God is involved, and I'm happy to be working for the union, especially because the religious leaders and their congregation are behind us. You don't know how inspiring that is. That's what it's all about, because God works through people. When man creates something, it's for a purpose. The light bulb – it's for a purpose. The telephone, telegraph, and internet, all were created for a purpose. God created each of us with a purpose and He created each of us individually. He gave us gifts. Each of us has our own gift and purpose. We are on this earth for

a divine reason. We have an earthly responsibility, and we have a divine responsibility. And it's our choice. We choose whether we say yes to it or no, whether we want to go to heaven or whether we go to hell. It's important to know God chose us first but He allows us to choose him back. I do feel that is a tricky statement to make because when God chooses you and puts a desire in you I often wonder who is really making the choices. That desire in me is so much stronger than me. We are also placed in this age because God knew each of us could live up to our full God-given potential in this age. All we need to live up to that potential is to have a heart after God. When we give our hearts to God we can trust Him and we know that He never loses a battle and He never fails. So it was with the hotel contracts.

I choose to be obedient. I can do better; I am not perfect. But I love working with the religious leaders who supported the Hotel Workers Rising campaign. They are very inspiring, not only to me, but to the other hotel workers. When the Hilton saw the religious leaders, I think that swayed the company in their decision to give us what we asked for. We didn't get everything but at least we tipped the scale. They saw it was not just those workers sitting in there. The company has to be concerned about the community, the community that's going to give them their money, their profit. That community consisted of the religious leaders and their congregation. The company knows we're not in this by ourselves.

Did it help the hotel workers when religious leaders delivered scrolls to the workers with all the signatures of the religious leaders who signed the letter of support?

Absolutely, it was encouraging. At first we thought we were going to strike, so naturally people were afraid. But when they saw the support of the religious leaders, everybody was willing to walk out. It really helped; it gave them courage. I think they saw themselves as grasshoppers and Hilton as this giant, and they are a giant, but we were no longer grasshoppers, we were giants against giants. That's what the religious leaders did for us; they gave us strength and courage. We know they would have been out there with us if we had to go on strike. We also know they never would have crossed the picket line. This came at the peak of the convention season. I'm still actively involved with the religious leaders so it's not over yet. God's work with me and us is not finished.

What did the workload reduction that you won in the 2006 campaign mean for your job?

It means not being injured, because they make you feel like you have to do all this work and all these dishes have to be washed. You feel like you have to get your job done for fear of being written up, suspended, or fired. So you're trying to overwork your body and anytime you do that you're going to be injured. Now, we know we're there to do an eight-hour job, and if the dishes don't get washed, they don't get washed. You don't have to be in fear that you're going to lose your job if all the work is not finished. The workers now are much more relaxed, not just in my department but in other departments as well. Workers are actually standing up for themselves regarding the workload. They know workload reduction was negotiated in the contract so workers are actually holding meetings and making the Hilton abide by the contract.

Are you still having problems even after the improvements you've made through the union?

We're still having problems. Because you have to look at this like this is years of injustice and it's not all going to change overnight. But it has gotten better and we're going to stand up. There are people in there who still want to take advantage of you. You know, a lot of our workers are immigrants; a lot of people do not speak the language. I had an incident there, where we were getting off at 10 p.m. We're supposed to work until 10:30 p.m., but they were allowing us to leave a half hour early if we didn't take a lunch. So this manager wrote up a co-worker and me because we left at 10 and left a lot of dishes behind. What he failed to realize was our time ran out on the clock. We gave up our lunch so we could leave at 10. He never asked us to stay and work overtime. So I wrote a letter and I explained what happened. I called the union rep and she said, "Get your co-worker to sign it," since I had put his name down too. So I went to him and he was afraid to sign his name on the letter. He said, "Me no speak no English. You can get a better job." And I understood that. That was why I included him in the letter and in the grievance I filed without going to him first. I understood his struggle and his fear. I ended up adding an extra page to the letter, explaining that he was afraid. I was just honest. They did an investigation, which actually surprised me. They went through all of our files, and they saw that it was routine for everybody in the department to leave at 10 p.m. So they threw out the write-ups for both of us. Everybody now has to take a lunch as a result of this and we all have to leave at 10:30 p.m.

What I don't understand is, when human resources comes in, they know that management is wrong, but they still support them. I always thought human resources was there to help us. Once you get a write-up, suspended, or fired it seems to me they should intervene first to see that justice is done before they send a person packing. However, you pack first, then the investigation starts. I once got suspended for eating a "Mike and Ike." After the union came in, a year later I got the money back. It took a year to get the money back after I filed the grievance.

So it's crazy stuff like that that goes on there. For you to be suspended for eating a "Mike and Ike." It's a little piece of candy the size of a "Good and Plenty." And they said, "you're eating on the job!" I was like, "What!" I got suspended for that. That's the kind of injustice … that's the kind of stuff that goes on in that place. It grieves me that people would treat each other like that. You know, we are all human beings; even management should be treated with respect. It often behooves me to think that that same person who is mistreating you has a son, or a daughter, or a mother or a brother … how can he treat someone else like that? It's amazing what people will do for money. Even the supervisors and the other managers know that it's wrong, but they get their orders from the top. Without God you see what happens. We need God to intervene on our behalf.

Do you think that your campaign helps the larger community as well as the workers?

It's a struggle for everybody. You don't know who's working in the hotels. It could be your family, friends or even a stranger, someone you don't know, and you wouldn't want them to be treated like that. We were the ones fighting, but this was everybody's fight. That's how it should be. Jesus didn't come to save one man, or the best ones, he came to save mankind, the good, the bad and the ugly. When you see someone struggling, the whole community should come to the rescue. The strong help the weak. In the end, the weak help the strong, so everybody gets help and then in the end, we help the bad guys, because we turn them around. So when they see us, it changes them, so everybody gets helped in this. I'm usually saying it's us against them, but really, everybody gets changed. All management can see is profit and we need to help them take the blinders off and see that we are human beings. A kind word, along with kind treatment of one another, goes a very long way. It always benefits everybody involved. We knew that the religious leaders as well as the community were there for us. Not only here in Chicago but across North America and beyond. Whenever something good comes out of something bad that's when God gets the glory.

Faith at Work in Miami

Rev. C.J. Hawking (2007)

South Florida Interfaith Worker Justice (SFIWJ) was formed in 1998 with a mission, based on our faith traditions, to "involve the faith community in issues that will improve the wages, benefits, and employment conditions of the workers, especially the low-wage workers of South Florida." The membership, which spans Miami-Dade and Broward counties, includes clergy, congregants, congregations and judicatories. SFIWJ's volunteer Board of Directors is comprised of eighteen faith leaders from a variety of religious and ethnic traditions. SFIWJ is one of 60 affiliates of Interfaith Worker Justice, clergy and lay people advocating for workers' rights across the United States.

One paid staff member had provided day-to-day operational support for SFIWJ but, knowing that union organizing campaigns were about to heat up, IWJ sent a consultant to Miami in August 2005. For a period of one year, the consultant commuted from the Midwest to Miami each Monday morning.

Condos Are to Miami as Cars Are to Detroit

In 2005, SFIWJ began a campaign to support and advocate for the 4,000 custodians in luxurious condominium buildings. According to a 72-page report from the Florida International University Labor Research Center, the average South Florida condo worker earns $7.10 an hour and lacks family health coverage and other basic benefits. Many have to work a second and third job to survive, taking precious time away from their families, communities and places of worship. In contrast, unionized janitors in New York and Chicago earn over $15 an hour with full benefits.

After hearing about condo workers being harassed, threatened and sometimes even fired for expressing interest in joining Service Employees International Union (SEIU) Local 11 in June 2005, SFIWJ marched to the headquarters of Continental, the major employer of condo workers in South Florida. When Continental refused to meet with the group of 30 clergy, they left bitter herbs, a symbol of the bitterness of the enslaved Israelites and the injustice that condo workers must endure.

Throughout autumn 2005 clergy "adopted" condo buildings that employ workers from Continental, writing and calling condo boards to ask to meet with them to discuss their workers' conditions. Most condo boards would not return the calls and those that did refused the request.

Finding Stride

On January 16, 2006 South Florida Interfaith Worker Justice brought together more than 400 people of faith to celebrate Dr. Martin Luther King Day with a spirited rally for the condo workers. Organizing an event that large in a place like Miami was not easy; the labor movement has never had a large presence in the city, and the entire Sun Belt has a long tradition of vehement anti-unionism by employers.

For the rally SFIWJ made a very intentional effort to reach out far beyond the people previously involved in the group's work by publicizing the rally at dozens of churches and synagogues. The group mailed information on the rally to a large list of clergy from around the Miami area, followed up with phone calls and then hand delivered over 40,000 bulletin inserts to interested congregations.

The event was a real breakthrough for SFIWJ in both its size and diversity. According to Father Jack Stanton, an Episcopal priest who served as chair of the task force that planned the SFIWJ rally, "the rally exceeded our wildest expectations. The church seats 400 and we were putting seats in the aisles and spilling out the front door." Religious leaders and congregants from all of Miami's racial and ethnic groups participated, and speeches were translated into Spanish and Creole.

Participants watched an excerpt from *At the River I Stand*, a powerful documentary on Dr. King's work supporting the Memphis sanitation strike. The Most Rev. Felipe Estevez, Auxiliary Bishop of the Roman Catholic Archdiocese of Miami, the Rev. Dr. Joaquin Willis, a respected leader in Miami's African-American community, and SEIU President Andy Stern all gave rousing speeches on Dr. King's economic justice work and framed the condo workers' campaign as a civil rights struggle. Two condominium workers, Marvin White and Jairo Garces, talked about the experience of being fired for supporting the union. A Jewish cantor, a Haitian choir and a Latino children's choir provided musical inspiration. The crowd then marched through the streets to a building managed by the target company, and workers led a ritual in which each participant poured a cup of saltwater into a large clay pot to symbolize the sweat and tears of the workers as well as the sea the Israelites had to pass through to get to freedom. All of the speakers received thunderous standing ovations.

Stanton, who attended Dr. King's 1963 March on Washington, remarked that the rally's appeal was that it gave Miami's religious community the opportunity to take action in the tradition of Dr. King. Economic justice was a central part of Dr. King's vision for society, and he believed the Civil Rights Movement and the labor movement were natural allies with "identical interests." During the last year of his life, King and the Southern Christian Leadership Council initiated a "Poor People's Campaign" that aimed to focus the nation's attention on economic inequality and the millions of Americans of all races living in poverty in the midst of the richest country in the world. Dr. King was supporting striking sanitation workers in Memphis, Tennessee, when he was assassinated in 1968. As Fr. Stanton stated, "This was not just another Martin Luther King Day event, where you have a parade and a speech. We were actually engaging Dr. King's work in a local justice issue."

The rally succeeded in both applying pressure to the employers and building momentum for SFIWJ. According to the master of ceremonies, Rabbi Rebecca Lillian, the event "showed that a large cross section of the community really cares about economic justice." SFIWJ Coordinator Sara Shapiro describes the rally as "just what the clergy needed in order to get energized." Most employers of condo workers still refuse to honor workers' right to a free and fair process for union recognition. SFIWJ has strengthened their task force in order to engage the religious community in the condo workers' struggle, which also now includes valets, security guards, and concierges, totaling over 8000 workers. After the upcoming 2007 Dr. King Day Interfaith Service, the congregation will march to show support to the janitors on Fisher Island, Miami Beach's most posh and exclusive community (a boat is required to get to the island) whose residents include Oprah and other famous billionaires.

University of Miami

While forming a clergy group to support the 410 janitors at the University of Miami, SFIWJ asked Fr. Frank Corbishley, an Episcopal priest serving a congregation of nearby residents and students at his University of Miami, to join. The janitors made $6.80 an hour, had no health care benefits, and wanted to form a union. SFIWJ also asked Corbishley if the workers could hold weekly meetings in his sanctuary. Corbishley assented.

The janitors were employed by UNICCO, a Boston-based company that was contracted to provide janitorial services at the University of Miami (UM) Coral Gables campus and at the university's hospital. The UM President is Donna Shalala, the former Secretary of Health and Human Services in the first Clinton administration. Ironically, she now refused to include health care, wage increases, and dignity on the job for the janitors covered under the UM-UNICCO contract.

After meeting with several workers and hearing their plight, the clergy group, with Corbishley as their chairperson, took a series of actions, including:

- Regularly provided meeting space for workers at the Episcopal Student Center on campus.

- Sent a letter to UM President Donna Shalala, requesting a meeting, which she declined.

- Took out a full-page ad in support of UM workers on Dr. King Day in the

- *Miami Herald, UM Hurricane* and *Coral Gables Gazette.*

- Offered prayers and a sermon at a UM student-led Dr. King Service

- Hosted workers in churches as speakers and gained over 600 signatures on postcards from Coral Gables residents, all of which were addressed to Shalala.

By late February the workers were ready to take a strike vote. Shalala had offered them an increase in wages and some health care benefits but the workers knew that they needed a permanent voice on the job. In short, they needed a union. But Shalala was trying to squash the increasing support from the faculty, students, community leaders and SFIWJ to support unionization.

Strike Sanctuary

On the evening preceding and the morning of Ash Wednesday, the UNICCO workers took a very brave step and walked off the job. By noon they were at the Ash Wednesday Mass at St. Augustine's Church and Student Center, adjacent to the UM campus. The support from St. Augustine's was not easy to come by. In fact, many advised SFIWJ to bypass the church altogether as the senior priest was known to be cautious and "not social justice-oriented."

SFIWJ decided instead to approach the associate priest, an Augustinian who had just returned from serving in Peru for 20 years and at St. Augustine's less than a year. Fr. Rich Mullen, the associate, was able to communicate all strategies and events to the senior priest. As it turned out, the senior priest encouraged Fr. Rich in his participation.

So the stage was set when hundreds of striking, purple-t-shirted workers sat scattered throughout St. Augustine's sanctuary at noon on Ash Wednesday.

Within the first days of the strike and at the request of the UM faculty, SFIWJ contacted neighboring churches and synagogues to request that alternative classroom space be made available to faculty who did not wish to cross the picket line. Over 200 UM classes were offered in alternative classroom sites.

Since Miami–Dade county gave $85 million annually to UM, SFIWJ President Episcopal Bishop Ottley met with Miami-Dade County Chairman Martinez to request his assistance. Martinez contacted Shalala but apparently she remained entrenched in her position to not allow the workers to unionize.

After the students returned from Spring Break and the strike was about to enter its second month, the clergy decided to join the workers in nonviolent civil disobedience.

Continuing the Legacy

> "You may well ask, 'Why direct action? Why sit-ins, marches, etc.? Isn't negotiation a better path?' Indeed, this is the purpose of direct action. It seeks to dramatize the issue so that it can no longer be ignored."
> Dr. Martin Luther King, Jr., Letter from the Birmingham Jail

Invoking the traditions of Dr. Martin Luther King and Mahatma Gandhi and after attending training in non-violent civil disobedience, 17 people were arrested as hundreds of supporters surrounded them on Tuesday, March 28.

After 300 supporters stopped traffic by securing the perimeter of the Dixie Highway and Granada intersection in Coral Gables, Bishop Ottley moved to the center of the intersection and began a prayer. One-half dozen workers then formed a circle in the intersection, followed by a group of clergy and community supporters. Among those participating in the action were: Rev. Bill Bailey of Sellers United Methodist Church; Rev. Renwick Bell of Metropolitan Community Church; Rev. C.J. Hawking of Interfaith Worker Justice; Fr. Roger Holoubek of St. Maurice Catholic Church; Rev. Guillermo Marquez Sterling of Coral Gables Congregational Church; Ms. Sara Shapiro of SFICWJ; and Rev. Frank Smith, retired pastor of the United Methodist Church, who wore a suit.

The individuals were handcuffed, put into a police vehicle and taken to the Coral Gables jail. Other than having little to no air in the vehicle, they were treated kindly, talked at length with a supportive police force, and were released on their own recognizance within four hours. They were charged with the misdemeanor of obstructing a highway and received a "Notice to Appear" at a date to be specified later. (About three months later the charges were dropped.)

As the above action was unfolding, Fr. Frank Corbishley joined a group of students in a simultaneously planned action to occupy the Admissions Office in the main administrative building on the University of Miami campus. The group occupied a room on the first floor which was surrounded by glass and right off the lobby, so that they were constantly visible to supporters in the lobby and outside the building.

Back on Dixie Highway, news of the occupation reached the 300 supporters and they quickly rushed over to the administration building. Several joined the sit-in being held in the Admissions Office and dozens of workers, faculty and students rallied in the lobby, shouting their support. Within an hour the supporters were cleared out of the lobby and by 5 pm all non-students had been asked to leave. This left 17 students, one legal observer, one young reporter and Fr. Corbishley.

Reports of pending arrests circulated hourly as the lobby and the building became filled with dozens of Coral Gables police officers. The supporters' group swelled at 5 pm, the time that the building officially closed, and a prayer of support was offered by Rev. Ren Bell, just released from jail.

President Shalala offered to meet with the group at 7:30 pm but only on the condition that Fr. Corbishley not be present. The group voted that they would not be forced to sacrifice Fr. Corbishley's presence. Shalala arrived. When she asked Fr. Corbishley to leave, he told her this was a group decision and that his faith was tied up with the students' faith. She abruptly left.

Shalala kept her demand and eventually the group acquiesced with the condition that Corbishley be able to return. Shalala returned throughout the night, for a total of four negotiation sessions with the students, each time demanding that Fr. Frank sit in a chair in the lobby, surrounded by the police officers who now rested comfortably in the chairs. Before the 14-hour siege ended, Shalala ordered the arrest of Fr. Corbishley. When the officer came in the room and looked at Corbishley, he refused. His superior did not force the issue and Shalala left exasperated.

On the eve of the subsequent meeting, SFIWJ held an abbreviated Labor Seder outside of Corbishley's church. The event, led by SFICWJ Board Member Rabbi Rebecca Lillian, drew over 200 people, including workers, clergy, faculty, students and community supporters.

The promised meeting, which Shalala did not attend, did not have any results.

Community support for the workers' struggle grew. In addition to significant newspaper coverage and SFIWJ's weekly listserv updates, SFIWJ Board Member Bishop Estevez interviewed Fr. Rich Mullen, a member of the clergy task force, on Radio Paz, the Catholic Spanish radio station, asking him about the struggle of the workers. Bishop Estevez had also previously interviewed a worker on the radio.

Hunger Strike

Six days after the civil disobedience action and on the anniversary of Dr. King's death, SFIWJ hosted a showing of *At the River I Stand* which chronicles King's time in Memphis on behalf of striking garbage collectors. This was in preparation for the hunger strike which was to be launched the next day.

Ten workers and seven students began a hunger strike, living and sleeping outside of the main UM gate and under the thundering Metro rail. "Freedom Village" was comprised of sprawling tents, a medical tent with a nurse, a meeting tent, art work, bands, entertainers, port-a-johns and a steady stream of media. Visitors to Freedom Village included Dolores Huerta, Ed Asner, Barbara Ehrenreich, former Senator and Vice Presidential candidate John Edwards, Teamsters President James Hoffa Jr. and President Charles Steele from the Southern Christian Leadership Conference.

Members of SFIWJ brought oil for anointing, choirs for singing, and prayers for sustaining the hunger strikers. In addition to the hunger strikers holding informal prayer circles each afternoon, a 30-minute bilingual service was held for the fasters and their families each evening.

Within the first ten days, five workers and a student were rushed to the hospital and medically ordered to leave the hunger strike. Faculty, community leaders and SFIWJ members then began fasting in solidarity with the hunger strikers, many sleeping overnight in the tents. In addition to her 77-hour fast, SFIWJ Board Member and Quaker Jeanette Smith provided steady e-mail updates for members and pastoral care to the hunger strikers.

Holy Week occurred during the hunger strike at Freedom Village. SFIWJ led a Palm Sunday Service, a foot-washing ceremony on Holy Thursday and Stations of the Cross on Friday. On Easter Sunday, St. Augustine's gave special recognition to the hunger strikers.

However, some clergy, faculty and community supporters were opposed to the hunger strike. Some said that the body should not be abused. Also, opposition to the methodology by which the janitors wanted to unionize – eliminating the cumbersome step of involving the National Labor Relations Board which can delay unionization for years and replacing the union voting process with government-sanctioned observers, called "card check" – surfaced.

By Day 17, with health declining and the clergy presiding, workers and students broke their fast with bread and soup at a prayer service. In their place, SEIU President Andy Stern and Vice President Eliseo Medina, began to fast and reside at Freedom Village. That evening Stern stepped away from Freedom Village to attend services at the most prominent synagogue on Miami Beach. Rabbi Kliel Rose, who completed a "Seminary Summer" union organizing internship arranged by IWJ one year prior to the strike, acknowledged appreciation of Stern, in spite of the congregation holding predominantly anti-union sentiments.

By the close of the weekend, Stern was called away, but Medina remained. Medina, a man of humility and grace, seemed to enjoy the fast and relax in ways that boggled the minds of friendly observers. "I love this," remarked Medina, a Catholic man of deep faith. "I get to be with the workers and not behind a desk or on a plane."

Nine days into Medina's fast, the news of a breakthrough with Shalala came.

"We won! We won!" The cheers went up from janitors, students, faculty and members of the SFIWJ on May 1 as the University of Miami janitors won card-check election after a two-month strike. The Service Employees International Union later negotiated a contract with 33 percent wage increases, affordable health care, and sick, holiday and vacation benefits. Perhaps most importantly 410 janitors now have a permanent voice and dignity on the job.

Coverage of SFICWJ's support appeared in *The New York Times, The National Catholic Reporter, The Miami Herald* and a "Sixty Minutes" segment profiling Andy Stern.

SFIWJ's Future

Two weeks later at an awards luncheon hosted for the clergy, SEIU Director of Building Services Stephen Lerner and Local 11 President Rob Schuler remarked on how the clergy's moral voice made a profound impact on the struggle. The clergy were acknowledged with plaques and eloquent speeches of gratitude. When the risks taken by Fr. Corbishley were outlined, the clergy and unionists jumped to their feet with long, thunderous applause. Bishop Ottley, who presided as bishop for all of Central America during the torturous 1980s, remarked that he never dreamed that he would get to be a part of a social movement like this again.

Having demonstrated their capacity to help bring about justice and social change and with the knowledge that additional large-scale union organizing campaigns are planned for South Florida, SFIWJ is in the process of hiring three additional staff members and tripling the budget.

Rev. C.J. Hawking, a United Methodist pastor, is the Executive Director of Chicago Interfaith Committee on Worker Issues.

A New Alliance between Religion and Labor?

The 2002 Graphic Communications International Union – *San Diego Union-Tribune* Newspaper Contract Negotiation

Robert B. Horwitz (2006)

Despite a largely successful, 15-year effort to get rid of its labor unions, in July 2002 the *San Diego* (California) *Union-Tribune* newspaper signed a contract with its pressroom workers that maintained the integrity of the Graphic Communications International Union as the legal bargaining agent. What was unusual was not simply that the company signed a contract after years of negotiations essentially designed to break the union, but that the contract was negotiated by a team of outsiders: three leaders of the San Diego religious community drawn from the executive board of the Interfaith Committee for Worker Justice, the Secretary-Treasurer of the San Diego-Imperial Counties Labor Council, and a prominent local businessman. The pressroom workers had dropped out of the negotiating and authorized these others to bargain on their behalf. Perhaps the most intriguing element of the episode was the role of the religious leaders. Adopting the pressroom workers' cause, they brought about the reopening of contract negotiations with the company and helped alter the character of discussion within the negotiations. The intervention of the religious leaders also facilitated the participation of local businessman Stephen Cushman, probably the key figure in the renewed contract negotiations. The case suggests that faith-based participation in labor conflicts can change the dynamics of the conflict because, one, the introduction of a religiously inflected discourse of social justice has the potential to insert ethical questions concerning fairness into negotiations, and two, faith-based participation opens a space for the involvement of important non-labor actors on labor's side.

The Context: The *Union-Tribune* and Its Decertification Campaign

The flagship paper of the Copley Press, Inc., the *San Diego Union-Tribune* became the effective monopoly daily newspaper in San Diego following the merger of the morning *Union* and the afternoon *Tribune* in February 1992, and the termination of the *Los Angeles Times'* San Diego edition that same year. The total average paid circulation of the *Union-Tribune* throughout the mid to late 1990s was about 375,000 daily and 450,000 Sunday, figures that placed the *Union-Tribune* as the 23rd to 26th largest circulation daily in the United States.[1]

A privately held corporation, the Copley Press, Inc. does not release financial information about itself, hence specific data on revenues and profits at the *Union-Tribune* are difficult to come by.[2] Hoover's Online, the business information website, reports 2001 revenues for Copley Press at $534 million, with a one-

---

1. Audit Bureau of Circulations, 2002 <www.accessabc.com/reader/102700_0702_RPRD.pdf>.

2. Also hard to come by was the company's perspective on its labor relations. *Union-Tribune* executives declined to speak with the author about the negotiations between the company and the GCIU. In response to a letter asking for an interview, President and CEO R. Gene Bell wrote, "Once we reached a contract last year, we all resolved to put the past behind us and not to rehash the events of the previous ten years. Given the fact that we have an ongoing bargaining relationship with the union and anticipate negotiating with the union again in 2005, I feel it would be inappropriate to discuss with a third party the 2002 negotiations." R. Gene Bell, Letter to author, November 4, 2003. The company clearly discouraged its employees from discussing labor relations with outside parties. Patrick J. Marrinan, Manager of Labor Relations for the *Union-Tribune*, declined author's invitation for an interview in much the same language. Patrick J. Marrinan, Letter to author, February 24, 2004.

year sales growth of 5.5 percent. Data for 2003 show revenues of $573 million, with a one-year sales growth of 8.1 percent.[3] In 2002 the Copley Press published nine daily, eight weekly, and one bi-weekly newspaper, and operates the Copley News Service. One can reasonably surmise that the financial performance of the *San Diego Union-Tribune* doesn't depart too far from that of comparable publicly owned newspapers in the United States. Although there is much pessimism about newspapers in the long term due to declining circulation and competition from other media sources, in the short term daily newspapers are a highly profitable industry. Operating margins for big city dailies, historically in the 10 to 15 percent range, can now range between 20 and 30 percent, a level of profit more than two to three times that of the average industrial corporation.[4] Newspapers have become highly profitable for a number of reasons, but two stand out. First, a long-term trend of declining competition and emergence of single newspaper towns has effectively resulted in local monopolies.[5] Second, a technological revolution that eventually computerized composition and platemaking in the 1970s and 80s resulted in fewer workers needed to put out a newspaper and also changed the balance of power between labor and management – largely because newspaper workers effectively lost the power to strike.[6] Together, these trends have allowed newspaper companies, increasingly consolidating through merger and acquisition under a publicly traded stock ownership model and focused on serving "shareholder value," to cut costs while charging advertisers more. Computerization not only eliminated entire classes of work at newspapers and reduced staffing in general, it also permitted newspaper companies to attack newspaper unions and effectively roll back wages. The average real hourly wage at US newspapers, according to US Department of Labor data, dropped 25.7 percent between 1976

and 2000, from $18.58 to $13.81, a far steeper drop than the average decline of the average manufacturing real hourly wage (6.8 percent) during the same time period.[7]

Many of these trends played out at the *San Diego Union-Tribune*. Not long after the 1992 merger of the *Union* and the *Tribune*, the company embarked upon a substantial overhaul of many of its operations. It refurbished its press capacity with a $34 million upgrade of its existing production facility, adding Goss Metro Tower units to existing equipment to double the color capacity and increase printing capacity. New formers, the machines that shape the paper on the press and assemble it into sections, were also introduced to each press line, increasing the number of sections that the press could handle at one time. The company brought in R. Gene Bell as President and CEO in 1993. Bell, a longtime newspaper executive, had been corporate vice-president for newspaper operations at the Tribune Company in the 1980s and helped transform the *Chicago Tribune* and *Orlando Sentinel's* production plants into state-of-the art printing facilities. Those achievements also included the wholesale restructuring of labor relations at those newspapers and resulted in high profits. Bell had been a player in the disastrous *New York Daily News* strike in 1990, a conflict prompted by the Tribune Company's heavy-handed efforts to wrest control over pressroom and delivery staffing from the unions.[8] Bell's move to San Diego signaled the increased standing of the law firm, King & Ballow, in the labor policies of the *San Diego Union-Tribune*. King & Ballow, which arrived on the scene at the *Union-Tribune* in the mid-1980s, was known within the industry for its hardball negotiating agenda. In labor's eyes, King & Ballow was notorious for its no-holds-barred union-busting tactics.

Six bargaining units represented workers at the *Union-Tribune* in 1993 when Bell arrived: the composing room and packaging (mail) room were separate units, each represented by the Communication Workers of America; drivers were represented by the Teamsters;

3. Hoover's Online <www.hoovers.com/free/co/factsheet. xhtml?COID=42556>, visited March 6, 2004; <www. hoovers.com/copley-press/--ID__42556--/free-co-factsheet.xhtml>, visited February 12, 2005.

4. Geneva Overholser, "Editor, Inc.," in Gene Roberts, ed., *Leaving Readers Behind: The Age of Corporate Newspapering* (University of Arkansas Press, 2001): 157-188.

5. Gilbert Cranberg, Randall Bezanson, and John Soloski, *Taking Stock: Journalism and the Publicly Traded Newspaper Company* (Iowa State University Press, 2001).

6. Catherine McKercher, *Newsworkers Unite: Labor, Convergence, and North American Newspapers* (Rowman & Littlefield, 2001).

7. Cited in Howard R. Stanger, "Newspapers: Collective Bargaining Decline Amidst Technological Change," in Paul F. Clark, John T. Delaney, and Ann C. Frost, eds., *Collective Bargaining in the Private Sector* (Industrial Relations Research Association, 2002): 179-216.

8. Kenneth M. Jennings, *Labor Relations at the New York Daily News: Peripheral Bargaining and the 1990 Strike* (Praeger, 1993); Richard Vigilante, *Strike: The Daily News War and the Future of American Labor* (Simon & Schuster, 1994).

the platemaking and pressroom units were represented by the Graphic Communications International Union; and the Newspaper Guild, the largest unit, represented reporters, editors, advertising and circulation workers, even janitors. Under the direction of King & Ballow, *Union-Tribune* management moved to transform the company's relationship to its workforce and by 1998, a mere five years after Bell's arrival, only two labor unions remained at the newspaper: the Teamsters and the GCIU. Management first went after the Newspaper Guild, in the late 1980s. King & Ballow knew from past experience that decertifying a Guild bargaining unit would be a long process, and approached the task in a staged offensive. The company attacked the "agency-shop" provisions of the contract, refusing to administer the collection of union dues through automatic deduction from the paycheck. As Craig Rose, president of the Guild local for two years in 1990s and chair of the bargaining committee in 1998, relates, once automatic dues deduction was eliminated, only about 50 percent of dues payers consistently paid their monthly union contributions. The consequences played out according to the King & Ballow plan: tensions between union stalwarts and erratic dues payers (or non-dues payers) about free-riding, and much less money available to the union. The loss of monetary resources made it hard for the union to pay lost wages when its members took off from work to engage in union business. Thus, much more union activity took place after hours, at night and on weekends, causing resentment within families and burn-out among union activists. The Guild nearly struck over the agency-shop issue but pulled back from the brink. The company's triumph regarding agency-shop and the corresponding reduction in union dues collections weakened the Guild bargaining unit considerably. The company then refused to negotiate across-the-board wage increases, insisting instead on a comprehensive merit pay system.[9]

Breaking the Newspaper Guild was a work in progress. *Union-Tribune* management had more definitive early success with the composing room bargaining unit, and won the second of two decertification votes in 1991. The decertification of the packaging room unit came next. Also on the company's hit list were the pressroom and platemaking workers, both represented by the Graphic Communications International Union. The company's contract with the pressroom workers expired October 1992. The pressroom workers' last pay raise was October 1991, and following the expiration of the contract, management reduced the wage by $40

per week. The company refused to increase its share of health insurance premiums in the face of rapid rise, even though it paid virtually the full cost of the premium for the company's non-union workers for equivalent insurance coverage. This was another part of the King & Ballow strategy: let unionized workers see that their non-union counterparts received yearly wage increases and better benefits.[10] As contract negotiations between the company and the pressroom workers proceeded, management put forward an offer that hit at the union's core: 1. a merit-based raise system that diluted the principle of seniority; 2. a two-tier wage scheme that would pay new employees 25 percent lower wages; 3. no pay raises for journeymen press operators; 4. the elimination of the long-standing apprenticeship program; 5. the elimination of company contributions to the union-run pension plan. Staffing – the crux of conflict in the *New York Daily News* struggle – was not directly at issue in the *Union-Tribune* labor negotiations. *Union-Tribune* management already had effective control over staffing levels in the pressroom, and since 1991 staffing had been reduced on each press. Nor was the impact of new

---

9. Craig Rose, Interview with author, August 6, 2003.

10. King & Ballow typically engage in a form of negotiating known in labor circles as "Boulwarism." Named after Lemuel Boulware, chief negotiator for the General Electric Company in the 1940s, this form of bargaining is commonly, if somewhat incorrectly, understood as "take it or leave it" bargaining. Boulwarism describes an employer who comes to the bargaining table and refuses to grant concessions on what the National Labor Relations Act deems mandatory subjects (that is, wages, hours, and terms and conditions of employment), while making promises if the workers go non-union (General Electric Co, 150 NLRB 192 [1964], enf'd, 418 F.2d 736 [2d Cir. 1969], cert denied, 397 U.S. 965 [1970]). As union attorney Richard Prochazka explains, this is a strategy of negotiating designed for the sole purpose of causing the employees in the bargaining unit to give up their support of the union. And as Richard Vigilante writes in his account of the *New York Daily News* struggle, King & Ballow characteristically operate just at the edge of the legal duty to bargain in good faith. The Supreme Court has held that an employer's unilateral implementation of terms violates the NLRA's required duty to bargain in good faith (NLRB v. Katz, 369 U.S. 736 [1962]). But in practice it is relatively easy for an employer to avoid a bad faith charge without ceding much ground in bargaining. King & Ballow lawyers negotiate in a way that threatens unions with effective destruction if they do not agree to their clients' substantive demands, and are willing to talk tough for years toward that end. Richard D. Prochazka, Interview with author, July 16, 2003; Vigilante, *Strike*; also see Martin Jay Levitt with Terry Conrow, *Confessions of a Union-Buster* (Crown Publishers, 1993).

printing technology on pressroom workers at issue, according to GCIU local president Jack Finneran.[11] Although the new press units served to digitalize most pressroom functions, pressroom workers in fact needed to be *more* skilled, because they were required to know both the old technologies and the new, and make possible their integration. But, whereas staffing was not at the center of the bargaining struggles, reduced staffing clearly was of concern to pressroom workers. They had to do more work, felt more exposed to a greater risk of discipline for equipment breakdowns or for production of low-quality papers, and felt at greater risk of injury caused by being required to perform too many tasks at the same time. This was one source of tension on the shop floor.

The company was victorious in its long effort to decertify the Newspaper Guild. After the Guild's fall in June 1998, a decertification petition was filed in the platemaking department. However, that petition was automatically blocked by a series of pending unfair labor practice charges relating to shop floor harassment in the pressroom. Richard Prochazka, who served as the attorney for several of the *Union-Tribune* bargaining units, pursued a legal approach of filing unfair labor practice charges against the company with the National Labor Relations Board – not so much on account of their own merits as part of a strategy against the newspaper's broader depredations against the union.[12] Under current NLRB practice, the actual remedies for most management violations of the National Labor Relations Act are, in Prochazka's judgment, trivial, an appraisal almost universally shared in the labor movement. Since the 1980s, accounts of management harassment of union leaders and advocates are legion, largely because the potential penalties companies face from the NLRB are so insubstantial and the immediate payoff of getting rid of union leaders so decisive. If companies are found at fault in firing union workers, they must merely rehire them with back pay – ordinarily after a period of months or years due to the length of NLRB proceedings, and hence, consequentially, well after the company has rid itself of union leaders during the crucial period of heated labor activity.[13] Judicial decisions have limited the remedy

for bad faith bargaining to no more than an order to bargain in good faith, rather than imposing monetary sanctions, requiring arbitration, or imposing terms.[14] On the other hand, if the NLRB investigates unfair labor practice charges and issues a complaint against management, any action to decertify a union is suspended until the complaint is settled, or adjudicated and remedied.

Thus began a cat and mouse game between the GCIU and the *Union-Tribune* management. The union filed many charges against the company for unfair labor practices, a good number of which were deemed worthy enough by the NLRB regional office to issue complaints. In the meantime, contract negotiations between the pressroom workers and the newspaper continued to be fruitless. The *Union-Tribune* declared "impasse" in negotiations in March 1999, withdrew recognition from GCIU Local 432-M as a bargaining unit, and imposed new work conditions in the pressroom.[15] In GCIU local president Jack Finneran's view, the company's strategy was to be both so intransigent and implacable in negotiations, and so provocative on the shop floor, that workers would either get fed up and strike – and thus be put in the position of being replaced – or lose faith in their union and thus become amenable to a decertification vote. Whether or not

---

Labor Relations Policy, 1947-1994 (Philadelphia: Temple University Press, 1995).

14. H.K. Porter v. NLRB, 397 U.S. 821 (1970); Ellen Dannin, "From Dictator Game to Ultimatum Game … and Back Again: Judicial Amendment Posing as Legal Interpretation," *University of Pennsylvania Journal of Labor and Employment Law* 6 (2004): 241-294.

15. *San Diego Union-Tribune*, "Wages, Hours and Terms and Conditions of Employment for Employees of the Union-Tribune Publishing Co Employed in Its Pressroom and Represented by Graphic Communications International Union, Local 432M" (March 8, 1999). In US labor law the aim of the bargaining process is to negotiate a collective bargaining agreement that will define the terms and conditions of employment of the represented workers during the term of the agreement. There is no duty to agree, however, and if the parties deadlock, or reach impasse, the employer is free to implement the last offer and modify the terms and conditions of the workers' employment (see Litton Financial Printing Div. v. NLRB, 501 U.S. 190 [1991]). Impasse implementation rights create incentives for an employer to bargain intransigently, declare impasse and implement its offer, hoping to provoke workers into a strike and making possible a lockout and the hiring of permanent replacement workers. See Dannin, "From Dictator Game to Ultimatum Game."

---

11. Jack Finneran, Interviews with author, February 24; July 9; September 26, 2003.

12. Richard D. Prochazka, Interview with author, July 16, 2003.

13. See Richard W. Hurd, *Assault on Workers' Rights* (Washington, D.C.: AFL-CIO Industrial Department, 1994); James A. Gross, *Broken Promise: The Subversion of US*

top management furnished shop floor managers with an authorized wink to engage in harassment isn't known, but it is safe to assume that reduced staffing, stalled contract negotiations, and the strained relations between union supporters and the company made for difficult relations in the pressroom. A series of squabbles, altercations, reprimands, suspensions, and terminations transpired during the years of contract negotiations. Many of these involved union leaders and/or the union's most vocal supporters. The GCIU's charges were consolidated in two sets of formal complaints filed by the NLRB against the *Union-Tribune*, and were taken to hearings before administrative law judges. In general the rulings were mixed, with the judges finding for the company in some instances, for the union in others.[16] The company was required to post notice of its violations in the pressroom. And, the complaints had achieved a key purpose: delay of decertification.[17]

---

16. United States, Before the NLRB Division of Judges, San Francisco Branch Office, Union-Tribune Publishing Co. v. Graphic Communications Union, Local 432-M, Graphic Communications International Union, AFL-CIO. Decision. Cases 21-CA-31124, 31812, 31893, 32033, 32261, 32488, 32716, 33042, 33114, 33162, 33199, 33223, 33253, 33254, 33331, 33447, 33469, 33545, 33579, July 27, 2001; United States, Before the NLRB Division of Judges, San Francisco Branch Office, Union-Tribune Publishing Co. v. Graphic Communications Union, Local 432-M, Graphic Communications International Union, AFL-CIO. Decision. Cases 21-CA-33611, 33641, 33684, 33708, 33774, 33798, 33799, July 26, 2001.

17. The *Union-Tribune* entered into a similar pattern of negotiations with its 45-member Teamsters bargaining unit. Like the pressroom workers, the drivers had not had a contract since the early 1990s (1993), and a parallel set of exasperating negotiations took place between the Teamsters and the company for several years. After many years of no wage increases and uncertainty over health, welfare, and pension matters, the drivers were fairly desperate for a contract. Teamsters' local president Phil Saal entered the negotiating sessions in 1999 and steered the talks toward settlement. But when it became clear to *Union-Tribune* Manager of Labor Relations and chief negotiator Patrick Marrinan that the Teamsters actually were set to accept the company's offer, Marrinan withdrew to caucus with his team and abruptly broke off bargaining, charging the union with "retrogressive bargaining" (an undefined term that appears only twice in the NLRB database). In Phil Saal's strong impression, Marrinan had called King & Ballow, who advised him to back out of negotiations. The fact that the company withdrew its contract offer after it was clear the Teamsters were poised to accept it is strong indication

In addition to the NLRB route, the GCIU engaged in other tactics. In 1996, then local president David Rubi sent letters to the advertising managers of businesses that customarily bought large ads in the newspaper, notifying them of labor troubles in the pressroom and how the absence of a contract and reduced staffing levels were undermining professionalism and the quality of work.[18] A year later, the GCIU augmented its public relations activities with a skunk mascot and a "Something Stinks at the *Union-Tribune*" campaign, urging *U-T* subscribers to boycott the newspaper and cancel their subscriptions because of the company's bad behavior in contract negotiations with the pressroom workers. Because paid subscriptions form the basis for the determination of advertising rates, the "Something Stinks" campaign aimed directly at the company's revenues. Depictions of "Stinky the Skunk" alongside the "Something Stinks" slogan could be seen on automobile bumpers, t-shirts, and newsstands during the five years of the boycott campaign. The union bought radio ads, gave media interviews, appeared on cable access television, made a "Something Stinks" video, and held "Something Stinks" rallies in front of the *Union-Tribune* building attended by several hundred unionists and their supporters. Union stalwart Jeff Alger wore a "Stinky the Skunk" outfit and marched in the annual Hillcrest neighborhood Gay Pride parade. The GCIU continued to try to get the *Union-Tribune's* advertisers involved, hoping to have major advertisers put pressure on the newspaper to settle a contract or even to withdraw advertising until a contract was signed. GCIU members handed out flyers just outside the business premises of major *Union-Tribune* advertisers. In a sour piece of irony, the *Union-Tribune*, an entity that should be devoted to free speech, went to Washington trying (unsuccessfully) to convince the NLRB to ban the workers from publicizing their dispute and engaging in its handbilling of advertisers.[19] Although the campaign attracted some media attention, according to union president Finneran the strategy had only limited practical success. Advertisers didn't respond or, when they expressed sympathy for the pressroom workers,

---

that the company never intended to settle and its goal was in fact to break the union. Saal's account was replicated by San Diego-Imperial Counties Labor Council Secretary-Treasurer Jerry Butkiewicz. Phil Saal, Telephone interview with author, September 9, 2003; Jerry Butkiewicz, Interview with author, August 27, 2003.

18. David Rubi, Letter on GCIU letterhead to advertising managers, June 27, 1996.

19. See James Kelleher, "Stop the Presses!" *San Diego Weekly Reader*. March 4, 1999: 4-8.

the effective monopoly position of *Union-Tribune* in San Diego precluded any action. As Joe Drew, owner of Drew Ford, told Finneran, "I'm in business. I need to sell cars. And when there's only one newspaper in town …" Still, Finneran maintained that the campaign hurt the image of the company in the community, a claim that had some plausibility in view of subsequent events.[20]

The GCIU's Turn to the Interfaith Committee for Worker Justice

The endurance and doggedness of the pressroom workers and their leadership were remarkable, but the years of sparring with the company took their toll. Attrition among journeymen pressroom workers at the *Union-Tribune* was significant. GCIU local president Jack Finneran, terminated by the company in August 2000, continued searching for allies to sustain the struggle. He began attending meetings of the San Diego Interfaith Committee for Worker Justice. The San Diego ICWJ is the local chapter of a loose confederation of national interfaith committees. A self-described "social action project of the San Diego faith communities" (Interfaith Worker Justice, no date), including over 75 religious leaders representing more than a dozen different religious traditions, the San Diego chapter of IWJ was established in August 1998 by Regina Botterill of the National IWJ and Donald Cohen, then political director of the San Diego-Imperial Counties Central Labor Council.[21]

In the beginning, the religious activists thought that their mere presence and their reasoning would sway

employers. Donald Cohen said it took about a year for them to realize that their moral arguments, absent the threat of coercion, would simply be dismissed or ignored by employers.[22] ICWJ now has its own lively executive board and organizes its own actions, at which unions and workers may be present. ICWJ members tend to be middle aged or older, yet very mixed in terms of race and ethnicity, and very balanced in terms of gender. Monthly meetings attract about 40 people, roughly balanced between men and women, and, although majority white, lots of Latinos and African-Americans. Some are active lay people; many are ordained clergy. The monthly meetings of the ICWJ feature presentations from workers that are as much testimonials as they are reports from the field. Local labor leaders also present progress reports, and CPI staffers report on research projects. ICWJ meetings feel less like union or political gatherings; they are more like a mélange of social action religious and support-group gatherings similar to the church-based Central America solidarity groups of the 1980s. Indeed, the model of worker testimonials to the ICWJ seems patterned after the narratives of Salvadoran or Guatemalan refugees to USA solidarity groups.

Like the effort to enlist *Union-Tribune* advertisers to pressure the newspaper to settle with the pressroom workers, GCIU president Jack Finneran turned to the ICWJ and religious leaders for similar kinds of assistance. He began reporting to the ICWJ at its monthly meetings on what was happening – or *not* happening – in negotiations with the *Union-Tribune*. In one telling meeting in the spring of 2002, a weepy Finneran told the ICWJ that the workers were at the end of their rope and about to give up and sign a bad contract. Eric Miller, a minister relatively new to the monthly ICWJ meeting, became distressed upon hearing Finneran's anguished testimonial. "We can't just let this happen," he declared, and called for prayer. The prayer, in Rabbi Coskey's recollection, produced a "spiritual zap" that energized the group and prompted it to adopt the pressroom workers' cause.

The ICWJ's involvement with the pressroom workers took two paths. The first, the public path, was to hold a prayer vigil at the *Union-Tribune* on behalf of the union. Forty to fifty people of various religious affiliations in prayer shawls or habits attended the vigil at the front entry of the *Union-Tribune* Mission

20. Jack Finneran, Interview with author, February 24, 2003.

21. Cohen's social movement background (he was coordinator of the San Diego chapter of the Committee in Solidarity with the People of El Salvador and founder of the Central America Information Center in the 1980s and was the coordinator of San Diego Neighbor to Neighbor in the early 1990s) is very much in keeping with what researchers describe as a new generation of labor activists who were strongly influenced by the social movements of the '60s and '70s, and who are described both as transformers of sclerotic union bureaucracies and as bridge-builders between unions and community groups. Lowell Turner and Richard W. Hurd, "Building Social Movement Unionism," in Turner, Katz, and Hurd, eds., *Rekindling the Movement: Labor's Quest for Relevance in the Twenty-First Century*, 9-26; Voss and Sherman, "Breaking the Iron Law of Oligarchy: Union Revitalization in the American Labor Movement"; Nissen, "The Effectiveness and Limits of Labor-Community Coalitions."

22. For the point in general on the relationship between morality and coercion, see Reinhold Niebuhr, *Moral Man and Immoral Society: A Study in Ethics and Politics* (Westminster John Knox Press, 1932).

Valley headquarters in June 2002. Participants offered prayers for both management and workers, and sang spiritual songs. Drawing loosely from the Jewish tradition of Passover, the Reverend Robert C. Ard, pastor of Christ Church San Diego, tried to offer a tray of bitter herbs to the *Union-Tribune* management. The bitter herbs were intended to symbolize both the pressroom workers' resentment and how difficult and bitter the contract negotiations had become for both sides. These ritually freighted actions were part of the ICWJ's protest playbook. Collected in a booklet called "Stand Up for Justice: An Interfaith Prayer Service," the booklet instructs activists how to invoke religious themes, language, and utilize widely recognizable rituals and attire in public actions.[23] Because no one would come out of the *Union-Tribune* building to accept the offering, Reverend Ard placed the tray of bitter herbs at the base of the company's flagpole. As the faith participants engaged in prayer, someone from the *Union-Tribune* called the police. With some discomfort, the police declared the rally unlawful but permitted the vigil to conclude. In the meantime, *Union-Tribune* management also called a towing company to remove illegally parked cars from its company parking lot. Many of these cars were those of vigil-attending nuns in habit, and the police intervened to give the nuns time to collect their vehicles.[24]

The behind-the-scenes path was to draft Jerry Butkiewicz, the Secretary-Treasurer of the San Diego-Imperial Counties Labor Council (CLC), to join the campaign. This was not a surprising move. Butkiewicz has a reputation in town as an effective spokesman for labor, someone who can get things done, and who is able to interact both with his union constituency and with local businessmen, politicians, and community groups.[25] San Diego labor politics had long been characterized by a combination of a largely invisible business unionism and punctuated labor militancy. Many San Diego labor unions, like many mature unions in the post-World War II period, became essentially servicing bureaucracies for their members,

isolated from communities and other natural allies in common cause against corporate power, quiescent and politically weak.[26] The San Diego-Imperial Counties Central Labor Council, particularly under the plodding leadership of Secretary-Treasurer Joe Francis in the 1990s, was ineffective. At the same time there had been considerable militancy among the industrial unions in San Diego in the late 1980s. Workers at General Dynamics, Solar Turbines, and National Steel and Shipbuilding all went out on strike – and all got beat.[27] The perception of Joe Francis as ineffective led to his ouster in 1996. Jerry Butkiewicz brought a social movement unionism perspective and political smarts to the San Diego labor scene, gradually transforming the largely dormant CLC into a vibrant organization, forging alliances with other communities, and involving itself in the nitty-gritty of local politics. Butkiewicz, originally from the Postal Workers Union, had served as the AFL-CIO's Labor Liaison to the United Way for over a decade, and was robustly networked in the business community. The new orientation of the San Diego-Imperial Counties CLC was consistent with a general transformation in the 1990s toward more activist CLCs.[28] Indeed, by the early 2000s, traditional San Diego power blocs and conservative political groups not only noted labor's new political clout in town, they were complaining about it.[29]

ICWJ Director Rabbi Laurie Coskey, who did

---

23. ICWJ, "Stand Up for Justice: An Interfaith Prayer Service."

24. Reverend Robert C. Ard, Interview with author, August 8, 2003; Kent Peters, Interview with author, July 22, 2003.

25. Libby Brydolf, "Union Boss: Jerry Butkiewicz Wants to Organize Your Employees Next," *San Diego Metropolitan Magazine* (May 1997); David Hicks, "A Voice for Workers: San Diego-Imperial Counties Council Butkiewicz Leads the Charge of Labor Unions Into the Political Arena," *San Diego Daily Transcript* (September 11, 2002).

26. In general see Kim Moody, *An Injury to All: The Decline of American Unionism* (Verso, 1988).

27. See Mike Davis, Kelly Mayhew, and Jim Miller, *Under the Perfect Sun: The San Diego Tourists Never See* (New Press, 2003).

28. Fernando Gapasin and Howard Wial, "The Role of Central Labor Councils in Union Organizing in the 1990s," in Bronfenbrenner, Friedman et al. eds., *Organizing to Win*: 54-67; Ray M. Tillman and Michael S. Cummings, eds., *The Transformation of U.S. Unions: Voices, Visions, and Strategies from the Grassroots* (Lynne Rienner, 1999).

29. The San Diego-Imperial Counties Labor Council includes 100,000 union members and approximately 110 affiliated labor groups (www.unionyes.org/about.htm, visited March 13, 2005); Philip J. LaVelle, "New Clout in Town: Political Pull in San Diego Used to Reside with a Few: Today, Unions and Tribes Lead a Diverse Array of Groups Sharing in the Power," *San Diego Union-Tribune* (Aug. 4, 2002): A-1; idem, "A Labor Leader Who Really Leads: Scrappy Figure Adds Unions to San Diego Political Mix," *San Diego Union-Tribune* (May 5, 2003): A1; Ray Huard, "New Council Expected to Be More Open: Skepticism, Demand For Information Also Likely, Observers Say," *San Diego Union-Tribune* (Dec. 2, 2002): B-1.

most of the organizing in the aftermath of the faith organization's commitment to the *Union-Tribune* pressroom workers, met with Butkiewicz about the *Union-Tribune* – GCIU contract negotiations. In the meantime, she placed a call to Patrick Marrinan, Manager of Labor Relations at the *Union-Tribune* and chief labor negotiator for the company. Coskey was hoping to arrange a meeting between Marrinan and some members of the ICWJ. In Coskey's retelling, Marrinan himself, rather than a secretary, unexpectedly answered the phone. In the course of their conversation, Marrinan told Coskey that he did not want to meet with ICWJ and did not want the clergy to hold the prayer vigil on *Union-Tribune* property. He did, however, pass along a surprising piece of information: the GCIU could put whomever they wanted on their negotiating team. Butkiewicz agreed to become involved on the condition that the GCIU membership voted to give him full authority to act on the union's behalf. With the cajoling efforts of Jack Finneran, the GCIU rank and file did so. Butkiewicz put together a new negotiating team, consisting of himself and three members of the ICWJ Executive Committee: Rabbi Coskey, Kent Peters from the Catholic Diocese, and Reverend Robert C. Ard, pastor of Christ Church. The final member of the reformulated GCIU negotiating team was the most surprising: Stephen P. Cushman, owner of various auto dealerships and among the largest advertisers in the *Union-Tribune.*

A longtime San Diego businessman with political, or, perhaps more accurately, public/community service inclinations, Cushman had served on scores of boards of community and business organizations. As Chairman of the Greater San Diego Chamber of Commerce, he instigated the Chamber's invitation of Jerry Butkiewicz to join its Executive Committee in 1997, a first for a labor leader in San Diego. A moderate Republican with a self-described "strange relationship with labor," Cushman came to know Butkiewicz through their mutual participation in community organizations. In Cushman's telling, the two men worked together, most often quietly, behind the scenes, bringing management and labor together on many issues. "Labor and I work very well together," he declared.[30]

Cushman also came to the bargaining table with an intimate knowledge of the newspaper business. His family had owned Independent Newspapers, a group of community papers that had operated as a union shop until the family sold the business some 35 years

ago. The family's ownership of Independent Newspapers meant that Cushman dealt with the unions from the management side. He knew the trades, the unions, and, importantly, he also was familiar with the work; he claimed to be able to run a traditional printing press. Because of the newspaper connection, Cushman's family had a 50-year friendship with the Copley family, owners of the *San Diego Union-Tribune.* Cushman had been approached by the GCIU a few years earlier in its campaign to get large advertisers to pressure the *Union-Tribune* to settle with the pressroom workers. He had not been pleased with the picketing of his auto dealerships, and he was somewhat offended by the "Something Stinks at the *Union-Tribune*" campaign, especially the union's occasional public nastiness toward the Copleys. In this regard, Cushman revealed his proclivity toward understanding politics as an elite affair, best conducted by pragmatic men of substance such as *Union-Tribune* CEO Gene Bell, Jerry Butkiewicz, and himself. When disputes range out of their proper ken, Cushman reflected, things not only get messy and ugly, but people lose the ability to "do business," compromise, and settle.

This is how Steve Cushman understood the strife at the *Union-Tribune.* Each side had come to hate the other, thus each side had painted itself into a corner. At the same time, Cushman showed compassion toward the plight of the pressroom workers. "They [the pressroom workers] were outcasts," he said, and "it wasn't fair that they weren't getting the same benefits as other workers" at the paper. Yet when asked why he thought the *Union-Tribune* management had engaged in more than a decade of what could only be described as ruthless union-busting activity, Cushman avoided passing judgment, replying that this was "their affair." In addition to his business connections to the *Union-Tribune,* his family friendship with the Copleys, and professional relationship with Jerry Butkiewicz, Cushman had other connections to the players involved in the *Union-Tribune* – GCIU controversy. He had a close professional relationship with and great respect for *Union-Tribune* CEO Gene Bell. He had recruited Bell to sit on a board associated with Sharp Hospital. Cushman also had a historic, if indirect, family connection to Rabbi Laurie Coskey. For many years he had been a congregant of Beth Israel, the premier Reform Jewish synagogue in San Diego. In his characterization, a high-dues-paying, but only two-day-a-year (Rosh Hashanah and Yom Kippur), somewhat reluctant congregant, Cushman's forebears literally built the first Beth Israel building, a one-room, simple but elegant wood structure, now a historical landmark

---

30. Stephen Cushman, Interview with author, August 5, 2003.

situated at Heritage Park in San Diego's Old Town neighborhood. Laurie Coskey had served as an associate rabbi at Beth Israel in the 1980s and had officiated at Cushman family funeral functions.

The new, curious GCIU negotiating team met the *Union-Tribune* team just twice, in sessions that each lasted three to four hours. Participating for the *Union-Tribune* were: Howard Kastrinsky, the King & Ballow attorney; Jane Matthews from Human Relations; and Carlos Stovall, Manager of Pressroom Operations. Patrick Marrinan, the *Union-Tribune's* Manager of Labor Relations, was supposed to participate, but a minor stroke kept him away from the first session. That session, in the judgment of the faith participants, was lighter than the second, in part because the company's negotiators initially thought the GCIU was kidding. In Reverend Ard's view, the *Union-Tribune* negotiators were amazed at the composition of the GCIU's team. Having the faith representatives as contract negotiators, while somewhat disorienting, was also seen as a bit of a joke. Indeed, Ard indicated that there was an ironic mismatch of perceptions. The new GCIU team actually had the authority to bargain and settle for the pressroom workers whereas the *Union-Tribune* team did not have full authority to settle for the newspaper, yet the *U-T* team questioned the mandate of their opponents.

In the judgment of the faith representatives, Cushman was the linchpin of the process. His newspaper background meant that he was knowledgeable not only about the business of running a newspaper, but was surprisingly well-informed with regard to the concrete tasks in a pressroom and what it took to turn out a daily paper. This, according to Coskey and Peters, was an enormous advantage inasmuch as the *U-T* negotiators could not challenge the GCIU team's business or technical expertise when discussing specific contract points. Furthermore, Cushman's social status was such that he could not be brow-beaten or fobbed-off by the *U-T* negotiators. Progress halted upon the return of Patrick Marrinan for the second negotiating session. In Cushman's recollection, each team's hackles were raised and there was a strong possibility that negotiations would cease. When the discussions got sticky or the *Union-Tribune* negotiators indicated that they did not have authorization to decide on a particular negotiating point, on more than one occasion Cushman became irritated, admonishing them not to waste his time. In Coskey's recollection, Cushman whipped out his cell phone during the sessions and called *Union-Tribune* CEO Gene Bell directly. On one occasion,

Cushman then turned to the *U-T* negotiators and related, "I'm told you can come to an agreement about this."[31] Cushman recalled phoning Gene Bell just once, during a break, when the second session was collapsing. He told Bell that the *U-T* negotiating team's position had hardened. Bell then called his team and advised them to be more pliant. After a half-hour recess, the teams were back to business and eventually reached a settlement.[32] In sum, Butkiewicz brought into the negotiations an intimate knowledge of union contracts; Cushman brought in connectedness, business acumen, and implied economic pressure. The fact that Cushman was among the *Union-Tribune's* largest advertisers was a looming presence in the sessions, never mentioned aloud, but with an implication that he might not want to give his business to a company that treated workers this way.[33] Cushman's knowledge of the newspaper business allowed the GCIU team to sign off on certain provisions, particularly issues around part-time work. Cushman assured the team that it wasn't a matter of having to trust the *Union-Tribune;* it was a matter of strict business sense that the newspaper would act in specific ways.

And what was the role of the faith participants? Coskey, Peters, and Ard downplayed their roles in the negotiating sessions. Peters reflected that without Butkiewicz and Cushman, there was no way the ICWJ participants could have negotiated a contract; they simply did not have the expertise.[34] But the faith participants were in many respects much too self-effacing in their assessment. It was their intervention that got the new negotiations going in the first place. And their intervention and participation brought a morality-based purpose to the negotiations that was difficult for the company to snub or ignore. Ard, Coskey, and Peters, in their diffident manner, did suggest that they affected the overall atmosphere in crucial ways. For one thing, the union's new negotiators noted the intense animosity and ill will that existed between Jack Finneran and his GCIU negotiating team and the *Union-Tribune* negotiators. After nearly ten years and over 100 futile sessions, the contract negotiators hated one another. All the original negotiators were

---

31. Rabbi Laurie Coskey, Interview with author, March 15, 2004.

32. Stephen Cushman, Interview with author, August 5, 2003.

33. Reverend Robert C. Ard, Interview with author, August 8, 2003.

34. Kent Peters, Interview with author, July 22, 2003.

"bruised, wounded, and bitter," in Coskey's words. Everyone concurred in this assessment. Jerry Butkiewicz remarked that the GCIU and *U-T* negotiators hated each other so much that they couldn't sit at a table and agree that the sky was blue. In the bargaining sessions, Coskey, Peters, and Ard toned things down by, in Coskey's words, "making nice," and by bringing a general sense of compassion to the process. In effect, they acknowledged the *U-T* participants' pain, stating outright, "this process has been awful for all of you." At the same time, they imparted a moral seriousness to the discussion, continually merging in their comments mundane contract issues with the language of justice, fairness, and equity. The ICWJ representatives came into the negotiating sessions talking about what was right, what was just for each party; Cushman could then follow with business sense, suggesting where the money could come from if the company agreed to particular contract provisions. Their presence had the effect of bearing witness and, in their account, of bringing a sense of humanity to the negotiating process. By continually posing the moral question of "what is the right thing to do?" Coskey, Peters, and Ard compelled the *U-T* negotiators to justify their proposals before the faith community. They thus succeeded in transforming a contract negotiation into a forum where the discourse of social justice held some sway.

This moral tone, especially embodied by Reverend Ard, had a particularly strong effect on pressroom manager Carlos Stovall. Stovall, a tough-minded African-American supervisor, had been brought in to bust the union, in Coskey's estimation. "But you could see that he was a good guy, and he seemed to care that the new GCIU negotiating team saw him as fair." According to Kent Peters, Stovall had stopped the harassment of pressroom workers on the shop floor. A man of faith, he prized the workers under him, and they had respect for him. Stovall was affected by Reverend Ard's presence. A large, deep-voiced African-American pastor, Reverend Ard projects, in Coskey's words, the sense that "God is watching you through his person." Ard acknowledged that Stovall and he struck up a relationship during the negotiating sessions. At the first session, Stovall was defensive, parroting the company's positions. He loosened up in the second session and supported a settlement because, in Ard's view, he saw that the faith participants were talking about the right things, and that they were not asking any more for the pressroom workers than was given to other *Union-Tribune* workers. The essential humanity of the issues was recognized.

Conclusion

In the end, the *Union-Tribune* – GCIU contract was similar to the company's last, best, and final offer, and thus can hardly be seen as an unequivocal victory on the part of the union. The union accepted the right of the company to hire part-time workers and it accepted merit pay over strict seniority system. In return, the company made several (albeit modest) concessions. But the key outcome was that the contract preserved the GCIU as the pressroom workers' legal bargaining agent – reversing ten years of the company's efforts to break the union.

Why did the *Union-Tribune* settle? In Jerry Butkiewicz's view, first, the company, like the union, was tired. Ten years of negotiations is a long time, and the GCIU had proved to be a formidable irritant, mobilizing the local labor movement and reaching out to the community in ways that the *U-T* found damaging to its reputation. While the subscription boycott and the "Something Stinks" campaign didn't have known, unambiguous effects on the *Union-Tribune's* circulation, they clearly had a negative effect on the company's public standing.[35] Second, the years of labor turmoil in the pressroom and the departure of significant numbers of skilled journeymen meant that paper wastage was up considerably. Finally, and perhaps most important, the reconstitution of the GCIU negotiating committee pulled three crucial groups to the table on labor's side, groups that need to be in place if labor is to succeed in this day and age: the community, in the form of the representatives from the Interfaith Committee for Worker Justice; advertisers, in the personage of Steve Cushman; and the united power of labor, in the form of active support from the Labor Council. Whether Cushman was in any way 'representative' of

---

35. The *Union-Tribune's* daily circulation slipped some 20,000-25,000 papers by the turn of the century, according to the Audit Bureau of Circulations. This drop isn't necessarily attributable to the boycott inasmuch as newspaper circulation in general has been declining as a long-term trend. Still, *Union-Tribune* circulation dropped even as the population of the San Diego metropolitan area had grown strongly. Whatever its precise impact on circulation, former Newspaper Guild local President Craig Rose asserted that the "Something Stinks" campaign did worry *Union-Tribune* management to the extent that the circulation department telemarketers were given a scripted response to read to subscribers who either called to cancel their subscriptions or who, when solicited to subscribe, asked about the ongoing labor strife. In contrast, the company's campaigns to boost circulation were notable failures.

advertisers needn't be addressed; the fact that a major advertiser sat at labor's side of the table in negotiations had to have a major psychological impact vis-à-vis *Union-Tribune* management.[36]

Two factors not elaborated by Butkiewicz but inherent to this analysis merit additional attention: the morality-based discourse brought to the negotiations by the ICWJ and the personal relationship and trust between Cushman and *Union-Tribune* CEO Gene Bell. The ICWJ's participation and its transformation of the negotiating dynamics could not *alone* have compelled the company to sign a contract. It is reasonable to conclude that the involvement of Stephen Cushman, given his peculiar position as a large advertiser and an associate of *Union-Tribune* CEO Gene Bell, was the single most important factor in getting the company to settle. But neither should the ICWJ's participation and its morality-based arguments be downplayed. The ICWJ not only transformed the nature of the talks, it altered their tone. The ICWJ's arguments established an ethical framework within which the give and take of interest-based demands and exercise of negotiating power took place. This is not to argue, naively, that the company responded sincerely to the ethical bid proffered by the ICWJ negotiators. The company, with the exception of pressroom manager Carlos Stovall, surely responded to the power politics of the moment. Given the peculiar array of groups and personalities negotiating for the pressroom workers, *Union-Tribune* management most likely saw its position as a probable public relations nightmare. The faith participants thus effectively parlayed their collective religious identity and their "interest-free" talk of social justice into a negotiating position of consequence: morality backed by coercion.[37] But the "conversion" of Carlos Stovall is a testament to the possibility that the faith participants' articulation of social justice *can* induce authentic reconsideration of position. Labor has lost the ability to speak credibly about social justice; faith-based organizations can do so.[38]

While the efficacy of religious community support in labor struggles should not be exaggerated, the resurrection of the social justice dimension of such struggles by groups such as the ICWJ can play an important part in those conflicts. Perhaps the key conclusion that can be drawn is that with the involvement of the faith-based community in a labor conflict it becomes possible to attract business and political figures – like Stephen Cushman – who would never get involved in such a conflict if it were only a union matter. Is the UT – GCIU story replicable? To what degree can a case study support a generalized conclusion? I think it is reasonable to propose that, while the specifics of participation will vary from situation to situation, the presence of religious leaders can be expected to open up space for the involvement of important non-labor actors on labor's side.

And nothing succeeds like success. One consequence for the ICWJ following its role in the *Union-Tribune* – GCIU contract negotiation was a new gravity in its participation in other labor disputes. The organization played an active role in the successful 2002-03 county Justice For Janitors struggle, and its efforts on behalf of janitors working at the seven Westfield America shopping malls in San Diego County concluded in the workers signing a favorable contract in March 2004.[39] Indeed, according to Donald Cohen, it was the ICWJ that ended the two-and-a-half-year fight to win union agreements at the Westfield malls. SEIU local 1877 had pulled back on the campaign; the ICWJ, after adopting the janitors, did not. They held more than 30 prayer vigils and sent delegations to management at the various Westfield properties. Rabbi Coskey addressed the Jewish-Australian Lowy family, owner of Westfield, and applied a religious-inflected public pressure and helped leverage an international morality-based campaign against the company. The Westfield campaign featured another organization, in part faith-based, the Los Angeles Progressive Jewish Alliance, which mobilized over 80 rabbis to sign a letter to Lowy arguing in favor of the unionization of janitors based on Talmudic interpretation of labor

---

36. Jerry Butkiewicz, Interview with author, August 27, 2003.

37. Because *Union-Tribune* employees declined to speak, the author concedes that the direct evidence for this conclusion is insubstantial. The point is that all the other evidence points to the conclusion as reasonable and, indeed, likely.

38. Reinhold Niebuhr's analysis in *Moral Man and Immoral Society* seems apt here: "Furthermore there must always be a religious element in the hope of a just society. Without the ultrarational hopes and passions of religion no society will ever have the courage to conquer despair and attempt the impossible; for the vision of a just society is an impossible

---

one, which can be approximated only by those who do not regard it as impossible. The truest visions of religion are illusions, which may be partially realized by being resolutely believed. For what religion believes to be true is not wholly true but ought to be true; and may become true if its truth is not doubted." Niebuhr, *Moral Man and Immoral Society: A Study in Ethics and Politics*: 81.

39. Michael Kinsman, "Mall Janitors Approve Labor Pacts," *San Diego Union-Tribune* (March 17, 2004): C3.

and justice. And unlike the GCIU – *Union-Tribune* intervention, the Westfield campaign featured no "enlightened capitalist" or "class traitor" such as Stephen Cushman; the faith-based organizations succeeded on their own. More recently, the San Diego ICWJ was a behind-the-scenes player in the lawsuit filed in March 2004 against Neighborhood House Association for cheating hundreds of its workers out of overtime pay. And ICWJ, along with CPI and the Labor Council, was one of the key players in the successful effort that galvanized the San Diego City Council to adopt a living wage ordinance in April 2005.[40] Local union leaders now try to leverage ICWJ's support and its morality-based arguments in negotiations with employers. ICWJ's involvement changes the nature of negotiations, according to Bridget Browning, lead organizer for the Hotel Employees and Restaurant Employees San Diego local. Management is more respectful of the workers and the workers feel more secure, more convinced in the righteousness of their cause and thus more apt to persevere.[41] In sum, if the San Diego experience is representative of an emerging alliance between labor and faith-based organizations such as ICWJ, the labor movement has much to gain from these new coalitions. Religious organizations have much to gain as well, but that is the subject for another paper.

40. Jennifer Vigil, "City Council Adopts Living Wage Ordinance," *San Diego Union-Tribune* (April 13, 2005): B1.

41. Bridget Browning, Telephone interview with author, March 31, 2004.

The Church, the Union and the Trinity

Rev. Darren Cushman Wood, Speedway United Methodist Church, Indianapolis, IN (2007)

Hired Hands

"The attitude of the employer is that we are just the 'hands' that they can use up, discard, and replace. We feel that we are at the mercy of management because they can change policies at a moment's whim, without consulting us, the workers. That's why we formed a union – so that management would have to meet with us as equals across a bargaining table and discuss our working, as well as wages and benefits."[1]

These sentiments of Tony Ogundiran expressed his and his coworkers concerns about their employer, Walker Methodist Health Center. Ogundiran, a Licensed Practical Nurse (LPN), had worked for Walker for eight years when he and his coworkers elected the American Federation of State, County and Municipal Employees (AFSCME) to represent them in two separate elections in May and July of 2003.

The run-up to the elections had been marked by management engaging in a series of "union avoidance" tactics which have become commonplace in American business: firing pro-union employees; harassment of pro-union workers; one-on-one meetings with employees to scrutinize their union sympathies; and requiring Registered Nurses (RNs) to convey anti-union sentiment. Management attempted to prevent key union leaders from voting. (In this case, the drive was led by the LPNs. The union relented and allowed for a second, separate vote by the LPNs.) They distributed anti-union literature, used an attorney who directed their anti-union strategies, and held mandatory meetings in which management expresses their opposition to unions (known as "captive audience meetings"). In one such meeting, management showed an anti-union videotape which included film footage of the violence during the 1934 Minneapolis Teamsters strike.

 AFSCME won the first election with over 60 percent of the vote, but management immediately appealed the results to the National Labor Relations Board (NLRB). This appeal caused the results of the second election to be sealed, but it was widely believed that the union won that election by an even higher percentage. The appeals process dragged on even though the regional labor board sided with the union on numerous occasions. Management kept appealing to Washington in hopes of getting a favorable ruling. Other cases around the country had been filling the docket, which, if the Washington board would rule in favor of management in those cases, might create a new legal context for Walker's case. However, the backlog has been so enormous that the net effect was that the appeals languished for years. It was a classic strategy of playing out the clock in the hope that pro-union employees would become discouraged or be fired.

During this time the Minnesota Annual Conference of the United Methodist Church passed two resolutions in support of the workers calling on Walker to end all appeals, recognize the votes, and negotiate in good faith. Walker, which is one of the largest nursing homes in Minnesota, has historic and informal ties to the annual conference, and symbolically represents the church. Formally, the board of directors includes the bishop as an ex officio member.

In the Spring of 2007 – four years after the original votes – the regional board took up the appeals once again and ruled in favor of AFSCME. In turn, Walker finally agreed to enter into negotiations for a first contract. As of the writing of this paper, a first contract has not been signed.

* * *

This story is representative of a larger crisis of workers' rights in America and the dilemma it poses for faith bodies who are both direct employers as well as indirect employers through church-related institutions. Walker is not unique within the United Methodist Church or other denominations. Over the past 30 years, "union avoidance" strategies have become the automatic reaction of the business community.[2] An

---

1. Testimony to the Concern for Workers Task Force, General Board of Church and Society and General Board of Global Ministries of The United Methodist Church, Tampa, Florida, November 21, 2003. For information concerning the task force see *The 2004 Book of Resolutions*, resolution 220.

2. For a survey of anti-union practices see Lance Compa, *Unfair Advantage: Workers' Freedom of Association in the United States under International Human Rights Standards* (Human Rights Watch, 2000); John Logan, "Consultants, Lawyers, and the 'Union Free' Movement in the USA since the 1970s," *Industrial Relations Journal* 33:3 (2002); Darren Cushman Wood, *Blue Collar Jesus: How Christianity Supports Workers Rights* (Seven Locks Press, 2005), chapter 2.

anti-union culture has emerged in corporate America which erases the post-World War II labor-management détente and renews an antagonism which is reminiscent of the Gilded Age. The attack on workers' rights is seen in a series of tactics, of which Walker is a typical example, that is driven by a multimillion dollar industry of union-avoidance consulting firms and attorneys. These tactics take advantage of the inherent flaws in the National Labor Relations Act, which has governed labor relations since 1935. Under the Bush administration, labor law has been severely strained by pro-business rulings overturning established case law. The net effect is that millions of workers have lost the right to organize and union elections resemble elections in Third World countries.[3]

Church-related institutions have been swept into this anti-union trend. These institutions rely upon the same organizational and business practices as their secular counterparts in order to maintain their professional standards and economic efficiency. But this unquestioned acceptance of our "culture" makes it very difficult to take a different path when faced with unionization. The anti-union prejudices in society combined with the anemic social teachings of their denominations make it nearly impossible for the leaders of these institutions to see an alternative.

It would be easy to conclude that this is only a problem for mainline Protestant denominations who have easily accepted societies' norms, but the same problems occur within more conservative Protestant and Roman Catholic traditions. The weight of paternalism, the unintended consequences of a "distinction of spheres of influence" or of "a spiritual-material dichotomy," and the presuppositions of social class among white-collar church leaders all combine to support anti-union managerial practices in their programs and institutions as well.

Workers' rights refer to three interrelated activities among workers. First, there is the right to just compensation, which includes wages and benefits. Second, there is the right to dignity and safety in the workplace. The right to leisure is derived from these two fundamental rights. Third, there is the right to organize collectively in order to express needs and concerns. This last right includes joining a labor union,

union representation in a grievance procedure, and collective bargaining. It also includes the right to engage in strikes and other forms of protest and political activity in order to secure the first two rights. By definition, then, the issue of workers' rights includes the question of labor unions. One cannot talk about workers' rights without affirming the right to engage in union activity.[4] The purpose of this paper is to explore the theological dimensions of the third set of workers' rights, namely the nature and role of labor unions.

The crisis raises serious questions. How can the church maintain its integrity in its relationship with workers? It goes without saying that the church should support workers' rights. But what should be the church's relationship with labor unions, which seek to promote those rights within the church? If the church needs to reform its employment practices in order to restore its integrity, what then is the role (if any) for a labor union in this process? Is the union a mere troublemaker causing conflict or is it an instrument of the Holy Spirit? If the union is a tool of divine providence, then what becomes of the unique role of the church in God's salvation of the world? In short, theologically speaking, what is a labor union? By extension, what is the theological basis for workers' rights?

The theological questions are more than a quandary over getting the right words in an ethical statement. This crisis also raises the question of what will enable the leadership of the church to discern what is the right response to this crisis in order to restore the integrity of the church. Any theological explanation of the relationship between the church and organized labor must also explain how the Spirit works in us. It must be more than just an exercise in theological ethics; it must describe and encourage the kind of spirituality that compels and directs the church and its leadership to act.

Just as these questions are imposed on us by the crisis of workers' rights, the answer to these questions is informed by the current state of organized labor in the United States. Currently, only seven percent of the private sector is unionized and when public sector employees are included twelve percent of American

---

3. For an overview of recent changes in American labor law, see The Honorable George Miller, *Workers' Rights Under Attack by Bush Administration* (Committee on Education and the Workforce, U.S. House of Representatives, http://edworkforce.house.gov/committee/publications/NLRBreport071306.pdf).

4. For an extended explanation of workers' rights, see Compa, p. 6-7; *Blue Collar Jesus*, chapter 1; Darren Cushman Wood, "To the Leadership of Peabody Energy and the United Mine Workers of America," 17 January 2007, letter for Interfaith Worker Justice; and Darren Cushman Wood, "The Idolatry of Helping the Poor," *Insights* Spring (2006): 21-24. See also *The Universal Declaration of Human Rights*, articles 23 and 24.

workers are union members, the lowest rate of unionization since the 1920s. Unionization still provides economic advantages for workers, but except for a few isolated situations most labor unions face an identity crisis. They are struggling to overcome internal problems of organization, strategy and vision. Since the election of John Sweeney as President of the AFL-CIO in 1995, organized labor has been searching for new direction. We are in a new era of labor history but it remains to be seen whether labor will successfully respond to this crisis.

Thus, this paper does not grant labor unions uncritical acceptance. Unlike an earlier generation of Social Gospelers, who might have romanticized progressive social movements, there is no way anyone can wax eloquent about the American labor movement. On the other hand, this paper presupposes that withdrawal is not an option. One cannot romanticize the church as a place or a people which are above or beyond the pale of sinful economic practices. I have met too many sinners in the union hall and in the sanctuary, and any theological assessment must acknowledge both.

Mouthpiece for Social Justice

According to United Methodist social teachings the problem with Walker Methodist should have been cut and dry. *The Social Principles* declare that we believe "in the right of employers and employees … to engage in collective bargaining," and in a series of resolutions *The Book of Resolutions* spells out how these matters should be handled.[5] But that did not stop management or encourage the religious leaders on the board of directors to do the right thing. *The Social Principles* and the resolutions only express what we believe but they do not fully explain why we believe it. Even less, they do not motivate anyone to do the right thing. Thus, they are a typical example of the paucity of Protestant reflections on workers' rights.

In order to discover a theological understanding of labor unions one must begin with Catholic social teachings because they are by far the most extensive reflections on the subject. For over 100 years, the Roman Catholic perspective developed through three main encyclicals: *Rerum Novarum, Quadragesimo Anno,* and *Laborem Exercens*. Each were responding to the challenges of their day – Leo XIII wrote *Rerum Novarum* in response to industrialization and the rise of socialism in Europe in 1891; Pius XI penned *Quadragesimo Anno* at the height of the Great Depression and in response to Communism in 1931; and John Paul II issued *Laborem Exercens* in 1981, in part as an affirmation of Solidarity in Poland.[6] It is essential to read all three together because Pius and John Paul's letters build upon and update *Rerum Novarum*. The Vatican II document *Gaudium et Spes* plays an important role in *Laborem Exercens* and as such needs to be referenced.

Throughout the tradition, labor unions have been affirmed and supported. Leo writes that "workers associations ought to be so constituted and so governed as to furnish the most suitable and most convenient means to attain … an increase in the goods of body, of soul, and of prosperity." *Quadragesimo Anno* speaks of "the innate right of forming unions" and that they are "glad signs of coming social reconstruction." And John Paul declares in *Laborem Exercens* that labor unions are "an indispensable *element of social life*" and that "they are indeed *a mouthpiece for the struggle for social justice.*"[7]

This affirmation of organized labor presupposes a particular understanding of work that is outlined in the encyclicals. Their understanding of work is grounded in Genesis One and the *imago Dei*. "The soul bears the express image and likeness of God," states *Rerum Novarum*, "and there resides in it that sovereignty through the medium of which man has been bidden to rule all created nature below him."[8] Even though work enables human domination of the earth, as com-

---

5. Resolution 237, "Rights of Workers" and resolution 238, "The Right to Organize and Bargain Collectively," *The Book of Resolutions of The United Methodist Church 2004* (The United Methodist Publishing House, 2004) 591-596. "The Economic Community," 163.B, "The Social Principles," *The Book of Discipline of The United Methodist Church 2004* (The United Methodist Publishing House, 2004)115.

6. John Paul II sought to give direction to Solidarity in Poland. He drew from the French personalist Emmanuel Mounier and German phonomenologists such as Max Scheler to offer an alternative to the Marxist interpretation of work. Gregory Baum, *The Priority of Labor* (Paulist Press, 1982) 15-19.

7. *Rerum Novarum 76; Quadragesimo Anno* I.3 and III.3; *Laborem Exercens* 20. Echoing this is Vatican II, "Among the basic rights of the human person is to be numbered the right of freely founding unions for working people. These should be able truly to represent them and to contribute to the organizing of economic life in the right way. Included is the right of freely taking part in the activity of these unions without risk of reprisal." *Gaudium et Spes* II.68. Herein after, *Rerum Novarum* – RN; *Quadragesimo Anno* – QA, *Gaudium et Spes* – GS, and *Laborem Exercens* – LE.

8. RN 57 and QA, II.2. See also, GS I.34 and II.67.

manded in Genesis, this is a part of God's ordering of creation. The *imago Dei* is an intrinsic part of this ordering. It is applicable for each human being while it is expressed uniquely by each human being.[9]

Each encyclical describes the dynamics of work by referring to dual aspects of labor based on the *imago Dei*. *Rerum Novarum* describes the two marks of work, which are "implanted by nature," as personal and necessary. Labor is "personal," which means that work belongs to the individual who did it and that it is an act of free will. But if this is the only dimension of labor then it leaves the worker vulnerable to being compensated at a rate which will not sustain life. Work is "necessary" in order to preserve the worker's life (and by extension his or her family members who are dependent upon him or her), and so this demands that work be compensated at a rate which will enable the worker (and his or her family) to live. Work has individual and social dimensions according to Pius, and thus the fruits of our labor should contribute to the common good.[10]

In *Laborem Exercens* work has an objective dimension, insofar as work changes "objects" (broadly defined) and produces new ones. But there is also a subjective dimension to work. As an expression of the image of God, a person is "a subjective being capable of acting in a planned and rational way ... with a tendency toward self-realization. ... *As a person, man is therefore the subject of work.*" This subjective dimension gives work an inherent ethical dimension.[11]

The natural revelation of work as defined by the *imago Dei* is confirmed by the witness of the Incarnation. The Incarnation affirms, according to *Laborem Exercens*, that "the primary basis of the value of work is man himself." Christianity introduced a new understanding of work infused with dignity because God in Christ Jesus spent most of his life engaged in manual labor. Leo states, "Although he was the Son of God and God Himself, yet he willed to seem and to be thought the son of a carpenter; nay, he even did not disdain to spend a great part of his life at the work of a carpenter" (see Mark 6:3). From this "Divine example" come two conclusions: poverty is not a sin or a result of sin, but that the poor have dignity because Christ came as a poor carpenter. *Gaudium et Spes* draws out the conclusions when it declares that God in the Incarnation has united with all of humanity. Because the particular form of the Incarnation is the carpenter Jesus, the dignity, equality and freedom of our work is rooted in his Incarnation. From this John Paul extrapolates how salvation and vocation are experienced in the realm of work, which he calls "the gospel of work."

Whether it is John Paul's "gospel of work" or Pius' literalist Jesus the carpenter, the dignity of labor comes from the *imago Dei* as confirmed by the Incarnation. The dignity of labor is further defined by four related principles which flow from and help qualify this definition of work.

First, there is the principle of the priority of labor. Implied in the other letters, *Laborem Exercens* makes explicit use of this term. "*The principle of the priority of labor* over capital is a postulate of the order of social morality" and "*the adequate and fundamental criterion* for shaping the whole economy."[12] This principle is derived from the primacy of the subjective dimension. It is "*the primacy of man over things*" because labor is the "efficient cause" while capital – the objective dimension of work (i.e. "objects") – is merely the instrument of the cause.[13]

The priority of labor becomes the basis for the critique of capitalism. All the encyclicals reject laissez-faire capitalism. For Leo, it is because it does not honor the necessary dimension of labor, and for John Paul it inverts the priority of labor and makes capital the subject. Free market capitalism creates a "materialistic economism" which treats the worker as a mere "instrument of production."[14]

The principle of the priority of labor points to the second principle: a just wage. Beginning in *Rerun Novarum*, Roman Catholic social teaching declares that there is "an element of natural justice ... that the wage shall not be less than enough to support a worker who is thrifty and upright." Rejected is the assumption that

9. LE 4.

10. QA II.4.

11. LE 6.

12. LE 15 and 17.

13. LE 12.

14. LE 7; RN 62; see also, QA II.5. The encyclicals chart a course between capitalism and socialism/communism. RN condemns socialism, as does QA, which lumps it together with communism and sees "Christian socialism" as an oxymoron. All of the letters defend private property as long as it is not an end in itself and contributes to a just wage and the common good. Only after Paul VI in *Populorum Progressio* is the option of a modified form of socialism acceptable, but clearly even as early as RN the vision of a cooperative economy has affinity with democratic socialism.

the only basis for setting wages is whether the amount has been freely agreed upon between the employer and the employee or by the market place. *Quadragesimo Anno* explains that "the wage-scale must be regulated with a view to the economic welfare of the whole person." A just wage is defined by the amount that is needed to support the worker's entire family, which, for John Paul, also includes other benefits such as health care, pension and disability insurance.[15]

Third, the principle of a just wage supports the principle of the common good. For *Laborem Exercens,* the just wage "is the concrete means of *verifying the justice* of the whole socioeconomic system" because the concept includes "various social benefits" which contribute to the welfare of the entire society.[16] It contributes to the good of society because it enables workers and their families to fully participate in society and to achieve human fulfillment. According to Pius, the common good is violated by a handful of elite owners who claim too much while their employees starve, but it is also violated by radical worker movements which claim that they have the right to all wealth.[17]

Finally, the common good is maintained when society is organized around the principle of the cooperative society. *Quadragesimo Anno* envisions society as "a truly social and organic body" which, according to natural law, reflects "mutual harmony and mutual support."[18] Society will be hierarchically ordered based on vocations or functions rather than incomes. While *Rerum Novarum* and *Laborem Exercens* share this harmonious view of society, they do not elaborate on the stratification as Pius does. John Paul states that "in no way can labor be opposed to capital or capital to labor" and "still less can the actual people behind these concepts be opposed to each other."[19] All of them state that capital (in this case, a reference to owners and managers) and labor cannot be separated from each other and thus one cannot receive all of the profits to the exclusion of the other.

---

15. RN 63 & 20; QA II.4.c; LE 19.

16. LE 19.

17. QA II.5.

18. QA II.4.

19. LE 12. It should be noted that there is a subtle but qualitative shift in the use of the term "capital" in both *Laborem Exercens* and *Quadragesimo Anno.* At times, it refers to the products of human labor and at other times it refers to a social class of managers and owners. For example, see LE 11 and 12.

Because harmony is at the fundamental core of society, the encyclicals see class conflict as an aberration. In contrast to Marxism, the conflict is not the inevitable product of historical forces or an essential aspect of the relationship between capital and labor. It cannot be if capital (the "objects" of labor) is nothing more than the sum of human labor. This is not to say that the conflict is not real. It is a "capital evil" as Leo states and a violation of "sacred law" according to Pius because one group is excluding the other group from their fair share of the profits.[20]

Where does the conflict come from? "The conflict originated in the fact that the workers put their powers at the disposal of the entrepreneurs, and these, following the principle of maximum profit, tried to establish the lowest possible wages for the work done by the employees." It was caused by owners and managers acting solely on the principles of "economism" (materialism) and not honoring or seeing the priority of labor as the subject of work.[21]

Thus, the real issue is the question of how capital is *used* and not the question of ownership. Regardless of who owns it, unless the subjective side of work is primary, capital will be misused. By not making the ownership question the primary focus, it allows John Paul to be able to critique both the Communist and capitalist systems, a dual criticism which is supported in varying degrees by the other encyclicals.[22]

The reality of class conflict necessitates a role for the state to intervene in the economy. According to *Rerum Novarum,* labor laws, regulations and arbitration are legitimate activities of the state to "protect equitably each and every class of citizens" in order to maintain distributive justice.[23]

But the state is not the sole unifying institution for society. An organic, harmonious society is comprised of a variety of other organizations and institutions which play a necessary role in maintaining the common good. Pius calls this the principle of "subsidiarity."[24]

At the heart of this variegated and harmonious view of society stands the family. The well-being of the family becomes the criterion for evaluating the relations of various societal entities and their functioning.

---

20. RN 28 and QA II.2.

21. LE 11.

22. Baum, *The Priority of Labor,* 25, 46.

23. RN 49. See also RN 54.

24. QA II.2.

Just as the standard of workplace justice was established in the holy family (Jesus learning his trade from his father), the legitimation of labor unions comes from their contribution to the welfare of the family.

When the encyclicals' understanding of work is combined with these four principles one can see why John Paul called labor unions a *"mouthpiece for the struggle for social justice."*

Drawing upon Aquinas, *Rerum Novarum* and *Quadragesimo Anno* see labor unions as legitimate organizations within an organic and harmonious society. Leo writes that they spring from a "natural propensity" to "form private societies." Because they are a natural right, the state should not outlaw their existence. Pius speaks of "vocational groups" that are social bodies composed of individuals in the same trade or occupations. At times the language is confusing, because it implies that both employees and employers are a part of the group, but Pius acknowledges that there are times when employers and employees must divide into separate groups for "protection against opposing interests."[25]

The most elaborate description of a labor union is found in *Laborem Exercens*. Because forms of work continue to change and because of the ever-present threats to the principles of the priority of labor and a just wage, "there is a need for ever new *movements of solidarity of* the workers and *with* the workers. ... The Church is firmly committed to this cause, for she considers it her mission, her service, a proof of her fidelity to Christ."[26]

Unions are not simply a reflection of class conflict. Labor solidarity is not an historical inevitability. It originates in conscious human efforts to oppose injustice, which reflect the subjective dimension of work. It is the struggle to restore the priority of labor over capital in society, and as such it is the struggle for social justice. "This struggle should be seen as a normal endeavor," for dignity and not just a struggle against an enemy.[27] It will be conflictual but the conflict must always be seen in the light of the goal of a greater common good.

Laborem Exercens posits an even more basic rationale for labor unions in the nature of work itself. "It is characteristic of work that it first and foremost unites

people. [It is] the power to build a community" among the workers and managers. But this unity does not negate the necessity for labor unions; rather, it brings to light their necessity when the workers' needs are denied in that community of work:

> *In the light of this fundamental structure of* all work – in the light of the fact that, in the final analysis, labor and capital are indispensable components of the process of production in any social system – it is clear that, even if it is because of their work needs that people unite to secure their rights, their union remains a constructive factor of *social order* and *solidarity,* and it is impossible to ignore it.[28]

John Paul presupposes the priority of labor in this relationship; he regards economism as an inversion of that relationship and the source of the conflict. Labor unions are *"a mouthpiece for the struggle for social justice"* because they are a necessary corrective to the sin of materialism, and the providence of God can use labor unions to contribute to the common good.[29]

All the encyclicals recognize the right of workers to form unions, but with that right come responsibilities. Just as employers have a responsibility to provide a just wage, safety and dignity, the employee must "perform entirely and conscientiously whatever work has been voluntarily and equitably agreed upon" and "to refrain from violence" in resolving conflicts.[30]

For all of the encyclicals, dialogue is the first step toward resolving labor disputes, but the affirmation of strikes varies. Pius states that "strikes and lock-outs are forbidden." Instead, arbitration by the state is the only solution. John Paul sees strikes as "a kind of ultimatum" which are "legitimate in the proper conditions and within just limits" as long as they do not threaten the common good of society as a whole. In a similar vein, *Gaudium et Spes* says that strikes are "a necessary, though ultimate, means for the defense of the workers' own rights and the fulfillment of their just desires."[31]

Both *Rerum Novarum* and *Quadragesimo Anno* envision the creation of "catholic unions" but permit Catholics to join secular trade unions as long as those

---

25. RN 72 and QA II.5.

26. LE 8.

27. LE 20.

28. Ibid.

29. Ibid.

30. RN 30.

31. QA II.5; LE 20; GS II.68. Oddly enough, in light of Solidarity in Poland, John Paul opposes strikes for political purposes.

unions allow for associations to be formed which will provide religious instruction to their Catholic members, "that these in turn may impart to the labor unions to which they belong the upright sprit which should direct their entire conduct. Thus will these unions exert a beneficent influence far beyond the ranks of their own members." Throughout the encyclicals there is affirmation for union participation and leadership as a legitimate Christian vocation.[32]

Transcripts of the Trinity

One could cite a number of problems with the encyclicals' description of work and society. First, the encyclicals do not acknowledge the qualitative difference between suffering caused by unjust working conditions and the hardships associated with the struggle for economic justice, and this failure can imply that the former is as ordained by God as the latter. We see this in John Paul's "gospel of work." *Laborem Exercens* is correct to trace a connection between the cross and human toil, which is caused by sin embodied in and channeled through economic exploitation. But the encyclical comes close to supporting the view that the worker should suffer quietly because Jesus suffered crucifixion. Insofar as it relies upon *Gaudium et Spes* it avoids this conclusion.

However, it would have been helpful if the encyclical was more specific: When we endure the toil of working for social justice we work in union with Christ for us and we collaborate with the Son of God for the redemption of humanity. Also, the encyclical implies that any form of toil is analogous to the cross. It fails to distinguish the voluntary suffering of the cross from the involuntary suffering of exploitation, leaving open the misidentification of the cross with acquiescence. Even though all kinds of labor are capable of embodying the "gospel of work," not all kinds of jobs can do this.

Second, John Paul (along with Pius and Leo) does not acknowledge that there may be some forms of work whose objective side makes them immoral per se, such as the production of cigarettes. The absence of this kind of prohibition leads one to assume that all occupations can be an expression of divine vocation.

Third, there is also a problem that stems from the overemphasis on the cooperative view of society. At times there is a naive trust in the state to be a neutral arbiter of labor disputes and an inability to acknowledge that the state is often an ally of capital. There is a seeming unwillingness to explore the extent and complexity of original sin in social structures. This is reflected in the ambiguous use of the term "capital" in *Laborem Exercens*. While class conflict should not be the norm, given the structural nature of the conflict it is more entrenched than the encyclicals seem willing to acknowledge.

Yet, these deficiencies can be corrected with a proper understanding of and emphasis on the other principles in the encyclicals – the principle of the common good and just compensation as a measure of that good; the defense of labor unions as legitimate associations within society. The history of Catholic labor activism in the United States bears this out. Time and again, Catholic leaders such as John Ryan, Charles Owens Rice and Vigil Michel interpreted and applied these papal letters in this manner.[33]

The principles in the letters (and the potential tensions that exist among them) are held together by the concept of natural law. In order to appeal to the widest audience, these letters posit work within the framework of natural law as reflected in Genesis One and the *imago Dei*. The Incarnation is evoked, but in many respects it often reads either like simple literalism or as an appendage.[34] Since the definition of a labor union is derived from their definitions of work, the justification for organized labor can be traced back to natural law.

---

32. QA I.3

33. RN influenced the creation of the Militia for Christ, which attempted to support and influence the AFL, and it inspired Msg. John Ryan to enter the priesthood. Later, QA was seen as a vindication of Ryan's ideas and activities. QA and RN were often used by Father Charles Owen Rice, "the Chaplain of the CIO," and Father John P. Boland, chairman of the New York State Labor Relations Board in the 1930s. It also gave inspiration and direction to the creation of the Association of Catholic Trade Unionists during the Great Depression, and both letters were used by Catholic trade unionists, such as Philip Murray, president of the United Mine Workers of America. See Neil Betten, *Catholic Activism and the Industrial Worker* (University Presses of Florida, 1976) 35, 41, 77, 85, and 113.

34. For an example of a literalist use of the Incarnation, see RN 37. There is a sense in which Jesus the carpenter is an appendage to John Paul's central definition of work in the way the letter is structured. *Laborem Exercens* lays out an extensive definition of work in the beginning of the letter utilizing solely natural law and only at the very end of the letter does it refer to the Incarnation. This may have been done in order for the letter to speak to the widest possible (secular) audience. See LE 24-27. In contrast, see GS I.22, 41 and II.67 for an example of the Incarnation playing a central role.

But the reliance on natural law, when combined with an acceptance of economics as an autonomous "science" of "facts," weakens the Church's teachings. The net result has been that the teachings can be used by all parties to justify their positions. The encyclicals attempt to speak to a broad audience beyond the Church, but, according to Stephen Long, in doing this they "did not develop out of specifically theological language capable of forming people within the church."[35] This broad appeal gave too much ground to modernist presuppositions, which assumed that the social sciences operate in a realm that is autonomous from theological virtues. As long as Catholic social teaching acknowledges that the natural can only be understood in light of the Gospel, then it can provide a compelling alternative economic vision. Only then do the church's teachings have the potential to form its members and institutions with this vision. But when it fails to do this the Church, its members and institutions, will tend to reproduce the false distinction between theology and economics that leaves the Church vulnerable to being taken captive by the values of the marketplace.[36]

Grounding the encyclicals' teachings in the Trinity enables us to avoid these problems and to place the nature and role of labor unions on more solid ground. The *imago Dei*, from which the definitions of work and workers rights spring, is best understood in light of the Trinity. A Charles Wesley hymn affirms that we are "ordained to be Transcripts of the Trinity."[37] As such, a trinitarian perspective affirms the purpose as well as challenges the role of organized labor in society.

In recent years, several theologians have explored the ethical dimensions of "social trinitarianism." Even though there are many variations, they follow the same logic of identifying the unity of the Persons of the Trinity and then looking for its correspondence in the human experience. Social trinitarian thinking makes the assumption that doctrine can and must be interpreted in light of its pragmatic value. M. Douglas Meeks' *God the Economist* is the best example of this for describing how the Trinity affirms the role of labor unions in society.

Meeks describes the doctrine of the Trinity as "a kind of logic of God's economy that creates access to livelihood by the gifting of God's righteousness, which is God's power for life."[38] For him, the doctrine enables us to "demythologize" the ideologies that justify exploitation. He points out that at the same time that market society was emerging, the doctrine of the Trinity was being labeled as pure speculation. In contrast, however, the Trinity is the proper name of God and as such it identifies where our loyalties lie in the modern economy. In contrast, when the concept of God remains a formal, empty concept then we can pour into it any justification for the economic status quo.

In speaking about ideologies which seek to legitimize dehumanizing work, Meeks states that when the doctrine of God is described in monistic terms it has "sometimes aided the camouflage of work ideologies, making them seem common sensical assumptions, generally agreed upon."[39] In contrast, the Trinity, as "the economic community of righteousness," provides us with a hermeneutic for critically assessing current patterns of work as well as for affirming ethical principles for work. From it, he derives four hermeneutical principles for critiquing ideologies of work.

The first principle demonstrates how the Trinity affirms *distinctive personal work*. The triune God's work of creation and salvation is common to all the Persons of the Trinity, but each one's work is distinctive ("proper") in relation to each other. Meeks concludes from this concept of "appropriation" that the Trinity affirms the unique worth of each person's vocation, and that "the Trinity is a criticism of all systems of work that exclude some people in the household from distinctive personal work."[40]

The second principle comes from the Trinity as a model of *cooperative* work. Each Person of the Trinity works in unity with the others for the common purpose of salvation. Each Person's work "coinheres in the work of the other members of the community" and is made possible by the cooperation inherent in the Trinity. Meeks concludes that "the Trinity is a criticism of all structures of work that atomize the worker by separating his or her work from the other members of the community, the worker from the product of his or her

---

35. *Divine Economy: Theology and the Market* (Routledge, 2000) p. 185.

36. Ibid., p. 209. See also, p. 217.

37. *A Collection of Hymns for a People Called Methodist, The Works of John Wesley: The Bicentennial Edition*, vol. VII (Abingdon Press), Hymn 7.

38. *God the Economist: The Doctrine of God and Political Economy* (Fortress Press, 1989), p. 70.

39. Ibid., p. 130.

40. Ibid., p. 133.

work, or working classes from nonworking classes."[41]

The third principle derives from the *egalitarian* quality of the triune relationships. Because there is no "hierarchy or stratification of work within the divine community" there can be no religious justification for "an authoritarian order of subordination for human work." Meeks goes on to summarize that "the Trinity is a criticism of all forms of work that incur relationships of domination."[42]

The fourth principle is the *self-giving* love inherent in the work of the triune God. God's unity is not maintained by uniformity or coercion but is expressed as sacrificial and life-affirming love. And so, the Trinity stands in judgment of all ideologies which seek to cover up or justify coercion and greed.

While he does not discuss labor unions, it is not difficult to see how these four principles enable us to see their relationship with the Trinity. When labor unions are a vehicle for resisting domination, coercion and greed (principles three and four), they reflect the triune God. When they perpetuate exploitation through corruption and violence, they too stand in judgment of the doctrine of the Trinity.

These principles provide a critique of the union-busting strategies of corporations. Such strategies are attempts to make invisible the collective identity of workers (the second principle) and to suppress the impulse of the image of the triune God. Behind this is the belief that the only form of community in the workplace should be the relationship of the individual worker to and through the corporation. Even if the corporation encourages cooperative forms of work (e.g. work-sharing schemes, work teams, etc.), the only forms of solidarity which are deemed legitimate are ones which are authorized or created by the corporation itself. On a smaller scale, this is seen in businesses in which the proprietor believes that he or she should determine whether or not his or her employees can join a union. Yet, the dynamic of power is the same on a larger, bureaucratic scale. In short, the company becomes the sole expression of human solidarity and as such it becomes a form of idolatry.

This is not to suggest that the modern corporation per se is idolatrous. Not all corporations are alike, in terms of either practices or governance. The case can be made in Catholic social teaching that the modern corporation can be a legitimate expression of a community of work which honors the image of the triune God in and among all its employees. However, the Trinity problematizes the corporation when the corporation seeks to be the sole expression of the *imago Dei*.

Up to this point, the legitimacy of labor unions has been based solely on the need to overcome injustice. For example, even when John Paul speaks of work as community his justification for labor unions is because they are a "mouthpiece for social justice." In essence, their existence is dependent upon a prior deficiency in the community of work, which implies that if this deficiency did not exist there would be no need for workers to organize themselves. Certainly, the desire to establish justice is a reflection of the triune God whose being is one of equality and unity.

However, the desire and necessity for worker solidarity is more than the impulse to rectify injustice. Beneath or saturated in this desire is the need to find fulfillment in community. When unions create solidarity among workers and enable people to participate in the economy, they reflect the values of the Trinity (Meeks' first and second principles). As "transcripts of the Trinity," our identity and existence finds completion in communities of love and justice. Woodie Wilson, a retired coal miner and Baptist preacher, expressed this to me at a Black Lung Association meeting: "I didn't join the union because I needed a job or more money. I could always get work, but I saw the union as a way for me to follow the Golden Rule." Even if a corporation does not exhibit unjust labor practices, the solidarity among workers is a legitimate expression of community which reflects the triune God. For example, this solidarity has taken the form of skill development through apprenticeship programs and benevolences for injured workers and their families.

When unions fail to create solidarity among workers and prevent some workers from full participation in the economy, the Trinity stands in judgment of the labor movement. Throughout labor history this has been seen in jurisdictional disputes and the perpetuation of racism and sexism within the ranks of organized labor. More recently, it is seen in timidity toward organizing, the lack of coherent strategies for organizing, and inadequate training for its members.

A trinitarian understanding of the *imago Dei* affirms the desire of workers to organize themselves into unions for the purpose of collective action both for resistance to injustice and for the establishment of community.

---

41. Ibid., p. 133.

42. Ibid., p. 133-134.

Yet, social trinitarianism runs the risk of misusing the Trinity as if the doctrine can be used to justify any number of human relationships which are mutually exclusive. For example, the Trinity is used by Michael Novak as a rationale for neoliberal economic policies.[43] Meeks would claim that there are inaccurate applications of the Trinity, such as Novak's, which can be discerned by the inner logic of the doctrine itself. Even if the right interpretation of the doctrine can be delineated, it still runs the risk of losing its critical potential. In the case of labor unions there are two potential pitfalls. One, the Trinity should not be used to romanticize the labor movement by diminishing or ignoring the problems within organized labor. Two, trinitarian accounts of secular movements such as organized labor cannot be used to relativize the role of the Church in God's work of salvation, as if the unique relationship of the Church and the triune God can be replaced by any other human organization.

Having noted these reservations, I agree, to some degree, with Meeks that a social application of trinitarian thinking is possible. The doctrine's potential application to the human experience is a possibility because we are created in the image of the triune God. We have the potential to become "transcripts of the Trinity" because God wills it and gives us the ability to fulfill it through grace in Jesus Christ. However, it is never a possibility as a pattern which we can reproduce as autonomous moral agents or as a perfect duplication of the triune life of God.

Even if one can discern the right formulation, there is still another, more serious problem with social trinitarianism. It is inadequate to sustain and guide our engagement in the struggle for workers' rights. No matter how precise and intricate Meeks' description may be, in the end it is essentially the same as the General Conference resolutions and papal encyclicals. It becomes an ideal to which we must aspire but which we can never attain. This impossibility leads to one of two strategies. Either we will become paralyzed by guilt for not having reached the trinitarian ideal or we will water down its critique in order to justify our status quo. In short, it leads to either anxiety or self-delusion. But it will not lead to a greater degree of justice or deeper commitment to that task because the forces of injustice are greater than our ethical pronouncements. Reinhold Niebuhr said it best:

> **Men will not cease to be dishonest, merely because their dishonesties have been revealed or because they have discovered their own deceptions. Wherever men hold unequal power in society, they will strive to maintain it. They will use whatever means are most convenient to that end and will seek to justify them by the most plausible arguments they are able to devise.[44]**

The development of public theology plays a role in increasing social justice, as Niebuhr would say, but it reminds us of its inevitable inadequacies.

The impotence of social trinitarianism stems from a fundamental misunderstanding of the relationship of the imago to the triune Dei. Social trinitarianism seeks to establish a correspondence and use it as a "pattern" for us to imitate. As Kathryn Tanner points out, because there is an unequal relationship between us and God the correspondence can only be an approximation, because our relationships with one another are not of the same kind as those within the Trinity. Human relationships are "at a distance" and thus the correspondence can be lost.[45]

The proper application of the doctrine of the Trinity to workers' rights does not begin with a "pattern" but with "participation." Through the Holy Spirit we participate in the triune life and work of God in the world, which is made possible by the Incarnation. Tanner writes, "Christian experience hereby takes on its own Trinitarian form: in the Spirit, who is given to us by the Son, we gain the Son, and through the Son, by the same power of the Spirit, we have a relationship with the Father."[46] Our relationships can reflect the Trinity because we participate in the life of Christ through the Spirit:

> *The condition for this inclusion of us in the dynamic of the Trinity's own life is our unity with Christ, which is also worked by the Holy Spirit as the Spirit of Christ, the Son, sent by him for the completion of the Father's work ad extra. It is as we are united to Christ by the Holy Spirit that we receive the perfections that Jesus received in his humanity.[47]*

43. *The Spirit of Democratic Capitalism* (Madison Books, 1982), p. 337-340.

44. Reinhold Niebuhr, *Moral Man and Immoral Society* (1932), p. 34

45. *Jesus, Humanity and the Trinity* (Fortress Press, 2001), pp. 45-46.

46. Ibid., p. 56.

47. Ibid., p. 53-54.

The Trinity can be our pattern for human relations when we participate in the triune life of God. Through this participation the pattern becomes understandable. By being assumed by Christ we find assurance and empowerment for "the completion of the Father's work." Instead of domesticating the doctrine to our social agenda, the experience of the Trinity challenges us and enables us to discern afresh when and how we serve God's will in the world.

The link between workers' rights and the Trinity resides in the incarnation. If the Son through whom we participate in "the dynamic of the Trinity's own life" is Jesus the Carpenter, as the encyclicals affirm, then our participation in the triune life of God includes working for the dignity and justice of workers. Because the Christ was a carpenter, our participation in the triune life of God is never merely a mystical experience aloof from the sufferings of workers. The doctrine of the Trinity cannot remain on an abstract intellectual level lest it become an empty concept into which the values of a sinful economic system can be poured. Instead, the struggle for workers' rights is an expression of our unity in Christ and of Christ living in us. The Spirit will push and prod the believer to activism. The Spirit will guide and direct the believer in that activism. And the Spirit will encourage and empower the believer to sustain activism which manifests the "pattern" of trinitarian relationships in the world.

The centrality of the incarnation for understanding and experiencing the triune God points to the greatest deficit in Meeks' social trinitarianism. His appropriation of the Trinity to economics runs the risk of abstracting the doctrine of the Trinity from the Gospel narrative of how Jesus Christ is the Son of God. The doctrine loses its coherence and its power when this happens. Not only can it be misused but, more importantly, we lose access to experiencing life in God through Christ which fosters our work for justice.

If advocating for workers' rights indicates participation in the triune life of God, what is the relationship between the labor union as a "mouthpiece for social justice" and the Trinity? The Trinity is not the exclusive experience of Christians. "Expressing this dynamic life outward in a grace of beneficent love for what is not God," Tanner writes, "the triune God brings about a variety of different forms of connection or union with the non-divine, for the sake of perfecting what is united with God." She goes on to speculate that "it is presumptuous to limit the workings of God's grace in Christ to explicitly Christian

acts of service."[48] In a similar and more positive vein, *Gaudium et Spes* states that:

> *Christ is now at work in the hearts of men through the energy of His Spirit, arousing not only a desire for the age to come, but by that very fact animating, purifying and strengthening those noble longings too by which the human family makes its life more human and strives to render the whole earth submissive to this goal.*[49]

In this sense, the labor union can be an instrument through which the Spirit works to establish the common good in society. Similarly, the desire for justice among union members indicates the presence of the Holy Spirit. This does not mean that the union or its members need to be aware of this dynamic in order for the Spirit to be present; nor does it mean that the Spirit's gracious presence is sufficient for their salvation without their faith. Rather, it means that the Spirit of Christ can and does use labor unions as instruments of the divine will and in so doing can begin to draw the workers, through his or her desire for justice, to salvation.

* * *

To return to the original question – From a theological perspective, what is a labor union? – there are several things one can affirm. When organized labor pursues just compensation and dignity for workers it has a rightful place in society and makes a contribution to the common good. This collective action is an expression of workers being created in the image of the triune God, and such action is inspired by the Spirit of the triune God. Organized labor is an arena in and an avenue through which the Holy Spirit stirs and sustains the *imago Dei* among workers, even if they are unaware that it is the Spirit at work.

If the Spirit is active in the labor movement, the relationship between the Church and the union is threefold. First, the Church is a partner with labor unions in working for justice in the workplace and for the common good. The Church joins in movements of solidarity as an expression of its mission and in so doing participates in the life of the triune God. These acts of solidarity are ways for the Church to "give internal strength to human associations which are just."[50]

---

48. Ibid., p. 35-36, 64.

49. GS I.38.

50. GS I.42. See also, LE 8.

Second, the Church bears witness for the Gospel to labor unions and their members. By affirming the work of individual trade unionists, the Church enables them to identify their desires and aspirations as experiences of the Spirit of Christ and direct them to salvation in Christ. On an organizational level, it is a relationship of constructive criticism. "These movements must be penetrated by the spirit of the Gospel and protected against any kind of false autonomy," as stated in *Gaudium et Spes*.[51] It is only, however, through sustained relationships of solidarity that the Church develops the integrity to be able to offer this kind of criticism.

Third, just as the labor union is the recipient of the blessings and the prophetic criticism of the Church, so too should the Church receive the challenge to reform from the labor union. The Church is to be a recipient of the Spirit's criticism through the union. If the union can be an instrument of the Holy Spirit in society, then it can also be a vehicle for the Spirit to confront the Church's hypocrisy and apathy. In the case of church-related institutions, such as Walker, God challenges the Church to restore the integrity of its mission by purging its institutions of those practices which violate the image of God in the work place.

---

51. GS I.41.

Future Religious Leaders Live Their Theology!

Joy Heine (2007)

Students and faculty in theological and religious schools across the country are embodying a living theology focused on justice and human dignity with workers. These leaders are engaging in education and action with workers through internships, student groups, courses and curricula. They are experiencing pastoral care, solidarity with workers and practical theology as a part of their theological training through Interfaith Worker Justice's mission to educate and mobilize the religious community on issues of worker justice.

As the founding board members of IWJ sat around the table beginning to build the organization, they realized that the incredible leaders in religion and labor work were all in their late 50s and 60s. There was a whole generation of leaders who had not been exposed to worker issues. They knew that one of the core valuess of IWJ had to be to engage future religious leaders in training and practical experiences focused on worker justice.

Seminary Summer

In order to involve young religious leaders, IWJ partnered with the AFL-CIO in 2000 to develop the first Seminary Summer program, which continues today. This internship program provided opportunities for Jewish and Christian seminarians to live out the economic justice teachings of their theology by working on labor union organizing campaigns. They started with an intensive training on religion and labor organizing, later spending the next eight and a half weeks working to build religious support for a local labor organizing campaign. Their last two days provided opportunities to reflect and debrief on their summer experiences. These students learned about the labor movement, the values of a religion-labor partnership and the power of collective action. Here are a few of their stories:

Rev. Teran Loeppke, now a graduate of Garrett Evangelical Theological Seminary, participated in the internship. Although he enjoyed his classes on theology, church history and Bible, he wanted to apply these teachings in a more practical way. In the summer of 2002, Teran worked with UNITE HERE! Local 1 on the union's hotel workers campaigns. Through this experience, Teran learned how to mobilize the religious community to support hotel workers. He teamed up with religious leaders, union organizers and hotel workers to develop the campaign "Hungry for Justice." For this part of the campaign they asked for the support of religious leaders to raise awareness in their congregations through a food drive. The food was collected in order to support workers and their families, should they have to strike during the campaign. As the food was coming in, Teran realized the support was overwhelming and he didn't have enough space for the food. He called the local interfaith committee to ask for suggestions on where to place it. They suggested he contact the local Teamsters, who had empty warehouses nearby.

Not only did the food collected show overwhelming religious support; the workers knew it meant they were not alone in the campaign. When the time came for the workers to decide if they would strike as a use of their collective power, they voted yes. The employers were forced to negotiate with the workers, because August is the busiest conference and tourist season for Chicago hotels. Together, the workers, their union representatives and the hotel owners sat down and negotiated a contract. The workers received not only a pay increase and better benefits; they gained back their dignity.

Sabira Alloo and Aqel Khan were two of the first Muslim students to participate in the program in 2004. They worked with Jobs with Justice, IWJ's local affiliate in Washington D.C., to educate the Muslim community about labor. They laid the foundation work to build a bridge between Islam and labor. In 2006, Gulsum Gurbuz participated in the program, interning in Phoenix with the Iron Workers and the AFL-CIO. She reached out to the religious community to support construction workers seeking better wages; however, the workers' most serious concern was lack of water on their job site. She partnered with Alison Rainey, summer intern, to plan an action called "Thirst for Justice." Leaders across religious traditions participated in supporting workers on the job and bringing them water for their thirst.

Undergraduate Summer Internships

After a successful first year of Seminary Summer, in 2001 IWJ staff, board members and affiliates realized that a key group of students to engage were Catholic students. The Catholic community has a long tradition of Catholic Social Teaching, which embodies the value of human dignity and supports living wages. IWJ partnered with Catholic universities and local interfaith affiliates to establish the Catholic Social Teaching internship. Fourteen students participated the first summer. Their experiences varied depending on whether they worked with a local interfaith affiliate or a worker center.

Edin Laurin, a student from DePaul University, spent hours mobilizing monks, rabbis, priests, nuns, laity and others to engage in worker justice issues. She described her summer as "a whirlwind," which enabled her to go from, "no idea what the 'labor movement' referred to" to "teaching grown adults about worker rights." It was "not a luxury, nor a vacation." Edin said the internships are "a necessity for any student, of any faith, in any field." She believes that they are "a chance to touch another's life, as well as their own, an opportunity to create change and become a spark in a movement that moves with passion." In 2004 the program expanded to include undergraduates from other faith perspectives. Students, like Joelle Abramowitz, interned with a local interfaith committee and engaged the religious community in supporting the Illinois living wage campaign.

Hugo Esparza interned at the Western North Carolina Workers Center, where he became a worker rights advocate. He organized to get back wages for workers. While helping one worker, Noel, Hugo reflected that "In some cases wages can be recovered without difficulty, but how do we mend the dignity of the workers? Through Noel I came to understand the objective of my work this summer. I cannot mend Noel's dignity, but I'm here to help remind people that all workers deserve it."

Seminarians for Worker Justice

Seminarians have talked about how their Seminary Summer experiences transformed their lives and compelled them to keep working for justice. In 2002, three Chicago interns formed the first Seminarians for Worker Justice (SFWJ) group to continue working for justice during the school year. They educated and mobilized their seminary colleagues on worker justice

through the Carousel Linen laundry workers campaign. Their first action was meeting the women who worked at Carousel Linen on their picket line. These women invited UNITE HERE! to represent them and began organizing themselves. As in most cases, the workers wanted the union and they signed cards to join. However, their employer, Scott Close, did not want them to unionize. He made life harder for them. He harassed workers who signed cards, docked pay from union supporters and decreased their hours to defeat their unified strength. These women stood strong and they voted to strike. That's when the newly forming SFWJ group was invited in to help.

Students organized their colleagues to walk the picket line with workers. They brought guitars to sing and always prayed with the workers. In turn, the women offered them food for lunch. The students tried to talk with Close, to hear his perspectives and voice their concerns, but he would not meet with them. The students also sought support from those who patronized Carousel Linen. Finally, Scott Close caved in and recognized the power of the workers' collective voice. The workers negotiated a contract that increased their wages, granted paid sick and vacation leave, a 401-K plan, time and a half pay after eight hours of work and improvements in their healthcare benefits.

The SFWJ group in Chicago continues to engage future religious leaders in worker justice issues. In 2003, Seminary Summer alumni formed the second SFWJ group with students at the Graduate Theological Union (GTU), a consortium of seminaries in Berkeley, California. This group decided to focus on immigration and living wages for workers. In May 2006, there was excitement throughout the country because of the impact of immigration rallies. The students were discussing the upcoming rally in San Francisco in the dining hall, when the immigrant workers in the kitchen overheard them. They wanted to go; however, they had to work and had little vacation or sick leave time. So the students marched over to the president's office and asked for permission for the workers to join with them in the rally. A group of students offered to work for them; however, the president agreed to let the workers go without a dock in pay or any threats to their employment. He worked with other presidents to close down one dining hall that day. The students and workers made it happen.

Students in Los Angeles and Boston have also formed Seminarians for Worker Justice groups to engage future religious leaders in actions and reflections on worker justice issues and campaigns.

Faculty Partnerships

Because of the incredible work of the summer interns and the Seminarians for Worker Justice groups, it became apparent that there was a need for partnerships with seminary faculty. Students wanted to return to their classrooms and reflect theologically on their experiences in order to help them be better religious leaders. However, there were few courses being taught about issues of work, labor and religion. So in 2003, Interfaith Worker Justice began to seek partners in this endeavor. IWJ developed the Religious Perspectives on Work project, which seeks to engage seminary faculty and institutions in developing new courses, incorporating worker justice issues into the classroom and providing more practical opportunities for students to learn from workers in their communities.

In 2004, faculty from seminaries across the country convened in Chicago to discuss possible ways to deepen the theological understandings of students around work.

Collectively, ideas emerged about ways to engage their students. They realized that they could incorporate worker justice issues into current courses by selecting specific books, like Barbara Ehrenreich's *Nickel and Dimed,* or by inviting workers and union organizers to speak or watching movies that focus on worker organizing. The faculty realized that networking with one another to share ideas and resources was key to incorporating worker issues into the classroom. After this meeting faculty members began thinking of new ways to engage students in worker justice issues.

During the summer of 2004, Dr. Joan Martin of the Episcopal Divinity School, and Dr. Mary Hobgood of Holy Cross College, partnered with IWJ to train and pastor students in Seminary Summer and Catholic Social Teaching. During that summer, they provided training for students to internalize and articulate their understandings on work, race and class. Dr. Martin also worked in collaboration with IWJ to develop the faculty resource section on IWJ's website. She has collaborated with the Religious Perspectives on Work project, the Boston Theological Initiative (BTI) and faculty in the BTI to form a working group of faculty invested in teaching their students about work and justice.

In January 2005, Dr. Richard Perry of the Lutheran School of Theology at Chicago, Dr. Kazi Joshua of North Park Theological Seminary and Rev. Mark Wendorf of McCormick Theological Seminary, along with IWJ staff in Chicago, teamed up to develop "Faith, Labor and Economic Life," the first course of its kind.

In Los Angeles, a consortium of seminaries participated in a faculty meeting organized by Clergy and Laity United for Economic Justice (CLUE). These faculty members, in partnership with students, planned the first Economic Justice Awareness Week across religious and denominational lines. Rev. Bridie Roberts, a former student from Claremont Theological Seminary and a Seminary Summer graduate, organized workers and labor leaders to participate in the week. She invited them to educate participants about the hotel workers campaigns and to participate in weekly worship services in each of the seminaries. Rev. Alexia Salvatierra, Executive Director of CLUE, engaged students and faculty on the crisis of working poverty.

In Berkeley, faculty and students formed the GTU Justice Collaborative. This group emerged out of a desire to highlight, strengthen and reinforce the GTU's commitment to addressing matters of economic and racial justice. They have developed an inventory of all the classes in the GTU consortium and at the University of California Berkeley that focus on race and economic justice. This resource is the beginning of the work they will continue to do in the next few years, such as networking, providing resources and developing new courses.

In Memphis, James Luvene, a student at Memphis Theological Seminary (MTS), has spent two years working with Rev. Rebekah Jordan, Director of the Mid-South Interfaith Network for Economic Justice, to build relationships with faculty and learn about the goals of the seminary and how the work of the Mid-South Network can benefit both workers and MTS. In the fall of 2005, they found a way. MTS wanted to develop a new and exciting course focused on justice in their curricula. They invited Rev. Jordan and Dr. Peter Gathke of MTS to teach a course called "Jesus was a Carpenter: Faith Perspectives on Labor." It will continue to be taught into the future as part of MTS' newly revised curricula, approved by the Association for Theological Schools.

Students, through their experiences organizing Seminarians for Worker Justice groups and participating in IWJ internships, have succeeded in persuading their seminaries and colleges to not only focus on the study of theology, but to integrate these teachings with praxis. They are inspiring their teachers to learn more about worker and labor issues. Faculty members are developing resources for the students to combine their experiences with their theology. Through this collaboration the next generation of future religious leaders will be prepared to address worker justice in their congregations and communities. There is a need to move further and to develop an academic discipline that focuses on the issues of work, especially as it relates to human dignity, worker justice and labor unions.

There is no time like the present to embody a living theology while teaching and learning about worker justice.

Conclusion

What You Can Do

The collaboration between religious and labor movements on issues that matter to workers has deep historical roots. There are differences between the ways the two movements operate, organize and mobilize, but the similarities outweigh the differences when workers' livelihoods are on the line.

In this reader you have had an opportunity to learn about the lives of workers, especially those in low-wage jobs; get a glimpse of religion-labor history; learn about religious perspectives on work; and understand some of the ethical and theological issues surrounding work. You have also been provided with examples of religious and labor leaders working together on improving working conditions and wages for working people.

Now you have the opportunity to get engaged in the religion and labor movement. Here are five ways you can get involved:

1. Connect with a Seminarians for Worker Justice group or an interfaith committee to get involved in campaigns that impact workers' lives. If there isn't a group close by, start one. Visit the Interfaith Worker Justice website (www.iwj.org) to find a group located near you.

2. Preach about worker justice in your congregation or school during Labor Day weekend as part of Interfaith Worker Justice's Labor in the Pulpits program. Invite speakers or members of your congregation to speak or preach on work. However,

don't limit yourself to once a year. Any time of the year is a great time to focus on worker issues and highlight the workers in your congregations and schools. For more information and resources visit www.iwj.org.

3. Engage in worker justice by participating in an IWJ-sponsored summer internship program, such as, Seminary Summer, Islamic Internship for Worker Justice, Catholic Social Teaching or Interfaith Worker Justice summer. Work with a union, local interfaith committee or worker center focusing on the issues that matter to workers. Visit www.iwj.org for more information.

4. Teach or write about worker justice. There are several resources available; however, there are not enough. People of faith do not all know or understand how worker and religious issues are interconnected. If you would like to teach or write about worker justice, visit the website of Interfaith Worker Justice (www.iwj.org) or call us at (773) 728-8400.

5. Pray for and with workers. Please use the resources on our website (www.iwj.org) in your congregations, places of business, schools and organizations.

Acknowledgements

Section 1: Crisis for U.S. Workers

"The State of Working America: Executive Summary," reprinted from *The State of Working America 2006/2007*, Lawrence Mishel, Jared Bernstein, Sylvia Allegratto. Copyright 2006 Economic Policy Institute. All Rights Reserved. Used with permission. Please visit www.epinet.org for more information about the Economic Policy Institute.

"Why Unions Matter." Copyright 2007 Interfaith Worker Justice.

"Globalization and Its Impact on Labor." Copyright 2007 Pamela K. Brubaker. All Rights Reserved. Used with permission.

"U.S. Demand for Immigrant Labor and Its Impact." Copyright 2007 Ana Bedard. All Rights Reserved. Used with permission.

Section 2: Religion-Labor History

"Historic Highlights of the Religion-Labor Movement." Copyright 1999 Interfaith Worker Justice.

"Negro Labor and the Church" (A. Philip Randolph). Copyright 1929 Macmillan Company. All Rights Reserved. Used with permission.

"Religion and Labor: Then and Now," from *Organized Labor and the Church: Reflections of a "Labor" Priest*. Copyright 1993 George Higgins. All Rights Reserved. Used with permission.

"At Work in the Vineyard: The Jesuit Labor Apostolate" (Edward F. Boyle). Copyright 2000 *In All Things*. All Rights Reserved. Used with permission of the Jesuit Conference of Social and Humanitarian Ministries.

"No Shvitz: Your One-Stop Guide to Fighting Sweatshops." Copyright 1993 Progressive Jewish Alliance. All Rights Reserved. Used with permission. For more information about the Progressive Jewish Alliance, please visit www.pjalliance.org.

"Charles Stelzle and the Workingmen's Department" (Richard P. Poethig), reprinted with permission from *Church & Society Magazine* (January/February 2003, Volume 93, Number 3). For further information go to www.pcusa.org/churchandsociety.

Section 3: What Our Religious Traditions Say about Work

"The Christian Vision of Economic Life: A Biblical Perspective," Economic Justice for All: Pastoral Letter on Catholic Social Teaching and the U.S. Economy, reprinted with permission from the National Conference of Catholic Bishops. All Rights Reserved. Used with permission.

"Unitarian Universalist Economic Justice Statements" – "Working for a Just Economic Community," a 1997 General Resolution, and "Economic Injustice, Poverty, and Racism: We Can Make a Difference!" a Statement of Conscience passed by the Unitarian Universalist Association of Congregations General Assembly 2000. All Rights Reserved. Used with permission.

"Resolution on Workers' Rights in the United States," Union for Reform Judaism. Copyright 2005 Union for Reform Judaism. All Rights Reserved. Used with permission.

"Sufficient Sustainable Livelihood for All." Copyright 1999 Evangelical Lutheran Church in America. Produced by the Department for Studies of the Division for Church and Society, 8765 West Higgins Road, Chicago, Illinois 60631-4190. Scriptural quotations from the New Revised Standard Version of the Bible are Copyright 1989 Division of Christian Education of the National Council of the Churches of Christ in the United States of America and are used by permission.

"Ethical Guidelines for Labor Relations in United Church of Christ Organizations and Related Organizations," United Church of Christ, 1995.

Section 3 (Cont.)

"Covenanting for Justice in the Economy and the Earth," World Alliance of Reformed Churches. This document is a report from the WARC 24th General Council Proceedings and is presented here by permission of the World Alliance of Reformed Churches (WARC) from *That All May Have Life in Fullness,* Accra 2004, Appendix 13, pp. 153-160, also found online at http://warc.jalb.de/warcajsp/news_file/doc-181-1.pdf.

"The Economic Community," *The United Methodist Book of Discipline.* Used with permission of UMC Publishing. Copyright 2004 "The Economic Community" from the Social Principles found in The United Methodist Book of Discipline.

"The *Qur'an* and Worker Justice." Copyright 2002 Interfaith Worker Justice.

 "Labor Statements," Presbyterian Church (USA)

Section 4: Theology and Ethics of Work

"God and Work," from *God the Economist* by M. Douglas Meeks. Copyright 1989 Fortress Press. Used with permission of Augsburg Fortress.

"Whose Work Ethic? A Womanist Reading of 'A Work Ethic' from the Bible to the United States," from *More than Chains and Toil: A Christian Work Ethic of Enslaved Women* by Joan Martin (Westminister John Knox Press). Copyright 2000 Joan Martin. Used with permission of Westminster John Knox Press.

"'And Demand Justice': A Jewish Response to the Business of Poverty." Copyright 2007 Aryeh Cohen. All Rights Reserved. Used with permission.

"The Living Wage: A Jewish Approach" (Jill Jacobs), reprinted from *Conservative Judaism*, vol. 55:3, Spring 2003, pp. 38-51.

"Distributors of Justice: A Case for a Just Wage" (Michael J. Naughton), reprinted with permission of America Press, Inc. Copyright 2000. All rights reserved. For subscription information, call 1-800-627-9533 or visit www.americamagazine.org.

Section 5: The Religion-Labor Movement Today

"Religion-Labor Partnerships: New Directions, New Opportunities" (Kim Bobo). Copyright 2007 Interfaith Worker Justice.

"Struggling for Justice, Sustained by Faith: A Hotel Worker's Words" (Cleopatria Kyles, interviewed by Will Tanzman). Copyright 2007 Interfaith Worker Justice.

"Faith at Work in Miami" (Rev. C.J. Hawking). Copyright 2007 Interfaith Worker Justice.

"A New Alliance between Religion and Labor?" Copyright 2006 Robert B. Horwitz. All Rights Reserved. Used with permission. A longer and more complete version of this paper was published in *Social Movement Studies*, Volume 6, Issue 3 (December 2007).

"The Church, the Union and the Trinity." Copyright 2007 Rev. Darren Cushman Wood.

"Future Religious Leaders Live Their Theology!" (Joy Heine). Copyright 2007 Interfaith Worker Justice.